YSEC Yearbook of Socio-Economic Constitutions

Volume 2022

The broad theme of the series revolves around the constitutional frameworks for economic activities and their interaction with the social sphere. It is this very interaction this Yearbook strives to focus on. At the same time, it is this focus which distinguishes it from other formats in the field. The reference to "constitutions" mirrors the Yearbook's ambition to contribute to a better understanding of those legal rules which provide the very foundations for our economic and social well-being within a community governed by a constitution, irrespective of whether on the local, national, regional, or global level. The Yearbook aims to, first and foremost, provide a forum for doctrinal legal treatment of the questions that various socio-economic constitutions are faced with in today's globalized context, while at the same time remain open to neighbouring disciplines to the extent that they inform the doctrinal treatment. For further information please visit https://www.ysec-yearbook.eu/.

Eva Storskrubb
Editor

YSEC Yearbook of Socio-Economic Constitutions 2022

Funding of Justice

Springer

Editor
Eva Storskrubb
Uppsala University
Uppsala, Sweden

ISSN 2662-7124 ISSN 2662-7132 (electronic)
YSEC Yearbook of Socio-Economic Constitutions
ISBN 978-3-031-38509-4 ISBN 978-3-031-38510-0 (eBook)
https://doi.org/10.1007/978-3-031-38510-0

This Springer imprint is published by the registered company Springer Nature Switzerland AG
The registered company address is: Gewerbestrasse 11, 6330 Cham, Switzerland

Introduction: Funding of Justice

Abstract The special part of the third volume of the YSEC yearbook focuses on funding of justice. As noted in our original call for the volume, funding of justice has significant consequences for the enforcement of rights and impacts directly on access to justice and the right to a fair trial as a constitutional right. However, access to justice logically also impacts also on the enjoyment of other types of rights, for example administrative and constitutional rights, since having the actual means to access a court, or other relevant dispute resolution body, and bring a claim in case of a potential breach of such rights strengthens that right since actual vindication of rights is arguably an important component of justice. In this volume that focuses on socio-economic legal perspectives, the types of rights that are raised in the contributions can be characterized as civil and commercial, administrative and public, as well as international and constitutional. Therefore, a broad panoply of rights and types of legal proceedings is dealt with in the respective contributions. By gathering contributions from different procedural contexts and jurisdictions the aim of this volume is to contribute to the comparative understanding of access to justice in light of the current challenges in funding of justice.

Background and Scope

The special part of the third volume of the YSEC yearbook focuses on funding of justice.[1] As noted in our original call for the volume, funding of justice has significant consequences for the enforcement of rights and impacts directly on

[1]The volume editor's contribution forms part of her involvement with the project *Affordable access to justice (subproject: From public to private funding)*, Project number VI.C.191.082 of the Vici Research Programme which is financed by the Dutch Research Council (NWO).

access to justice and the right to a fair trial as a constitutional right.[2] For example, if a potential litigant in a civil or commercial case does not have the financial means to bring or defend a claim in court, because the litigant is not eligible for legal aid or cannot use private forms of litigation funding, that litigant is effectively deprived of access to justice. However, access to justice logically also impacts also on the enjoyment of other types of rights, for example administrative and constitutional rights, since having the actual means to access a court, or other relevant dispute resolution body, and bring a claim in case of a potential breach of such rights strengthens that right since actual vindication of rights is arguably an important component of justice. In this volume that focuses on socio-economic legal perspectives, the types of rights that are raised in the contributions can be characterized as civil and commercial,[3] administrative and public,[4] as well as international and constitutional.[5] Therefore, a broad panoply of rights and types of legal proceedings is dealt with in the respective contributions, though logically not addressing the criminal justice sphere that is excluded from the analysis in this volume.

Access to Justice

Underlying the special part of this volume of the yearbook is the notion of access to justice. Historically, the most comprehensive comparative work on access to justice remains the 'Florence project' launched by Mauro Cappelletti and Bryant Garth.[6] They showed that procedural reforms in the late eighteenth and nineteenth centuries focused on the formal right to litigate or defend a claim, based on a notion of a liberal society that led to an individualistic conception of rights. Thus, there was no focus on the practical ability to vindicate rights, and the state was passive in relation to the potential inability of litigants to do so. Equally, they observed that procedural scholarship mainly focused on more theoretical and systematic concerns, not on the real problems of the justice system.[7] However, according to Cappelletti and Garth a new focus on actual accessibility emerged in the twentieth century. This development was linked to the development of a modern concept of human rights as well as the emergence of social rights in the welfare state and was a trend that they identified worldwide. Thus, effective access to justice and more affirmative state action in this respect gained importance. In the words of these seminal authors in

[2] See Storskrubb and Ziller (2007) for an overview of the modern development of access to justice as a constitutional right.

[3] For example, the contributions of Cabral and Cao in this volume.

[4] For example, the contributions of Schaks and Wejedal (in this volume).

[5] For example, the contributions of Ghinelli and Sahani (in this volume).

[6] Cappelletti et al. (1978–1979). See also Cappelletti et al. (1982), pp. 664–665 regarding the main publications of the project.

[7] Cappelletti and Garth (1977–1978), pp. 183–184.

1978: 'Effective access to justice can thus be seen as the most basic requirement – the most basic "human right" – of a modern, egalitarian legal system which purports to guarantee, and not merely proclaim, the legal rights of all'.[8]

Cappelletti and Garth also argued that these changes entailed a change in procedural scholarship, that a focus on access to justice invariably leads to a broadening and a deepening of the aims and methods of scholarship. For example, they noted that the focus of procedural scholarship should not only be on courts but also include alternative means of dispute resolution.[9] The latter point is uncontroversial today and is also reflected in the contributions in this volume. The types of venues of justice addressed in the contributions include a multitude of bodies and varied proceedings, such as court systems, international treaty arbitration and enforcement mechanisms. This diversity reflects the realities of today. Several decades after the work of Cappelletti and Garth many accesses to justice issues are still not resolved, rather they remain crucially topical and are still debated and analysed in traditional procedural contexts. In addition, they are also intensely being considered in more recent and even in emerging dispute resolution contexts such as investment-treaty conflicts and climate change litigation. The purpose and hope of this volume was to attract a broad spectrum of contributions to highlight this diversity, which is reflected in its content. However, insights from one context may also be valuable for another context. By gathering contributions from different contexts and jurisdictions, a further aim is to contribute a comparative understanding of access to justice and its current challenges.

The precepts of the access to justice project of Cappelletti and Garth became a point of debate and also met with different avenues of criticism and discussion in the subsequent international procedural doctrine.[10] Its authors were also acutely aware of the necessity to be aware of and keep abreast of new developments and sought to assess how these impacted on access to justice, for example asking whether financial crisis could impede its expansion.[11] Naturally, societies have evolved since the late 1970s. One such evolution, identified as the starting point for this volume, is that public funding is in decline and market liberalization even in the field of justice increases. Public funding of justice has come under pressure due to the reality of financial austerity measures and the tightening public budgets in many countries across the globe. This has contributed to privatization and marketization of funding for venues and parties in ever more jurisdictions.[12] Ideally, such privatization and marketization can provide more access to justice than before. However, crucial questions arise related to the rule of law, access to justice and social and economic development, in the intersection between states, citizens and business. Two of the

[8] Cappelletti and Garth (1977–1978), pp. 184–185.

[9] Cappelletti and Garth (1977–1978), pp. 185–186.

[10] Cappelletti et al. (1982), pp. 664–672.

[11] Cappelletti et al. (1982), pp. 671–672.

[12] See amongst other Uzelac (2014), pp. 11–12, Kramer and Kakiuchi (2015), pp. 143–145. See further Hodges et al. (2010).

contributions in the volume, those of Usín and Sahani, take a broader, systematic and more theoretical approach to access to justice taking into account the current context of increasing privatization of funding of justice.

Usín notes in her contribution that the role of the state and private actors is still being redefined in the post-welfare state. Therefore, she raises a two-fold question; to what extent does the state remain responsible for guaranteeing access to justice, and what is the role of private actors in this scenario? She also refers to the third wave of constitutionalism with a connected solidarity shift. Further, she proposes an analytical framework, applied from human rights theory, and proceeds to analyse the three duties to *respect*, to *protect* and to *fulfil* access to justice, in order to establish the responsibilities that may be relevant for states and private actors. Sahani conducts a thought experiment in her contribution to identify areas of law and categories of parties where the promise of private funding may fall short regarding expanding access to justice. After outlining these complexities, she presents potential solution for funding the identified categories of long-shot winners, expensive winners, respondent winners, non-financial winners and political winners – depending on the facts and circumstances of the disputes. As both these contributions demonstrate when market liberalization in the field of justice increases, crucial questions related to the rule of law, access to justice and social and economic development, in the intersection between states, citizens and business are raised. Therefore, it becomes paramount to consider how equality of access can be fostered whilst at the same time protecting market freedom and the right to business. The quest for such a balance is not an easy task, but one which the contributions of Ucín and Sahani seek to provide tentative solutions for as well as provoke further discussion on. If such a balance is not addressed, there is a risk that the relevant dispute resolution system loses its legitimacy.

The Three-Wave Metaphor

The first task of the Florence project was to identify barriers to access to justice, which were grouped under the following headings: (1) costs of litigation, (2) relative party capability and (3) diffuse (i.e., collective or fragmented) interests.[13] Thereafter, the comparative research conducted identified and analysed basic approaches, devices and solutions adopted by legal systems across the world, this process being characterized in terms of the now famous 'wave' metaphor. The *first wave* comprised legal aid and other solutions to address litigation poverty, the *second wave* related to reforms to support litigation of diffuse claims such as class action or representative action and the *third wave* went beyond courts and encompassed the development of non-judicial alternatives (i.e. ADR).[14] The research was broader

[13] Cappelletti and Garth (1978), pp. 186–195.

[14] Cappelletti and Garth (1978), pp. 197–227.

than mere procedural rules encompassing also the structure of the courts and other dispute resolution bodies as well as the role of the legal profession and other actors in the justice system. Connecting the wave metaphor of the access to justice movement to the theme of the special part of our yearbook, funding of justice, as well as the current privatization development, is obviously interesting to reflect upon with respect to issues connected to the first wave of access to justice. However, it is also relevant for the second and third waves of the access to justice movement. As we will see below, the funding of dispute resolution in the context of class or representative actions is a very topical issue at present, for example, in relation to collective climate change actions. In addition, non-judicial dispute resolution mechanisms, that are sometimes characterized as private litigation venues, have formed one central arena in which private funding tools have evolved. In particular, in the context of arbitration one form of private funding, so-called third-party funding (TPF), has become a central and potential funding tool for certain parties.

However, it is first pertinent to reiterate that the costs of litigation and the first wave of the access to justice movement remain central. Many reforms and idealistic models developed in the 1970s have been challenged since public funding is not unlimited. In the present context of the recent financial crises and ensuing public austerity measures also justice systems have been under pressure in many jurisdictions. As noted by commentators, austerity primarily influences the overall financing of the judicial system, the provision of legal aid and court fees. However, pressure on public finances can also often result in a strive to introduce or expand simplified court procedures with the aim of lower costs for both courts and the litigating parties.[15] A general economic downturn can also increase the number of unrepresented litigants in jurisdictions that allow self-representation, the so-called litigants in person. The contribution of Wejedal in this volume deals with the growing number of litigants in person and the lure of simplified procedures from the specific perspective of Swedish administrative proceedings. He notes the key problem of litigants in person is either insufficient litigation skills, to be solved by compelling litigants to rely on qualified counsel, or the level of complexity inherent in court litigation, to be solved by simplifying the procedure. However, as Wejedal notes mandating counsel will not lower party costs, ultimately someone must pay. Thus, legislators may instead attempt to simplify the procedure with the customary result that the court must assist the unrepresented party. This is in turn not uncontroversial since it may contradict basic principles of procedural law. Therefore, he asks whether simplification of procedure is a realistic alternative to lawyer-conducted litigation which he responds to based on empirical data regarding litigation outcomes.

In addition to the cost of the primary substantive litigation, a further question of costs and funding arises in the potential subsequent enforcement proceedings.[16] Such proceedings ensue when a judgment creditor is obliged to resort to formal

[15] Kramer and Kakiuchi (2015), p. 143.

[16] For a recent comparative work, see Kennett (2021).

enforcement proceedings to realize and execute the judgment. The contribution of Cao deals with the costs of enforcement proceedings in China. He notes that the allocation of enforcement costs between the state court and the enforcement creditor is related to the efforts of the court during enforcement proceedings. The application fee for enforcement does not have to be prepaid, thus the operation of enforcement proceedings is promoted and financially supported by the courts. However, the enforcement creditor must pay the fees for judicial identification of assets in advance which are then recoverable after successful enforcement. Although the court pays principle is prevailing, he posits that doubts can be raised based on the interests of general taxpayers. Furthermore, as explained by Cao, some public enforcement services are paid by the creditor and privatized enforcement systems appear to be evolving. Thus, a balance between the input of public resources of the state and the costs borne by the parties should ideally be accomplished.

The contribution of Shaks relates to a very fundamental advancement of access to justice identified in the first wave, namely legal aid. Historically legal aid and other types of public schemes assisting litigants were focused on providing access to natural persons who could not afford to litigate.[17] Shaks raises a more modern facet and discussion in relation to legal aid, namely the availability of legal aid, hence the availability of access to justice, for legal persons in administrative proceedings. More specifically, he addresses the question of where in German constitutional law the entitlement to legal aid is rooted and what effects this has on the entitlement to legal aid for legal persons. He posits that legal aid is not anchored in the constitutional principles of social welfare, equality under the law or the general principle of the rule of law. Contrary to the general opinion, he argues that legal persons may also have a right to legal aid on constitutional grounds based on Article 19 [4] sentence 1 of German Basic Law, which guarantees legal recourse. Furthermore, he posits that statutory law that makes individual legal protection for legal persons dependent on the interest of the public or third parties creates an unnecessary burden and may therefore be deemed unconstitutional.

The contribution of Cabral tackles the problem of the funding of civil justice determined by contract between the litigating parties. He explains that procedural agreements can potentially be used as a tool to define the costs distribution between the parties, for shifting or modifying statutory provisions on costs, to assign or sell claims, as well as appointing third parties responsible for the costs associated with judicial procedures (litigation expenses insurance and third-party funding). He highlights the varied possibilities for such agreements to transfer costs of civil litigation available in the Brazil and further analyses some of the main related issues related thereto. Cabral deals with the issues of potential conflicts of interest, duties of information and disclosure, the risk of shadow litigants and the normative effects that are expected to derive from the interaction of third parties with both the parties and the court. He demonstrates that depending on the values underpinning the legal system many of these issues can be resolved. The four contributions of Wejedal,

[17] Cappelletti and Garth (1978), pp. 197–209.

Cao, Shaks and Cabral demonstrate that at the domestic level many issues are still being debated and evolving in relation to costs and access to justice. In addition, they demonstrate the difficult balance between the public and private interests involved.

In addition, for diffuse and fragmented claims the second wave of the access to justice movement envisaged reforms and facilitation. The specific issues and challenges of public interest litigation clearly fell under the second wave and were at the time considered to be one of the most important developments of procedural law, and environmental protection was recognized as one of the specific fields of relevance for this development.[18] Now many decades later, we can see that despite reforms being envisaged, and despite progress, many problems of access to justice remain for environmental cases, evidenced by the recent surge of climate change disputes. This is illustrated by two contributions in this volume. Ghinelli argues that traditional standing, justiciability and evidence rules hinder access to climate justice, making it uncertain and potentially expensive for plaintiffs. He notes that in a number of jurisdictions cases have been rejected based on procedural grounds. In addition, procedural rules still appear unsuitable for fragmented nature of climate change harm. He argues that the 2020 Model Statute for Proceedings Challenging Government Failure to Act on Climate Change, drafted by the International Bar Association, might offer viable solutions for procedural law reform to decrease the hurdles identified for climate justice. Van Durme and Nicòtina specifically deal with the situation in Belgium noting that legislative amendments seem to have improved the legal standing of litigants acting in the collective actions. However, they focus on whether the legal framework ensures a satisfactory level of equality when it comes to access to funding for parties acting in environmental cases. Based on an exploratory study, they offer an overview of the funding instruments and modalities used in practice to bring environmental protection cases before Belgian courts. Based on their findings, they argue that the legal framework on legal aid currently in place is unable to guarantee access to justice in environmental matters, resulting in litigants having to turn to other, often private, sources of funding.

International Levels of Funding of Justice

Funding of justice is not an exclusively domestic issue but has increasing importance also for the supranational and international level of markets, actors and regulators. At the EU level, this has been evidenced recently by the ongoing implementation of the rules on private so-called third-party litigation funding (TPF) in Directive 2020/1828/EU on representative actions for the protection of the collective interests of consumers (RAD) and the Report of the European Parliamentary Research Service "Responsible private funding of litigation: European added value assessment" published in 2021 with a recommendation of the European Parliament to the

[18] Kötz (1981), pp. 85–89.

Commission to pursue further legislation in field. The Commission has chosen not to so at the moment and according to its mandated answer to the European Parliament it has chosen to wait for the domestic implementation of RAD in the Member States after which it will commission a further study on the regulation and practice of TPF across Europe in order to gage whether further action will be taken at the EU level.[19]

However, the Commission notes the concerns raised by the European Parliament following the increase of TPF also in Europe but is not sure whether any problems will materialize at the EU level. Historically, TFP has met with opposition and concerns since privatization of funding may raise difficult principled questions of conflict of interest and how to ensure independence of the adjudicator, or how to ensure a basic level of equality of access.[20] However, a further central question is how to deal with relevant concerns and what are the appropriate means and level of regulation. The contribution of Skog in this volume deals with the abovementioned Report, which was prepared to provide the Members of the European Parliament with an objective and authoritative analysis of litigation funding and its effects in order to consider policies for the TPF market, which remains unregulated at the EU level. Skog raises concerns with respect to the Report itself. He presents the lack of a clear and comprehensive taxonomy for the litigation funding practice in the Report. In addition, he shows that several critical conclusions on the purported drawbacks of litigation funding set forth in the Report are not founded in the research presented in the Report itself but rather contradict its actual findings. The findings of Skog thus mirror the currently more cautious approach of Commission and appear aligned with the idea of further and deeper analysis of the market after RAD has been implemented. We can though be certain that the debate on regulation of TPF in the EU will continue.

In the EU another means of controlling funding of justice, particularly public funding of justice, is the Justice Scoreboard. Published since 2013 by the European Commission, the annual Scoreboard is a means for the Commission to annually collect information on the justice systems of the Member States and to evaluate certain indicators for key components (quality, independence and efficiency) that are considered relevant to achieve an efficient judicial system.[21] The information is collected in the context of the EU's economic term and enables the Commission and ultimately the Council to make country-specific recommendations and have a dialogue with EU Member States on procedural reforms when allocating funds in the annual budget process via the EU Structural and Investment Funds.[22] The contribution of Dori explores how the Commission understands the role of adjudication costs and highlights how this tool addresses access to justice from an

[19] Letter of the Commission, 1 December 2022.

[20] See amongst other Cordina (2021) on the concerns raised in a European context.

[21] All Scoreboard editions are available at the European Commission's webpage https://ec.europa.eu. For the most recent Scoreboard, see COM(2023) 309 final.

[22] See, for example, COM(2014) 155 final, p 6 and COM(2018) 364 final, p 3 and 7. For a discussion on the evolution of the Scoreboard, see also Dori (2015).

economic point of view. She shows that the Scoreboard's reporting on costs has evolved gradually. It has shifted away from generic considerations on government expenditure (the supply-side) to adopt qualitative evaluations on the allocation of resources for litigants (the demand-side). Based on these findings, the contribution critically assesses the value judgements underpinning the Scoreboard and submits observations on its nature and function as a policy tool.

Finally, at the international level, private costs funding, TPF has been actively debated the past years in the context international arbitration, both commercial and investment-treaty arbitration. The contribution of Sahani mentioned above deals with access to justice in an investment-treaty context. The contribution of Maricante also investigates whether the TPF can facilitate access to justice for potential claimants in investor-state dispute settlement (ISDS). The chapter focuses on the possible identification and recognition of the right of access to justice in investment arbitration, notably through the indirect analysis of denial of justice and the relevance of bilateral investment-treaty provisions. The problematic nature of high costs in investment arbitration procedures is discussed, which sometimes represents a real obstacle to access to justice, especially for small and medium-sized enterprises (SMEs). The overall conclusion reached is that, although TPF facilitates access to justice, there are several complexities that could make its use difficult in ISDS. The chapter ends with some recommendations to overcome the main obstacles.

Uppsala University, Uppsala, Sweden Eva Storskrubb

References

Cappelletti M, Garth B (1977–1978) Access to justice: the newest wave in the worldwide movement to make rights effective. Buffalo Law Rev 27(2):181–292

Cappelletti M, Garth B, Weisner J (1978–1979) Access to justice (six volumes). Giuffrè and Sijthoff

Cappelletti M, Garth B, Trocker N (1982) Access to justice – variations and continuity of a world-wide movement. Rabels Zeitschrift für ausländisches und internationales privatrecht 46(4):664–707

Cordina A (2021) Is it all that fishy? A critical review in concerns surrounding third party litigation funding in Europe. Erasmus Law Rev 4:270–280

Dori A (2015) The EU justice scoreboard – judicial evaluation as a new governance tool. Max Planck Institute Luxemburg working paper

Hodges C, Vogenauer S, Tulibacka M (2010) The costs and funding of civil litigation. Bloomsbury

Kennett W (2021) Civil enforcement in a comparative perspective. A public management challenge. Intersentia

Kramer X, Kakiuchi S (2015) Austerity in civil procedure and the role of simplified procedures. Erasmus Law Rev 4:139–146

Kötz H (1981) Public interest litigation: a comparative survey. In: Cappelletti M, Weisner J, Seccomber M (eds) Access to justice and the welfare state. Sijthoff, Bruylant, Klett-Cotta and Le Monnier, pp 85–117

Storskrubb E, Ziller J (2007) Access to justice in European comparative law. In: Francioni F (ed) Access to justice as a human right. Oxford University Press, pp 177–203

Uzelac A (2014) Goals of civil justice and civil procedure in the contemporary world. In: Uzelac A (ed) Goals of civil justice and civil procedure in contemporary judicial systems, Springer, pp 3–31

Contents

Part I : Specific Part: Funding of Justice: Access to Effective Justice in Times of Marketisation of Justice and Shrinking Public Budgets

Revisiting the Concept of Access to Justice as a Human Right in the Post-welfare State

María Carlota Ucín

Contents

Abstract Access to justice — as defined here — is linked intrinsically to the different forms of the welfare state and social constitutionalism. However, due to the crisis currently confronting the welfare state, a change is occurring in the role of states and in the cut-off involving many social programmes, including the ones providing legal aid as part of access to justice programmes. This new scenario has led to an increase in the number of private actors playing the role of 'third party litigation funders' (TPLF). The main, twofold question I propose to answer in this article is to what extent does the state remain responsible for guaranteeing access to justice, and what exactly are the duties of private actors. For this purpose, I analyse from an argumentative perspective the concept of access to justice as a human right in the European system of human rights, and I suggest that the framework of three degrees of obligation (duty to respect, to protect and to fulfil human rights) should be applied for a better understanding of the topic. In this context, I examine the different soft law instruments that regulate access to justice, and I suggest certain gaps that should be filled in applying the human rights approach.

This publication is part of the project Affordable access to justice (subproject: From public to private funding), Project number VI.C.191.082 of the Vici Research Programme which is financed by the Dutch Research Council (NWO). Contact: ucin@law.eur.nl.

M. C. Ucín (✉)
Erasmus School of Law, Erasmus University, Rotterdam, Netherlands
e-mail: ucin@law.eur.nl

E. Storskrubb (ed.), *YSEC Yearbook of Socio-Economic Constitutions 2022*,
YSEC Yearbook of Socio-Economic Constitutions (2023) 2022: 3–28,
https://doi.org/10.1007/16495_2023_49, Published online: 4 July 2023

1 Introduction

In certain discursive contexts, or when we delve into some of the literature, it may seem superfluous to highlight that access to justice is — and should be — recognised as a human right. Whether we are diving into civil procedure or into constitutional texts, the claim would seem obvious. However, what tends to happen with obvious statements is that they do not require further justification. Likewise with this one. Moreover, if we were asked eventually for a quick justification, it may suffice to argue that our claim has support in positive law instruments. We might then affirm that it is a human right recognised in many international instruments, such as Articles 8 and 10 of the Universal Declaration of Human Rights; Articles 2.3 and 14 of the International Covenant on Civil and Political Rights; Articles 6 and 13 of the European Convention on Human Rights; and Article 47 of the Charter of Fundamental Rights of the European Union. And of course the right is incorporated in other international instruments that are imperative worldwide.

However, even if this were to satisfy our interlocutor, another issue could arise, since they might ask what precisely is our understanding of access to justice. In effect, it becomes clear that the main term *access to justice* is ambiguous, and has diverse meanings, depending on the context. The words *access* and *justice* are especially ambiguous, and it is necessary at this point to define the sense in which I will use the phrase in this article. The word *access* is related to the second term, *justice*, and we normally understand that — in a general sense — it refers to the way we reach a place. It is then essential to start defining what we mean by *justice* as a goal.

In a broad sense, justice may be equivalent to fairness, and it can then be related to certain material conditions that to some extent concern equality and wellbeing. This more substantive notion of justice addresses broad questions, such as whether a society ensures equal access to opportunities and benefits, and whether all individuals have the ability to live a just life.[1] In the same vein, it has been said that substantive justice can be related to the sense of a fair outcome or to getting something to which one has a right.[2]

However, we can also define the word *justice* more strictly, and relate it to the judicial branch and its adjudicative procedures, or, eventually, include also the alternative dispute resolution methods. From this perspective, justice can be seen as the processes that are available to help people enforce their rights under the law, and as the effectiveness of these processes.[3] In this regard, some authors affirm that access to justice can be understood as the possibility for the individual to bring a claim before a court and have it adjudicated within a due process of law. This means

[1] Larson (2015), p. 1.

[2] Friedman (2010), p. 2.

[3] Larson (2015), p. 1.

that the case is heard and judged in accordance with substantive standards of fairness and justice.[4]

In this paper, I will use the term *justice* in the more strict and procedural sense: that is, I will interpret it as being the procedural method of settling conflicts and adjudicating rights. Then, linking justice with the concept of *access,* I will allude to the opportunity of bringing our claims to the courts, or to any other triadic mode of dispute settlement, and to be decided by a third party within a reasonable time, and while respecting the other conditions relating to a due process of law.

However, access can also be subject to a formal or material interpretation. From a formal standpoint, we can relate it to the right to have our conflicts decided in a trial, no matter how effective this right is in practice insofar as it is recognised as being applicable to everyone. The negative aspect of this right implies the duty of providing a legal and judicial system as well as avoiding any interference in our protected sphere.

In the second sense — the material interpretation — we need to consider the effectiveness of the right in practice. In this approach, the right of access to justice may imply the imposing of additional positive duties on the state or other subjects to guarantee that the right is enjoyed at a practical level. Consequently, we may be forced to confront obstacles that prevent each person or group of people from having real access to the courts or to alternative bodies of dispute resolution.

Summing up my argument thus far, I will interpret the term *access* in the material sense presented above, and *justice* in its more restricted and procedural sense. Therefore, I will analyse the right to have *concrete and effective access to the courts, or to any other adjudicative institution, in order to have our conflicts decided by an impartial body*. This definition can be rooted in the decision of the European Court of Human Rights (hereinafter also ECtHR) in *Golder v. The United Kingdom,*[5] where the Court states that Article 6.1 secures for everyone the right to have any claim relating to his or her civil rights and obligations brought before a court or tribunal. Therefore, the Article embodies the 'right to a court' where the right of access — that is, the right to institute proceedings before courts in civil matters — constitutes only one aspect. This concept must be integrated with the other guarantees laid down in Article 6.1, and related to the organisation and composition of the court and the conduct of the proceedings, constituting the right to a fair hearing.

Therefore, going back to our imaginary dialogue, and notwithstanding the examples given, when we want to support the claim that access to justice — as stated above — is recognised in international instruments, we may face certain difficulties. In effect, when we go deeper into the textual content of these instruments, we may realise that access to justice is not always denoted explicitly. For instance, the ECHR does not use the term 'access to justice' expressly.[6] Instead, it contains provisions on

[4]Francioni (2007), p. 1.

[5]ECtHR, *Golder v. The United Kingdom, no.* 4451/70, §36, 21 February 1975.

[6]The same happens with Articles 2.3 and 14 of the International Covenant on Civil and Political Rights, and with Articles 8 and 10 of the Universal Declaration of Human Rights.

a fair trial and the right to a remedy. It was the case law that provided a full understanding of the phrase.[7]

Indeed, this notion has only recently been incorporated into human rights treaties.[8] Likewise, the inclusion of access to justice as an explicit concept in national constitutions is in response to a recent trend, probably linked to the works of Mauro Cappelletti and his research team, as pointed out by Storskrubb and Ziller.[9] Following this trend, we may find a clear and explicit mention of the right to access to justice in the Charter of Fundamental Rights of the EU (Article 47) as well as in the Treaty of Lisbon. This Treaty stipulates in Article 67 (4) that 'the Union shall facilitate access to justice in particular through the principle of mutual recognition of judicial and extrajudicial decisions in civil matters'. And according to established case law of the Court of Justice of the European Union, access to justice is one of the constitutive elements of a Union based on the rule of law.

These two levels of recognition indicate a progression that leads to the present and ample content of this right, either through explicit norms or through court interpretations. This process illustrates the impact of what I will call the *social shift* on the recognition of rights. This approach permeated the interpretation of the international instruments, and led to the explicit recognition of this right on several levels. As I will explain below, access to justice is a derivation of the right to a fair and public hearing, and in the second half of the twentieth century it grew in tandem with the expansion of state functions.

This means that even if there may not always be an explicit recognition of legal aid, or any alternative way of subsidising effective access to the courts, the interpretation of the right to a fair trial could still provide a wide understanding that includes the notion of access to justice. This is the case with the European System of Human Rights and the European Court of Human Rights case law. From its early jurisprudence, elaborated in the *Airey v. Ireland* case,[10] the ECtHR ruled that states were obligated to assure 'effective' access to courts when it was demonstrated that, without financial means, it would be impossible for the claimant to have *real* access to justice.

We can observe how the several waves of constitutionalism have modified the way that rights are understood, through positive recognition or via interpretation. As metaphors can be useful, I suggest illustrating this progression in terms of several geological layers that overlap each other, providing incremental protection of a right by way of new and different interpretations that are enriched by reconstructed values. This statement, however, may imply that if the evolution of rights and its interpretation can be influenced by the consensus at a given time, we may also have to accept that this is a dynamic movement that may never end. Therefore, we should be flexible in understanding the new forms that the rights may assume, while the role

---

[7] European Union Agency for Fundamental Rights – FRA (2011), p. 14.

[8] Gerards and Glas (2017), p. 13; Francioni (2007), p. 24.

[9] Sotrskrubb and Ziller (2007), p. 178.

[10] ECtHR, *Airey v. Ireland,* no. 6289/73, 9 October 1979.

of the state and its obligations also change in response to the demands of the society. However, these changes can never imply a restriction on the rights themselves, since there are imperative principles that govern the direction of this evolution, such as the progressive realization, which is applicable to social rights.

This is in effect what we are currently observing. Let us note that although most modern Constitutions and international treaties recognise this right of access to justice, either explicitly or implicitly, many countries are reshaping the role of the state in a direction that deviates from the welfare model. And it is clear now that the crisis involving this deviation has led many states to delegate some of their functions to private actors while they limit their own capacities to provide social goods. It may suffice to observe the privatisation movement, where many public services began to be provided by private enterprises as the state moved away from a number of sectors, such as the provision of healthcare, education, certain aspects of social security, and even prisons and security services.[11]

This phenomenon of privatisation is also starting to develop in connection with access to justice. Even if development of the ADR methods as a kind of privatisation of justice is not a novelty, I turn my attention to another interesting shift that involves moving access to justice from being an exclusive public responsibility to a scenario in which private actors are gaining relevance as they begin to take on the role of 'third party litigation funders' (TPLF). This concept includes several forms of enterprise that see in litigation another way of doing business, but novel forms of solidarity are also taking place in the form of crowdfunding. These forms are being developed rapidly, not only in Anglo-American countries but also in many others, including European ones.[12]

Underlying this problem, however, is another interesting level of analysis that suggests an understanding of the extent to which these private actors may also be liable for their actions in the field of access to justice. In other words, worth considering is that the shift in the role of states may not change the nature of access to justice, conceived as a human right. The extent of the responsibilities of private actors when they are gaining material profit in this arena should then be determined.

At this stage, it is reasonable to wonder whether we may have to renounce the entire extent of the protection provided by the social dimensions involving human rights. My immediate response is no, we do not need to; on the contrary, in fact. Now —

[11] Hocking (1999), p. 277; Teubner (1999), p. 51.

[12] In particular at the EU level, it is worth mentioning Directive 2020/1828/EU on representative actions for the protection of collective interests as well as the ELI-UNIDROIT Model European Rules of Civil Procedure, both of which deal with the topic of TPLF as an emerging practice. Also noteworthy is the Study of the European Parliament 'Responsible private funding of litigation: European added value assessment' (European Parliament 2021). These soft law instruments highlight concerns about the conflict of interest that can occur in these cases, and they focus mainly on the conditions that should be met to allow private actors to finance litigation without destroying the necessary balance within the process. Note: While the text was under revision, on 13 September 2022, the European Parliament adopted a resolution with recommendations to the Commission regarding a Directive on the responsible private funding of litigation.

more than ever — we should go back to the basis of the human rights theory to understand society's new dynamics, and to be guided by the values enshrined in human rights instruments.

Therefore, the main question, which is twofold, is to what extent does the state remain responsible for guaranteeing access to justice, and what is the role of private actors in this scenario. To answer this, I suggest that the framework of three degrees of obligation — applied in human rights theory for determining the content of the rights — would be useful. I then argue that the duty to respect, to protect, and to fulfil should be applied to access to justice, in order to establish the different responsibilities that may be of concern to states and to private actors in contributing to making this right effective. By doing so, we could provide arguments to feed future debates dealing with the regulation of these instruments. This article may not provide definitive solutions but aims to set the foundations for future works on the topic.

To this end, I will present in the following section a definition of access to justice that takes into account its social dimension, and shows that its content has been shaped through the several stages of constitutionalism. Touching on the recognition of this right in the European Charter of Human Rights (ECHR) and its case law, I will examine that progression and its link to the transforming role of the state. In Sect. 3, I will indicate a few problems that derive from the privatisation process, and will show that the matrix of three levels of duty can be useful for finding to some extent a balance in future regulations involving privatised systems. In Sect. 4, the matrix will be tested with respect to the right to access to justice as I explore certain preliminary guidelines for the prospective regulation of TPLF. Lastly, in Sect. 5 I will offer a number of provisional conclusions.

2 The Concept of Access to Justice as a Human Right

As previously stated, the recognition of access to justice can be found — either explicitly or through interpretation — in many of the instruments that recognise human rights. For the purpose of this article, I will confine my analysis to the system built upon the European Convention on Human Rights and the case law described by the ECtHR. In particular, I will focus on the field of civil law.

As previously mentioned, Article 6 of the Convention does not include explicitly the right to access to justice, although its text enumerates several elements that can be integrated into the notion of due process. Under the title of a right to a fair trial, the legal norm includes the right to have a fair and public hearing within a reasonable time and by an independent and impartial tribunal established by law. This applies not only to criminal charges but also to the determination of civil rights and obligations.

The following sections of Article 6 are restricted to criminal law guarantees, and it is in these paragraphs that the right to free legal assistance — for instance, if the person does not have the means to pay — is mentioned. Despite the restrictive outreach of this norm, its text can be read as giving a minimal content to the right, stipulating a kind of threshold, because nothing prevents states from including in their legislations legal aid schemes for civil cases. The key point, nevertheless, is to determine when the lack of access to legal aid in civil matters can constitute a violation of Article 6 in civil rights cases.

In the classic *Airey v. Ireland* case, the ECtHR said explicitly that Article 6 does not oblige the state to provide free legal aid with regard to every dispute relating to a civil right. But then the Court added:

> However, despite the absence of a similar clause for civil litigation (related to criminal free legal aid), Article 6 paragraph 1 may sometimes compel the state to provide the assistance of a lawyer when such assistance proves indispensable for an effective access to court either because legal representation is rendered compulsory, as is done by the domestic law of certain Contracting States for various types of litigation, or by reason of the complexity of the procedure or of the case.[13]

Additionally, it is worth mentioning that the Court said that legal aid schemes are possible options for guaranteeing access to justice but certainly not the only ones, and it was not the role of that body to determine which system the state should implement.[14] This explains why Article 6 was interpreted as recognising the right to access to justice in a broad sense and not just the right to a certain degree of legal aid. This is absolutely relevant, because, as we know, access to justice has to overcome many obstacles, not all of which are related to the costs and the funding of litigation.

It is also interesting to see how the Court assumed that the social rights approach was at stake in the case. In paragraph 25, the Court expressed that sometimes the fulfilment of a duty under the Convention necessitates positive action on the part of the state. Moreover, the Court argued that the Convention must be interpreted in the light of current conditions, and it is designed to safeguard the individual in a real and practical way with regard to those areas with which it deals. And regarding the text, it added:

> Whilst the Convention sets forth what are essentially civil and political rights, many of them have implications of a social or economic nature. The Court therefore considers, like the Commission, that the mere fact that an interpretation of the Convention may extend into the sphere of social and economic rights should not be a decisive factor against such an interpretation; there is no water-tight division separating that sphere from the field covered by the Convention.[15]

This paragraph allows me to introduce the argument involving the connection between access to justice and social constitutionalism. I am not saying here that the distinction between civil or political rights on the one hand and economic and social rights on the other hand has real importance if we look into the nature of these rights and their enforceability. However, I still find it interesting to maintain these categories in order to demonstrate the historical evolution that is more visible on the constitutional level. I contend that the progressive recognition of rights illustrates

---

[13] ECtHR, *Airey v. Ireland*, no. 6289/73, §26, 9 October 1979.

[14] Idem.

[15] ECtHR, *Airey v. Ireland*, no. 6289/73, §25, 9 October 1979.

the way in which reconstructed values amplify the protection of certain legal assets. I will try to explain these ideas with an example.

The right to healthcare can be seen as a typical social right, and no one would hesitate to include it in the social rights catalogue, even if the catalogue serves only pedagogical purposes. However, if we look into the core of that social right, we see that human life is the legal good that is being protected, which in turn is protected as a typical civil right. Furthermore, if we analyse the right to a healthy environment or to sustainable development, we may also find the link with the right to a healthy life, which includes present and future generations. My argument is that the main legal asset — every individual's life — is protected on many different levels that interplay and overlap like geological layers. And what gives support to these different levels of protection are the philosophical conceptions related to the role of the state and civil society, and which are behind the successive constitutional movements.

The concept of liberalism guided a constitutional architecture that has provided a shielded sphere for the functioning of civil society. It then became important to keep the power of the state within certain limits. But during what is referred to as social constitutionalism, there appeared the need to intervene in the economic sphere by guaranteeing some minimal levels of protection to every citizen or to any other person. Consequently, the role of the ideal state changed, suggesting the need to give it more power so that it could intervene in the economy and in the market. This explains why the content of many rights was augmented, and a number of positive obligations became part of their substance.

Therefore, returning to the aforementioned example of the growing protection of the right to life, we observe that life initially needed to be protected through law in order to avoid arbitrary intrusions from the state and, eventually, from other actors. Subsequently, the right to life as a civil right was to create an area of autonomy protected from any unfair intervention. Instead, in the social paradigm, the need to help citizens who were in extreme need of assistance appeared evident. Thus, the notion of the right to life also included a positive dimension that guaranteed at least a minimal level of health to every citizen. In parallel, the state began to take on this duty of protection by providing public healthcare services in many countries, because the welfare state was growing worldwide. In this context, the notion of social security was also well developed as a way of protecting citizens form all the risks related to life and health.

Nowadays, protected goods may be threatened not only by the state but also through the action of private actors that in some instances are even more powerful than the states. This is clearly visible in the globalised economy, where environmental pollution and the destruction of unrecoverable resources may be generated by the actions of multinational companies. As a result, the last stage of constitutionalism — enacted in the recent constitutional reforms — shows a perspective that is grounded in solidarity. It takes into account the need to protect goods, such as the environment, that are indivisible, and that are of prime concern to present and future generations. This last approach has a tremendous impact on the right to life and health, and to the protection of these domains it adds consideration of the environment as a social good that is indispensable for present and future generations.

I do not deny that the right to life, to enjoy certain level of good health, and to a balanced environment, can be seen as different rights, integrated into different catalogues (i.e. civil, social, and solidarity rights). However, by viewing them in this manner we would be disregarding the process that I find relevant and want to highlight here. And even if this taxonomy were useful for some purposes, I posit that if we carry out this reconstructive exercise, we may be able to trace the different values that permeate the growing protection of many human rights. By doing so, we can find the core values that support a certain interpretation of a right, and then be able to modify it in accordance with the present requirements, just as the ECtHR did in its time.

Moving on to the topic of this article, I maintain that this same evolution applies to the right to a fair trial and the due process of law. The right to a fair trial is no doubt part of the rule of law concept, and subsequently can be seen as a civil right stricto sensu. As this right was infused with the political philosophy of liberal individualism and the laissez-faire doctrine, these rights began to be protected in negative terms, although this does not mean that some positive duties were not implied, such as organising courts and instituting legal procedures.[16] In the context of the liberal states, a right to access to judicial protection meant essentially that individuals had a formal right to litigate or to defend a claim. In this context, the protection remained passive or blind to the concrete ability of a party to recognise their legal rights and to defend them adequately. From this perspective, the right to a fair trial and due process of law are oriented to limit the public power of the state by setting down negative obligations.

Within the social shift, this right to access to judicial protection begins to take into account the material conditions in which the right was recognised. Thus, it also included the notion of 'effectivity' in order to guarantee real access to the courts for everyone, regardless of their socioeconomic situation. This approach took into consideration that for large parts of society, their civil and political rights, as recognised in the constitutional declarations, were insufficient to provide *real* access to the courts. This same interpretation follows from the *Airey* case within the ECtHR as it was expressed in *Artico v. Italy.*[17] In paragraph 33 of the decision, it is stated that:

> The Court recalls that the Convention is intended to guarantee not rights that are theoretical or illusory but rights that are practical and effective; this is particularly so of the rights of the defence in view of the prominent place held in a democratic society by the right to a fair trial, from which they derive (see the Airey judgment of 9 October 1979, Series A no. 32, pp. 12–13, par. 24, and paragraph 32 above).

The right to effective access to justice — as stated here — has emerged as part of a greater movement initiated by the recognition of social rights. During the last half of the twentieth century, this approach emphasised the impact of socioeconomic disparities and other forms of inequalities on accessibility to the legal system. It

[16] Weston (2006), p. 21.

[17] ECtHR, *Artico v. Italy,* no. 6694/74, §33, 13 May 1980.

highlighted the substantial gap that exists between, on the one hand, the promise of liberal ideals like equality before the law and the rule of law and, on the other hand, the ability of members of different groups in society to effectively enjoy them.[18]

Connected to that movement, the Florence Project led by Cappelletti and Garth was involved during the 1970s with judicial reforms that were related to the welfare state. They referred to a society with considerable governmental involvement in an essentially private economy, and with a governmental commitment to ameliorating the economic and social conditions of the disadvantaged.[19] And it was within this context that the problem of effective access was studied using the metaphor of the three waves. These waves included reforms concerned with the economic, territorial, and cultural obstacles to access to justice; the protection of collective interests; and the idea of access to material justice through alternative and appropriate forms of providing solutions with regard to claims.[20]

According to the above-mentioned evolution, access to justice is linked to the welfare state ideal, and it broadens the spectrum relating to the responsibility of the state to provide support and funding to less fortunate litigants.[21] In this context, the problem of access to justice meant the problem of access to a complex social and administrative machinery, as well as the difficulty regarding control of the fairness of the decisions made within this machinery.[22]

However, all the social institutions that provided some form of aid to people in need became financially unsustainable in several countries.[23] Therefore, it is necessary today more than ever to go back to the basis of fundamental rights and see how we can create sustainable systems that provide access to justice. Considering the historical perspective introduced in this section, and its relevance for understanding the extent of rights and duties, we must acknowledge that we are living in the context of the post-welfare state, where the role of the state and private actors is still being redefined.[24]

At the same time, it must be taken into consideration that we are immersed in the third wave of constitutionalism. As mentioned earlier, its main characteristic is the prevalence of solidarity concerning the public values to be protected. This new *solidarity shift* also tells something about the role of private actors in providing

---

[18] Mor (2017), p. 1.

[19] Cappelletti and Garth (1981), p. 20.

[20] Cappelletti and Garth (1978), pp. 3–124.

[21] Storskrubb and Ziller (2007), pp. 178 and 179.

[22] Tunc (1981), p. 337.

[23] Storskrubb and Ziller (2007), p. 188.

[24] According to Baeten et al. (2015), the term post-welfare state refers to a new configuration of the welfare state characterised by the decentralisation of welfare provision to lower government levels, like cities, and to the private market. Government becomes governance and enters various novel relations and negotiations with private welfare providers that need some form of regulation. Post-welfarism therefore can be understood as a way of organising the provision of state welfare more in line with market principles (p. 209).

access to justice in cooperation with the state. This topic will be developed in the following section. Beforehand, however, I will add a complementary comment.

The previous presentation, provided to illustrate the several ways in which human rights have been shaped historically, can be related to the notion of the three generations of rights advanced by Karel Vašák. In this typology, the three generations are linked to the three themes of the French Revolution: namely, the first generation of civil and political rights is connected to the value of freedom (*liberté*); the second generation of social rights is related to the value of equality (*egalité);* and the third generation of rights is linked to the value of solidarity (*solidarité*).[25] These three generations overlap, and are cumulative, interdependent, and interpenetrating.[26]

Karel Vašák's framework was controversial as well as topical in the theory of human rights, and it is currently argued to be insufficient to comprehend the discourse on human rights.[27] However, and because of the similarity to my proposal, I need to state that without denying the limited utility of these categories, I emphasise the notion of progression and the cumulative effect of the several waves of recognition of rights. I do not suggest with this that there is either a priority between generations or a lack of development or infancy relating to the latest rights. I only try to show family ties within the duties included at a certain moment that pertain to the scope of a right, and to demonstrate at the same time the parallel understanding of the role of the state and society. In my view, this understanding is not static, and I therefore suggest in this paper the need to consider a new balance for the post-welfare state.

3 A New Balance for the Post-welfare State

In the previous section, I stated that in the last few decades we have witnessed a redefinition of the role of the state. After the crisis involving the welfare state, the tendency has been to apply many restructuration measures that led to privatisation or to the marketisation of public services, as well as to some branches of industry and commerce being deregulated. Examples include the decrease in the ownership of the state through genuine privatisation, the contraction of public services, and their delegation to private entities governed by market rules. The reduction in social security placed more responsibility on market-based solutions and on the family.[28]

In this context, it has been noted that:

[25] Vašák (1977), pp. 29 and 32.

[26] Weston (2006), p. 21.

[27] Domaradzki et al. (2019), pp. 423–443.

[28] Wilhelmsson (1999a), p. 4.

> Pressures of globalization and technological changes combined with the neo-liberal policies of national governments, both conservative and progressive, have created a transnational wave of privatisation.[29]

This can explain why this phenomenon is not a *rara avis*, but a common note with regard to many of the contemporary states. The fact is that the social needs that justified and explained the development of the various types of social assistance have not disappeared, and they still need to receive some level of response. In this same vein, it has been observed that even though the level of state-produced welfare services is sinking, some basic welfare expectations remain in European societies because of the adherence to welfarist ideals. Therefore, this should be taken into account when considering the basis of the post-welfarist society.[30]

Given the above, the still latent question concerns *what role should the state enact and how could private actors be integrated into this new picture*. Under these circumstances, it is usual to start thinking about a combination of state resources and the market, which together can provide the expected level of welfare. Ultimately, there is a need to expand the space for intersections within public and private spheres. And while the market economy may learn how to construe the fulfilment of social and ecological goals, players in the political arena must learn to use profit to reach these goals.[31]

As Wilhelmsson suggests, the interesting question is not whether we should have these kinds of mixes, but what should the proportions of the ingredients be. [32] In my opinion, this enquiry is central, and applies to the future regulation of third-party litigation funding. In legal terms, the author suggests that it is relevant to study the implications of the decline of the welfare state with regard to private law, and how new responses from this area of law can be given.[33] Moving a little further, I contend that it is relevant to introduce the human rights perspective into private law, particularly when confronted with the need to regulate these new forms of funding civil litigation.

If we keep a broad view of historical processes, we can better understand that the welfare state was only an intermediate and urgent response to social problems, while solidarity still needs to be integrated into the market mechanisms and other domains of civil society. At the same time, the division between private and public law starts to fade, as the phenomenon of the constitutionalisation of legal systems well illustrates, and the horizontal effect of human rights begins to permeate areas of private law.[34]

The same tendency is visible in the increasing development of public interest litigation, which is driven by civil society as a way of enacting constitutional values

[29] Teubner (1999), p. 51.

[30] Wilhelmsson (1999b), p. 242.

[31] Wilhelmsson (1999a), p. 9.

[32] Wilhelmsson (1999a), p. 5.

[33] Idem.

[34] Colombi Ciacchi (2006), pp. 167–180; Kay and Fisch (1998), p. 512.

through the courts. The increase in the recognition of human rights makes it clear that they are infiltrating the civil law discourse, as well as being the basis for making companies and other private actors liable for their actions. In effect, within the domain of private law, liability is seen as the key to holding private actors responsible. It has been stated:

> Liability law would have to emphasise not only physical security but also solidarity, taking into account expectations of economic security and equality.[35]

This has also become evident within climate change litigation and its related discourse, as the courts are using the human rights framework to uphold the responsibility of companies in the fulfilment of international norms, such as the Paris Agreement.[36]

The situation can also be analysed from another perspective, suggesting that every particular domain of the private sphere requires a regulation that fits its goals and is aligned with their inherent values. In Teubner's understanding, contemporary social practices can no longer be analysed in terms of the single binary (public/private), so it is not useful to think in terms of the impact of public logic on the private sphere, and vice versa. At the same time, it is important to state that the private sphere — defined as the area in which individuals interplay — cannot be reduced to the idea of any action that is guided by profit. Instead, it should be seen as a more sophisticated arena that includes social relationships, culture, art, and other matters involving individual decisions.[37]

Teubner argues that many of these areas were regulated previously under the dominance of a political party, and now that they have been privatised they tend to be regulated according to the rules of economy. However, this creates a mismatch between their internal logic and that of the market.

> While the new market regime liberates a whole set of sociocultural activities that had been stifled within the old regime public service provision, in the long run privatisation tends to create fatal mismatches with those sociocultural activities that are economically non-viable, even if they are central to the full achievement of their proper rationality and normativity.[38]

According to Teubner, it is not a matter of insisting on the tension between public services and the market in each area of autonomy. Instead, it is necessary to check each area's specific requirements and values in order to understand how they fail to align with the profit-related logic imposed by the market. This view can be linked to Sandel's ideas with regard to showing all the assets that money should not be able to buy. The author presents two independent objections to markets within the debates about the marketisation of some areas of life.

The *fairness objection* focuses on the inequality that market choices may reflect, since real freedom of choice may be an illusion. This objection points to the injustice

[35] Wilhelmsson (1999a), p. 26.

[36] Ucín (2021).

[37] Teubner (1999), pp. 53 and 54.

[38] Teubner (1999), p. 61.

that can arise when people buy and sell things under certain conditions of inequality. In turn, the *corruption objection* takes into account the attitudes and norms that market relations may damage or dissolve. It focuses on the degrading effect of market valuation and exchange regarding certain goods and practices. According to the corruption objection, certain moral and civic goods are diminished or corrupted if they are bought and sold. This argument is independent of the previous one, since it may apply under conditions of equality or inequality alike. This objection highlights the contrast between the goods at stake and the aim of profit and other values that guide the market, and evaluates the risk of corruption of the goods in question. This can be analysed in many examples, such as, among others, education, the adoption of children and organ donation.[39]

Even if the above-mentioned authors come from different conceptual frameworks, in the end Sandel's second objection to marketisation meets Teubner's idea of what constitutes a mismatch. And, if we agree with this view, it may not only be a matter of working on the conflicts between the political rationality of the public services and the economic rationality of their privatised successor. It is also a question of identifying areas of conflict where the logic of the market collides with fundamental principles of the social sub-systems involved.[40]

As a preliminary conclusion, I consider it relevant to bear in mind the idea that the state is still responsible for operating this balance through legislation. The new regulations should avoid the prevalence of economic interests over those purposes and values that support certain newly privatised areas. In the case of certain public services, it could be crucial to protect the value of solidarity against the pure aim of profit. This is because, ultimately, privatised public and other related services are simultaneously part of two social systems: the economic and the social system in which they perform their services. Private law therefore has to balance economic and social interests. In practice, this can mean enforcing by law its non-economic aspects against the logic of economic calculation.[41]

Taking a step into the analysis of access to justice, we should consider what values it serves, and provide regulation that can protect them. What must be avoided is any corruption emerging from the prevalence of the profit aim, which may grow if it is not constrained. Access to justice may not be a pure example of a public service, but it is protected as a human right. Additionally, it should be highlighted that access to justice provides the opportunity to enjoy the right to a fair trial, which is in effect a public service, and therein also lies its importance. At the same time, programmes like legal aid are also clear examples of public services, and, by analogy, the services provided by private actors as third-party funders could be considered likewise.

However, there are no absolutes in this growing arena where public and private spheres intersect. The expansion of private funding for civil litigation is a natural development of private autonomy, which in itself is not a bad thing, and should also

[39] Sandel (2012), pp. 110–114.

[40] Teubner (1999), p. 64.

[41] Teubner (1999), p. 75.

be protected. In this regard, it is necessary to establish a balance that considers the particularities of the different areas in which TPLF can interplay and provide appropriate regulations. Therefore it is essential to consider values like participatory democracy, rule of law, and equality in order to guide the regulation of these emergent forms of private action within a field that used to be guided entirely by public values.

Before delving deeper into this argument, however, I feel it is also relevant to comment on the human rights perspective, and on how this can also orientate future regulations regarding TPLF. Within the doctrine of human rights, it is topical that the complete fulfilment of each kind of right involves the performance of three types of duties that are transversal and apply to every right, regardless of whether it is categorised as positive or negative. This transversal perspective explains that the duties to respect, to protect, and to fulfil apply to every right.[42]

It must be noted, however, that this does not mean all these duties should be performed equally by the same actors or institutions.[43] And although human rights refer to norms concerning the relationship between individuals and the state, there is still room to include the responsibilities of private actors. Indeed, it can be accepted as evident that in order to protect and fulfil human rights, the state is entitled to impose duties on individuals through the law.[44]

In this vein, it has been pointed out that over the past few decades a paradoxical development has taken place in the international community. While the obligations of states have become increasingly detailed, the international standards of relevance to transnational corporations have moved in the opposite direction, by providing benefits but without imposing parallel duties in their regard.[45] However, under Article 29 of the Universal Declaration of Human Rights, everyone has a duty to the community. And for corporations, this entails two levels of responsibility: to the local community in their area of operation and to the national society in which they function. Therefore, it becomes urgent to spell out the boundaries of these responsibilities.[46]

It appears to be timely to build up a framework of duties that are appropriate for regulating TPLF. In this way, access to justice can be protected from the *corruption* of its values, a risk that may derive from the prevalence of the aim of profit. From this perspective, we could also establish a better distribution of roles between the state and private actors. It is obvious that a balance that may have worked during the period of the welfare state may no longer be suitable.

In effect, as described earlier, we are witnessing a shift in the role of the state. The decline in investment in some public services implies the intervention of new actors, such as corporations or civic society itself. In any case, the change in the role of the

[42] Shue (1980), pp. 52–64; Eide (1984, 2006); Alston (1984).

[43] Shue (1980), p. 52.

[44] Eide (1984), p. 154; Eide (2006), p. 175.

[45] Eide (2001), p. 560.

[46] Eide (2001), p. 560.

state must not imply abandoning a certain protection of individuals and respect regarding fundamental rights. It is relevant to re-evaluate the role of the law, and to embrace it as the main instrument for guiding conduct with respect to human rights.

Going back to the three levels of obligation, we have to define the duty to respect, to protect, and to provide aid or fulfil.[47] The *duty to respect rights* or to avoid depriving the protected good means that subjects should avoid doing harm to or depriving others of the protected good. This duty applies generally to everybody in a civilised society. However, it is reasonable to foresee that this duty may be infringed upon, and it is the role of the state, through the law, to establish norms defining crimes or the conditions of civil liability that follow the violation of this first duty.

The *duty to protect* the right is linked strongly to the first one. From the state's perspective, this duty implies two levels of obligation. The first level implies maintaining law enforcement by the police and by any criminal or administrative prosecution. But the second level entails the duty to design social institutions that do not exceed the capacity of individuals and organisations, including private and public corporations, to conduct themselves in an appropriate manner. This includes chronic threats that require imaginative legislation and long-term planning.[48] In this vein, to avoid violation, the law may also try to prompt compliance by providing incentives and indirect burdens, which can come in the form of subsidies, tax discounts, or exceptions.

Finally, it is crucial to consider that, despite every effort, there may be instances where certain people may need practical assistance. And here is where the *duty to fulfil* comes into play. This is the typical situation with regard to social benefits in general and within the scope of this paper; it refers to the arena where we can observe the development of legal aid or other forms of TPLF. It is precisely at this level that the previously analysed shift in the role of the state is taking place.

In particular, the debate on access to justice under the present circumstances implies that new forms of providing access must be considered for those in need, and who are beyond the protection of legal aid programmes. If we consider that in many countries these systems have undergone budgetary cuts, it is logical that their beneficiaries are being affected, and may suffer under these restraints. However, we should consider not only people that may be left out of legal aid schemes but also those in other situations in which the costs and benefits of filing a claim do not provide a positive result.

In this context, we are witnessing the emergence of several forms of third-party litigation funding that tend to complete the scene of the financing of access to justice. Under these circumstances, we should see that not only legal aid schemes — and therefore not only the states — are involved in the third category of duties. When profit-oriented private actors intervene in this arena, they must at the same time respect human rights. This standard should then guide future regulations with regard to these private funding schemes.

---

[47] Shue (1980), pp. 52–64; Eide (1984), p. 154.

[48] Shue (1980), p. 62.

As I will show in the next section, this is not the only element to be taken into account by legislators. According to Teubner's ideas, private law should mediate in order to limit profit-related goals while protecting the logic that is related to access to justice as a human right. On the one hand, this will contribute greatly to limiting some of the ethical problems of the market, such as inequalities, discrimination, asymmetry of information, and so forth. On the other hand, it will help to avoid the market logic with regard to corrupting the internal values of democratic participation, access to justice, and rule of law.

Actual regulations, coming particularly from soft law instruments, focus mainly on some of the conflict of interests between parties and the funders. However, the importance of including protection of the core values of access to justice appears to have been overlooked. I therefore argue the urgency of including a human rights approach to this regulation, which would prompt the development of social responsibility on the part of enterprises when they provide public goods or services, and would tend to reduce any possible discrepancy within these systems. I will develop this idea in the following paragraphs.

4 The Regulation of TPLF and the Human Rights Perspective

Over the last few years, we have witnessed a considerable development of various forms of third-party litigation funding. Truth is that the first wave of development has taken place in commercial areas associated mainly with financing the costs of arbitration.[49] But this does not mean there are no other marginal cases, and that this scheme cannot also expand to provide financial support regarding small consumer claims or other types of civil cases as well as public interest litigation claims.[50]

In a broad sense, TPLF can be defined as a process whereby a funder — with no direct interest in a piece of litigation — pays the legal fees of one of the parties, and receives a return on that investment. This is normally contingent upon the success of the case, and is paid to the funder from the proceeds of the action.[51] In a simplistic presentation, we can say that these contracts may be based on a non-recourse basis,

[49] Rowles-Davies (2014), p. 2. According to the European Parliament Research Service Study (2021), the most commonly funded claims are arbitration claims, claims pursued by insolvency practitioners, intellectual protection claims, investment recovery, anti-trust claims, and collective consumer claims. This document also shows that TPLF is commonly used to enforce judgments, especially in the context of cross-border litigation (p. 4).

[50] Rowles-Davies (2014), p. 10. Mendez claims that third party litigation financing may allow more middle class and less advantaged Americans to engage in civil litigation and seek redress for wrongs perpetrated against them, therefore increasing access to justice for those plaintiffs who cannot afford to pay a lawyer on an hourly basis. See Mendez (2021), p. 107.

[51] Rowles-Davies (2014), p. 4; Mendez (2021), p. 102.

which means that the amount that is borrowed will only be repayable if the case is successful and an award of damages is received.[52]

The third-party funder can be a bank, a hedge fund, an insurance company, or some other entity or individual.[53] If we keep the definition very vague, it could include crowdfunding alternatives and insurance companies as well as the attorneys providing funding in cases of contingency-fee agreements. For the purpose of this article, however, I will restrict the definition by referring exclusively to those agreements where the funder is an investor, irrespective of whether it is a bank or another entity. Other forms of third-party funding will be excluded.

Despite the growing expansion of this market, many countries within the European Union have no specific regulations with regard to TPLF, with the exception of Slovenia, where this kind of financing of litigation is permitted, and is regulated in accordance with the principles set out in the 2013 Commission Recommendation on collective redress. At the same time, TPLF is prohibited in Greece and Ireland, while in Germany, the German Federal Court prohibited the use of TPLF in actions for confiscations or profit pursuant under the Unfair Competition German Act.[54]

Directive 2020/1828/EU of the European Parliament and of the Council on representative actions for the protection of the collective interests of consumers refers to the funding of representative actions in Article 10. It states in paragraph 1 that — provided this is allowed by national law — Member States shall ensure that where a representative action is funded by a third party, conflicts of interest are prevented. It refers mainly to the tension between the economic interest of the funders and the protection of the collective interest of the consumers. To this end, in the second paragraph of Article 19, the directive establishes that states shall ensure that the decisions of the qualified entities in the context of the procedures, including settlement agreements, are not influenced by a third party in a manner that would be detrimental to the collective interests. The norm is also concerned with preventing the representative action being brought against a defendant that is a competitor of the funder, or even against a defendant on whom the funder is dependant (Article 10.2a, b). To achieve these aims, it prescribes that the courts or administrative authorities should be competent to assess these extremes.

This norm is focused on the eventual conflict of interest that may exist between the funder's goal and the values that support the right to a fair trial and the rule of law. It tries to prevent some forms of mismatch between the aim of profit and the public interest that is implied in access to justice and judicial review. On the one hand, it tries to avoid any unfair influence on the claim of consumers that could contribute to a limitation of their right to access to justice and to have a fair trial. On the other hand, it tries to avoid the prevalence of spurious interests on the part of funders, which are geared to prejudice the defendant. At this point, the norm is

[52] Idem.

[53] Sahani (2020), p. 615.

[54] European Parliament (2021), p. 1.

tackling an eventual corruption of civil justice by the introduction of private interests that may collide with those related to justice, rule of law, accountability, and, ultimately, to consumer rights and collective redress.

In the same vein, Rule 245 (2) of ELI-UNIDROIT Model European Rules of Civil Procedure[55] specifies that funding arrangements must not contain any terms that could be detrimental to the party that is receiving financial aid, by imposing a disproportionate amount in return or by giving the funder an undue influence over the conduct of the proceedings, which may eventually prevent the party from entering a settlement that could represent their best interests. Therefore, and to allow a certain assessment of this aspect, the rule establishes that any party who receives funding from a professional third-party funder or a crowdfunder shall disclose this fact, as well as the identity of the funder (Rule 245 (1)). This duty goes further in the case of collective procedures, where Rule 237 (2) allows courts to require a qualified claimant to disclose the details of any funding agreement that pertains to the instance at stake.

The approach exhibited by these norms is interesting, since it demonstrates awareness of the possible tension between the aim of profit and other values such as those mentioned above. However, many other issues that go beyond these situations need to be taken into account in future regulation. A few of these issues are analysed in the Study of the European Parliament 'Responsible private funding of litigation: European added value assessment'.[56] This document explores the gaps and the potential policy options for improving the EU framework, and it considers the contractual, ethical, and procedural aspects of TPLF.[57] Not all of the gaps mentioned there are focused on the link that exists between TPLF and access to justice. In this domain, the document presents the eventual conflict of interest and the need to disclose the agreement under certain circumstances.[58] It addresses the question of fairness relating to excessive rates of return,[59] and also examines the risk of an expansion of frivolous claims being made through unregulated third-party funding.[60] As with the examples analysed previously, these cases could also be perceived as a mismatch between the aim of profit and fair access to the court.

Moving ahead, I would like to rethink the dynamics of TPLF in connection with the matrix of duties. As I implied earlier, these contracts are the result of citizens exercising their autonomy. And for this reason, they should not per se be limited by the state. Autonomy as well as freedom of contract should be protected, and, in order

[55] ELI-UNIDROIT (2020).

[56] European Parliament (2021). Note: While the text was under revision, on 13 September 2022, the European Parliament adopted a resolution with recommendations to the Commission regarding a Directive on the responsible private funding of litigation. The resolution follows some of the points of the study and report, while it detaches on others from that previous text.

[57] European Parliament (2021), pp. 17–23.

[58] European Parliament (2021), p. 21.

[59] European Parliament (2021), p. 22.

[60] European Parliament (2021), p. 20.

to respect these rights, the state should *avoid interfering* in this domain. At the same time, the right to conclude contracts in this field should also be *protected* by legislation. This entails not only the protection of the provider but also, and I would say especially, of the consumer. As a result, both aspects of the contract may be accorded a balanced safeguard. However, when we analyse the content of these contracts, we see that they are providing services relating to another human right: namely, access to justice. This private activity, geared towards the aim of making a profit, is growing in an area that was once monopolised by the state. It is easy to envisage how the aforementioned risks associated with privatisation can occur.

When applying the matrix of obligations to understand the content of access to justice, we can see the following. There is a duty to *respect* this right by preventing harm or any limitation to it. This duty applies not only to authorities but also to private actors, especially if they are going to offer financial services in this area. The duty to respect implies, for example, the forbidding of any form of discrimination, and this can plausibly lead to a special new field opening up with regard to this regulation. In addition, special attention should be paid to the selection criteria that funders apply in choosing the cases they will support. It may also be related to the duty of respect, the consideration regarding fairness, and the forbidding of excessive rates of return.

Considering the duty to *protect* access to justice, we may move to the responsibility of states to exercise their legislative powers reasonably. In this regard, it is public responsibility to establish a coherent system that can provide everyone with affordable access to justice. I need not emphasise that at the moment this is the major challenge facing states. This suggests distributing charges and benefits within groups in society while protecting the rationale of the right to access to justice in these mixed systems. The regulation of TPLF cannot and should not be seen as an isolated matter, but in connection with the existing forms of public legal aid.

Consequently, the way a sustainable system can be built up is linked to the budget the state is willing to devote to legal aid programmes. This places us in the third level of obligation, related to the *duty to provide aid* to those in need. In times when the public budget is shrinking, the growth of private initiatives may be stimulated. But the *duty to protect* this right still falls into the category of state responsibility, and therefore a system should be created that safeguards respect towards human rights standards. Provided that the newly designed system is sustainable and respects human rights, it may respond to social needs. For this, however, the state should take into account the tensions and mismatches that may arise, especially with the privatisation of this domain. In this case, conflicts of interest may derive from the fact that private investors or enterprises will be dealing ultimately with the fulfilment of a human right.

However, this is not the only level on which human rights should be considered. Legislation should also take into consideration the incorporation of some degree of solidarity in the regulation of business actors. Third-party funders are not only providing a financial service but are also interacting in an area that is strictly linked to the right to a fair trial and access to courts. Consequently, they come very close to providing a public service.[61] This situation places them in a delicate role, and their duties must be defined from a human rights perspective. Legislation should be imaginative in order to conceive of proper ways of establishing some kind of solidarity in this area. This could be enacted through taxation, in case this can add some level of solidarity to the system.[62] Eventually, some form of pro bono activities could be encouraged by legislation.[63]

While states have the primary responsibility, there are certain situations in which they are unable or unwilling to provide public services such as legal aid. It then becomes necessary to address this situation without undermining human rights values.[64] A realistic view of the actual powers and resources of state and non-state agents must take into proper account the effects of globalisation, and the ways in which power has been reconfigured in this new scenario.[65] I would argue that it is necessary to introduce protective standards into the habitual contracting terms. This should be done through private law, but may also imply a compromise among judges in the interpretation of the law and contracts.

This approach is in line with the UN Guiding Principles on Business and Human Rights.[66] This document is also based on the three levels of duty to respect, to protect, and to provide aid. The principles contained therein are grounded on recognition of the well-known obligations of states, but also on the duty of business enterprises to respect human rights. The UN Guiding Principles mention the duty of states to protect human rights against abuse within their territories by third parties, including business enterprises. The way this can be done includes by means of the regulatory and policy functions. For enterprises, Principle 13 also establishes that the duty of respect implies that business enterprises must avoid causing or contributing to adverse impacts on human rights through their activities, and address such impacts when they occur. The Principle also establishes that enterprises seek to prevent or mitigate adverse impacts that are linked to their operations, products, or services. This last element can be related directly to the above-mentioned role of private investors funds that provide TPLF.

On the basis of what has been presented here, there are two types of matters to be addressed by legislation. The first type is related to the general functioning of

[61] In a similar vein, Mendez has argued that the states should promote a healthy and responsible litigation finance industry. This implies a consideration of the particular elements of this contract, and leads to the conclusion that simply using the consumer protection laws may be insufficient for the industry as well, as it is also inadequate to treat financiers as simple lenders. See Mendez (2021), p. 119.

[62] Although at this preliminary stage I cannot present definitive proposals, the redistributive effects of taxation could be thought as useful to enact solidarity in this domain. This does not necessarily or exclusively mean to tax the funders, but could include the beneficiaries. The proceeds of such taxation could improve the public aid programs finance, for example.

[63] Sahani (2020), p. 330.

[64] Brown (2016), pp. 71–80.

[65] Brown (2016), pp. 63–70.

[66] United Nations (2011).

fairness within the judicial process as well as the protection of the values implied in judicial review. We note that the main topics analysed in the instruments referred to earlier could be related to this broad matter. However, it is still possible to add other topics that can contribute to TPLF's final legal shape. The second type of matters is related in particular to the role of private actors in the respect of access to justice conceived as a human right, and to the definition of their particular duties in providing some degree of fulfilment of this right.

As I argue here, with regard to the three levels of duty, the regulations should also provide a key to guide the conduct of private actors on every level. Being that the state is principally responsible, it should not only respect this right but also, and in particular, facilitate the regulation of a well-balanced system that guarantees not only legal aid for individuals in need but also a fair contractual atmosphere for those who would apply for these financial services. The litigation funding provided by third-party funders places these investors in the role of providers of a service protected as a human right. Therefore, they are placed voluntarily in the area covered by the duty to fulfil the right to access to justice, the third level in the aforementioned matrix. The specific regulation of TPLF provided by the state should take into account the duty of third-party funders to respect the right to access to justice, and to provide aid in a way that balances both of the interests in question: namely, the aim of making a profit and the protection of a human right.

5 Concluding Remarks

It is difficult to reverse the idea that human rights are a construction based on the responsibility of the state. We have human rights as shields against state action or omission to act. And this is true — or particularly true — if we look into the origins of the recognition of fundamental rights in written instruments. However, we live now in a more complex world. We need to be protected not only *from* the state but also *by* the state. Owing to the increase in globalisation, we are seeing an expansion of multinational corporations whose power is not only equivalent to but arguably greater than that of the states. And even if this phenomenon is not entirely new, the legal shift is still incomplete, which is why it is relevant, even imperative, to start laying down some pertinent points in the discussion.

It is necessary to expand the protection of human rights, not only because private actors are now posing certain risks but also because the states are becoming weaker, and may not be able to produce the necessary changes effectively if society is not involved. As presented here, one of the duties of the state is to prevent harm perpetrated by others. This prevention can be in the form of legislation, which may imply the sanctioning of criminal offences but also the design of a wide range of programmes that promote respect for human rights, and even their promotion by private agents. This could be done, in general, by means of incentives, taxes, and other ways relating to civil or administrative responsibility.

Nevertheless, the domain of private action is huge, and the state cannot and may not regulate everything. Therefore, a wide range of activities exist in the private sphere that need to develop with some degree of freedom, but at the same time must be guided by the values inherent in human rights. This is a matter of urgency, since in many areas, such as the increasing dangers of climate change, we do not have time to waste. In other areas, like access to justice as reviewed here, urgency is relative but still present. Providing the means to afford concrete access to justice is necessary, and is an appropriate domain for the expansion of certain businesses. However, in some areas, certain compromises from actors with high standards regarding the protection of human rights may be required, and this should be guided carefully by regulation.

The state then needs to regulate and take all the actions necessary to protect citizens from any restriction of their rights. And in connection to access to justice, this implies that the core values of this right — namely, equal access to a fair trial under dignified conditions of treatment without any trace of discrimination — are balanced with the enterprise's aim of making a profit. The role of the state is to guide private action and to create, if necessary, incentives to promote compliance with human rights. The model of the welfare state is probably no longer a viable option, but the compromises are not erased; the methods may be changed, but the social contract is not rescinded. Private actors may interact in this new arena, with strong compromises regarding these values as necessary conditions for reproducing a liveable society. Peace is something we build every day by means of small actions; rule of law is an institutional way to facilitate this, and businesses must cooperate in maintaining the balance, not only for the sake of others but also for their own interests.

To build a sustainable system that regulates access to justice means focusing not only on individuals in need of legal aid but also on those in other tiers of society that are out of the reach of these programmes. Considering the three levels of obligation, it can be seen as a duty of the states to provide legal aid to people who are in need. Beyond these extreme cases, however, we should also consider a balanced regulation that assigns responsibilities to private actors that are willing to provide financial services. The three levels of duty still apply here, and their complete regulation would coordinate the role of states and private agents. Because it is difficult to expect business corporations or investors to comply spontaneously with these duties, it is the state's responsibility to provide innovative legislation that supports and ensures these ways of proceeding.

In the shift from public to private forms of intervention in many areas of social development, it is more important to discuss new ways in which private actors should proceed than to talk about how states have changed shape. And this must be deliberated also by taking into consideration the values inherent in human rights: mainly dignity and equality linked by solidarity. This suggests considering not only the eventual conflict of interests but also evaluating the rationale for selecting the cases to be financed. What about the claims that are too risky, or that are not profitable but essential for rule of law? Or what about cases that might go against some personal or sectorial interests? In other words, and as Sahani argues, would real access to justice need to involve TPLF in the financing of indigent or even innocent defendants or righteous injunctions with no monetary recovery?[67]

Some alternatives have been introduced in the present paper. Taxation is likely to play a role, not only for guiding action but also as a way to trigger redistributive effects and to have a positive influence on the judicial system, or eventually to help the legal aid systems. On a parallel level, private action can also be nudged to work on pro bono lines, supporting cases where the public interest is at stake. In any case, further reflection is needed as well as a broader analysis that examines some of the actual legislations in light of the previously mentioned conceptual matrix.[68] These are only a few preliminary ideas open to discussion, but there is still a great deal of work to be done. Because in determining a way to create a sustainable system for access to justice in the twenty-first century, an appropriate balance needs to be found between fairness and profit.

References

Alston P (1984) International law and the right to food. In: Eide A, Eide WB, Goonatilake S et al (eds) Food as a human right. The United Nations University, pp 162–174

Baeten G, Berg LD, Lund Hansen A (2015) Introduction: neoliberalism and post-welfare Nordic states in transition. Geografiska Annaler: Series B, Hum Geogr 97(3):209–212

Brown G (2016) Responsibility for human rights. In: Brown G (ed) The universal declaration of human rights in the 21st century: a living document in a changing world, vol 2, 1st edn. Open Book Publishers, Cambridge, pp 71–80. http://www.jstor.org/stable/j.ctt1bpmb7

Cappelletti M, Garth B (1978) Access to justice: the worldwide movement to make rights effective. A general report. In: Cappelletti M, Garth B (eds) Access to justice, A world survey, vol I. Sijthoff and Noordhoff/Dott. A. Giufré Editore, Alphen aan den Rijn/Milan, pp 3–124

Cappelletti M, Garth B (1981) Access to justice and the welfare state: an introduction. In: Cappelletti M (ed) Access to justice and the welfare state. European University Institute, Florence, pp 1–24

Colombi Ciacchi A (2006) The constitutionalization of European contract law: judicial convergence and social justice. Eur Rev Contract Law 2(2):167–180. https://doi.org/10.1515/ERCL.2006.013

Domaradzki S, Khvostovai M, Pupovac D (2019) Karel Vasak's generations of rights and the contemporary human rights discourse. Hum Rights Rev 20:423–443

Eide A (1984) The international human rights system. In: Eide A. Eide W.B., Goonatilake S et al. (eds), Food as a human right, The United Nations University, pp 152-161

Eide A (2001) Obstacles and goals to be pursued in economic, social and cultural rights. In: Eide A, Krause C, Rosas A (eds) Economic, social and cultural rights. A textbook, second revised edition. Martinus Nijhoff, The Hague, pp 553–562

Eide A (2006) Economic, social and cultural rights as social rights. In: Claude RP, Weston BH (eds) Human rights in the world community. Issues and action, 3rd edn. University of Pennsylvania Press, pp 170–179

ELI-UNIDROIT (2020) Model European rules of civil procedure

[67] Sahani (2020), p. 614.

[68] I tackle this aspect in a forthcoming article: *How can business best approach human rights in third-party litigation funding? Guidelines for future regulations* (under review process).

European Parliament Research Service (2021) Responsible private funding of litigation. European added value assessment

European Union Agency for fundamental rights – FRA (2011) Access to justice in Europe: an overview of challenges and opportunities

Francioni F (2007) The rights of access to justice under customary international law. In: Francioni F (ed) Access to justice as a human right. Oxford University Press, pp 1–55

Friedman LM (2010) Access to justice: some historical comments. Fordham Urb Law J 37:3

Gerards JH, Glas LR (2017) Access to justice in the European Convention on Human Rights system. Netherlands Q Hum Rights 35(1):11–30

Hocking BA (1999) Can we, should we, use private law as a means of regaining governmental provision of services and care for citizens? In: Wilhelmsson T, Hurr S (eds) From dissonance to sense: welfare state expectations privatisation and private law. Ashgate Publishing, Farnham, pp 277–299

Kay R, Fisch WB (1998) The constitutionalization of law in the United States, Faculty articles and papers 512. https://opencommons.uconn.edu/law_papers/512

Larson DA (2015) Access to justice, encyclopedia of law and economics. Springer Science +Business Media, New York

Mendez C (2021) Welcome to the party: creating a responsible third-party litigation finance industry to increase access and options for plaintiff. Mississippi Coll Law Rev 39(1):102–123

Mor S (2017) With access and justice for all. Cardozo Law Rev 39:611

Rowles-Davies N (2014) Third party litigation funding. Oxford University Press

Sahani V (2020) Rethinking the impact of third-party funding on access to civil justice. DePaul Law Rev 69:611–632

Sandel MJ (2012) What money can't buy. Penguin Books, London

Shue H (1980) Basic rights. Subsistence, affluence and U.S. foreign policy. Princeton University Press, New Jersey

Storskrubb E, Ziller J (2007) Access to justice in European comparative law. In: Francioni F (ed) Access to Justice as a human right. Oxford University Press, pp 177–203

Teubner G (1999) After privatisation? — The many autonomies of private law. In: Wilhelmsson T, Hurr S (eds) From dissonance to sense: welfare state expectations privatisation and private law. Ashgate Publishing, Farnham, pp 51–82

Tunc A (1981) The quest for justice. In: Cappelletti M (ed) Access to justice and the welfare state. European University Institute, Florence, pp 315–359

Ucín MC (2021) Milieudefensie vs. Shell. O sobre las nuevas formas de la justicia, Sup. Innovación y Derecho 2021 (octubre), 1, LA LEY 2021-F

United Nations (2011) Guiding principles on business and human rights: implementing the United Nations "Protect, Respect and Remedy" framework

Vašák K (1977) A 30-year struggle; the sustained efforts to give force of law to the Universal Declaration of Human Rights, The UNESCO Courier: a window open on the world, XXX, 11, pp 28–29, 32, illus

Weston BH (2006) Human rights: concept and content. In: Claude RP, Weston BH (eds) Human rights in the world community. Issues and action, 3rd edn. University of Pennsylvania Press, pp 17–26

Wilhelmsson T (1999a) Welfare state expectations, privatisation and private law. In: Wilhelmsson T, Hurr S (eds) From dissonance to sense: welfare state expectations privatisation and private law. Ashgate Publishing, Farnham, pp 3–36

Wilhelmsson T (1999b) Private law 2000: small stories on morality through liability. In: Wilhelmsson T, Hurr S (eds) From dissonance to sense: welfare state expectations privatisation and private law. Ashgate Publishing, Farnham, pp 221–251

The Impact of Third-Party Funding on Access to Justice

Victoria Shannon Sahani

Contents

Abstract Third-party funding advantages funded parties because funded parties already tend to be calculable winners on the merits rather than parties likely to lose on the merits. Thus, parties likely to win on the merits are even more likely to win with third-party funding, but not all winning parties can secure third-party funding. Hence, the overarching question is as follows: if funders pick winners among the winners, what does real access to justice look like in an era of third-party funding? For example, would real access to justice need to involve third-party funders funding indigent or innocent respondents, expensive long-shot claimants, righteous injunctions with no monetary recovery, or unprofitable cases that espouse some worthy yet controversial position?

This chapter uses a thought experiment to identify areas of law and categories of parties where the promise of third-party funding may fall short regarding expanding access to civil justice. After outlining the thorny needles of this problem, this chapter presents a potential solution for funding long-shot winners, expensive winners, respondent winners, nonfinancial winners, and political winners—depending on the facts and circumstances of the disputes.

V. S. Sahani (✉)
School of Law, Boston University, Boston, MA, USA
e-mail: sahani@bu.edu

E. Storskrubb (ed.), *YSEC Yearbook of Socio-Economic Constitutions 2022*,
YSEC Yearbook of Socio-Economic Constitutions (2023) 2022: 29–52,
https://doi.org/10.1007/16495_2023_55, Published online: 28 July 2023

1 Introduction

Third-party funding[1] is unbalancing our notions of party-driven dispute resolution processes and even-handed tribunals.[2] Aspirationally, an arbitrator or judge oversees the proper administration of the proverbial "scales of justice" in an orderly manner and "balances" out party-power differentials calmly through procedural evenhandedness. However, third-party funding greatly advantages funded parties, particularly since funded cases already tend to be calculable winners on the merits, and for-profit third-party funders generally do not fund parties likely to lose on the merits.[3] Thus, parties likely to win on the merits are even more likely to win with third-party funding, but not all winning parties can secure third-party funding for several reasons.

[1]An in-depth working definition of "third-party funding" is provided later in this chapter. See infra Sect. 2.1 and accompanying text. For now, third-party funding can be simply defined as a financial arrangement between a party involved in a dispute and an outside entity through which the party seeks funding for its legal representation instead of self-financing. For a more thorough and nuanced description of third-party funding, see generally Bench Nieuwveld and Sahani (2017). See also Steinitz (2011), pp. 1270, 1275–1277; Burke Robertson (2011), pp. 161, 167; Sebok (2011a), p. 453; Bond (2002), p. 1298; Cain (2014), p. 12; Shukaitis (1987), p. 329; Freeman Engstrom (2014), p. 379; Freeman Engstrom (2013), p. 112; Wendel (2018), pp. 2–3; Wendel (2016), p. 725; Wendel (2014), p. 656; Glover (2016), pp. 918, 922–923; Chamblee Burch (2015), p. 823; Hensler (2011), pp. 320–322; Hensler (2014), pp. 500, 509–510; Shannon (2015a), p. 863, n.1, p. 869; Sahani (2016), p. 390; Sahani (2017a), p. 407.

[2]See, e.g., Hamby (2016); Eberhardt (2013); Eberhardt and Olivet (2012); Kontorovich (2016): "Anyone who donates to the ACLU or a Legal Aid fund is basically underwriting third-party litigation. Most recently, private profit-motivated litigation finance has emerged as an industry in its own right, unburdened by any concern over the old common law rules . . . . By current standards, [such] funding should raise no eyebrows — unless one also wants to revisit public interest litigation, class actions and contingent fees . . . . But if the lawsuit is not frivolous, it is hard to see how the motivations of funders are relevant (or discernible). One would not say a civil rights organization could not accept donations from philanthropists angered by a personal experience with discrimination. All [this] has done is cut out the middleman."

[3]However, see Brown de Vejar and Baldwin (2019), p. 541: "Certainly, third-party funders have no incentive to back a losing claim, and they generally have skilled teams of lawyers who assess the claim before determining whether to invest. But studying the form guide doesn't mean that the punter will pick the winning horse. The fact that the third-party funder has studied what is known about the case at a certain point (usually before anything is known of the respondent State's position) and is financially incentivized to bet on a winner does not mean that because the funder decides to invest, the case is bulletproof, or even that it is likely to end in a result favourable to the investor. It also does not mean that a fundamentally unmeritorious claim, which should never have been brought, will not receive third-party funding.") (parentheses in original); Nieuwveld and Sahani (2017), p. 25 ("[I]t helps to look at a third-party funder's motivations. At any point in time, the third-party funder will be determining on which one of three paths the litigation sits: (1) is the third-party funder still likely to make a significant profit; (2) if not, does the third-party funder have a decent chance of emerging with some or all of its original investment intact (and possibly a modest profit) if it continues to fund; or (3) is it likely that any new money invested will be wasted, alongside the old money? Only in the latter case (path 3) is it likely that the third-party funder will want to terminate.").

First, traditional for-profit third-party funders only fund cases from which they can make a profit.[4] Thus, many merit-based winners whose claims are too expensive to pursue relative to their claim value are turned down. Second, it is likely that long-shot winners—cases too risky even for a third-party funder—are less likely to be funded as well. These cases include those that rightfully argue for a change in the law or rely on creative theories that require mental and verbal jujitsu to convince the decision-maker of their merit (i.e., the topics of Hollywood films about courageous lawyers and citizens fighting against impossible odds). Third, respondent winners are less likely to receive funding unless those respondents already have funds at their disposal to either pay the funder a periodic premium or pay the funder from their own pockets (rather than from the proceeds of an award) upon winning the case. However, if a respondent winner already has that much cash on hand, they are more likely to finance their own representation rather than seek funding. Fourth, non-financial winners—parties seeking non-financial remedies—are unlikely to receive funding unless they are willing to pay the funder from their own pockets since there will be no monetary judgment upon winning the case. Fifth, political winners are unlikely to receive funding, as many funders choose not to fund controversial positions, parties, or cases involving governments. Funders avoiding political disputes could be considered courageous or cowardly, depending on the type of party or issue at stake in the case.

The previous examples collectively engender a broader, fundamental question: If funders pick likely winners—and more specifically, winners that suit their profit-making business model—then what does real access to justice look like in an era of third-party funding? For example, would real access to justice need to involve third-party funders funding indigent or innocent respondents,[5] expensive long-shot claimants, righteous injunctions with no monetary recovery, or unprofitable cases that espouse some worthy yet controversial position?

Much has been written about access to justice in civil litigation.[6] This chapter contributes to the conversation by presenting a theoretical framework to assess the current level of access to justice and determine pathways to increase access to justice. Moreover, this chapter proposes working definitions of "third-party funding" and "access to justice," and it presents a thought experiment to assess which parties currently have access to justice and which parties may lack such access. Finally, this chapter concludes by suggesting some next steps in increasing access to justice in civil proceedings.

[4]Cf. Nieuwveld and Sahani (2017), pp. 33–34 (describing traditional commercial third-party funding investments as seeking "three times" or "3X" return on investment, at a minimum).

[5]This chapter uses the term "respondent" to encompass both defendants in civil litigation and respondents in international arbitration.

[6]See generally Galanter (1994); Galanter (2010); Galanter (1999); Goodwin and Lindsay (2019); Buhai (2009); Abel (2009); Weinstein (2017); Steinberg (2015); Rogers (2015); Dautaj and Gustafsson (2017); Kudrna (2013); Butler and Herbert (2014); Daly and Melikian (2013), pp. 211–224; Francioni (2009), pp. 729–747.

2 Assumptions Made

2.1 Defining "Third-Party Funding"

What is third-party funding? Put simply, third-party funding is an arrangement in which a party involved in a dispute seeks funding from an outside entity for its legal representation instead of financing its own legal representation.[7] The outside entity—called a "third-party funder"—finances the party's legal representation in return for a profit.[8] The third-party funder could be a bank, hedge fund, insurance company, or some other entity or individual.[9] If the funded party is the plaintiff, then the funder typically contracts to receive a percentage or fraction of the monetary award from the case if the plaintiff wins.[10] Unlike a loan, the funded plaintiff does not have to repay the funder if it loses the case or does not recover any money.[11] If the funded party is the respondent, then the funder contracts to receive a predetermined payment from the respondent—similar to an insurance premium—and the agreement may include an extra payment to the funder if the respondent wins the case.[12] In addition to these traditional third-party funding structures, many other innovative third-party funding transaction structures can be used, the analysis of which is outside the scope of this chapter.[13]

To cast the widest net, this chapter adopts the ICCA-Queen Mary Task Force on Third-Party Funding[14] definition of "third-party funding," which reads as follows:

> The term "third-party funding" refers to an agreement by an entity that is not a party to the dispute to provide a party, an affiliate of that party or a law firm representing that party,
>
> (a) funds or other material support to finance part or all of the cost of the proceedings, either individually or as part of a specific range of cases, and
> (b) Such support or financing is either provided in exchange for remuneration or reimbursement that is wholly or partially dependent on the outcome of the dispute, provided through a grant [i.e., *pro bono*] or in return for a premium payment.[15]

---

[7] A party may also engage both a contingency fee attorney and a third-party litigation funder to work together simultaneously on its case.

[8] Nieuwveld and Sahani (2017), p. 1.

[9] Nieuwveld and Sahani (2017), p. 3.

[10] Nieuwveld and Sahani (2017), pp. 4–5.

[11] Nieuwveld and Sahani (2017), pp. 4–6.

[12] Nieuwveld and Sahani (2017), pp. 3–5.

[13] *See generally* Sahani (2017a), discussing innovative third-party funding transaction structures including funder-client and funder-law firm partnerships.

[14] This Task Force on Third-Party Funding was organized as a collaboration between the International Council for Commercial Arbitration (ICCA) and Queen Mary University of London School of Law between 2013 and 2018. See ICCA, *Third-Party Funding*, https://www.arbitration-icca.org/third-party-funding-task-force.

[15] ICCA, *ICCA Queen Mary Task Force Report on Third-Party Funding in Litigation, ICCA Rep. No. 4* (Apr. 2018), https://www.arbitration-icca.org/icca-reports-no-4-icca-queen-mary-task-force-report-third-party-funding.

This definition encompasses traditional for-profit third-party funding investments and not-for-profit third-party funding, in which profit-making is not the primary motive.[16]

Third-party funding is widespread around the world in both litigation and arbitration. A large and growing number of banks, hedge funds, and other financial institutions are funding the legal representation of parties to litigation as a type of investment. This phenomenon is growing exponentially and is already estimated to be a multibillion-dollar industry domestically and internationally.[17] In addition, depending on the structure of the funding arrangement, the funder may legally control or influence aspects of the legal representation or may completely take over the case and step into the shoes of the original party.[18] The United States is home to dozens of funders of consumer disputes, such as personal injury and other tort claims, and funders of large, complex corporate disputes.[19] In light of its increasing prevalence, there is a fascinating debate regarding the place of third-party funding both in the American legal system and in the context of international dispute resolution.[20]

There are four main drivers of the third-party funding industry worldwide. First, funders help some—but not all—individual plaintiffs bring claims that they would not otherwise be able to bring, which—in theory—supports the public policy ideal of

[16]See Sahani (2017b).

[17]See, e.g., Smith (2014): several funders have several hundreds of millions of dollars in assets under management; Smith (2013): "Gerchen Keller Capital LLC, a Chicago-based team that includes former lawyers . . . has raised more than $100 million and says there is plenty of room for newcomers given the size of the U.S. litigation market, which they put at more than $200 billion, measuring the money spent by plaintiffs and defendants on litigation."; O'Connell (2011): "The new breed of profit-seeker sees a huge, untapped market for betting on high-stakes commercial claims. After all, companies will spend about $15.5 billion this year on U.S. commercial litigation and an additional $2.6 billion on intellectual-property litigation, according to estimates by BTI Consulting Group Inc."

[18]See Nieuwveld and Sahani (2017), pp. 6–7: explaining that some third-party funding arrangements are structured as an assignment in which the third-party funder becomes the claimant in the case and the original party is no longer involved. For an in-depth treatment of assignment and insurance policies in the third-party funding context, see generally Sebok (2011b); Bond (2002); Cain (2014); Shukaitis (1987).

[19]Regarding consumer disputes, there are over 30 third-party funding companies funding consumer claims as members of the American Legal Finance Association (ALFA), as well as several other third-party funding companies that are not members of ALFA funding consumer disputes. See ALFA, http://www.americanlegalfin.com/. Regarding commercial disputes, see Smith (2014); Smith (2013); O'Connell (2011).

[20]See, e.g., Rodak (2006), pp. 504, 508, 513–523, 523, n. 113, 526–527; Martin (2004), pp. 56–57, 68–69, 72, 74, 77; Martin (2008), pp. 83–84; Sebok (2011b), p. 72, n. 36, p. 139; Barksdale (2007), p. 735; Steinitz (2011), pp. 1325–1336; Lyon (2010), pp. 608–609; Radin (1935), pp. 74–75: arguing for the regulation of contingency fees in a way similar to today's arguments for regulating third-party funding; Molot (2009), pp. 377–439: proposing defense-side funding in the United States that would be similar to after-the-event insurance in Europe; Shaltiel and Cofresi (2004), pp. 350–361: proposing a statute to regulate third-party funding for individual consumers.

increasing access to justice for indigent or disadvantaged persons.[21] However, third-party funding's contribution to increasing access to justice for plaintiffs does not reinforce the rights of civil respondents to present an adequate defense, which will be addressed later in this chapter. Second, many insolvent companies and small companies seek means to pursue valid claims that they could not otherwise afford to pursue and that are too risky for a contingency fee attorney to accept.[22] Third, many large companies are frequently sued (such as insurance companies or manufacturers of dangerous products) and seek means to smooth out the litigation line item on their balance sheets; funders can offer them a fixed-payment system for managing their litigation costs as respondents.[23] Fourth, the worldwide market turmoil over the past decade since the 2008 global financial crisis and the economic uncertainty in the aftermath of the COVID-19 pandemic have led many investors to seek investments that are not dependent upon financial markets, stock prices, or company valuations.[24] Each litigation or arbitration matter is separate and independent from market conditions regarding the value of the underlying harm or liability.[25] This independence shields the third-party funder's investment and potential profit from the general uncertainty present in the global financial markets.[26]

---

[21] See Abrams and Chen (2013), p. 1076, n. 3, p. 1077, n. 6, p. 1077, n.7: reporting the results of their study on public data on third-party funding available in Australia.

[22] See Raconteur Media, *Raconteur on Legal Efficiency*, The Times (Supp. Mar. 25, 2010), pp. 7–9; Steinitz (2011), pp. 1275–1276, 1283–1284; Martin (2004), p. 67, n. 93; Martin (2008), p. 685; Dana Jr. and Spier (1993), pp. 365–366; Lindeman (2010).

[23] See, e.g., LaCroix (2013): "Litigation funding proponents contend that the funding arrangements helps to level the playing field by allowing litigants to pursue lawsuits against better financed opponents, or simply allowing litigants to keep litigation costs off their balance sheet. It seems clear that as the litigation funding field grows, the funding companies are offering new approaches – for example, the defense side option that the Gerchen Keller firm will be offering, or the 'defense costs cover' that provided protection for prospective RBS claimants sufficient for them to be able to take on litigation in the U.K. notwithstanding the 'loser pays' litigation model that prevails there."; Lat (2013): "Ashley Keller [of Gerchen Keller Capital]: You're certainly right that a lot of these clients have balance sheet capacity and could fund out of pocket. Notwithstanding their balance sheet capacities, there might be institutional constraints. If a company has a $5 billion claim, it will pursue it. But what if it has a $50 million or $100 million claim? If you're a general counsel, a lot of C-suite executives are viewing your office as a cost center. It's not that easy to walk to the CFO's office and ask for $5 million or $10 million to finance offensive litigation. That will immediately hit the P&L of the company and affect earnings per share, but the outcome is uncertain and contingent. We think a fair number of meritorious claims are being left on the table notwithstanding balance sheet capacity."

[24] See Steinitz (2011), pp. 1283–1284.

[25] See Nieuwveld and Sahani (2017), p. 11.

[26] Id.

2.2 Defining "Access to Justice"

What is access to justice in civil litigation?[27] Access to justice can be defined in many ways depending on the context. For this chapter, simple working definitions are appropriate. Therefore, this chapter assumes that "justice" means that the system of civil dispute resolution, viewed as a whole, reliably and regularly decides cases in a fair and enforceable manner that upholds the due process of the law for all parties involved, leaving aside the idiosyncratic errors or biases of individual judges or arbitrators. Of course, this is a naively rosy assumption that could rightly be challenged by those critical of the civil litigation system. Nevertheless, such an assumption is necessary for this thought experiment—like a mathematical constant, if you will—to examine access to justice from a purely financial perspective.

Moreover, it is important to note that the definition of "justice" used in this chapter does not address the merits of a particular claim or defense. In other words, this chapter assumes that losers have just as much right as winners to bring their claims or marshal their defences and, therefore, losers deserve as much *procedural* justice as winners do—even though losers' substantive arguments on the merits may be less convincing to a judge or arbitrator. Again, such an assumption could be challenged, but this chapter adopts this assumption as necessary for the conclusions of this thought experiment, discussed further below.

This chapter also assumes that "access" relates to the *financial* ability to proceed forward in court proceedings. Thus, "access" in this context does not address nonfinancial barriers to adequate representation, such as jurisdictional requirements, unfavorable precedents, inadequate remedies, nonparticipating parties, the certifiability of a class, or any similar nonfinancial barrier. In sum, for the sake of argument, this chapter limits the phrase "access to justice" to mean having or acquiring the *financial* resources needed to bring your claim or muster your defense in court or arbitration.

In applying this definition, there are countless ways a party could have or acquire financial resources to pursue a claim or defend against it. For example, many parties self-finance their claims or defences. Parties may also acquire liability insurance or

---

[27] This chapter does not address third-party funding as a way to increase access to justice for criminal defendants, because third-party funding is illegal in criminal cases in over 60 jurisdictions worldwide in which this Author has conducted research. See Nieuwveld and Sahani (2017), presenting research on third-party funding laws in over 60 jurisdictions. Nevertheless, it is undisputed that severe access to justice problems exist for criminal defendants as well. See e.g., Goodwin (2016); Goodwin (2004); Bergmanis (2016); Luna (2005a); Luna (2005b). As a farfetched hypothetical, if third-party funding of criminal defense were allowed—and, to be clear, it is expressly *illegal* in all jurisdictions globally—criminal defendants might be able to subsidize the cost of their criminal defense using their related civil damages claims, with the financier funding both the criminal and civil proceedings. This would likely be prohibitively expensive and unprofitable, however, and therefore would not be an attractive target for investment by for-profit dispute financiers.

political risk insurance,[28] which may pay the costs of litigation or arbitration. Subsidiaries may be able to tap into the resources of their parent corporations. States or national governments may use their internal legal teams or tap into their treasuries to pay external law firms. A client may hire an attorney or law firm on a contingent or conditional fee basis. In addition, there's third-party funding.

Given the plethora of financing options, this chapter must draw an arbitrary dividing line in the sand to assess access to justice. On one side of that line, the party definitely has access to justice; on the other side, the party could potentially lack access to justice. It is important to note that this is not simply a line between the "haves" and the "have nots." Instead, it is a line between those who most certainly have access to justice and those whose access to justice is predicated on the outcome of the decision-making process of a financier not present at the time the dispute arises. Thus, this thought experiment draws the line where the party's dispute financing is based on a *preexisting* financial relationship with the financier *before* the event that led to the claim in the dispute. Of course, this line could be defined by other characteristics of a party or its case. Nevertheless, since this chapter focuses on *financial* access to justice, the choice to draw the line according to the status of the source of a party's funding seems most appropriate.

To illustrate how this line functions, the simplest example is that a party with the financial resources to self-finance litigation has a preexisting relationship with itself (the financier) before the claim arose; thus, that party has access to justice according to this chapter's definition. Similarly, a subsidiary has a preexisting relationship with a parent corporation before the dispute arises. If the parent corporation can and will provide financial support for a viable claim or defense, then the subsidiary has access to justice. Furthermore, if a party acquires liability insurance, political risk insurance, or legal expenses insurance at the outset of a contract or before entering into a commercial relationship, and if such insurance covers the costs of dispute resolution, then the party has access to justice.

On the other hand, an attorney or law firm will not enter into a contingent or conditional fee arrangement with a client until after the event that gives rise to the claim has taken place. Thus, if the party needs such a contingent or conditional fee arrangement to pursue litigation, then the party is in danger of not having access to justice if it cannot obtain such an arrangement. Similarly, third-party funding—as traditionally envisioned—is tied to the existence of events that give rise to a claim.

It is important to note that since the definition of access to justice articulated above involves engaging the machinery of court procedures, this chapter assumes that types of outside funding not tied to the existence of a dispute are more in the realm of corporate finance transactions and are not contemplated within this chapter's definition of access to justice. The assumption here is that if a party has the

[28] Political risk insurance insures an investor against a (usually foreign) government taking an action that harms or devalues the investors investment. See e.g., U.S. International Development Finance Corporation, *Political Risk Insurance*, https://www.dfc.gov/what-we-offer-our-products/political-risk-insurance.

means to enter into a corporate finance transaction independent of any pending disputes, then it also likely has access to adequate resources to pursue a claim or defend itself in litigation. Therefore, according to this chapter's narrow definition, it has access to justice. Furthermore, any insurance agreement entered into *after* the event that gives rise to the claim has taken place, which is often termed "after-the-event insurance,"[29] is categorized on the same side of the line as third-party funding and contingent or conditional fee arrangements.

This line in the sand is crucial because the "access" in "access to justice" indicates possibility, not certainty. In other words, having access to justice means that a party *could* financially pursue litigation even if it chooses not to do so or is unable to do so for other nonfinancial reasons. For example, if a subsidiary could bring a viable claim with the help of the parent corporation but chooses not to do so for business reasons, then the subsidiary has access to justice, according to the definition in this chapter. In addition, if the subsidiary could bring the claim with the help of the parent corporation, but the parent corporation believes that the claim is not viable enough to bring, then the subsidiary has access to justice, according to the definition in this chapter. Furthermore, if a party is a respondent with sufficient financial resources to self-finance and nevertheless *refuses* to participate in litigation (e.g., thinking that the claim is bogus), then the party has access to justice, according to the definition in this chapter.

On the other hand, if a party is the *respondent* and does *not* have sufficient financial resources to self-finance while wanting to participate meaningfully in the litigation, then whether such a respondent has access to justice depends on the type of financier that could finance the respondent's defense. If the respondent can obtain a financier through a preexisting financial relationship, such as a family member, a parent corporation, or a preexisting insurance agreement, then the respondent has access to justice. However, if the respondent's financial relationship with the financier arises after the event that led to the claim in the litigation—such as a contingent or conditional fee arrangement with a law firm, after-the-event insurance, or traditional third-party funding—then the respondent may have no access to justice if it is unable to create such a financial relationship.

This highlights a crucial point about access to justice regardless of the definition. Any proper assessment of access to justice must examine the situation of parties that have no choice in the matter: respondents. Respondents in all types of adjudication have no choice regarding whether the adjudicated result will bind them, regardless of whether they are financially able to participate in the proceedings or not. Thus, respondents *must* have access to justice—obtaining the financial resources needed to muster their defenses in litigation—for the system to be considered "just" at all.

---

[29] After-the-event insurance often overlaps with third-party funding and is also offered by third-party funders. See e.g., Allianz, *Allianz Legal Protection*, https://www.allianz.co.uk/business/legal-protection.html ("After the event (ATE) insurance will provide cover against the financial burden incurred if a legal action is unsuccessful, including opponent's solicitor's costs, expert reports, barrister's fees and court fees.").

2.3 Cost as a Component of "Access to Justice"

There is also a cost component to access to justice, namely, whether the financier's willingness to pay the costs of litigation is predicated on some relationship between the amount of the costs of litigation and the value of the claim. Some types of financiers—such as self-financiers, parent corporations, and liability insurers—will pay litigation costs regardless of the amount of the claim or the type of defense because of their preexisting relationship. Other types of financiers—such as third-party funders or after-the-event insurers—might only agree to pay the litigation costs if the costs are a fraction of the claim amount or if the party provides the financier with an alternative form of remuneration. Attorneys on contingent or conditional fees likely fall somewhere between those two extremes. A contingent-fee attorney may turn down a case that might be too expensive to pursue relative to the expected contingent fee if the party wins the case, especially since most jurisdictions have a legislative cap on attorney contingent or conditional fees.[30] In light of this, the cost of litigation is a crucial component to consider in determining whether a party has adequate access to justice.

To further complicate the matter of costs, it is nearly impossible to calculate precisely how much a case will cost in advance. The only exception may be that some financiers, such as third-party funders or law firms working on a contingent or conditional fee, may include provisions in their contracts capping the amount the funder will spend on litigation costs. In addition, there are different fee provisions under the various arbitration rules—whether calculated on an hourly or daily rate or based on the amount in dispute—and, for *ad hoc* arbitration,[31] the basis for the fees is even more variable. Moreover, some claims or remedies may require more extensive resources, such as class litigation, or may require the services of an emergency judge or arbitrator (in addition to the one deciding the merits of the case), such as an injunction. In addition, the costs in such proceedings may be highly variable and not connected to the case's economic value. Furthermore, some remedies may have no damage award attached to them, such as injunctive or declarative relief. The costs in cases with non-monetary judgments and awards will always mathematically outweigh the dollars recoverable from the claim, even if the claim is otherwise worthy, winnable, and has intrinsic value. Finally, there is the question of

---

[30] See generally Nieuwveld and Sahani (2017), citing contingent or conditional fee caps in the Canada, China, New Zealand, South Africa, the United Kingdom and United States. There are also likely many other countries that cap contingent or conditional fees, but which were not included in the aforementioned book due to the lack of information available from those countries regarding the availability of third-party funding.

[31] *Ad hoc* arbitration is arbitration administered solely by the arbitrator or arbitrators and is not overseen by the auspices of an arbitration institution or other administrative body. See e.g., United Nations Commission on International Trade Law (UNCITRAL), *UNCITRAL Arbitration Rules (with new article 1, paragraph 4, as adopted in 2013)*, https://uncitral.un.org/sites/uncitral.un.org/files/media-documents/uncitral/en/uncitral-arbitration-rules-2013-e.pdf (exemplifying arbitral rules commonly used for *ad hoc* international arbitration).

timing and settlement. If all other parameters are equal, a case that settles early usually results in cheaper costs than a case that goes all the way to an award, which also results in cheaper costs than a case that leads to enforcement or appeal proceedings after the judgment or award.

In sum, a case may be wildly expensive or may settle cheaply. Usually, one cannot predict in advance exactly which of these scenarios will happen in a particular case. Therefore, considering the high variability in cost structures and amounts, the thought experiment in this chapter makes a simple assumption about costs. It assumes that the costs for a hypothetical party to a case are reasonable and proportional to the type of case and type of claim or defense at issue, even though many cases may be extraordinarily expensive or surprisingly inexpensive. This assumption regarding costs is necessary to draw generalizable conclusions regarding access to justice from this thought experiment.

2.4 Other Assumptions

There are a few less controversial assumptions in this thought experiment as well. First, this chapter addresses only three types of parties: a corporation, a state, or an individual. A state-owned corporate entity is treated the same as a private corporation in this chapter.[32] Multi-party actions—such as class, mass, or representative actions—are not contemplated. Furthermore, this chapter categorizes the relief requested by a claimant as either damages or nonfinancial relief, such as an injunction, specific performance, or declarative relief. For respondents, the relief requested (that is, the respondent's "claim") is characterized as "no liability" (namely, asking the tribunal to decide that the respondent is not liable for the injury the claimant alleges) to consider respondents and claimants together in this chapter. Parties may request other hybrid, unusual, or less common types of relief, but the aforementioned categories encompass most types of claims or defences.

Finally, since it is virtually impossible to predict with certainty the outcome of a case, this chapter addresses only two possibilities concerning the outcome—likely winner or likely loser. However, a party is just as likely to win or lose in reality. This chapter addresses only those two possibilities because all parties, including those who are self-financing, engage in some analysis regarding the likelihood of winning the case when deciding whether or how to proceed. Most parties or their legal counsel have at least some expectation regarding whether the party is more likely to win or more likely to lose the case, and funders analyse this question and draw their conclusions often before the litigation has even commenced. Moreover, some

[32]For reasons beyond the scope of this chapter, the Author takes the view that states and state-owned entities that are parties in a contractually-based international commercial arbitration are in a fundamentally different position than respondent states sued in investment treaty arbitration. For example, one key difference is that contractual rights are bilateral whereas rights under classic investment treaties are unilateral in favor of investors and against states.

financiers enter the case in the middle of the proceedings or finance enforcement proceedings at the end of the case. Those financiers will have a different viewpoint regarding the likelihood of winning than the financier who considers the case at the outset. Thus, the categories "likely winner" and "likely loser" are rough and inexact but help draw another necessary line in the sand, similar to this chapter's aforementioned arbitrary dividing line for defining access to justice.[33]

3 A Thought Experiment on Access to Justice

This section presents a thought experiment based on the assumptions above to assess what types of parties are in danger of not having access to justice. This thought experiment begins by excluding parties whose preexisting relationships provide access to justice. From the foregoing assumptions, any party with a preexisting financial relationship with the financier *before* the event that led to the claim has access to justice. Thus, any party with the guaranteed ability to self-finance or obtain funding from a parent corporation or preexisting insurance contract (liability insurance or before-the-event insurance) has access to justice. This is true regardless of the likelihood of winning or losing, the type of claim, and whether the party is a claimant or respondent. This is also true if the party chooses not to pursue the claim or defense, despite having adequate financial resources.

In contrast, a party in danger of lacking access to justice must enter into a new financial relationship *after* the event that gives rise to the claim. Thus, the thought experiment will focus on avenues for financial support for litigation that are available only after the event that gives rise to the claim has happened. These avenues include contingent or conditional fee agreements with attorneys, after-the-event insurance agreements, bank loans, and traditional third-party funding arrangements.

The second phase of the thought experiment narrows the categories of litigation parties that need dispute financing by separating those likely to win from those likely to lose. Most available options for dispute financing after the event are tied to the likelihood of winning. Attorneys and law firms will generally only enter into a contingent or conditional fee agreement if they believe the case is a likely winner. Similarly, after-the-event insurers and third-party funders will generally only enter into an arrangement in which they expect to make money, usually tied to the party winning the case or receiving a settlement. There are some structures for third-party funding or after-the-event insurance (often, but not exclusively, on the defense side) where the financier receives some remuneration even if the party loses the case.[34] In

[33] See supra Sect. 2.2.

[34] These structures normally involve either the respondent making periodic fixed payments to the funder while the funder pays for the fluctuating legal costs, or the respondent making a "success payment" to the funder if the respondent wins the case and avoids liability, or both. See e.g., Sahani (2017a).

most situations, however, financiers that enter into a postdispute agreement with a party want to fund likely winners on the merits rather than likely losers if such a characteristic can be gleaned at the outset. Thus, in contrast to the situation described in the prior paragraph, in which the party is virtually guaranteed access to justice, a party with no preexisting financial relationship with the financier and who is also likely to *lose* its claim or defense has almost no access to justice. The word "almost" is used because there may be rare instances of financiers willing to back a case with a slight chance of winning (a "long shot"). However, regularly backing cases likely to lose would not be lucrative for such financiers and may frustrate their investors. Thus, parties likely to lose will remain largely unfunded unless a preexisting financier is available. Therefore, according to the framework presented in this chapter, such parties are likely to lack access to justice.

This lack of access to justice for these "likely losers" can be viewed in two different ways. On the one hand, one could argue that claimants who have a high likelihood of losing should not be able to bring their claims, perhaps (for example) because those claims might be frivolous. Similarly, one could argue that respondents who have a high likelihood of losing should not need the money to muster a zealous defense, perhaps because they genuinely did injure the claimant and the magnitude of that injury is equal to the relief that the claimant alleges. On the other hand, one could argue that both claimants and respondents may have a high likelihood of losing, not because the claim or defense is invalid or frivolous but rather due to a defect in the law applied to the case, the party's lack of access to evidence to submit to the tribunal (for example, if the opposing party possesses the majority of the vital evidence), or the party's (perhaps less expensive) legal counsel being inexperienced in litigation or arbitration. In addition, even losers deserve the opportunity to zealously advocate for reducing the magnitude of their losses by arguing in favor of a set-off claim, a partial award, a lower cost award to the winner, or a lower interest rate on the damages (if applicable).

Nevertheless, the lived experience of "winning" and "losing" feels more like a spectrum than polar opposites because all parties involved lose time resolving the matter, and most lose some money on costs. Thus, this chapter focuses purely on winners or losers on the *merits only*, rather than degrees of winning or losing measured by cost allocation or award set-offs. The result is that likely losers on the merits that need dispute financing typically do not obtain such financing and, therefore, lack access to justice. This is the first access to justice problem that this thought experiment has uncovered: *How can we provide access to justice for "unfunded losers"?*

If we set aside the parties with preexisting access to funding and the unfunded losers, we are left with what this chapter terms "unfunded winners," namely, claims or defences that are likely to win on the merits if the party can obtain dispute financing. In civil litigation, the parties are all fungible, meaning that any party can be on any side and bring any claim or counterclaim. Corporations, individuals, and states can all serve as either claimants or respondents in civil disputes. In addition, respondents in civil disputes can bring counterclaims or set-off claims, which gives them the ability to serve as claimants while also serving as respondents simultaneously. Therefore, the type of party is irrelevant in determining whether access to justice is available to unfunded winners in civil litigation. This is also true in domestic arbitration and international commercial arbitration, although it is not true in international investment treaty arbitration for reasons beyond the scope of this brief intervention.[35]

Instead, one must examine the type of claim to assess access to justice for "unfunded winners" in civil litigation. Damages claims are understandably attractive to dispute financiers because there will be a pot of money to share if the party wins. Nonfinancial claims and "no liability claims" (defenses) are less attractive or might be utterly unattractive. Such claims do not automatically create a pot of money to share, even though such claims may be worthy of merit. Dispute financiers that arrive on the scene after the dispute has arisen are typically looking for a cash profit. This is where the access to justice problem arises in civil litigation. The one exception is what one may call "not-for-profit" funders, which are funders that take an interest in the specific merits outcome of the case for nonfinancial reasons and do not expect to make a profit.[36] However, "not-for-profit" funders are not

[35] Under traditional international investment treaty arbitration, corporations or individuals are always claimants, and states are always respondents in investment arbitration. For arguments in favor of granting states jurisdiction to bring claims in investment arbitration, see, e.g., Shannon (2015b); Laborde (2010). This is because traditional investment treaties do not provide for rights of the respondent state. For a basic explanation of jurisdiction in investment treaty litigation, see, e.g., Schreuer (2014). However, some investment treaties negotiated in modern times do contain rights of respondent states and corresponding obligations of the individual or corporate investor. See, e.g., Gazzini (2017), describing the innovations in this treaty, including putting obligations on investors to comply with the laws of the host state and providing a state the opportunity to sue an investor in the courts of its home country for violations of the treaty obligations. While this treaty does not allow for a state to bring an investment litigation claim against an investor, the treaty does provide a judicial route through which the state may be compensated for any wrongs the investor commits under the treaty. In addition, the treaty is silent regarding whether states may bring counterclaims against investors in investment treaty litigation, which may open the door to jurisdiction over such claims. The effects of these provisions will be tested if a case is eventually commenced under the treaty. Furthermore, jurisdictional constraints restrict the types of claims that can be brought. The treaty must specifically name the substantive rights that claimants may vindicate in investment litigation. In vindicating those rights, the claimant may request damages or non-financial relief, such as restitution in kind or specific performance, but only if such remedies are allowed by the treaty. See, e.g., Schneider (2011); Allen (2011); Schreuer (2004). Under more modern investment treaties, respondent states may have the jurisdictional ability to bring substantive counterclaims and the corresponding rights within the treaty that may be vindicated in investment litigation. For some examples of how tribunals have responded in cases in which host states have tried to bring counterclaims under traditional investment treaties, see Kalicki (2012). Nevertheless, the right to bring a counterclaim is necessarily predicated on the claimant bringing the original claim first. Thus, it is exceedingly rare to see a host state bring an initial claim (rather than a counterclaim) against an investor under a treaty. As mentioned in the main text above, such a scenario would most certainly be possible in a contractually agreed domestic arbitration or international commercial arbitration.

[36] Cf. generally Sahani et al. (2018): "In addition, not-for-profit funding may be a viable option for respondents in international arbitration—particularly respondent States in investment arbitration—since a financial return on investment would not normally be required." Sahani (2017b); Sahani (2022). For example, in *Philip Morris v. Uruguay*, Uruguay's defense was funded by a not-for-

general market players in this space; they typically fund cases on a one-off, case-by-case basis and cannot be counted on to fund large categories of cases. Thus, "not-for-profit" funders cannot provide a generalizable solution to civil disputes as a whole and, therefore, cannot solve the problem of access to justice in civil litigation. This brings us to our second access to justice problem that this thought experiment has uncovered: *How can we provide access to justice for "unfunded winners" with non-damages claims or defenses?*

Turning to investment arbitration, the picture becomes more complicated. "Unfunded winners" in investment arbitration must first be divided by party. Due to jurisdictional constraints, corporations or individuals are almost always claimants in investment arbitration, and states are almost always respondents in investment arbitration.[37] Furthermore, jurisdictional constraints restrict the types of claims that can be brought. The treaty must specifically name the substantive rights claimants may vindicate in investment arbitration. In vindicating those rights, the claimant may request damages or nonfinancial relief, such as restitution in kind[38] or specific performance, but only if such remedies are allowed by the treaty.

Traditional investment treaties do not provide for the rights of the respondent state,[39] although some investment treaties negotiated in modern times do contain the rights of respondent states and corresponding obligations of the individual or corporate investor.[40] Under traditional investment treaties, the respondent state has no right to bring a counterclaim. The only "claim" a respondent state could have is a

profit funder called the Campaign for Tobacco-Free Kids, and the Anti-Tobacco Litigation Fund (a Bloomberg Foundation and Gates Foundation collaboration) is funding respondent states facing similar challenges. *See* Bloomberg Philanthropies, *Bloomberg Philanthropies & The Bill & Melinda Gates Foundation Launch Anti-Tobacco Trade Litigation Fund*, Press & Media (Mar. 18, 2015), https://www.bloomberg.org/press/bloomberg-philanthropies-bill-melinda-gates-foundation-launch-anti-tobacco-trade-litigation-fund/. The Bloomberg and Gates Foundations are not-for-profit funders, however, which invites the question, should only not-for-profit funders fund respondent governments? This chapter argues for answering this question in the negative, but cogent arguments could be made on the other side. For example, in the political campaign finance arena, arguments have been raised about the impropriety of corporate influence over elections and governmental functions through lobbying and financial contributions; one could argue that for-profit third-party funders funding governments, generally, could yield similar negative effects.

[37] For arguments in favour of granting states jurisdiction to bring claims in investment arbitration, see, e.g., Shannon (2015b); Laborde (2010).

[38] See, e.g., Schneider (2011); Allen (2011); Schreuer (2004), pp. 325–332.

[39] For a basic explanation of jurisdiction in investment treaty arbitration, See, e.g., Schreuer (2014).

[40] See, e.g., Gazzini (2017), describing the innovations in this treaty, including putting obligations on investors to comply with the laws of the host state and providing a state the opportunity to sue an investor in the courts of its home country for violations of the treaty obligations. While this treaty does not allow for a state to bring an investment arbitration claim against an investor, the treaty does provide a judicial route through which the state may be compensated for any wrongs the investor commits under the treaty. In addition, the treaty is silent regarding whether states may bring counterclaims against investors in investment treaty arbitration, which may open the door to jurisdiction over such claims. The effects of these provisions will be tested if a case is eventually commenced under the treaty.

claim of "no liability," which translates as its defense as defined above. Under more modern investment treaties, respondent states may have the jurisdictional ability to bring substantive counterclaims and the corresponding rights within the treaty that may be vindicated in investment arbitration.[41] Nevertheless, the right to bring a counterclaim is necessarily predicated on the claimant bringing the original claim first. Thus, it is exceedingly rare to see a host state bring an initial claim (rather than a counterclaim) against an investor under a treaty. As discussed above, such a scenario would most certainly be possible under a contract. Therefore, in pure treaty arbitration under traditional investment treaties, the host state appears to be perpetually stuck in the respondent role with almost no jurisdictional or substantive access to counterclaims. This means that the respondent always has a "no liability" claim but rarely will have any other type of claim under a traditional investment treaty.

In contrast, the individual or corporate investor can bring damages and nonfinancial claims in investment treaty arbitration. If the respondent state could overcome a jurisdictional challenge to a counterclaim, then the investor would also have a "no liability" claim vis-à-vis that counterclaim. This means that the individual or corporate investor can subsidize the cost of bringing nonfinancial claims through damages claims. Thus, the individual or corporate investor claimant is more likely to have access to justice in investment treaty arbitration than the respondent state.

4 Suggestions for Increasing Access to Justice

The thought experiment above has raised the following question: *How can we provide access to justice for two types of parties in civil dispute resolution: unfunded losers and unfunded winners with non-damages claims or defences?* Both of these categories also include respondent states in investment arbitration. This chapter concludes with a few ideas regarding how to address this question and thereby improve access to justice in civil dispute resolution both domestically and internationally.

The first step is for our global society to decide whether the concept of the procedural due process requires that unfunded losers and unfunded winners have adequate access to dispute financing. This is more of a philosophical question and, thus, is largely beyond the scope of this brief chapter. The short answer, from this author's point of view, is that the right to adequate resources for loss mitigation—i.e., a party's right to argue for a judge or arbitrator to reduce the amount of the party's loss—is a right that society should recognize as part of the concept of procedural due process. Arguing in favor of loss mitigation may take the form of pursuing a claim that is likely to lose, requesting an injunction or other non-monetary

[41] For some examples of how tribunals have responded in cases in which host states have tried to bring counterclaims under traditional investment treaties, see Kalicki (2012).

relief, arguing for paying lower costs despite losing on the merits, or presenting a viable defense, including mitigating factors.

Note that likely losers, as mentioned in this paragraph, may include plaintiffs and respondents—a long shot could be on either side of a case. However, long shots can change the world, as we have seen in cases in which the right of minority groups facing long-shot odds and unfavorable laws have led to judicial victories that have changed the course of history. In addition, even in the criminal context, the loser has the opportunity to mitigate their loss of liberty by taking a plea agreement to reduce the length of their prison sentence. Should losers in the civil context not have equal access to loss mitigation resources? Losers have the right to "lose well," including presenting the most robust case they can for their side, even if those arguments do not sway the decision-maker regarding the final decision on the merits. This author believes that loss mitigation is as fundamental to assessing access to justice as the idea of meritorious claims. Thus, for the sake of argument, this chapter will assume that society would agree that the concept of procedural due process requires that unfunded parties in the three categories outlined in this chapter have adequate access to dispute financing to proceed to the next step in this analysis. However, this author recognizes that compelling arguments could undoubtedly be made on the opposing side.[42] Assuming that unfunded losers and unfunded winners have a right to adequate financing for their claims or defences, the next step in this analysis is determining how to pay for this. This chapter presents four categories of possible solutions.

The first potential solution is for the unfunded party to bring more than one claim in litigation or arbitration. A party in civil litigation can subsidize the cost of bringing a nonfinancial claim or a lower damage claim via a higher damage claim such that the marginal cost of bringing two (or three) claims instead of one is significantly reduced. In fact, most plaintiffs bring at least one damages claim even if they intend to raise nonfinancial claims. Thus, the potential recovery on the damages claim could be enough to cover the costs of the additional nonfinancial claims or low damages claims such that a dispute financier might agree to finance the representation. A drawback of this solution is that it would be limited to unfunded parties with more than one viable claim, one of which is a damage claim that would be attractive enough to a dispute financier. Therefore, this would not include unfunded parties who may only have a nonfinancial claim that the court would entertain, even if the nonfinancial claim is strong on the merits.

Since both claimants and respondents in investment arbitration may have damages and nonfinancial claims, the problem is not the type of claim but rather the type of party. Unsurprisingly, respondents in investment arbitration are generally not

[42]For example, in *Essar Oilfields Serv. v. Norscot Rig Mgmt.*, [2016] EWHC 2361 (Comm), the High Court upheld an ICC tribunal's ruling requiring the respondent to pay the claimant's cost of third-party funding in addition to paying the underlying damage award, because the court found that the respondent so damaged the claimant's financial position as to require the claimant to seek third-party funding in the first place. For a description of the *Essar* case, see, e.g., Szymanski (2016).

attractive targets for investment by for-profit dispute financiers.[43] This brings us to the third and final access to justice problem that this thought experiment has uncovered: *How can we provide access to justice for respondents in investment arbitration?* The term "respondents" may be more appropriate than "respondent states" because, although exceedingly rare, a few treaties permit a host state to initiate a claim against an investor.[44]

The second category of potential solutions involves donations of time or money. For example, third-party funders and after-the-event insurers should engage in pro bono funding for a subset of meritorious claims or defences that may be long shot winners, which are seemingly worthy but likely to lose, or non-damages claims. One could include worthy claims against judgment-proof respondents in this category, meaning that the plaintiff would likely win the case but might be unable to collect the award from the respondent. Thus, an unpaid judgment or award could have a symbolic, political, or public value that would make the endeavor worthwhile for non-monetary reasons. Additionally, it could result in positive reputational effects for the funder or insurer that supports the plaintiff *pro bono* in the case. A drawback of this solution is that it would require a likely unrealistic paradigm shift in the for-profit dispute financing industry to embrace its role in promoting widespread access to justice beyond its primary profit-making motive. Whether such a transition is possible remains to be seen.

Another way to frame this solution is by analogizing dispute financing pro bono efforts to attorney pro bono obligations. For example, the attorney bar in many countries asks attorneys to donate a small percentage of their annual hours (e.g., fifty hours per year on average in the United States)[45] to pro bono efforts or for attorneys to donate money to the pro bono efforts of other attorneys instead of performing the work directly. Similarly, law firms regularly take on some litigation cases pro bono, without any expectation of reimbursement. By analogy, third-party funders or after-the-event insurers should donate some small percentage of their portfolio funds toward pro bono efforts without expecting a return on investment. In addition, a defense fund for needy respondents could be established, perhaps even from the funds donated pro bono by third-party funders, law firms, and after-the-event

---

[43] There is potentially one dispute financier that would finance a respondent state's "no liability" claim (i.e. its defence), but one dispute financier is not enough to solve a systemic, structural problem. Narghis Torres, Co-Founder and CEO of LexFinance, publicly stated that his firm regularly finances respondent states in investment arbitration at an event titled "Third-Party Funding in Investor-State Dispute Settlement" hosted by Columbia Law School on 17 Oct. 2017. This Author was in attendance at the event.

[44] See note 35 describing the 2016 Morocco-Nigeria BIT which allows host state claims against investors in national courts and, arguably, may allow host state counterclaims in an investment arbitration initiated by the investor under this treaty.

[45] See Amer. Bar. Ass'n, Model Rules of Prof'l Conduct, r. 6.1 ("Every lawyer has a professional responsibility to provide legal services to those unable to pay. A lawyer should aspire to render at least (50) hours of pro bono publico legal services per year . . . . In addition, a lawyer should voluntarily contribute financial support to organizations that provide legal services to persons of limited means.") (parentheses in original).

insurers.[46] Finally, crowdfunding by multiple individual donors—which already exists—may provide a potential solution in this context.[47]

The third category of potential solutions involves changes in the law or litigation rules. For example, courts and arbitral institutions could adjust their fee scales to give indigent parties a discount on the fees. Alternatively, courts and arbitral institutions could adopt a rule that a party against whom an injunction or declaratory relief is granted must pay the litigation costs of the winning party. This latter solution would allow law firms to take on injunction or declaratory relief cases on a contingent or conditional basis; their attorney fees will be repaid if the party is granted the requested relief. However, the drawback of this solution is that it would only help parties likely to have their injunctions or declaratory relief granted, i.e., unfunded winners; this solution would not assist unfunded losers.

Another more controversial change, which is also less likely to be implemented, is the renegotiation of investment treaties to allow for host-state claims against investors and counterclaims by respondents. This one is much harder to implement since many countries no longer have the political will to ratify a renegotiated treaty, no matter how problematic the existing treaty may be. Nevertheless, countries whose investment treaties have expired, who are engaged in renegotiating their treaties for other reasons, or who are entering into new treaties could consider including provisions to allow for host state claims. In addition, the European Court of Justice decision in *Slowakische Republik v. Achmea BV* signals that all the investment treaties in Europe will likely need to be renegotiated, at least in part.[48] Provisions for host-state claims against investors and counterclaims by respondents could be included in those renegotiated treaties or in any EU-wide investment treaty that may be negotiated in the future.

Finally, a fourth category of solutions involves financiers modifying their criteria when deciding which cases to fund. For example, a third-party funder might modify its algorithms and decision-making processes to include other factors in determining whether to fund a case to increase access to justice in litigation. One of those factors could be ensuring that respondents have access to third-party funding. Notably,

---

[46]For a proposal for funding developing states in WTO dispute settlement, see, e.g., Nagelmueller (2017), proposing that for-profit dispute financiers should provide financing to developing states in WTO dispute settlement proceedings.

[47]See, e.g., Gomez (2015); Perry (2018).

[48]See *Slowakische Republik v Achmea BV*, Case C-284/16, Decision of the Court of Justice of the European Union (6 Mar. 2018). For a description of the decision and its impact, See, e.g., Court of Justice of the European Union, *Press Release: No. 26/18 – The arbitration clause in the Agreement between the Netherlands and Slovakia on the protection of investments is not compatible with EU law* (6 Mar. 2018), https://curia.europa.eu/jcms/upload/docs/application/pdf/2018-03/cp180026en.pdf; Reuters, *EU Court Rules Against Tribunals Settling Intra-EU Disputes* (6 Mar. 2018), https://www.reuters.com/article/us-eu-court-arbitration/eu-court-rules-against-tribunals-settling-intra-eu-disputes-idUSKCN1GI1AY; Center for International Environmental Law, *Press Release: New European Court of Justice (ECJ) ruling could signal end of intra-EU investor-state dispute settlement* (6 Mar. 2018), https://www.ciel.org/news/new-european-court-justice-ecj-ruling-signal-end-intra-eu-investor-state-dispute-settlement/.

respondents can fall into all categories of unfunded parties mentioned in this chapter's introduction. Respondents can be long-shot winners, respondent winners, nonfinancial winners, and political winners all at the same time, depending on the facts and circumstances of the dispute. Respondents—particularly those with viable counterclaims—can also be merit-based winners whose claims are too expensive to pursue relative to their claim value when offset by the cost to defend against the investor's original claim.

Furthermore, third-party funders have a much more dubious reputation in investment arbitration than in commercial arbitration. Gallons of ink have been spent arguing against allowing third-party funding in investment arbitration for various reasons.[49] If third-party funders financed respondents more regularly, then perhaps the participation of third-party funders in dispute settlement would be viewed as more balanced, perhaps even viewed positively. In addition, investment arbitration, as a whole, may be viewed as more legitimate if respondent states have more regular access to third-party funding. If third-party funders in litigation choose to take the first step toward genuinely contributing to access to justice, that first step should be to fund respondent states in investment arbitration and civil respondents.

To address a broader question, the solutions presented in this chapter depart from the poverty paradigm that is often used to argue that dispute financiers should modify their choices regarding which cases to fund to promote access to justice.[50] For example, since so few respondent states are currently being funded, to this author's knowledge, both poor and wealthy respondent states alike are equally denied third-party funding from most for-profit funders. Instead, this chapter argues that assessing worthy, nonfinancial aspects of a case may be the proper foundation of "access to justice" that funders should espouse and support financially, such as upholding the health and safety laws of a country,[51] defending against abusive investment practices, ensuring the stability of a country's legal system, stopping damaging environmental practices of investors, clarifying the meaning of ambiguous treaty language, and so on. This chapter argues that those are worthy ideals worth pursuing and financing regardless of the wealth or poverty of the respondent nation or the potential for profit (or lack thereof).

---

[49] See note 35.

[50] See, e.g., United Nations Office of the High Representative for the Least Developed Countries, Landlocked Developing Countries and Small Island Developing States (UNOHRLLS) and the International Development Law Organization (IDLO), *Investment Support Programme for the Least Developed Countries (ISP/LDCs): Programme Document*, p. 5 and fn. 11 (6 Sep. 2017), https://res.cloudinary.com/lbresearch/image/upload/v1506335575/isp_ldcs_programme_document_6_september_258117_1133.pdf (proposing a system for providing support to poor states for, among other endeavours, "[f]oreign investment-related dispute settlement between the Client and a foreign entity, including arbitration or any other alternative dispute resolution proceeding" and "if the applicable rules to the dispute allow, the ISP/LDCS may also seek to identify and field the Client's party-appointed arbitrator").

[51] See note 36 for an example of a non-profit funder supporting a state's laws regarding packaging of tobacco products for public health and safety reasons.

5 Conclusion

This chapter has argued that if funders decide to fund only one additional category of parties to increase "access to justice"—even if such funding cuts against the funder's profit-seeking interests—then respondents are an excellent place to begin. This is because respondents in civil litigation and arbitration, by definition, do not commence the dispute. Therefore, in theory, the third-party funder did not stir up the litigation itself (i.e., maintenance, champerty, or barratry). In addition, this chapter has proposed that worthy aspects of the case in addition to financial value may be the proper foundation of "access to justice" that funders should espouse and support financially. Finally, this chapter has presented a few ideas regarding how a funder might modify its algorithms and decision-making processes to include some of these aspects as factors to weigh in determining whether to fund the various categories of "unfunded winners" to help rebalance the scales of justice.

The thought experiment presented in this chapter intends to provoke discussion and deep thought about the legitimacy crisis in our global system of dispute resolution as viewed through the lens of financial access to justice and in light of new options for parties to access capital for their cases. Although the assumptions made herein may seem rudimentary and the solutions presented may seem idealistic, this chapter provides a solid starting point for a global discussion wherein targeted solutions could be developed that may be more viable to implement than the solutions proposed herein.

References

Abel LK (2009) Evidence-based access to justice. Univ Pa J Law Soc Change 13:295

Abrams DS, Chen DL (2013) A market for justice: a first empirical look at third party litigation funding. Univ Pa J Bus Law 15:1075

Allen BE (2011) The use of non-pecuniary remedies in WTO dispute settlement: lessons for arbitral practitioners. In: Performance as a remedy: non-monetary relief in international arbitration: ASA special series no. 30

Barksdale CR (2007) Note, all that glitters isn't gold: analyzing the costs and benefits of litigation finance. Rev Litig 26:707

Bergmanis E (2016) Justice underfunded is justice denied. J Mo B 72:4

Bond P (2002) Making champerty work: an invitation to state action. Univ Pa Law Rev 150:1297

Brown de Vejar K, Baldwin C (2019) The economics of access: systemic imbalances in ISDS. In: Kalicki J, Raouf A (eds) Evolution and adaptation: the future of international arbitration. Wolters Kluwer

Buhai SL (2009) Access to justice for unrepresented litigants: a comparative perspective. Loy Los Angeles Law Rev 42:979

Burke Robertson C (2011) The impact of third-party financing on transnational litigation. Case West Reserve J Int Law 44:159

Butler P, Herbert C (2014) Access to justice vs access to justice for small and medium-sized enterprises: the case for a bilateral arbitration treaty. N Z Univ Law Rev 26:186

Cain T (2014) Third party funding of personal injury tort claims: keep the baby and change the bathwater. Chic Kent Law Rev 89:11

Chamblee Burch E (2015) On regulatory discord and procedure. N Y Univ J Law Bus 11:819
Daly BW, Melikian S (2013) Access to justice in dispute resolution. In: Scheffer KN (ed) Poverty and the international economic legal system: duties to the world's poor. Cambridge University Press
Dana JD Jr, Spier KE (1993) Expertise and contingent fees: the role of asymmetric information in attorney compensation. J Law Econ Organ 9:349
Dautaj Y, Gustafsson B (2017) Access to justice: rebalancing the third-party funding equilibrium in investment treaty arbitration. Kluwer Arbitration Blog, 18 November 2017. http://arbitrationblog.kluwerarbitration.com/2017/11/18/access-justice-rebalancing-third-party-funding-equilibrium-investment-treaty-arbitration-2/
Eberhardt P (2013) A response to the critics of "profiting from injustice". Kluwer Arbitration Blog, 2 January 2013. http://arbitrationblog.kluwerarbitration.com/2013/01/02/a-response-to-the-critics-of-profiting-from-injustice/
Eberhardt P, Olivet C (2012) Transnational Institute and Corporate Europe Observatory, profiting from injustice, Brussels/Amsterdam, November 2012. https://corporateeurope.org/sites/default/files/publications/profiting-from-injustice.pdf
Francioni F (2009) Access to justice, denial of justice and international investment law. Eur J Int Law 20(3):729–747
Freeman Engstrom N (2013) Re-re-financing civil litigation: how lawyer lending might remake the American litigation landscape, again. UCLA Law Rev Discourse 61:110
Freeman Engstrom N (2014) Lawyer lending: costs and consequences. Depaul Law Rev 63:377
Galanter M (1994) Predators and parasites: lawyer-bashing and civil justice. Georgia Law Rev 28:633
Galanter M (1999) "Old and in the way": the coming demographic transformation of the legal profession and its implications for the provision of legal services. Wis Law Rev 1999:1081
Galanter M (2010) Access to justice in a world of expanding social capability. Fordham Urban Law J 37:115
Gazzini T (2017) The 2016 Morocco–Nigeria BIT: an important contribution to the reform of investment treaties. Investment Treaty News, 26 September 2017. https://www.iisd.org/itn/en/2017/09/26/the-2016-morocco-nigeria-bit-an-important-contribution-to-the-reform-of-investment-treaties-tarcisio-gazzini/
Glover JM (2016) Alternative litigation finance and the limits of the work-product doctrine. N Y Univ J Law Bus 12:911
Gomez MA (2015) Crowdfunded justice: on the potential benefits and challenges of crowdfunding as a litigation financing tool. U S F Law Rev 49:307
Goodwin M (2004) Race as proxy: an introduction. Depaul Law Rev 53:931
Goodwin M (2016) The pregnancy penalty. Health Matrix 26:17
Goodwin M, Lindsay M (2019) American courts and the sex blind spot: legitimacy and representation. Fordham Law Rev 87:2337
Hamby C (2016) Secrets of a global super court: a BuzzFeed news investigation. Buzzfeed.com, 28 August to 12 October 2016. www.buzzfeed.com/globalsupercourt
Hensler DR (2011) The future of mass litigation: global class actions and third-party litigation funding. George Wash Law Rev 79:306
Hensler DR (2014) Third-party financing of class action litigation in the United States: will the sky fall. Depaul Law Rev 63:499
Kalicki J (2012) Can states assert counterclaims against investors in BIT proceedings? Kluwer Arbitration Blog, 16 January 2012. http://arbitrationblog.kluwerarbitration.com/2012/01/16/can-states-assert-counterclaims-against-investors-in-bit-proceedings/
Kontorovich E (2016) Peter Thiel's funding of Hulk Hogan-Gawker litigation should not raise concerns. Washington Post, 26 May 2016
Kudrna J (2013) Arbitration and right of access to justice: tips for a successful marriage. Transnational Notes Blog, 22 February 2013. https://blogs.law.nyu.edu/transnational/2013/02/arbitration-and-right-of-access-to-justice-tips-for-a-successful-marriage/

Laborde G (2010) The case for host state claims in investment litigation. J Int Disput Settlement 1: 97
LaCroix K (2013) What's happening now? Litigation funding, apparently. The D&O Diary, 9 April 2013. http://www.dandodiary.com/2013/04/Essays/securities-litigation/whats-happening-now-litigation-funding-apparently/
Lat D (2013) Litigation finance: the next hot trend? Abovethelaw, 8 April 2013. http://abovethelaw.com/2013/04/litigation-finance-the-next-hot-trend/
Lindeman R (2010) Third party investors offer new funding source for major commercial lawsuits. Bureau of National Affairs: Daily Reports for Executives, 6(42). https://perma.cc/39WX-8PQX
Luna E (2005a) System failure. Am Crim Law Rev 42:1201
Luna E (2005b) The overcriminalization phenomenon. Am Univ Law Rev 54:703
Lyon J (2010) Revolution in progress: third-party funding of American litigation. UCLA Law Rev 58:571
Martin SL (2004) The litigation financing industry: the wild west of finance should be tamed not outlawed. Fordham J Corp Fin Law 10:55
Martin SL (2008) Litigation financing: another subprime industry that has a place in the United States market. Villanova Law Rev 53:83
Molot JT (2009) A market in litigation risk. Univ Chic Law Rev 76:367
Nagelmueller M (2017) Guest post: dispute finance for sovereigns in WTO disputes - access to justice for developing countries. International Economic Law and Policy Blog, 12 September 2017. https://worldtradelaw.typepad.com/ielpblog/2017/09/dispute-finance-for-sovereigns-in-wto-disputes-access-to-justice-for-developing-countries.html
Nieuwveld LB, Sahani VS (2017) Third-party funding in international arbitration, 2nd edn
O'Connell V (2011) Funds spring up to invest in high-stakes litigation. Wall Street Journal, 3 October 2011. https://www.wsj.com/articles/SB10001424052970204226204576598842318233996
Perry R (2018) Crowdfunding civil justice. Boston Coll Law Rev 59:1357
Radin M (1935) Maintenance by champerty. Calif Law Rev 24:48
Rodak M (2006) Comment, it's about time: a systems thinking analysis of the litigation finance industry and its effect on settlement. Univ Pa Law Rev 155:503
Rogers CT (2015) Access to justice: new approaches to ensure meaningful participation. N Y Univ Law Rev 90:1447
Sahani VS (2016) Judging third-party funding. UCLA Law Rev 63:388
Sahani VS (2017a) Reshaping third-party funding. Tul Law Rev 91:405
Sahani VS (2017b) Revealing not-for-profit third-party funders in investment arbitration. Oxford University Press: Investment Claims. https://oxia.ouplaw.com/page/third-party-funders
Sahani VS (2022) Third-party funders. In: Bjorklund A, Ferrari F, Kröll S (eds) Cambridge compendium of international commercial and investment arbitration. Cambridge University Press
Sahani VS, Smith M, Deniger C (2018) Third-party financing in investment arbitration. In: Beharry C (ed) Contemporary and emerging issues on the law of damages and valuation in international investment arbitration
Schneider ME (2011) Non-monetary relief in litigation: principles and litigation practice. In: Performance as a remedy: non-monetary relief in international arbitration: ASA special series no. 30
Schreuer C (2004) Non-pecuniary remedies in ICSID litigation. Arbitr Int 20:325
Schreuer CH (2014) Jurisdiction and applicable law in investment treaty arbitration. McGill J Disput Resolut 1:1
Sebok AJ (2011a) Betting on tort suits after the event: from champerty to insurance. Depaul Law Rev 60:453
Sebok AJ (2011b) The inauthentic claim. Vand Law Rev 64:61
Shaltiel Y, Cofresi J (2004) Litigation lending for personal needs act: a regulatory framework to legitimize third party litigation finance. Consumer Fin Law Q Rep 58:347

Shannon VA (2015a) Harmonizing third-party litigation funding regulation. Cardozo Law Rev 36: 861

Shannon V (2015b) The structural challenge of investment litigation viewed through the lens of third-party funding. Oxford University Press: Investment Claims, 9 June 2015. https://oxia.ouplaw.com/page/491/the-structural-challenge-of-investment-litigation-viewed-through-the-lens-of-thirdparty-funding

Shukaitis MJ (1987) A market in personal injury tort claims. J Leg Stud 16:329

Smith J (2013) Investors put up millions of dollars to fund lawsuits. Wall Street Journal, 7 April 2013. https://www.wsj.com/articles/SB10001424127887323820304578408794155816934

Smith J (2014) Litigation investors gain ground in U.S. Wall Street Journal, 12 January 2014. https://www.wsj.com/articles/SB10001424052702303819704579316621131535960

Steinberg JK (2015) Demand side reform in the poor people's court. Conn Law Rev 47:741

Steinitz M (2011) Whose claim is this anyway - third party litigation funding. Minn Law Rev 95: 1268

Szymanski M (2016) Recovery of third party funding ordered by ICC tribunal and confirmed by the English High Court – an under-theorised area of the law. Kluwer Arbitration Blog, 8 October 2016. http://arbitrationblog.kluwerarbitration.com/2016/10/08/recovery-of-third-party-funding-ordered-by-icc-tribunal-and-confirmed-by-the-english-high-court-an-under-theorised-area-of-the-law/

Weinstein I (2017) Coordinating access to justice for low- and moderate-income people. N Y Univ J Legis Public Policy 20:501

Wendel WB (2014) Alternative litigation finance and anti-commodification norms. Depaul Law Rev 63:655

Wendel WB (2016) Litigation trolls. N Y Univ J Law Bus 12:725

Wendel WB (2018) Paying the piper but not calling the tune: litigation financing and professional independence. Akron Law Rev 52:1

The Supply and Demand of Justice: What Policy Implications from the EU Justice Scoreboard?

Adriani Dori

Contents

This publication is made possible by the funding of the Vici project 'Affordable Access to Justice: towards sustainable cost and funding mechanisms for civil litigation in Europe' (project no VI. C.191.082), financed by the Dutch Research Council (NWO). See www.euciviljustice.eu.

A. Dori (✉)
Erasmus School of Law, Rotterdam, The Netherlands
e-mail: dori@law.eur.nl

E. Storskrubb (ed.), *YSEC Yearbook of Socio-Economic Constitutions 2022*,
YSEC Yearbook of Socio-Economic Constitutions (2023) 2022: 53–86,
https://doi.org/10.1007/16495_2023_51, Published online: 3 August 2023

Abstract What is the right price for adjudication? The influence of prices in determining access to justice makes this question all the more problematic, as the free interaction between supply and demand for judicial services has notoriously a limited role in this area due to the pervasive role of state-determined tariffs. Fixing prices at too low a level is an easy way to satisfy the need for justice, but it may come at the cost of overlitigation, which squanders resources. Fixing prices at too high a level is an easy way to make justice quicker, but it may neglect the costs of reducing access to justice. Using the EU Justice Scoreboard—a unique policy instrument to measure the performance of EU national justice systems—the paper explores how the European Commission understands the role of adjudication costs. In so doing, it highlights how this tool addresses access to justice from an economic point of view. The paper's findings show that the Scoreboard's reporting on costs has evolved gradually. It shifted away from generic considerations on government expenditure (which involve a supply-side analysis) to adopt qualitative evaluations on the allocation of resources for litigants (which involve a demand-side analysis). Based on this interpretation, the paper critically assesses the value judgements underpinning the EU Justice Scoreboard and submits some observations on its nature and function as a policy tool.

1 Introduction

"The Price is Right" is one of the longest-running game shows in television history. The main concept, albeit simple in its essence, captured the zeitgeist of its epoch brilliantly: the contestants had to guess the actual retail price of the good offered. Those bidding closest, without going over, won the prizes. Spreading capitalistic optimism (at its finest) within a prosperous post-war society made the quiz show wildly popular worldwide.

Since the program first aired in the mid-50s in the USA, many beliefs have changed in our society. But some have been proven remarkably resilient over time. Despite some failed attempts—which according to some authors, might have marked "*the end of history*"[1]—western liberal democracies have always relied upon some shared basic economic principles. And while there is still plenty of room for contemporary discussions on how to regulate modern market economies, there is a common agreement on two essential points: resources are limited, and prices are an efficient way to drive their allocation, although not a perfect one.

What is the right price for adjudication? The influence of prices in determining access to justice makes this question all the more problematic, as the free interaction between supply and demand for judicial services has notoriously a limited role in this area due to the pervasive role of state-determined tariffs. Fixing prices at too low a

[1] Fukuyama (1989).

level is an easy way to satisfy the need for justice, but it may come at the cost of overlitigation, which squanders resources. Fixing prices at too high a level is an easy way to make justice quicker, but it may neglect the costs of reducing access to justice.

Instead of guessing, as the quiz show contestants do, this paper examines how the European Commission (EC) understands the price of justice services. To do so, it analyses the EU Justice Scoreboard (hereafter "Scoreboard"), a unique policy instrument created by the Directorate-General for Justice (DG Justice) which provides on an annual basis quantitative and qualitative data on the performance of EU national justice systems.

The paper focuses on the Scoreboard predominant economic philosophy. Following the underlying idea of effective access to justice as a determinant of growth, the Scoreboard considers costly (and lengthy) judicial proceedings as the main impediment(s) to access to justice and offers a benchmarking analysis with various data to depict Member States' performance in that regard.

The paper provides a targeted survey on all variables included in the Scoreboard that address the costs of justice (hereinafter also: "cost-related variables/indicators"). It also explores how the tool understands, reports, and quantifies adjudication costs for both the supply and demand of judicial services. Ultimately, the paper shows how the way those data are measured and reported unveils the overall philosophy underlying the Scoreboard but also the EC's perception on the costs of access to justice. Based on this interpretation, it then submits some observations on the nature and function of the Scoreboard as a EU justice policy tool.

To answer all these research questions, the paper combines theoretical, empirical and statistical methods. Section 2 offers a brief account of the Scoreboard twin-track philosophy between the rule of law and economic considerations and sets the basis for understanding better the role of costs within. Section 3 zooms in on the costs of adjudication and offers the readers some of the typical Scoreboard findings on costs grouped in five categories: (1) public budgets, (2) court and legal fees, (3) cost-shifting, (4) legal aid and consumer access to justice and (5) availability of information on costs for the litigants. Sections 4 and 5 provide a more systematic analysis of the cost-related variables of the Scoreboard by classifying them according to their structure and, respectively, by highlighting the evolving role of litigation costs within the Commission's annual monitoring exercise. Section 6 draws some general lessons on the importance of costs and the policy messages, the value judgements, and the concept of access to justice underpinning the Commission's annual monitoring exercise set forth with the Scoreboard. The paper concludes with a summary of the relevant findings.

2 The Scoreboard Underlying Philosophy and the Role of Costs

2.1 Between Rule-of-Law and Economic Considerations

Empirical research is no longer *terra incognita* in the field of comparative law.[2] Nowadays, policymakers are increasingly relying on documents assessing and comparing the effectiveness of courts through indicators, judicial statistics and empirical evaluations.[3]

The EU Justice Scoreboard (hereafter Scoreboard) represents the first attempt of the European Commission to venture into this field. Created by DG Justice in 2013 and issued annually, it provides data on the efficiency, quality, and independence of EU Member States' judicial systems.[4] The official narrative defines the Scoreboard as a non-binding monitoring instrument reflecting the Commission's efforts to map the functioning of national courts, draw up an inventory of potential challenges, and incentivise judicial reforms through peer pressure and benchmarking exercises.[5]

The Scoreboard has not appeared as a novel policy instrument out of thin air. It was the result of a political and economic impetus in the Union. The creators behind the initiative have built the tool's launch and public promotion upon a twin-track policy narrative.

The Scoreboard was first coupled with political fermentations which took place after 2010 within the Union. They were all driven by the importance of the rule of law for the EU political process, and they were instigated by multiple "*rule-of-law crises*"[6] that occurred in EU States. The "*voluntary*" repatriation programme for the Roma population in France,[7] and the systematic crackdowns on judicial independence first observed in Romania[8] and Hungary,[9] have demonstrated the limited ability of the European Commission to address systematic democratic backsliding and to protect the fundamental values of Article 2 TEU. More importantly, at the political level, they have jeopardised the internal legitimacy and the external credibility of the EU to act as a rule of law promoter.[10] Given the importance of justice systems in upholding the Article 2 values, the Scoreboard has been portrayed as an

---

[2] See e.g., Michaels (2009); Spamann (2015).

[3] Hess (2021), paras 2.93ff.; Gascón Inchausti (2017), pp. 41ff.; Siems (2018) pp. 180ff.

[4] All Scoreboard editions are available at the European Commission's webpage https://ec.europa.eu.

[5] EU Justice Scoreboard 2020, p. 3.

[6] The term "rule-of-law crisis" has been widely used by the (at the time) Justice Commissioner *Viviane Reding* to describe disruptions of check and balances and crackdowns in the independence of national justice systems; See Reding (2013); Konstantinides (2017), p. 142.

[7] See Parker (2012); Gunther (2012); Konstantinides (2017), pp. 146 and 148.

[8] See Perju (2015); Dawson (2017), pp. 161–166; Budó (2014), pp. 5ff.

[9] Halmai (2018).

[10] Conan (2016), p. 172.

additional instrument of the EU apparatus for monitoring and safeguarding the rule of law within the Union.[11]

At the same time, the Scoreboard was also connected to the EU attempts to boost growth and enhance competitiveness.[12] In the aftermath of the economic crisis, the Union's justice policy had been steered to become a means to stimulate growth, attract investors and restore Europe's competitiveness.[13] Following this reasoning, a policy tool measuring and benchmarking national courts' performances had been conceptualised as a part of a broader EU plan for the completeness and the modernisation of the Internal Market. For that reason, it was also ordered institutionally under the EU annual cycle of economic policy coordination, the so-called European Semester[14] and became a key reference for it.[15] The ultimate goals of the European Semester were to ensure sound public finances, avoid excessive public debt, prohibit macroeconomic and fiscal imbalances, mitigate inconsistencies, and support reforms.

The inclusion of national justice-related performances in the European Semester reflected the broader idea that economic convergence among the EU States—one of the crucial determinants of the EMU resilience[16]—does not depend on budgetary measures alone. Therefore, focusing exclusively on Maastricht-like parameters of deficit and debt ratios to the Gross Domestic Product (GDP) cannot ensure macroeconomic stability. Instead, the assumption underlying the renewed convergence tools relied on the fact that economic growth and financial stability result from multivariate dynamics.[17] These encompass a broad array of development metrics in different economic sectors and national institutions, such as the quality of education, the efficiency of labour markets, or the effectiveness of health services. Among these factors, the justice sector maintains a key role, as it determines the Member States' ability to reduce litigation costs and ensure credible enforcement mechanisms to the benefit of legal certainty. These factors are crucial to determining the competitiveness of economic institutions within a country.

In this general context, improving the effectiveness of national justice systems became one of the European Semester priorities.[18] The Scoreboard intended to help the Member States to achieve this priority.[19] In more detail, its findings assist the Commission in identifying possible shortcomings of judicial systems and

[11] "*We as a European Union need to stand firm on our values and on the rule of law, and that is why I think that we need to put in place an objective mechanism to assess the judicial systems in all of our 27 Member States*": Reding (2012a), p. 8.

[12] "*The judicial system lies at the heart of a healthy market*": Reding (2012b).

[13] See European Commission (2014a), p. 5.

[14] See EU Justice Scoreboard 2013, p. 21.

[15] See EU Justice Scoreboard 2020, Foreword.

[16] De Grauwe (2020), pp. 123–129.

[17] Hinarejos (2020), p. 580.

[18] See also European Commission (2012), pp. 12f.

[19] See Hess (2021), para 2.96; Althammer (2015), p. 6.

incentivising judicial reforms through non-binding Country-Specific-Recommendations for the Member States.[20]

Contrary to the Commission's initial rhetoric, the Scoreboard did not live up to the expectations regarding its task to monitor and protect the rule-of-law. A bird's eye view of the academic literature shows that references to the Scoreboard appeared to be made mostly *in passim* when examining the insufficiencies of the EU's rule-of-law arsenal.[21] Such insufficiencies included the political nature of Article 7 TEU,[22] the non-binding Commission's "new EU Framework to strengthen the rule of law",[23] or the limitations of infringement actions under 258–260 TFEU.[24] This literature's approach should not come as a surprise since the first Scoreboard annual editions offered only a mono-dimensional analysis. The indicators were selected exclusively based on their input for the economy. This included, for instance, an analysis of the variables that could decrease business risks or affect consumers' choices and an assessment of the business perception of judicial independence. Despite the recurring calls by the European Parliament (EP) to re-focus the Scoreboard on rule-of-law considerations,[25] and the critical voices from the academia questioning the Scoreboard's ability to address those matters,[26] the Commission did not tone down its economic reasoning and maintained the Scoreboard's focus on its role in fostering reforms that facilitate economic development.[27]

Progressively, the Commission's rhetoric abandoned the Scoreboard connections to the EU rule-of-law agenda and classified the tool under the EU policies pertaining to economic governance.[28] Dysfunctional justice systems with lengthy and costly judicial proceedings were considered primarily friction factors for the EU economic integration, financial market development, entrepreneurship and innovation, and ultimately growth. Throughout all editions, emphasis was given to the negative correlation between efficient enforcement of contracts on the one hand and opportunistic behaviour as well as transaction costs on the other,[29] and on the economic implications of lengthy legal enforcement of claims and the difficulties of retrieving payments or penalties.[30] Following similar studies of international organisations

[20] EU Justice Scoreboard 2021, p. 3.

[21] See e.g. Dawson and Muir (2012); Janse and Gramatikov (2012); Balfour and Stratulat (2012); Carrera et al. (2013); Carrera and Guild (2014); Hirsch Ballin (2016), p. 140.

[22] European Commission (2003); Sadurski (2010), p. 394.

[23] European Commission (2014b); Pech and Scheppele (2017).

[24] Scheppele et al. (2020); Bogdanowicz and Schmidt (2018).

[25] European Parliament (2013, 2014).

[26] Van Rijckevorsel (2016), p. 444; Sedelmeier (2017), p. 347; Strelkov (2019), p. 15.

[27] European Commission (2015).

[28] "*The EU Justice Scoreboard is an information tool which feeds the European Semester process and covers civil, commercial and administrative justice as these areas are key drivers for growth.*": European Commission (2015).

[29] EU Justice Scoreboard 2014, p. 4; EU Justice Scoreboard 2021, p. 3.

[30] E.g. EU Justice Scoreboard 2013, p. 6; EU Justice Scoreboard 2014, p. 8; EU Justice Scoreboard 2015, p. 8; EU Justice Scoreboard 2016, p. 4.

(IMF, World Bank), the Scoreboard maintained in its initial years a predominant economic orientation.

By all accounts, the situation shifted after 2018. The escalation of the attacks against the Polish judiciary appeared to have played a crucial role in the post-2018 Scoreboard formation. In the following editions, the Scoreboard started to direct more attention to the importance of monitoring justice reforms, the rule of law, and Poland's ongoing political and legal developments. New indicators on structural judicial independence were added, which appeared to have been created specifically to capture Poland's disrupted checks and balances.[31]

To conclude, efficiency and quality of an independent judiciary secure and promote the rule of law as a shared value within the EU. At the same time, well-functioning justice systems restore economic growth and foster competitiveness. The policy narrative on the Scoreboard revolves around this two-pronged reasoning, shifting from one to another, depending on the general political or legal context.

The contrast between economic and rule-of-law considerations characterises the public debate surrounding the Scoreboard. Policymakers emphasise the tool's economic philosophy, whereas the vast majority of scholars analyse it from the perspective of its rule-of-law dimension. This is not a surprise either, since the starting point depends on the commentator's objectives and focus. On the one hand, the Scoreboard's underlying economic reasoning and its linkage to the Internal Market support the Commission's political ambitions to function as the regulator of national justice systems[32] and to intervene in sovereignty-sensitive policy fields, such as the organisation and management of the judiciary, with policy guidelines that have a more solid basis in the EU Treaties. On the other hand, academics have always shifted their attention to the EU-wide rule-of-law challenges and the Scoreboard's contribution in fostering the Union's values of Article 2 TEU. Although the Internal Market and the rule of law are not entirely antagonistic,[33] this antithesis reflects the Scoreboard's two-faced nature and confusing identity.

2.2 *The Role of Costs*

This framework that combines rule-of-law and efficiency considerations, sometimes in an uneasy fashion, can also shed light on the role of litigation costs within the Scoreboard. As the remainder of the paper demonstrates, the analysis of the costs within the Scoreboard reflects the twin-track philosophy underlying the document.[34] The prevalence of one or the other of its prongs often reflects the overall

[31] E.g. EU Justice Scoreboard 2018, Figs. 60 and 64–68; EU Justice Scoreboard 2021, Figs. 52–58.

[32] Hess (2016), p. 10; Storskrubb (2017), p. 333.

[33] Dawson and Muir (2013), p. 1965.

[34] For a more detailed analysis of the providers, reliability and comparability of cost-related data included in the Scoreboard see Dori (2021).

development of the Commission's exercise. This is hardly surprising if one considers that, after all, the costs of accessing a court perform some of the essential functions of prices. Even in an environment where the 'price of justice' is determined by administrative acts, users of justice services will consider such price as one of the elements driving their decisions to litigate—together with more obvious ones like the value of the claim and the probability of success.[35]

Unfortunately, the relationship between costs, on the one hand, and rule-of-law or efficiency, on the other, is not always linear. Take the impact of costs on the length of proceedings. Material growth in the costs of accessing justice will likely reduce, at the margin, the number of lawsuits brought before a court.[36] Increasing costs results in a barrier that can restrict access to justice so that their impact on the rule of law is explained, in this regard, as one of inverse proportionality. At the same time, however, and all else equal, reduced access to courts and inflow of cases may lead to quicker decisions,[37] which is beneficial to the rule of law. In this regard, the relationship between costs and the rule of law can be described, instead, as one of direct proportionality.[38]

Which effect prevails between direct and indirect proportionality is to a large extent a matter of value judgment. For instance—moving now from the rule of law to efficiency—whether a judicial system is more efficient when it delivers a smaller volume of decisions in a relatively shorter time or when it can handle a larger caseload in a lengthier fashion depends on the preferences of citizens and policymakers, including on distributive concerns.

Further complicating the picture is that court fees are only part of the picture. As court fees are in no European country the only source of funding for the function of justice, the resulting imbalance is typically covered through recourse to public budgets. The relationship between public budget and court fees is also quite complex, as it determines the allocation of costs between litigants, on the one hand, and taxpayers, on the other. The matter would require a more extensive analysis, which cannot be carried out in this paper. Suffice it to mention that the limited role of arbitration and ADR does not remove the quasi-monopolistic nature of justice services provided by courts and that in this market structure, subsidies can help reach allocative efficiency by narrowing the distance between prices (court fees) and marginal costs.[39] On top of this, some form of subsidisation may play a role in fostering the positive externalities of court-administered justice (just like in a

[35] For more on the motives to use the legal systems see Shavell (1997).

[36] Mora-Sanguinetti and Martínez-Matute (2019); Esposito et al. (2014); OECD (2013), p. 4; Vereeck and Mühl (2000); Shavell (1997), pp. 586f. and 591.

[37] OECD (2013), p. 7; Esposito et al. (2014), p. 6; Buscaglia and Ulen (1997), p. 288. Other factors that can increase productivity of courts include ICT, training, new case processing design and cultural changes, se Dakolias (1999), pp. 53ff.

[38] Priest (1989), pp. 533ff.; cf. Voigt (2016), p. 202.

[39] Decker (2014), pp. 20 and 71f.

negative Pigouvian taxation).[40] Examples of these positive externalities are the social stability that an efficient justice can deliver (*ne cives ad arma ruant*) and the value of precedent that judicial decisions can play in favour of third parties.[41]

In the following sections, the paper will show how the Scoreboard records this complex relationship between costs, rule-of-law and efficiency from the point of view of public budget expenditure and court and legal fees. Indeed, the way costs and their impact on proceedings are measured is not neutral because the decision to focus (or even just to highlight) one or the other implication of litigation costs can reveal a lot about the overall understanding of the relationship between rule-of-law and efficiency in the Scoreboard.

3 Zooming in: Some Findings of the Scoreboard on the Costs of Access to Justice

3.1 Introduction

This section shows some findings of the Scoreboard on the allocation of the costs of justice. Reflecting the non-systematic nature of their source, the findings are selected based on their ability to illustrate the kind of results the Scoreboard typically displays. The results are organised as follows: (1) the role and the allocation of public budget resources in the funding of justice; (2) fees and their impact on the length of proceedings; (3) cost-shifting and recoverability of lawyer fees; (4) the availability of information on costs to the litigants; (5) legal aid and consumer access to justice. To provide some chronological depth to the analysis, those results are drawn from different editions of the Scoreboard.

3.2 The Role of Public Budget in Funding Justice

A standard Scoreboard measure is the allocation of budget to justice. Typically, the Scoreboard confined itself to a mere description of the data, accompanied by general statements on the importance of adequate financial and human resources for the quality and independence of justice systems.

The most obvious figure is the annual total government expenditure for law courts, determined in absolute value and *per capita*. The first Scoreboard editions (2013–2014)—which heavily relied on CEPEJ data—showed that States spent on average roughly around 60 EUR per inhabitant, though a closer look into the data

[40] Lambert (2017), pp. 36ff.

[41] Landes and Posner (1979), p. 248; Gico (2020), p. 649.

revealed significant divergences among jurisdictions.[42] The subsequent editions could identify trends in this respect. For instance, the 2015 analysis showed relative stability in public expenditure for justice within the Member States, with an overall slight increase.[43] More recently, the amount of public resources allocated to justice increased in most Member States. In 2021, according to the Commission's assessment, such an increase involved the actual government total expenditure per inhabitant and, sometimes, also the expenditure as a percentage of GDP.[44] Nevertheless, the actual amounts, both in EUR *per capita* and as a percentage of GDP, varied significantly across the Members States.[45]

The Scoreboard analysis over the years also went beyond these essential figures and included information on the decision-making power, within the State, on the allocation of budget. This information includes whether the decisions are taken at the executive, legislative, or judicial level and the criteria applied to determine courts' resources.[46] As regards the criteria, the Scoreboard findings had sometimes shown (as in the 2017 edition) that deficiencies in timely courts proceedings were not handled uniformly within the Member States. Some countries considered the allocation of additional financial and human resources as the standard follow-up measure to ensure compliance with time standards, while others did not.[47]

Additional information that the Scoreboard editions report is the detail of the allocation of resources within the broader label of "justice".[48] Figures often showed significant differences in the spending patterns across the Member States. For instance, in the 2019 edition, while compensation of employees (wages and salaries) represented the biggest share in most judicial systems, the budget allocated to fixed assets, such as court buildings or ICT infrastructure, was relatively low or even absent in some cases. Similarly, operating costs (e.g. building rentals, legal aid and other consumables) showed significant discrepancies across systems, and the expenditure on legal aid was considerably higher in a few Member States.[49]

3.3 *Court Fees and the Efficiency of Proceedings*

Particularly important are the Scoreboard results on the impact of litigation fees on the length of the proceedings. A good example is the 2016 edition on the Spanish experience. When presenting data on national courts' efficiency and comparing

[42] EU Justice Scoreboard 2013, Fig. 20; EU Justice Scoreboard 2014, Fig. 24.

[43] EU Justice Scoreboard 2015, pp. 3 and, 36.

[44] EU Justice Scoreboard 2021, Figs. 29–30.

[45] EU Justice Scoreboard 2021, p. 38.

[46] E.g. EU Justice Scoreboard 2015, Fig. 50; EU Justice Scoreboard 2016, Figs. 50–51.

[47] EU Justice Scoreboard 2017, Fig. 49.

[48] EU Justice Scoreboard 2019, Fig. 31.

[49] See EU Justice Scoreboard 2019, p. 42.

present to previous trends, the 2016 Scoreboard emphasised the positive developments in many Member States, which faced particular challenges and a high number of incoming and pending cases in the past.[50] Even though the Commission refrained from using concrete examples and was neither complimenting nor naming and shaming specific countries, Spain had the highest drop in incoming and pending litigious cases in 2015.[51] It, therefore, contributed significantly to the Commission's overall optimistic assessment of the EU-wide trends. The Commission was particularly interested in the "*volatility in the results, which may improve or deteriorate in Member States from one year to another*".[52] Such trends were justified with occurred changes in the national data collection methods,[53] whereas sudden deteriorations were explained with some vague references to "*contextual factors*" or "*systemic deficiencies*" of the justice systems but with no additional information.[54]

However, a better look into the Spanish trend shows a more complex reality than the Scoreboard would tell.[55] As mentioned only in a footnote and with small letters, the drastic drop in the number of incoming cases in Spain was attributed (next to methodological changes in the collection of national data), also to "*the introduction of court fees for natural persons*".[56] Indeed, a strong correlation existed between the stipulation of court charges and the findings for Spain, as statistics showed a reduction in the number of incoming cases in almost all national courts affected by the adoption of the Spanish new measures on court fees.[57] What the Commission had considered *in passim* and with an asterisk as a standardised policy lever to adjust the volume of filed and pending actions within a system constituted in Spain one of the most controversial justice reforms of the past decades.[58]

3.4 Cost Shifting and Recoverability of Lawyer Fees

The final allocation of lawyers' fees plays a crucial role in determining the costs of access to justice.[59] A rational litigant will decide whether to file a claim (if plaintiff) or submit a defence (if defendant) based on her action's actualised future net

---

[50] EU Justice Scoreboard 2016, p. 16.

[51] Ibid., Figs. 10 and 12.

[52] Ibid., p. 16.

[53] So e.g., the drop observed between 2013 and 2015 in the number of incoming cases in Spain was also attributed to the exclusion of payment orders; EU Justice Scoreboard 2016, Figs. 3 and 10.

[54] Ibid., p. 16.

[55] Mora-Sanguinetti and Martínez-Matute (2019).

[56] EU Justice Scoreboard 2017, p. 5.

[57] See also European Parliament (2015a), p. 65.

[58] Ibid, pp. 62ff; European Parliament (2015b), pp. 101ff.

[59] For the differences of access that litigants have to funds for their court cases and more generally to legal advice in the USA see Galanter (1974).

expected benefits, discounted for the probability of winning or losing the dispute. The recoverability of lawyer fees from the counterparty and the corresponding risk to pay for the counterparty's fees belong to the elements that such equation factors in.

Despite its importance, only in 2020 did the Scoreboard include for the first time an assessment of the cost-shifting principle for lawyer's fees and only for B2B litigation in a specific scenario of a cross-border commercial dispute of a claim of 20,000 EUR.[60] The analysis has revealed significant differences across jurisdictions. In the States with a statutory fee system, representing the first group of jurisdictions, the reimbursement of legal fees varied significantly (between 2400 and 1370 EUR)[61] depending on the level of statutory fee envisaged for the services provided. In the second group of States, those without a statutory fee system, the reimbursement of lawyer's fees was either full or partial. Finally, in the third group, the recoverability of lawyer's fees had been left at judicial discretion and was decided on a case-by-case basis.

3.5 *Legal Aid and Consumer Access to Justice*

Legal aid is a key determinant for access to justice by low-income litigants. Therefore, accessibility and size of legal aid are variables the Scoreboard measures when dealing with litigation costs. For instance, the 2016 edition found that, even though some legal systems left the question of legal aid eligibility at the court's discretion,[62] the applicant's income constituted in most jurisdictions the primary criterion for granting legal aid.[63]

A detailed analysis of the findings concerning legal aid can be found in the 2017 edition.[64] According to the Commission's analysis, applicants with an income ranging on average between +40% and −30% of the respective national at-risk-of-poverty threshold were eligible to receive legal aid in most jurisdictions. Even though the Scoreboard figures displayed thresholds only between these two values (+40% to −30%), a better look at the data exposed bigger gaps across the EU countries. Some systems were particularly generous and granted legal aid even to applicants with an income between +40% to +154% above the poverty level.[65] By contrast, other States appeared stricter and granted legal aid at an income threshold

[60] See EU Justice Scoreboard 2020, Fig. 26.

[61] The disparities appeared prima facie higher when considering the figures from Austria (2950 EUR) and Malta (682 EUR). However, while the scenario was not fully applicable to the Austrian system of reimbursement, lawyer's fees in Malta are calculated based on the value of the claim; ibid., p. 29.

[62] EU Justice Scoreboard 2016, p. 19.

[63] Idem.

[64] EU Justice Scoreboard 2017, Fig. 21 and p. 35.

[65] Denmark, Germany, Ireland, France, Croatia, Lithuania, Netherlands, Portugal, Finland and Sweden; ibid., p. 19.

that ranged between −30% and −68% below the domestic at-risk-of-poverty threshold.[66]

Regarding the trends in legal aid availability, the disparities between the Member States increased according to the 2018 Scoreboard. The income threshold determining eligibility for legal aid ranged in this evaluation cycle between −41% below and +357% above the domestic at-risk-of-poverty threshold, clearly showing different-gear systems EU-widely.[67] The Commission has also drawn attention to the fact that the income threshold for legal aid remained unchanged while the poverty threshold had increased. This, combined with the level of court fees—which appeared to remain largely stable since 2016 or even partly increased—constituted a significant challenge to access to justice, especially for citizens in or at risk of poverty.[68]

The 2019 edition further highlighted the difficulties in accessing justice for citizens in poverty.[69] Court fees, calculated as a percentage of the claim value, rose in several Member States, also due to an increase in the minimum court fee to file a claim.[70] Accessibility to legal aid became more difficult in many Member States. According to the Commission's findings, people below the poverty threshold were not always eligible to receive legal aid.[71] Restrictions in legal aid accessibility on the one hand, and the significant levels of court fees in some Member States on the other, dissuade access to justice, especially for people at risk of poverty.[72]

Consumer claims deserve a separate mention. These are also typically subject to some forms of subsidy with reduced tariffs. The rationale for the preferential treatment lies with the consideration that high entry costs relative to the small value of the claim would result in underenforcement. Here, a good example can be found in the 2017 Scoreboard edition.[73] Overall, very few states (Spain, France, Luxembourg, and Romania) provided unrestricted charge-free access to justice for consumers. In two countries (Bulgaria and Greece), court charges appeared to be set as a fixed percentage of the value of the claim.[74] Except for one State (Slovakia), in all other countries that had provided data, court fees calculated as a percentage of the claim value were significantly higher for low- than high-value consumer claims.

For each scenario, the amounts of court charges are only displayed as a share (in %) of the total claim value. Therefore, reverse engineering of the Scoreboard findings to understand the underlying functions of court fees is not possible. This prevents tracking with sufficient confidence the original formula of court charges in

[66] Hungary, Romania, and United Kingdom (Scotland only); idem.

[67] EU Justice Scoreboard 2018, Fig. 26 and p. 39.

[68] Ibid., p. 39.

[69] See EU Justice Scoreboard 2019, p. 41.

[70] Ibid., Fig. 22.

[71] Ibid., Fig. 21.

[72] Ibid., p. 41.

[73] EU Justice Scoreboard 2017, Fig. 22.

[74] This conclusion can be loosely inferred from the fact that the level of court fees remained stable in the two scenarios selected for a high- and low-value consumer claim; idem.

each system (e.g., flat tariffs, percentage tariffs, a combination of the two systems, tapering up to a certain amount). With the same caveat on reverse engineering, data also reflect some economies of scale and suggest that fixed tariffs were the standard method in most jurisdictions, at least for low-value consumer claims.

The combined reading of the two indicators on legal aid and court fees for consumer cases[75] showed that access to justice in some Member States remained challenging. Consumers with an income significantly below the domestic Eurostat poverty threshold were not always eligible for legal aid. Where court fees represent a significant share of the claim value, as is the case with low-value consumer claims, restrictions in the access to legal aid were particularly dissuasive for exercising the right to justice.[76]

3.6 *Availability of Information on Court and Legal Fees*

Finally, search costs, as a subset of transaction costs, are part of the information that prospective disputants would include in the equation of the decision to litigate. Therefore, the Scoreboard has also paid attention to the accessibility of information on litigation costs.

For instance, following the national trends for the availability of online information on costs and legal aid,[77] the 2016 edition complimented the Member States which had developed advanced and user-friendly solutions, for instance, through interactive online tools that allowed potential applicants to calculate the likelihood of being eligible for legal aid.[78]

In 2018, the Scoreboard registered that the results in this field were somewhat disappointing, as only eight Member States were equipped with online tools that made information on litigation costs accessible.[79] In any event, the autonomous relevance of these data within the Scoreboard is likely to decrease. The 2021 edition has broadened the scope of its analysis on digitalisation—as a natural consequence of the new setting Covid-19 imposed on the management of judicial proceedings—and has therefore absorbed the data on the availability of cost-related information into broader overarching variables.[80]

---

[75] See e.g. EU Justice Scoreboard 2018, Figs. 26–27.

[76] Ibid., p. 35.

[77] EU Justice Scoreboard 2016, Fig. 18.

[78] Ibid., p. 33.

[79] See EU Justice Scoreboard 2018, p. 39.

[80] See EU Justice Scoreboard 2021, pp. 31ff.

4 Towards a Taxonomy System of the Scoreboard Cost-Related Information

4.1 Background

The previous part described some of the Scoreboard findings on the allocation of the costs of justice. The upcoming part offers a more systematic analysis of all variables the Scoreboard adopted to report costs.[81] By so doing, it highlights the evolving role of litigation costs within the Commission's annual monitoring exercise.

Following the underlying idea of court effectiveness through timely and less costly proceedings, the Commission often uses arguments based on reducing costs to justify the selection of data presented in the Scoreboard. Typical examples are the indicators for ICT availability for courts,[82] electronic submission of claims,[83] online small claim proceedings,[84] or ODR options for consumers.[85] As a consequence of the Covid-19 pandemic, the latest 2021 publication has been augmented with further extended data. The focus has been placed on digital-ready procedural rules that allow for distance communication and submission of evidence in digital format (e.g. witnesses, experts or parties' testimonies),[86] and reduce the need for paper-based communication and physical presence of all participants.[87]

However, economic efficiency and costs of proceedings are not used only as a theoretical basis for including various indicators in the Scoreboard. They are also examined in an autonomous context with cost-related variables which measure different aspects of access to justice. The analysis below will show that cost-related quantitative or qualitative data are first displayed in the Scoreboard as components of various synthetic indicators (Sect. 4.2).

Quantitative or qualitative cost-related data are also presented in the form of individual indicators. The Scoreboard follows the classic dichotomy between the supply and demand side of judicial services. The supply side is essentially the State, which preserves the role of the monopolistic provider of judicial services. By contrast, the demand side encompasses all users of judicial services, namely natural and legal persons, including consumers and businesses. In this respect, the price at which adjudication is provided is reflected in court fees, but these are just one of the main financial sources that cover the cost of adjudication. The main remaining sources are subsidisation of the justice system through state budget contributions and subsidisation of disputants through legal aid. These contribute to determining

[81] For a more detailed and critical assessment of the Scoreboard data providers and the overall quality of the cost-related data they provide see Dori (2021).

[82] See e.g. EU Justice Scoreboard 2013, p. 13; EU Justice Scoreboard 2021, p. 35.

[83] See EU Justice Scoreboard 2016, p. 20; EU Justice Scoreboard 2020, p. 25.

[84] See e.g. EU Justice Scoreboard 2016, Fig. 22.

[85] See EU Justice Scoreboard 2017, Figs. 29 and 31.

[86] See EU Justice Scoreboard 2021, Fig. 40.

[87] Ibid., Figs. 41–42.

the nominal level of court fees (state budget contributions to the judicial system) or their actual value (legal aid).

Consequently, cost-related data are presented in the Scoreboard as a measure of three main quantities: State subsidies (Sect. 4.3), fees paid by the users of judicial and legal services (Sect. 4.4), and legal aid schemes that are made available in the different legal systems with information on their availability, eligibility criteria and effectiveness (Sect. 4.5).

For the sake of exposure, the remainder of the paper considers direct subsidisation by the State to the budget of the justice system as pertaining to the supply side—indeed, it reduces the cost of providing justice and, therefore, skews the supply curve of the market for adjudication services. For the same purpose, legal aid is classified as a demand-side element, as it increases the disputants' willingness to purchase judicial and legal services for any given level of court or legal fees. Additionally, legal aid frequently ends up becoming a means to shift the costs of litigation from the State to (younger) lawyers and (smaller) law firms, who accept the covered amount of legal aid, aware that it will only partially compensate for the actual legal services they provide.[88] Last but not least, court fees represent the price for adjudication services and are at the crossroad of the supply and demand side of the market. They are classified under the demand side because they are borne by disputants.

4.2 *Components of Synthetic Indicators*

Synthetic indicators allow more complex and multi-dimensional aspects of the courts' functioning to be summarised and measured. Synthetic indicators are built from different individual metrics (components) that are compiled and quantified into a single value (indexing). Indexing is used in the Scoreboard primarily—but not exclusively—to measure the quality of justice.

In this general context, the Commission has selected various cost-related variables (mostly qualitative) as components of synthetic indicators, which prima facie did not seem to tackle financial issues of litigation. For instance, the synthetic indicators designed to measure the incentives for the voluntary use and promotion of ADR[89] consider—among other factors—financial variables, such as the availability of legal aid for ADR, the revocability of court charges in case of a successful ADR outcome, the mandatory participation of lawyers in ADR schemes, or the possibility of online payment of applicable ADR fees.

Similarly, from 2015 the accessibility of online information on legal aid and legal costs became a component of the relevant Scoreboard synthetic indicator.[90] The Scoreboard publications after 2019 further enhance the relevance of this requirement

[88] Dori and Richard (2017), pp. 326f.

[89] See e.g. EU Justice Scoreboard 2015, Fig. 34; EU Justice Scoreboard 2021, Fig. 27.

[90] See e.g. EU Justice Scoreboard 2015, Fig. 26; EU Justice Scoreboard 2021, Fig. 44.

by indexing the availability of interactive online simulation tools to assess eligibility for legal aid.[91] Other examples of synthetic indicators that—while measuring the quality of justice—factor in cost-related variables can also be found where the Scoreboard maps courts' communication practices and indexes, for instance, free-of-charge access to judicial decisions.[92] In a similar vein, the Scoreboard assesses the level of digitalisation of proceedings, including the availability of online payments of court fees and electronic applications for legal aid.[93]

Synthetic indicators with cost-related variables as components can also be found outside the field of quality of justice. The indicators used after 2016 to map justice reforms[94] also itemise legislative and regulatory activities on legal aid, court fees, and regulation of legal services as separate categories. This demonstrates the Commission's interest in making the domestic developments within these policy fields subject to discrete surveillance. Similarly, the Commission builds connections between the budget for the judiciary and the independence of courts and examines the managerial powers of the Councils of the Judiciary to determine financial and human resources for courts.[95]

4.3 *States' Subsidies*

The Scoreboard displays cost-related data for the supply and demand side, though not with the same intensity. The first editions followed a one-dimensional approach. The initial focus was placed almost exclusively on the providers of judicial services, on States' subsidies, and on how much the operation of courts weighed in the public budget. In this light, the notion of access to justice was understood as a public good, which was made available to all society members, was administered by governments, and was collectively paid for through taxation.

The emphasis on the deployment of public means should not come as a surprise. The Scoreboard was linked to the EU's attempts to support structural reforms, boost growth, and enhance competitiveness. For these reasons, it was also placed institutionally under the EU economic governance and surveillance cycle of the European Semester.[96] The focus on the volume of public investments allocated to the justice sector was fully justified within this context. Consequently, the level of States' subsidies became from the very beginning subject of the Scoreboard analysis. As it will be described immediately, the Scoreboard's reporting shows a progressive

[91] EU Justice Scoreboard 2019, Fig. 20; EU Justice Scoreboard 2020, Fig. 22; EU Justice Scoreboard 2021, Fig. 39.

[92] See e.g. EU Justice Scoreboard 2015, Fig. 29; EU Justice Scoreboard 2021, Fig. 47.

[93] EU Justice Scoreboard 2021, Fig. 44.

[94] Figure 1 of all EU Justice Scoreboard editions from 2016 to 2021.

[95] See e.g. EU Justice Scoreboard 2015, Fig. 50.

[96] See Sect. 2.1.

evolution moving subtly from generic considerations on Governments' expenditure to qualitative evaluations of the allocation of resources.

From the first 2013 edition, the Commission presented figures on Governments' expenditure (per capita) for judicial systems.[97] The following publications further explored budgetary developments with more refined data on the amounts of public investments displayed as a percentage of the GDPs,[98] and later on with categorisations of the total expenditure for the maintenance and operation of law courts.[99]

During this first phase, the reporting followed a neutral approach. Domestic policies concerning the judicial budgets were not assessed or evaluated. Instead, they were described with quantitative data, which aimed at highlighting trends in the management of budgetary constraints.[100] It is also worth noting that the Commission refrained overall from recommending solutions that could enhance the effectiveness of national courts for all Member States. Identifying the proper amount of public resources to be allocated within each system would have required an in-depth assessment of the domestic situation, an exercise in which the Commission understandably did not endeavour. Therefore, better regulation toolboxes, improving impact assessments, and subjecting court activities to monitoring and evaluating became the priorities for the Commission, rather than the amount of public expenditure as such.[101]

In 2015, the Commission developed an increasing interest in qualitative assessments of States' subsidies and broadened the analysis beyond the mere reporting of quantitative budgetary data. The issue at stake was not solely to examine how much money was invested in national courts but also to explore the decision-making processes in this area through synthetic indicators. Next to the sums of public funds, the 2015 Scoreboard turned its attention to more substantive matters, starting with identifying the governmental branch in charge of allocating resources.[102] More importantly, the Commission showed also its intention to explore the motives that drove budgetary decisions at the domestic level by mapping the criteria national Governments apply when determining judicial budgets.[103]

Finally, from the 2017 edition onwards, the Scoreboard started to zoom in on the direct relationship between courts' resources and performances. Critical cases in the operation of a justice system (in terms of delays and unmet time standards) were selected to explore such connections. The issue was now to examine with qualitative

---

[97] See EU Justice Scoreboard 2013, Fig. 20.

[98] See e.g. EU Justice Scoreboard 2014, Figs. 25–26; EU Justice Scoreboard 2015, Figs. 40–41; EU Justice Scoreboard 2016, Figs. 28–29.

[99] See EU Justice Scoreboard 2019, Fig. 31; EU Justice Scoreboard 2020, Fig. 34; EU Justice Scoreboard 2021, Fig. 31.

[100] See e.g. EU Justice Scoreboard 2015, Figs. 38–41.

[101] Ibid., p. 36.

[102] EU Justice Scoreboard 2015, Fig. 50.

[103] Idem.; EU Justice Scoreboard 2016, Figs. 50–51.

data how States responded to shortcomings of courts,[104] and more particularly if deployment of additional resources was considered a policy choice in case of underperformance.[105]

To conclude, the first Scoreboard editions are characterised by a one-dimensional focus on the costs of adjudication for the supply rather than for the demand side of judicial services. Access to justice was primarily examined as a public good made available from the State to society as a whole. When handling delicate issues of allocation of public resources, the Commission followed a neutral approach presenting the public sums invested in each legal system. However, moving the focus from mere reporting on figures and trends to a more qualitative assessment also reveals a subtle transition from general budgetary surveillance to a more substantive evaluation of the allocation of public resources.

4.4 Litigants' Fees

The imbalance between the supply and demand side in the reporting of adjudication costs started to ease in the later Scoreboard editions, particularly after 2017. The cooperation of DG Justice with the "Council of Bars and Law Societies of Europe" (CCBE) worked as a catalyst for change. It opened up the Scoreboard analysis at least to a part of the demand side dealing professionally with judicial services.[106] It is yet uncertain whether the Commission plans to include more perspectives from the demand side, specifically the end users of courts like businesses and citizens. This inclusion would help counterbalance any potential biases that vested interests may have in the current data collection process.[107] Nevertheless, the cooperation with CCBE resulted in the production of indicators that addressed the price of judicial services, borne by the demand side of the market relating to court and lawyers' fees paid by the litigants, with more precise quantitative data.

Judicial services are provided by the State, acting as a monopolistic supplier on the public market of adjudication to all members of society. Natural or legal persons, consumers, and businesses willing to entrust public judicial institutions are potential court users and constitute the demand side of judicial services. Disputes among them may arise in different fashions. They may occur between businesses and consumers (B2C), between businesses (B2B), or between citizens under their private capacity in a classical civil litigation setting. As business and consumers represent the building blocks of the EU's core—the Single Market—the Scoreboard turned its attention first to costs arising from B2C disputes. Costs related to B2B disputes (commercial litigation) were included only at a later stage.

---

[104] EU Justice Scoreboard 2017, Figs. 47–48.

[105] Ibid., Fig. 49.

[106] Dori (2021), p. 292.

[107] Idem.

After defining the personal scope, the next question is to determine which kind of costs for the demand side became subject to the Scoreboard analysis. Given that the party initiating judicial proceedings pays entry fees to access judicial services in almost all European jurisdictions, the focus was first placed on plaintiffs' payments in the form of court fees.

Court fees represent the contribution (or reimbursement) for the use of State courts and are paid to provide resources to the administration of justice. Nevertheless, litigants' payments are usually not sufficient to cover the costs of judicial services in each specific dispute as States typically offer access to courts at rates that do not match the actual costs of the judicial system. Therefore, court fees can also be seen as a form of taxation. This could also explain why court charges are often calculated in legal systems based on the amount in controversy ("costs to case value ratio"), which represents a rough but cheap estimate of the value of the goods and services underlying the dispute, rather than an assessment of the costs to run a procedure. Lastly, court fees can additionally affect the demand for judicial services, and policymakers can use variations in the price of access to justice to influence the volume of litigation.

Following the same non-sophisticated approach that characterises the Scoreboard, the indicators at hand did not delve into the function of court fees across jurisdictions, nor did they provide insights on the formulas used in each system to calculate court charges. Instead, they presented mere numerical data on the level of court fees paid by consumers to initiate judicial proceedings.[108] Based on specific scenarios with low- and high-value consumer claims, the amounts of payable court fees were displayed as a percentage of the claim value.[109]

With the publication of 2020, the Scoreboard broadened its scope and included the costs of adjudication for business. Consideration paid to the financial aspects of B2B litigation, albeit with delay, was grounded on the importance of contract enforcement for the whole economy.[110] Similar to consumer disputes, the Scoreboard targeted the market for adjudicating services provided by the State and presented quantitative data on court fees in a specific scenario of a cross-border commercial dispute of a claim of 20,000 EUR.[111] The level of court fees was displayed in absolute amounts (in EUR).

Nevertheless, regarding commercial disputes, the Commission also decided to examine the costs arising from the private market of legal services and presented for the same hypothetical B2B scenario additional information on the recoverability of lawyers' fees for the successful litigant.[112] The indicator considered legal fees borne during the litigious phase and presented qualitative and quantitative data on the

---

[108] See EU Justice Scoreboard 2017, Fig. 22.

[109] Dori (2021), pp. 292f.

[110] See EU Justice Scoreboard 2020, p. 28; EU Justice Scoreboard 2021, p. 23.

[111] EU Justice Scoreboard 2020, Fig. 25; EU Justice Scoreboard 2021, Fig. 25.

[112] EU Justice Scoreboard 2020, Fig. 26; EU Justice Scoreboard 2021, Fig. 26.

recoverability of lawyer's fees in national systems, with or without a statutory fee envisaged for the legal services provided.

By looking at how the Scoreboard addresses the costs of adjudication for the demand side, we can draw some general conclusions. The Commission examined B2C and—later on—B2B disputes and completely neglected civil litigation among ordinary citizens. When comparing cost-related data for consumers and businesses, two main differences emerge. The first one is related to the scope of the analysis. For B2B disputes, the Scoreboard looked at the price for the use of both public and private market services and covered court charges and lawyers' fees. We do not know the reasons why lawyer's fees had not been examined for consumer claims, though the growing trend of litigants in person might have played a role.[113] It is also interesting to note that additional costs which might often occur in legal proceedings, such as the remuneration of other service providers (bailiffs, translators, court-appointed experts, and others), have not been examined in the Scoreboard, either for commercial or for consumer disputes.

The second difference between the reporting on costs for B2C and B2B disputes concerned the presentation of data. Court fees displayed as a percentage of the claim value provide information on the relative size of the amount due and emphasise the price of justice in a specific scenario. By contrast, the presentation of court fees in absolute amounts (in EUR) underlines the volume for which fees contribute to State revenues. In this general context, court fees for consumer disputes were displayed as a percentage of the claim's value. In contrast, court fees for commercial disputes were displayed in absolute amounts (in EUR). The Scoreboard does not delve into substantive matters of court fees within national legal systems. Therefore, we do not know if this difference in the Scoreboard layout had its roots in the formulas Member States apply when setting the price for the court system's use. Different formulas may involve, for instance, the calculation of court fees as a fixed amount or as a percentage of the value of the claim, a combination of the two systems, tapering, and others. However, the difference in the reporting of court fees in B2C and B2B disputes was evident, and, as often happens with the policy choices surrounding the tool, the Commission did not provide explanations.

Regardless that the current relevant data collections on litigants' fees come solely from the CCBE,[114] the fact remains that the Scoreboard moved its focus progressively from the costs of adjudication for the providers to the users of judicial services. It did so by gradually considering the actual sums paid by litigants to use services from the public (courts) or the private market (lawyers). This shift also signalled a change in the understanding of the notion of access to justice, from a public good provided by the State to all members of society to a service consumed by its users, the litigants.

[113]See Biard et al. (2021), pp. 9f.

[114]For the lack of neutrality regarding the Scoreboard data providers of cost-related indicator see Dori (2021), pp. 287f.

4.5 Legal Aid

The last area with cost-related variables presented in the Scoreboard is legal aid. As mentioned, questions on legal aid availability or eligibility can be addressed as components of synthetic indicators measuring different aspects of the quality of justice systems. For instance, the indicators on effective courts' communication policies map the availability of online information on legal aid,[115] including interactive online simulation tools to assess eligibility for legal aid.[116] Similarly, legal aid availability for ADR is also considered when evaluating the domestic incentives for the voluntary use of out-of-court dispute resolution in the different legal systems.[117]

In this part, however, we only consider the indicators of the Scoreboard, which have directly targeted legal aid.

The first two Scoreboard editions (2013–2014) did not tackle questions of legal aid directly. In some cases, aggregated figures provided by the Member States on the public budget allocated to the functioning of all courts included the amounts invested in legal aid. However, the lack of homogeneity of national data and the presentation of figures in an aggregated form did not allow cross-country comparisons.[118]

The Scoreboard eventually began, with the 2015 edition, to dedicate direct attention to legal aid. Reform initiatives in legal aid started to be mapped,[119] whereas the indicators reporting data on the public budget allocated exclusively to legal aid[120] gave a more comprehensive overview of the sums invested in each legal system (per capita). However, concentrated as it was on the total amount of subsidies for the supply side, the Scoreboard reporting remained abstract. Its inquiries did not report on the distribution of legal aid amongst beneficiaries and per case, the conditions and the amount of legal aid granted to successful applicants, or the type of fees (court or legal) covered through legal aid.

Starting in 2016, the cooperation with new data providers enriched the Scoreboard with more precise information on the eligibility criteria and the amount of legal aid granted in each system.[121] Representative disputes were selected again from the field of consumer law. Given the complexity of domestic legal aid schemes, the indicator created by the DG Justice and the CCBE set as a reference point the applicant's income, as this is the most common criterion in different jurisdictions when granting legal aid. It presented the income threshold in each system for legal aid eligibility compared to the domestic at-risk-of-poverty threshold. Additionally, the indicator provided qualitative information on the amounts of litigants' costs covered through legal aid (full or partial coverage of costs). In this way, the indicator

---

[115] See *supra* n. 90.

[116] See *supra* n. 91.

[117] See *supra* n. 89.

[118] Dori (2021), p. 293.

[119] EU Justice Scoreboard 2015, Fig. 1.

[120] Ibid. Fig. 39.

[121] EU Justice Scoreboard 2016, Fig. 19.

combined information on legal aid schemes and domestic economic conditions in consumer cases and, since 2016, has been reproduced in all the editions,[122] however without offering additional information as to the type of costs covered by legal aid (legal and/or court fees).

To conclude, the use of autonomous indicators in the field of legal aid is also characterised by a gradual development and a growing interest in the demand side. From displaying figures on the level of States' funds dedicated to legal aid, the Scoreboard moved the focus progressively to the evaluation of the effectiveness of domestic legal aid schemes. This assessment was not made in abstract terms but in the context of the domestic incomes and living conditions for litigants—particularly those lacking sufficient means to access justice. In this light, from a State's subsidy enabling access to justice for the whole society, legal aid began to be analysed as a concrete means at the disposal of litigants to facilitate access to justice.

5 Highlighting Trends

5.1 Progressive Development Identified

In the previous part, the paper has classified the Scoreboard variables relating to costs into four categories. Cost-related variables can appear either as components of synthetic indicators tackling different aspects of the functioning of courts or as various autonomous cost indicators.

Tracking down the progression of autonomous cost indicators throughout all editions showed that the Scoreboard had analysed the notion of access to justice, from a financial point of view, based on the triptych of States' subsidies, litigants' fees, and legal aid. At the same time, the reporting on all these three areas followed parallel patterns, shifting from more generic considerations to qualitative evaluations, and from supply to demand. The main takeaway of the analysis is that the assessment of access to justice from a financial point of view moved the focus gradually away from public budgets and Member States' economic performances towards a more user-oriented direction, emphasising the significance of costs for the actual litigants.

[122] EU Justice Scoreboard 2017, Fig. 21; EU Justice Scoreboard 2018, Fig. 26; EU Justice Scoreboard 2019, Fig. 21; EU Justice Scoreboard 2020, Fig. 23; EU Justice Scoreboard 2021, Fig. 23.

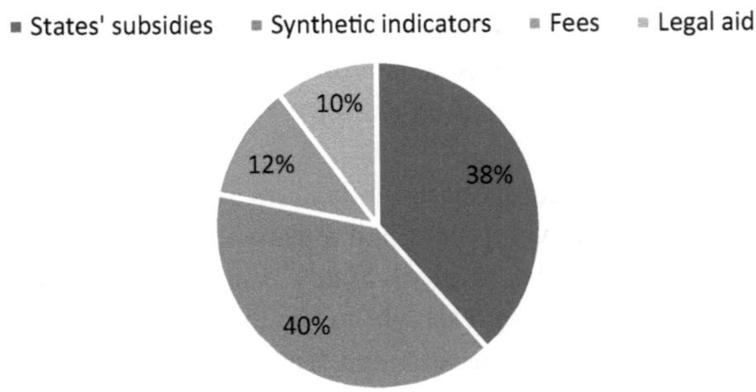

Fig. 1 The categories of cost-related indicators (aggregated 2013–2021) (Source: Author's calculations)

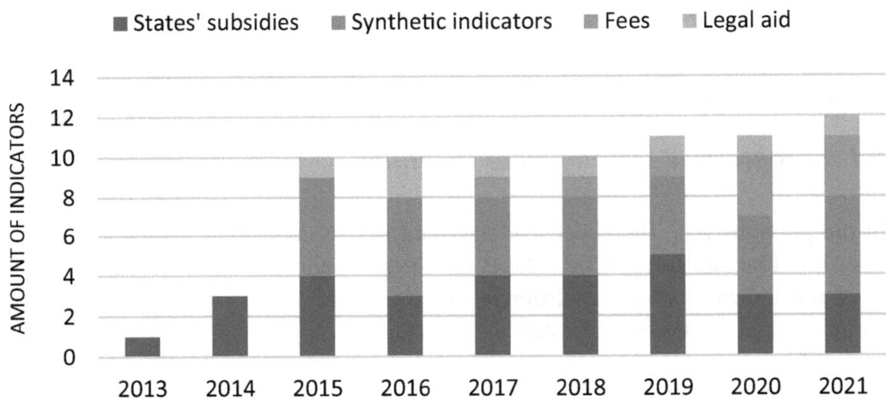

Fig. 2 The categories of cost-related indicators (per year) (Source: Author's calculations)

5.2 The Gradual Shift of Focus Towards the Demand Side

The Scoreboard's initial predominant focus on the costs of adjudication for States is still reflected in the aggregated figures of cost-related data. The first chart (Fig. 1) shows how cost-related data from all Scoreboard editions are distributed under the four different categories we have identified in the previous part (synthetic indicators with cost variables, States' subsidies, litigants' fees, and legal aid). Apart from synthetic indicators with cost variables (which address various aspects and therefore are not always easy to be categorised based on their content), budgetary data have appeared almost twice as frequently as the information on court fees and legal aid cumulatively.

Nevertheless, this general impression is relativised when the same data is presented per year of publication (Fig. 2). Besides synthetic indicators reflecting cost variables, which were introduced in 2015 and have followed a more or less stable trend ever since, the development of the rest of the cost indicators confirms the

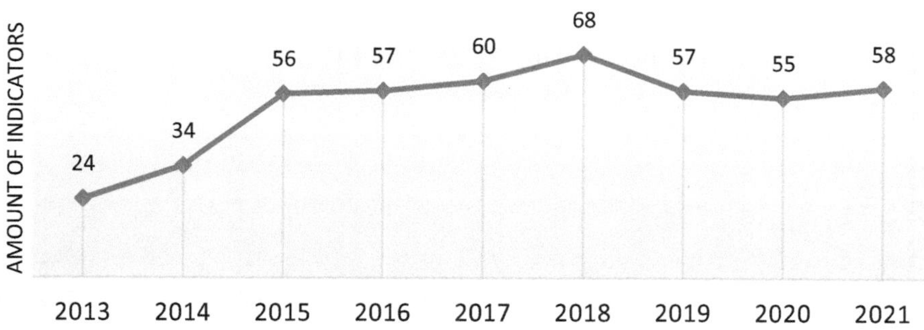

Fig. 3 The progression of all Scoreboard indicators (Source: Author's calculations)

Commission's gradual interest in the perspective of the demand side indeed, either in terms of fees paid by litigants or availability, eligibility and effectiveness of national legal aid schemes. The shift of interest first occurred in 2015 and became particularly evident in the 2020 edition. For the first time, the total number of indicators on fees and legal aid surpassed those on the Member States' budgetary performance. The same tendency also continued in the latest edition of 2021.

5.3 *The Growth of Data*

Already from its first 2013 edition, the Scoreboard pinpointed the difficulties in presenting indicators on the performance of courts in a comparative context. Addressing the data gaps became the main challenge.[123] As anticipated with the second edition,[124] the Commission started to rely progressively on new data providers. The new synergies led to expanding the available data in all fields reported in the Scoreboard. The more-is-better Commission's approach is clearly shown when looking at the progression of the total amount of all indicators over time (Fig. 3). The 2015 edition was characterised by a massive expansion of the available data. The increasing trend continued until 2018, and the total amount of Scoreboard indicators skyrocketed from 24 in 2013 to 68 in 2018.

The same data growth is also reflected in the field of costs. The synergies with new data providers[125] borne fruits and the 2015 edition was enriched with additional information and more precise key findings (e.g. legal aid budgets, criteria applied for determining courts' resources, other synthetic indicators, etc.).[126] As the next chart

[123] EU Justice Scoreboard 2013, p. 20.

[124] EU Justice Scoreboard 2014, p. 27.

[125] For more on the Scoreboard data providers in general and particularly for cost-related indicators see Dori (2021).

[126] Ibid., pp. 283ff.

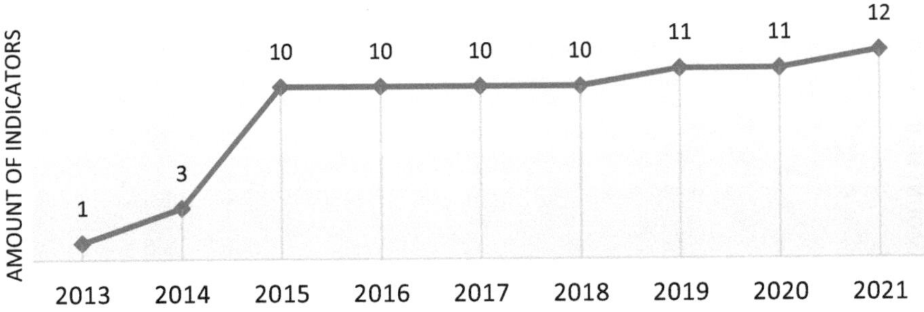

Fig. 4 The progression of cost-related indicators (Source: Author's calculations)

demonstrates (Fig. 4), the total amount of cost-related indicators tripled between 2014 and 2015. However, after 2015 it remained—more or less—stable.

5.4 The Commission's Experimental Approach

The stagnation in the amount of cost-related indicators that occurred after 2015 (see again Fig. 4) might create the impression that the post-2015 publications continued reporting on costs with minor modifications. However, this impression is misleading. As previously described, the Commission's interest in costs was neither coincidental nor temporary.

Overall, the costs of adjudication (together with judicial independence) constitute the most dynamic fields regarding the modification and experimentation of the relevant Scoreboard indicators. The next chart (Fig. 5) focuses precisely on the variations in cost-related data. It displays the changes in the construction of indicators from one edition to another and reveals a continuous adjustment even in a

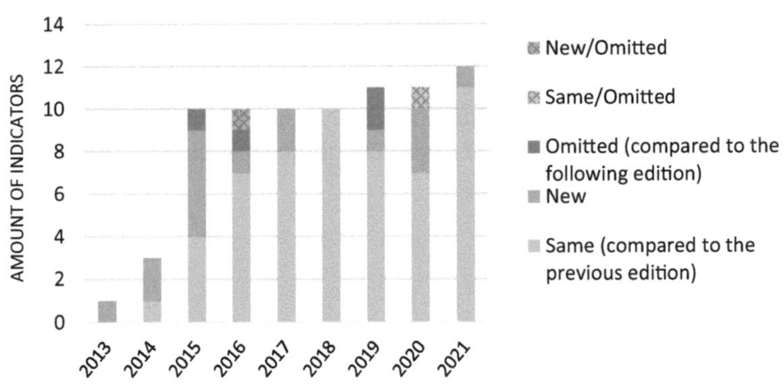

Fig. 5 The variations in cost-related indicators (Source: Author's calculations)

context where changes in the Scoreboard measures did not lead to a net increase in the information provided to the reader. Therefore, even though the numbers after 2015 remained—more or less—stable from a quantity perspective, the Commission demonstrated some willingness to experiment by exploring new measures from a qualitative point of view. Compared with the previous one, each new edition included additional indicators designed with the help of new data providers.

6 Zooming Out: The Role of Cost-Related Information in the Concept of Access to Justice

The last two parts zoomed in on the Scoreboard data on costs. They offered a classification system and highlighted trends. The following final part zooms out and looks at the broader picture by examining the relevant importance of costs for the Scoreboard. The way costs are reported also conveys a subtle but clear message on the concept of access to justice underlying the Scoreboard.

The main idea behind the Scoreboard creation is that the effectiveness of justice systems is a structural component for a healthy investment environment.[127] Following this reasoning, lengthy and costly judicial proceedings are considered as the main impediments to access to justice. The Scoreboard offers a benchmark analysis with quantitative and qualitative data in both directions. Judicial efficiency is measured primarily against the length of trials, for instance, with indicators about the disposition time, clearance rate, number of pending cases or bottlenecks at national courts. Costs of judicial proceedings are examined with figures on States' subsidies, litigants' fees, legal aid, or other synthetic indicators with cost-related variables. Aggregated calculations show that almost half of the Scoreboard indicators have dealt with aspects of judicial efficiency and costs (Fig. 6).

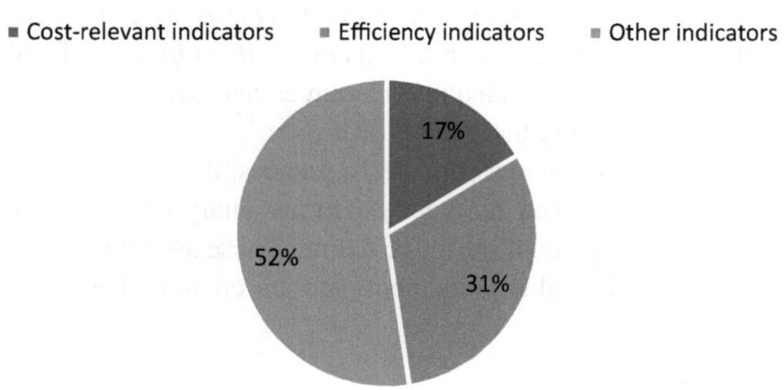

Fig. 6 Justice Scoreboard indicators per category (aggregated 2013–2021) (Source: Author's calculations)

[127] EU Justice Scoreboard 2014, p. 4.

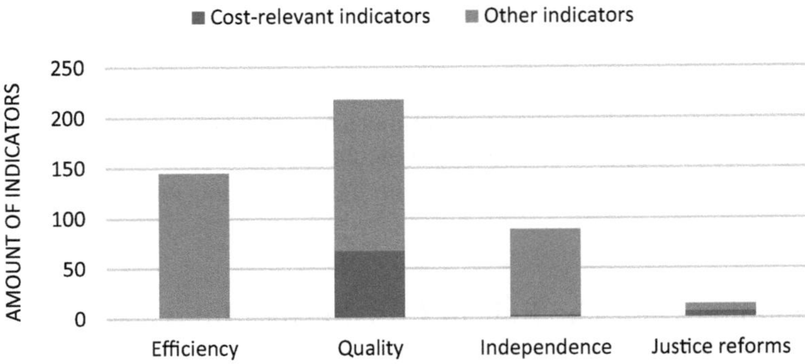

Fig. 7 Cost-related indicators—relative weight (aggregated 2013–2021) (Source: Author's calculations)

However, when assessing efficiency and costs, the Scoreboard does not build connections between the two notions.[128] The structure and the content of the indicators listed under judicial efficiency show that the Commission measures efficiency exclusively by the trial length and that courts' performance and courts' resources are presented in total isolation from each other.[129] In this respect, efficiency in the pages of the Scoreboard is understood as the output of judicial systems in terms of volume (quantity of decisions) and time (length of proceedings). In other words, the Commission measures the effectiveness of judicial systems and not the economic efficiency nor the efficient use of resources to achieve the desired output.

The missing link between efficiency and costs appears even more clearly if one takes a closer look at the Scoreboard structure (see Fig. 7). The Scoreboard part on efficiency of national justice systems does not include data on costs. Indicators reflecting cost variables do not constitute a separate (sub)category, either. Apart from very few exceptions, cost-related data can all be found in the Scoreboard part on the quality of justice systems. In more detail, data about States' subsidies are usually classified under the subcategory entitled "*resources*", and data about legal aid and litigants' fees are presented under "*accessibility of justice*". The Commission standard argumentation is that adequate resources and accessibility for courts are relevant factors for improving the quality of justice.[130]

However, when measuring systems' performances, the way costs for the supply and demand side of any given market system are analysed always reflects some assumptions, despite its apparent objective nature. These assumptions depend on the aim of the surveys and the value judgements of their creators. But at the same time,

[128] See also Ontanu et al. (2017), pp. 15f.

[129] The only exception has been the synthetic indicator presenting follow-up measure to ensure compliance with unmet time standards, which examined to what extent allocation of additional financial and human resources is foreseen in cases of lengthy judicial proceedings.

[130] See e.g. EU Justice Scoreboard 2021, pp. 21 and 26.

they also show an understanding of the main concepts underpinning such surveys and the policy message they seek to deliver.[131]

Factoring costs in the measure of efficiency would rest on the premise that the output of any given system always comes at a cost.[132] Efficiency, in this way, is understood as the relationship between the system's input (allocation of resources) and the system's output (volume and length of the production process) for any given amount of resources.[133] Therefore, a judicial system is efficient if it can produce with minor costs the desired output, meaning that it can deliver a higher volume of courts decisions for any period.[134] The allocation of resources as such does not have an absolute value but is always relevant to the produced output. On the other hand, the underlying idea behind costs being classified as a measure of quality is that the system's input (allocation of resources) is always determinant for the quality of the services provided. Therefore, the amount of resources invested in a system becomes an absolute value. Its positive contribution is taken for granted, regardless of opportunity costs.

Of course, in any given system, a different budget delivers a different quality. A higher amount of resources will most likely lead to a better quality of the services provided, even in those judicial systems that fall short the most in all Scoreboard rankings. A typical example is the allocation of resources for ICT and the electronic modernisation of courts.[135] However, a positive correlation between input and quality does not necessarily mean that the system becomes at the same time efficient. Investing more resources might increase the quality of justice. However, such policy choice might not be regarded as optimal especially when it is not paired with a parallel increase in the system's output in terms of courts' productivity.[136]

Furthermore, when analysing the input of judicial systems, the Scoreboard differentiates depending on the origin of the resources and measures the volume of public investments (public budget) and the accessibility of judicial systems in terms of legal aid and litigants' fees. However, the prices for accessing national judicial markets, either through public or private contributions, are equally qualified in the Scoreboard as elements of quality. In this light, the Scoreboard promotes the idea of the input of judicial systems as a matter of quality.

Therefore, evaluating costs under efficiency or quality is not just a matter of classification. On the contrary, it uncovers the policy messages underpinning evidence-based studies. And in the case of the Scoreboard, the Commission starts from the premise that a combination of a higher amount of public investments and

[131] See also Ippoliti and Tria (2020), p. 387.

[132] Voigt (2016), pp. 185ff.; Månsson et al. (2022), p. 432.

[133] Law (2016), entry "*economy, efficiency, and effectiveness*": *Efficiency measures how successfully the inputs have been transformed into outputs. Effectiveness measures how successfully the system achieves its desired outputs.*

[134] See also Månsson et al. (2022), p. 432.

[135] OECD (2013), p. 5.

[136] Voigt and El-Bialy (2016), pp. 195ff.

low entry fees for litigants reflects the Member State's commitment to achieving a higher quality of judicial services.

However, the Scoreboard exercise relies on evidence-based surveys which aim to measure the efficiency of national courts, have been created under a predominant economic philosophy, and are grounded on the ability of the judiciary to determine economic performances. Therefore, one would expect a deeper analysis of the correlation between input and output of a judicial system. This could be achieved, for instance, with the help of indicators capturing the courts' productive process based on the triangular relationship among costs for the justice production, volume of decisions, and length of proceedings. Unfortunately, the Scoreboard does not explore this path. The structure and the content of the Scoreboard benchmark analysis show that the Commission is not looking so much at the ability of a judicial system to be economically efficient. It instead looks at the ability of citizens to have access to justice. More importantly, the constitutional and procedural principle of access to justice is understood as an absolute value. Such an understanding of the notion of access to justice is based on a single value judgement, which, however, might not be the only available or optimal one.

In an ideal system with indefinite resources, reasoning in absolute values and setting unrestricted access to justice as the desired policy aim would be sustainable and require no justification. Unfortunately, economic reality hits hard. A policy that combines a high public budget with low entry fees implements the principle of access to justice with no limitations. However, removing entry fees eventually may generate overlitigation, congestion, delays, and ultimately, lower quality of the services provided as a negative externality.[137] Consequently, it will also result in wasting resources, whether public or private, which would be managed inefficiently. In other words, opportunity costs matter.

Therein lies the paradox of the Scoreboard. On the one hand, it promotes the idea of access to justice by using predominant economic reasoning and emphasising the economic implications of the inefficient enforcement of claims. But, on the one the other hand, it assesses the notion of access to justice based on value judgements that neglect that state-funded justice is prone to a common pool resource problem,[138] which exposes public subsidies to inefficiencies that may squander budgetary resources.

Evidence-based tools created to assist policy-making processes cannot look at the different policy areas in total isolation from each other. They need to evaluate policies against their ability to reach socially optimal results. In a social welfare system, an appropriate policy decision-making process based on evidence requires taking into account opportunity costs and the hazard of squandering resources. Justice policies are neither excluded nor immune from such evaluations, all the more in times of economic downturn and austerity. This is precisely the reason why studies like the Scoreboard would greatly benefit from an assessment of the overall

[137] See also Gico (2020), pp. 658ff. (with further references).

[138] Ibid., pp. 646 and 660 (with further references).

results of national systems in granting access to justice efficiently and look at the way justice is managed to maximise the benefits of society. However, whether and how governmental policies can grant access to justice while also ensuring a satisfactory level of economic efficiency is the elephant in the room, and the Scoreboard leaves this most critical question untouched.

7 Conclusions

Effective judicial protection is a prerequisite for the rule of law enforcement and economic development. The EU Justice Scoreboard is the tool the European Commission adopted to shed light on these overarching policies. With the help of indicators, it measures the performance of national courts in terms of efficiency, quality, and independence.

Although the Scoreboard data are gaining momentum and are used as a basis for academic studies, policy-making, and even case law, targeted research on the specific information in that tool is limited. This paper focused on one of the most significant areas of the Scoreboard datasets, namely the one dedicated to the costs of the adjudication.

Following the underlying idea of effective access to justice as a growth component, the EU Scoreboard is based on an economic approach to adjudication. Within this general context, it considers costly and lengthy judicial proceedings as the main impediments to access to justice and offers a benchmarking analysis with various data to depict Member States' performance in that regard. Nevertheless, the Scoreboard fails to build connections between the two elements of rule-of-law protection and economic efficiency.

The progression of cost indicators throughout all editions showed that the Scoreboard analyses the notion of access to justice from an economic point of view based on the triptych of States' subsidies, litigants' fees, and legal aid. At the same time, the Scoreboard reporting in all these three areas follows parallel patterns, shifting from more generic considerations to qualitative evaluations, and from supply to demand of judicial services. Along these lines, the Scoreboard gradually moved its focus away from public budget considerations towards a more user-oriented direction, emphasising the significance of costs for litigants.

However, the evolving role of litigation costs within the Scoreboard has also highlighted some of its weaknesses. On the one hand, the tool promotes the idea of access to justice by using predominant economic reasoning and emphasising the economic implications of the inefficient enforcement of claims measured exclusively by trial length. But, on the other hand, it assesses the notion of access to justice based on value judgements that neglect that state-funded justice is prone to a common pool resource problem, which exposes public subsidies to inefficiencies that may squander budgetary resources. In this light, the European Commission understands the constitutional and procedural principle of access to justice in absolute terms. Such an understanding of the notion of access to justice is based on a single value judgement which, however, disregards economic efficiency and opportunity costs and might therefore not be the optimal approach in all circumstances.

By not building connections between costs of adjudication and effectiveness of courts, the Scoreboard fails to answer the most critical question, namely whether and how governmental policies can grant access to justice while also ensuring a satisfactory level of economic efficiency.

References

Althammer C (2015) Mindeststandards und zentrale Verfahrensgrundsätze im deutschen Recht. In: Weller M, Althammer C (eds) Mindeststandards im europäischen Zivilprozessrecht. Mohr Siebeck, Tübingen, pp 3–31

Balfour R, Stratulat C (2012) The enlargement of the European Union. European Policy Centre, Discussion Paper, 10 December 2012

Biard A et al (2021) Introduction: the future of access to justice – beyond science fiction. In: Kramer X et al (eds) New pathways to civil justice. Springer, Berlin, pp 1–20

Bogdanowicz P, Schmidt T (2018) The infringement procedure in the rule of law crisis: how to make effective use of Article 258 TFEU. Common Mark Law Rev 55:1061–1100

Budó (2014) EU common values at stake: is Article 7 TEU an effective protection mechanism?. Barcelona Centre for International Affairs, Documents CIDOB, n. 1, May 2014

Buscaglia E, Ulen T (1997) A quantitative assessment of the efficiency of the judicial sector in Latin America. Int Rev Law Econ 17:275–291

Carrera S, Guild E (2014) The Juncker Commission: a new start for EU Justice and Home Affairs policy?. CEPS Essays, No. 15, 18 September 2014

Carrera S et al (2013) Rule of law or rule of thumb? A new Copenhagen mechanism for the EU. CEPS Policy Brief n. 303, 20 November 2013

Conan R (2016) Strengthening the rule of law at the supranational level: the rise and consolidation of a European Network. J Contemp Eur Stud 24:171–188

Dakolias M (1999) Court performance around the world: a comparative perspective, vol 23. World Bank Publications

Dawson M (2017) The governance of EU fundamental rights. Cambridge University Press, Cambridge

Dawson M, Muir E (2012) Enforcing fundamental values: EU law and governance in Hungary and Romania. Maastricht J Eur Comp Law 19:469–476

Dawson M, Muir E (2013) Hungary, EU fundamental rights and the rule of law. German Law J 14: 1959–1979

De Grauwe P (2020) Economics of monetary union, 13th edn. Oxford University Press, Oxford

Decker C (2014) Modern economic regulation: an introduction to theory and practice. Cambridge University Press, Cambridge

Dori A (2021) In data we trust? Quantifying the costs of adjudication in the EU Justice Scoreboard. Erasmus Law Rev 2021(4):281–297

Dori A, Richard V (2017) Litigation costs and procedural cultures – new avenues for research in procedural law. In: Kramer XE, Hess B (eds) From common rules to best practices in European civil procedure. Nomos, Baden-Baden, pp 303–352

Esposito G et al (2014) Judicial system reform in Italy—a key to growth. IMF working papers 14/32, International Monetary Fund

European Commission (2003) Article 7 of the Treaty on European Union – respect for and promotion of the values on which the Union is based (COM (2003) 606 final)

European Commission (2012) Annual Growth Survey 2013 (COM (2012) 750 final)

European Commission (2014a) The EU Justice Agenda for 2020 – strengthening trust, mobility and growth within the Union (COM (2014) 144 final)

European Commission (2014b) A new EU framework to strengthen the rule of law (COM (2014) 0158 final)

European Commission (2015) Follow-up to the European Parliament resolution on evaluation of justice in relation to criminal justice and the rule of law, adopted by the Commission on 25 June 2015 (SP(2014)457-0)

European Parliament (2013) Report on the EU Justice Scoreboard – civil and administrative justice in the Member States, (2013/2117(INI)), 5 December 2013

European Parliament (2014) Resolution of 4 February 2014 on the EU Justice Scoreboard – civil and administrative justice in the Member States (2013/2117(INI))

European Parliament (2015a) The impact of the crisis on fundamental rights across Member States of the EU – country report for Spain. European Parliament, Brussels

European Parliament (2015b) The impact of the crisis on fundamental rights across Member States of the EU - comparative analysis. European Parliament, Brussels

Fukuyama F (1989) The end of history? Natl Interest 16:3–18

Galanter M (1974) Why the haves come out ahead: speculations on the limits of the legal change. Law Soc Rev 9:95–160

Gascón Inchausti F (2017) Comparative perspectives in procedural law: some remarks and proposals. In: Cadiet L et al (eds) Approaches to procedural law – the pluralism of methods. Nomos, Baden-Baden, pp 13–46

Gico I (2020) The tragedy of the judiciary: an inquiry into the economic nature of law and courts. German Law J 21:644–673

Gunther C (2012) France's repatriation of Roma: violation of fundamental freedoms? Cornell Int Law J 45:205–223

Halmai G (2018) The application of European constitutional values in EU Member States – the case of the fundamental law of Hungary. Eur J Law Reform 20:10–34

Hess B (2016) The state of the civil justice union. In: Hess B et al (eds) EU civil Justice – current issues and future outlook. Bloomsbury Publishing, London, pp 1–20

Hess B (2021) Europäisches Zivilprozessrecht, 2nd edn. De Gruyter, Berlin

Hinarejos A (2020) Economic and Monetary Union. In: Barnard C, Peers S (eds) European Union Law, 2nd edn. Oxford University Press, Oxford, pp 573–597

Hirsch Ballin E (2016) Mutual trust: the virtue of reciprocity – strengthening the acceptance of the rule of law through peer review. In: Closa C, Kochenov D (eds) Reinforcement of the rule of law oversight in the European Union. Cambridge University Press, Cambridge, pp 133–146

Ippoliti E, Tria G (2020) Efficiency of judicial systems: model definition and output estimation. J Appl Econ 23:385–408

Janse R, Gramatikov M (2012) Monitoring and evaluation of the rule of law and justice in the EU: status quo and the way ahead? Concept paper, The Hague: HiiL, June 2012

Konstantinides T (2017) The rule of law in the European Union. Bloomsbury Publishing, London

Lambert T (2017) How to regulate: a guide for policymakers. Cambridge University Press, Cambridge

Landes WM, Posner RA (1979) Adjudication as a private good. J Leg Stud 8:235–284

Law J (ed) (2016) A dictionary of business and management. Oxford University Press, Oxford

Månsson J et al (2022) What lessons can be learned from cost efficiency? The case of Swedish district courts. Eur J Law Econ 54:431–451

Michaels R (2009) Comparative law by numbers? Legal origins thesis, doing business reports, and the silence of traditional comparative law. Am J Comp Law 57:765–795

Mora-Sanguinetti JS, Martínez-Matute M (2019) An economic analysis of court fees: evidence from the Spanish civil jurisdiction. Eur J Law Econ 47:321–359

OECD (2013) What makes civil justice effective?. OECD Economics Department Policy Notes, No. 18, June 2013

Ontanu A et al (2017) How many cases? Assessing the comparability of EU judicial datasets. Paper presented at the Conference Ius Dicere in a Globalized World XXIV Bi-Annual Colloquium of the Italian Association of Comparative Law (AIDC), Naples, 15–17 June 2017

Parker O (2012) Roma and the politics of EU citizenship in France: everyday security and resistance. J Common Mark Stud 50:475–491

Pech L, Scheppele KL (2017) Illiberalism within: rule of law backsliding in the EU. Camb Yearb Eur Leg Stud 19:3–47

Perju V (2015) The Romanian double executive and the 2012 constitutional crisis. Int J Constitutional Law 13:246–278

Priest G (1989) Private litigants and the court congestion problem. Boston Univ Law Rev 69:527–559

Reding V (2012a) Speech to the European Parliament. Doc. 13780/12, PE 413, Annex III, Strasbourg, 11 September 2012

Reding V (2012b) Weathering the storm together: justice for growth, justice for citizens. SPEECH/12/XXX, Institute for International and European Affairs, IIEA/Dublin, 25 September 2012

Reding V (2013) The EU and the rule of law – what next?. Speech/13/677, CEPS/Brussels, 4 September 2013

Sadurski W (2010) Adding bite to a bark: the story of Article 7, EU enlargement, and Jörg Haider. Columbia J Eur Law 16:385–426

Scheppele KL et al (2020) EU values are law, after all: enforcing EU values through systemic infringement actions by the European Commission and the Member States of the European Union. Yearb Eur Law 39:3–121

Sedelmeier U (2017) Political safeguards against democratic backsliding in the EU: the limits of material sanctions and the scope of social pressure. J Eur Public Policy 24:337–351

Shavell S (1997) The fundamental divergence between the private and the social motive to use the legal system. J Leg Stud 26(2):575–612

Siems M (2018) Comparative law. Cambridge University Press, Cambridge

Spamann H (2015) Empirical comparative law. Ann Rev Law Soc Sci 11:131–153

Storskrubb E (2017) Civil justice: constitutional and regulatory issues revisited. In: Fletcher M et al (eds) The European Union as an area of freedom, security and justice. Routledge, London, pp 303–326

Strelkov A (2019) EU Justice Scoreboard: a new policy tool for "deepening" European integration? J Contemp Eur Stud 27:15–27

Van Rijckevorsel E (2016) The European Union and the "indirect promotion of its values": an analysis of the Justice Scoreboard and the Roma Framework. Journal européen des droits de l'homme 3:444–468

Vereeck L, Mühl M (2000) An economic theory of court delay. Eur J Law Econ 10:243–268

Voigt S (2016) Determinants of judicial efficiency: a survey. Eur J Law Econ 42:183–208

Voigt S, El-Bialy N (2016) Identifying the determinants of aggregate judicial performance: taxpayers' money well spent? Eur J Law Econ 41:283–319

Illusory Truths and Frivolous Claims: Critical Reflections on a Report on Litigation Funding by the European Parliamentary Research Service

Johan Skog

Contents

Abstract This paper presents a close reading of the European Parliamentary Research Service's (EPRS), report 'Responsible private funding of litigation', which was prepared to assist the Members of the European Parliament with an objective and authoritative analysis of litigation funding and its effects in order to consider implementing policies on a yet unregulated market. The report raises significant

---

J. Skog (✉)
Kapatens, Stockholm, Sweden
e-mail: js@kapatens.com

E. Storskrubb (ed.), *YSEC Yearbook of Socio-Economic Constitutions 2022*,
YSEC Yearbook of Socio-Economic Constitutions (2023) 2022: 87–118,
https://doi.org/10.1007/16495_2023_44, Published online: 25 February 2023

concerns with respect to, *inter alia*, the alleged lack of a clear and comprehensive taxonomy for the litigation funding practice, as well as the perceived risk for frivolous claims and conflicts of interest whereby funders allegedly corrupt justice by influencing funded parties in settlement situations. However, through careful analysis of the report, it is shown in this paper that several critical conclusions on the purported drawbacks of litigation funding set forth in the report are not founded in the research presented in the report itself but rather contradict its actual findings.

1 Introduction

Third party litigation funding (TPLF)—i.e. the funding of dispute costs by a third party in exchange for a share of any successful recovery—is a business which is unregulated within the EU and which has increased significantly over the last years. It has now attracted some attention at EU level, as seen, *inter alia*, in the rules on TPLF in Directive 2020/1828/EU on representative actions for the protection of the collective interests of consumers. Further, in July 2022, the EU Committee on Legal Affairs presented a report with recommendations to the Commission on Responsible private funding of litigation (the so-called Voss Report), which suggests detailed regulation of TPLF through a draft Directive. In September 2022, the European Parliament voted in favour of adopting the draft Directive. At the time of writing this paper, the Voss Report and the draft Directive is yet to be considered by the European Commission. The Voss Report, which contains rather strong language on the practice of litigation funders as actors seeking profit maximization at the expense of claimants, concludes that the EU should act to "*stop the further erosion of our justice system*".[1] As one of the few sources on which the Voss Report relies with respect to the perceived dangers of TPLF, reference is made to a broad study of litigation funding by the European Parliamentary Research Service (EPRS), entitled *Responsible private funding of litigation*.[2] The EPRS report, which was explicitly "*prepared for, and addressed to, the Members and staff of the European Parliament as background material to assist them in their parliamentary work*",[3] consists of two parts. The first main part provides policy recommendations following analysis and conclusions which are built upon a study on litigation funding annexed thereto.[4] The

[1]Committee on Legal Affairs' Report with recommendations to the Commission on Responsible private funding of litigation, 2020/2130(INL), 25 July 2022, p. 33.

[2]European Parliamentary Research Service (2021). The EPRS is "*the European Parliament's in-house research department and think tank. Its mission is to assist Members in their parliamentary work by providing them with independent, objective and authoritative analysis of, and research on, policy issues relating to the European Union.*" https://knowledge4policy.ec.europa.eu/organisation/eprs-european-parliament-research-service_en.

[3]The EPRS report, preface.

[4]The EPRS report, p. I. The annex is entitled *State of play of the EU private litigation funding landscape and the current EU rules applicable to private litigation funding*.

report in its entirety (including both parts) is hereinafter referred to as "the EPRS report" or "the report".

It may be presumed that the EPRS report and the suggestions therein will provide a substantial part of the basis on which both the EU's and individual member states' policy makers will carry out their analysis in respect of which policy, if any, that should be put in place as regards the emerging TPLF market. It is thus an important document that may affect the business of funders, the potential claimants considering whether to use TPLF as well as the overall disputes services market within the EU. Against that background, it may be of interest to review the findings and conclusions of the EPRS report to get an understanding of the reasoning behind the policy suggestions that may lead to future legislation. My remarks in that respect are presented below.

2 The EPRS Report's General Findings and Conclusions on TPLF

Although the EPRS report states that TPLF "*may represent a tool to support private citizens and businesses in accessing justice and constitute a mechanism for transferring the risk of the uncertain outcome of the dispute to the litigation funder*",[5] its general overall view of TPLF is rather negative:

> At the same time, it may pose risks and entail conflicts of interests. If not properly regulated, it could lead to excessive economic costs and to the multiplication of opportunity claims, problematic claims and so called 'frivolous claims'. It could also be used for the pursuit of strategic goals by competing businesses, and the cost and time wasted in frivolous litigation in some instances could also potentially directly affect aggregate productivity and competitiveness.[6]

Against that background, it is established that the EU needs to take action:

> In light of the analysis, it has emerged that TPLF involves finding a balanced approach between the need to enhance access to justice and the need to prevent large risks, costs for businesses and significant potential for conflicts of interests. Accordingly, the study concludes by putting forward some recommendations for responsible TPLF in the EU and pinpoints the need for EU action in this respect.[7]

With respect to the above and the finding that "*a regulatory safety net for TPLF is needed*",[8] the following is suggested as regards such regulation:

> **Responsible TPLF regulatory framework** should aim at lowering costs, simplifying unnecessary procedures, increasing the predictability of costs, and delivering efficient services at costs that are proportionate to the amounts in dispute. It has also to ensure access

[5]The EPRS report, p. I.

[6]The EPRS report, p. I.

[7]The EPRS report, p. 82.

[8]The EPRS report, pp. 2 and 91.

> to the judicial system for all legitimate claims, while making sure that opportunistic, excessive, and frivolous claims do not develop and that TPLF is not purely motivated by financial gain or employed for businesses' strategic objectives.[9]

The EPRS report also sets out a comprehensive list of supposed risks associated with TPLF and certain policy measures deemed adequate to deal with such risks.[10] In summary, some of the key findings in the report is that (1) there is a risk for frivolous claims, that (2) there is significant potential for conflicts of interests, and that (3) it is set out to be crucial that key concepts and terms are adequately defined in order to bring about uniform and effective EU legislation. These items will be discussed below.

3 The Litigation Funding Taxonomy Used in the EPRS Report

3.1 Introduction

With respect to the terms and definitions used when discussing the TPLF market, the EPRS report sets out the following:

> Defining more precisely what the terms 'third party funder' and 'third party funding' means is a prerequisite for any attempt to propose comprehensive policy options in this field. However, TPLF funders and funding currently take a variety of different forms and encompass a large number of situations. There is therefore always the risk that a uniform definition may be over- or underinclusive. As such, clarifying the scope and providing a comprehensive taxonomy of the various forms of third-party funding accepted at EU level would allow for successful regulation for cohesion and uniformity across the EU.[11]

It is thus set forth that clear and precise definitions of the terms third party funder and third party funding, respectively, is necessary to allow for successful regulation.

3.2 The EPRS Reports' Definition of Third Party Litigation Funding (TPLF)

In the section where the EPRS report intends to clarify the terminology with respect to TPLF, the following is set out:

> This paragraph attempts to define some of the fundamental concepts discussed in the study and to clarify some terminology used.

[9] The EPRS report, p. 33.

[10] The EPRS report, p. 18.

[11] The EPRS report, p. 19.

> **'Third Party Litigation Funding (TPLF)'** refers to the professional practice of an entity, which is not a party to the dispute, in funding all or part of the costs of domestic or cross-border proceedings. The funding is provided in exchange for a reimbursement of the 'investment' and for remuneration that is (a) wholly or partially dependent on the outcome of the dispute ('percentage approach') or (b) provided through a success fee ('multiple approach').[12]

3.2.1 The TPLF Definition Used in the EPRS Report Seems Not to Include Portfolio Funding

The above quoted definition resembles other frequently used definitions. However, it seems to be entirely focused on the funding of single cases (cf. the references to "*the dispute*" above), whereas other leading definitions such as the one suggested by the ICCA-Queen Mary Task Force on Third-Party Funding is careful to add language which also comprise portfolio funding.[13] From the wording of the EPRS definition as such, it is therefore not clear whether portfolio funding actually falls within the term. The fact that the EPRS report has instead suggested a separate definition of portfolio funding indicates that such a practice was not in fact considered to fall within the general definition of TPLF.[14] It is therefore reasonable to assume that the term TPLF as defined in the EPRS report does not comprise the practice of portfolio funding. This has important implications with respect to the general assertions in the report that TPLF—which may thus be understood to include only single claims funding—may lead to frivolous claims (see Sect. 4 below).

3.2.2 The TPLF Definition Used in the EPRS Report Confuses the Relevance of Successful Outcome Under Different Remuneration Models

With respect to the second sentence of the definition of TPLF, which deals with reimbursement and remuneration, it is unclear how the two different remuneration approaches relate to each other and why it has been deemed important to separate them. As regards subsection (a), it refers to situations where remuneration is "*wholly or partially dependent on the outcome of the dispute ('percentage approach')*". However, a structure where the remuneration is in such way dependant on the

[12] The EPRS report, p. 43.

[13] Cf. "*either individually or as part of a specific range of cases*". Report of the ICCA-Queen Mary Task Force on Third-Party Funding in International Arbitration, 2018, p. 50.

[14] Thus, the EPRS report sets out in a separate definition that "***'Portfolio Litigation Funding (PLF)'*** *refers to the professional practice of funding a portfolio of disputes for business purposes*." (The EPRS report, p. 43.) The reason to define portfolio funding separately is unclear, particularly as the acronym PLF is used only twice in the EPRS report (pp. 60 and 73); whereas the full term "Portfolio Litigation Funding", stated to be one of "*the fundamental concepts discussed in the study*" (p. 43), is actually never used in the report.

outcome of the dispute is one of the key elements of any litigation funding agreement whatsoever, irrespective of how the remuneration is calculated. Thus, the language used in subsection (a) (percentage approach) with respect to the outcome of the dispute would apply equally for the type of remuneration that is set out as the defining factor in subsection (b) (multiple approach), since there would be no remuneration under a multiple approach mechanism unless there was a wholly or partially successful outcome of the dispute. What the definition seems to be aiming at is instead shown by the sub-definitions used within brackets to define the respective mechanism, i.e. "*percentage*" and "*multiple*" approach, respectively. The difference between those two mechanisms is that under a percentage model, the funder is entitled to payment which reflects a specific share or percentage of the recovery as such, whereas under the multiple approach, the funder is entitled to payment which is based on a multiple of the committed or paid-in capital under the litigation funding agreement ("LFA"). These models may be used interchangeably, and both require that the funded party, wholly or partially, succeeds on its claim (i.e. the defining language that however only is used for subsection (a) in the definition used in the EPRS report).

The language of the working definition is thus imprecise because a success fee can in fact be paid based on a percentage of the recovered amount, whereas remuneration dependant on the outcome of the dispute can be paid based on a multiple on the committed capital (i.e. the other way around with respect to the language suggested in the EPRS report). A reader of the definition not familiar with these different models would thus not be guided but rather confused by the allegedly clarifying definition presented in the EPRS report in this case. As comparison, it may well be noted that the ICCA-Queen Mary Task Force on Third Party Funding in its definition of third party funding refers to "*financing. . .in exchange for remuneration or reimbursement that is wholly or partially dependant on the outcome of the dispute*".[15] Such language comprises both the percentage and multiple based approaches. The fact that both approaches require a successful outcome is however made unclear by the definition used in the EPRS report.

3.2.3 The TPLF Definition Used in the EPRS Report Does Not Correspond with the Concept of Third Party Funding in EU Regulation

The definition of TPLF used in the report relates only to "*the professional practice of an entity*". *Professional practice* usually refers to the business carried out by persons who belong to a learned profession, whose occupation requires a high level of training or, more broadly understood, a company which has a certain level of expertise and frequency within a certain type of business. It may thus be presumed

[15] Report of the ICCA-Queen Mary Task Force on Third-Party Funding in International Arbitration, 2018, p. 50.

that funding activity carried out by a non-professional actor, i.e. any company not in the business of funding claims, seems not to fall within the definition of TPLF as suggested in the EPRS report (just as a natural person is not "an entity" and would also not fall within the definition, wherefore new forms of crowdfunding of litigation by a large number of natural persons would not constitute TPLF under this definition). This means that the definition used does not reflect or correspond with the provisions in Directive 2020/1828/EU on representative actions for the protection of the collective interests of consumers, which sets out to limit conflicts of interests also when a trader is funding an action.[16] A trader funding an action and considered a third party funder under the Directive would thus not be carrying out TPLF and be the subject of any applicable legislation based on the definition of TPLF as provided in the EPRS report (as it is not providing funding as part of its professional practice). One of the main concerns highlighted in the executive summary of the EPRS report is that "*TPLF* [...] *could also be used for the pursuit of strategic goals by competing businesses*".[17] However, under the definition of TPLF used in the report itself, that could not refer to a claim funded by any non-professional funding company (i.e. carrying out any other type of regular business) on the EU market, as provided for in the Directive, but only to a claim which would be funded by a professional litigation funder against another litigation funder (since otherwise the funder and the defendant company would not have competing businesses). It may be presumed that such was not the intention of the EPRS report.

3.3 The EPRS Reports' Definition of Third Party Litigation Funder

With respect to the definition of litigation funder, the EPRS sets out the following:

> '**Third Party Litigation Funder**' (or 'Third Party Funder', 'Litigation Financier', 'Litigation Funder', 'Litigation Fund' or 'Funder') indicates any entity that is not a party to a dispute, or a lawyer or insurer of such a party, which bears the costs of the dispute in exchange for a percentage of the financial recovery, only if the case is won.[18]

[16] "*The direct funding of a specific representative action by a trader operating in the same market as the defendant should be considered to imply a conflict of interest, since the competitor could have an economic interest in the outcome of the representative action which would not be the same as the consumers' interest.*" Directive 2020/1828, item (52). See also Article 10, Section 2 (b).

[17] The EPRS report, p. I.

[18] The EPRS report, p. 43.

3.3.1 The Third Party Litigation Funder Definition Used in the EPRS Report Does Not Cover All Entities Carrying Out TPLF as Defined in the EPRS Report

First, it should be noted that the definition of Third Party Litigation Funder is so narrowly drafted that it does not cover any and all entities carrying out TPLF as defined in the EPRS report (see Sect. 3.2 above), but only insofar as such activity may fall within subsection (a) of the TPLF definition, which relates to remuneration being paid under the so called percentage approach. As discussed above, the TPLF definition in the EPRS report also has a subsection (b) which relates to a multiple based remuneration model. However, as Third Party Litigation Funder is defined, any entity carrying out funding operations where success fee is payable not as a percentage of any recovery (but under a multiple based approach in relation to the committed or paid-in capital) thus seems not to fall within the definition, as such entity has not borne any costs "*in exchange for a percentage of the financial recovery*"—which is the definition of Third Party Litigation Funder as used in the EPRS report. It may also be noted that a funder entering into an arrangement whereby it funds a company seeking declaratory relief, or a defendant party, in which the remuneration in case of success would not come from any financial recovery but could be payable in shares or future revenues of the company etc., would not be considered a Third Party Litigation Funder.

3.3.2 The Third Party Litigation Funder Definition Used in the EPRS Report Does Not Cover Non-commercial Funders or Entities Funding Claims for Abusive Purposes

Another remark is that the definition of Third Party Litigation Funder as suggested in the EPRS report comprises only entities involved in commercial funding ("*in exchange for a percentage of the financial recovery*") and would not refer to any non-commercial funder or entity carrying out funding activity for policy or abusive reasons or any other purpose (including so called revenge funding) where the funder is not entitled to any remuneration from the funded party even if the case succeeds. Thus, the EPRS definition deviates also in this respect from the established definition used by the ICCA-Queen Mary Task Force,[19] and would not cover funding activity carrying out frivolous claims for harassment purposes. It is difficult to assess whether this omittance of funding practices carried out by actors not incentivised by claimants being awarded recovery so that the funder will be accordingly remunerated was intended and, if so, for what reasons. It is particularly odd considering

[19] Cf. "*. . .such support or financing is either provided in exchange for remuneration* [. . .] *or provided through a grant* [. . .]". Report of the ICCA-Queen Mary Task Force on Third-Party Funding in International Arbitration, 2018, p. 50.

the fact that much of the EPRS report's concerns seem related to the risk for abusive and frivolous claims funded by non-serious actors.

3.3.3 The Third Party Litigation Funder Definition Used in the EPRS Report Is Unclear with Respect to Whether Insurers and Lawyers May Fall Within the Definition

Further, it is unclear whether lawyers and/or insurers fit within the Third Party Litigation Funder definition, as the term "*indicates any entity that is not a party to a dispute, or a lawyer or insurer of such a party, which bears the costs of the dispute in exchange for a percentage of the financial recovery...*". The unclear language may be construed such as covering a non-party entity, a lawyer and an insurer to fall within the definition of Third Party Litigation Funder if bearing the costs of the dispute. However, considering that the report elsewhere sets out that the Code of Conduct for European Lawyers "*implies that a lawyer cannot act as a funder*",[20] it may be presumed that the intention is that a lawyer and an insurer should *not* fall within the definition and that an implied "nor" should be read before "*lawyer*" and "*insurer*", respectively. It is therefore interesting to compare the definition used in the report with the one proposed and used by Gian Marco Solas in a leading treatise on third party funding (cited in the EPRS report) which refers to "*any entity not a party to a dispute, which is neither a lawyer nor an insurer of that party, that professionally maintains the disputes' costs in exchange for a share of the sum recovered...*".[21] When comparing the language provided by Solas and by the EPRS report, it seems clear that the definition in the latter relies heavily on the definition suggested by Solas (whom is referred to several times in the EPRS report), but that the language has been adjusted in the EPRS report so that (1) the negation prior to the words "lawyer" and "insurer" ("*neither...nor*"), and (2) the word "*professionally*" (or similar) are not used. With respect to (1), the omittance of the negation, it is indeed peculiar that the EPRS report criticises the existing taxonomy on TPLF, yet uses and adjusts such earlier suggested definitions by leading TPLF scholars by in fact making the language more confused. With respect to (2), the omittance of the word "professionally", that circumstance is commented upon in the below Sect. 3.3.4.

The unclear language aside, if presuming that an insurer should not fall within the definition of Third Party Litigation Funder even if such entity is carrying out business which in fact falls within the EPRS definition of TPLF (which may very well occur), one may ask why that should be the case. Whether such entity is licenced as or otherwise deemed to be an insurer under applicable legislation should have limited bearing on a number of the issues dealt with in the EPRS report, such as

[20] The EPRS report, p. 76.

[21] Solas (2019), p. 4.

whether a funder should be liable for opposing party's legal costs and whether it should be required to post security for costs, etc.[22]

3.3.4 The Third Party Litigation Funder Definition Used in the EPRS Report Does Not Correspond with the TPLF Definition Used in the Very Same Report

As noted above, there is no reference to "*professional*" practice in the definition of Third Party Litigation Funder. The EPRS report's definition of Third Party Litigation Funder thus seems not to fit the report's previously defined concept of TPLF very well, as TPLF refers only to "*the professional practice of an entity*" in funding costs of proceedings, whereas the definition of Third Party Litigation Funder refers to "*any entity*" carrying out such practice, i.e. irrespective of whether professional or not. Thus, if a company not normally within the funding industry decides to carry out a one-off litigation funding deal, such company would be considered a Third Party Litigation Funder under this definition, but its funding deal would not be considered Third Party Litigation Funding under the TPLF definition. This has further implications with respect to actions carried out by a non-professional entity involved in third party funding, such as a trader, as commented upon in Sect. 3.2 above.

As it is particularly underlined in the EPRS report that the existing definitions of third party funding and third party funder are not satisfying and in need of clarification, it must be presumed that the carefully drafted suggestions in the EPRS report itself are intended to improve the use and understanding of the defined terms by deviating from the language used by the ICCA-Queen Mary Task Force and Solas, or other leading scholars in their definitions. However, that does not appear to be the case.

[22] If the intention of the EPRS report instead is that the definition should not be read such as to exclude insurers *per se*, it should be noted that there are some grammatical issues which provide further uncertainty, as the definition does not refer to any "*insurer*", but "*insurer of such a party*". Only insurers of a certain party ("*such a party*") may thus fall within the definition of TPLF. One would of course presume such party to be the insured or funded party. However, that is not what the definition says. Rather, there is only one party mentioned which could be referred to when using the language "*such party*", and that is an "*entity that is not a party to a dispute*". Thus, if narrowly construed in accordance with its letter, the definition states that an insurer of a non-party which bears the cost of the dispute in exchange for a percentage of the financial recovery would be considered a funder. Of course, that could not be the intention of the EPRS and it must be the case that the modifier in the definition is simply misplaced.

3.4 *Conclusion Regarding the Fundamental Concepts Defined in the EPRS Report*

Following the analysis in Sects. 3.2 and 3.3, respectively, several issues arise with respect to the key terms as defined in the EPRS report. In summary, with respect to the term (a) Third Party Litigation Funding (1) it is unclear whether the term shall comprise both single claim and portfolio funding, (2) the language is unprecise and provides a misconception with respect to whether remuneration for the funder is dependent on the outcome of the dispute also under the so called multiple approach, and (3) it relates only to "*the professional practice of an entity*", which means that the definition does not correspond with the provisions in EU regulation nor the definition of funder provided in the EPRS report itself (which means that a non-professional funder would not be considered to carry out TPLF); and with respect to the term (b) Third Party Litigation Funder (1) it is so narrowly drafted that it does not cover all entities carrying out TPLF as defined in the report itself, (2) it does not cover non-commercial funders not seeking remuneration (such as funding policy claims, abusive claims or carrying out revenge funding, even though the report deals with the alleged problem of revenge funding), (3) the language is grammatically problematic and it is therefore unclear whether lawyers and insurers may be covered by the definition, and (4) there is no reference to professional practice, which means that the definition of funder does not correspond with the definition of TPLF—thus, a trader could be entering into litigation finance deals and be considered a funder under the proposed definition and yet not be considered to carry out TPLF under such definition.

Since the EPRS report puts considerable weight on the need to provide a solid taxonomy of key funding terms, one would have expected somewhat more careful thought on the definitions used in the EPRS report itself, particularly when deviating from the most commonly used definitions already established by in fact providing more confusing, vague and unclear language.

4 The Perceived Risk for Frivolous Claims

4.1 *The EPRS Report's Conclusions Regarding Risk for Frivolous Claims as an Effect of TPLF*

As mentioned in Sect. 2 above, there are serious concerns raised in the EPRS report with respect to the risk for frivolous claims as an effect of TPLF. It is not set out in the report what is meant by the term "*frivolous claims*", but elsewhere the EPRS has referred to such claims as a form of "*abuse*".[23] According to Blacks' Law

[23]European Parliamentary Research Service (2017), p. 18.

Dictionary, "*frivolous*" means "[l]*acking a legal basis or legal merit; not serious; not reasonably purposeful*", whereas a "*frivolous claim*" is defined as "[a] *claim that has no legal basis or merit, esp. one brought for an unreasonable purpose such as harassment*." Generally, the term frivolous is thus understood as an adjective describing a claim that is worthless and in effect constitutes an abuse or harassment. The bar for any claim to be so considered is exceptionally high—and notably significantly higher than the mere finding by a court that a claim shall be rejected.

In the executive summary of the EPRS report, the following is set out:

> **Why should the EU act?**
>
> TPLF could offer some benefits if the associated risks are mitigated. In particular, it may represent a tool to support private citizens and businesses in accessing justice and constitute a mechanism for transferring the risk of the uncertain outcome of the dispute to the litigation funder. At the same time, it may pose risks and entail conflicts of interests. If not properly regulated, it could lead to excessive economic costs and to the multiplication of opportunity claims, problematic claims and so called 'frivolous claims'. It could also be used for the pursuit of strategic goals by competing businesses, and the cost and time wasted in frivolous litigation in some instances could also potentially directly affect aggregate productivity and competitiveness.
>
> Furthermore, there could be a tendency by some funders to move away from a traditional form of litigation funding to a much wider range of funding models such as complex portfolio funding. [---][24]

One of the key goals of the regulatory policies suggested in the EPRS report is indeed to ensure that "*in particular opportunistic, excessive and frivolous claims would be significantly reduced.*"[25] As part of its section on qualitative assessment of the effects of the suggested legislation on TPLF, the EPRS report sets out the following:

> By keeping the costs of litigation from rising uncontrollably, it could make it less costly for businesses to defend themselves against opportunistic, excessive and frivolous claims. Avoiding sometimes unnecessary, costly and lengthy proceedings could allow businesses to save resources or to direct them to more productive activities. Furthermore, by reducing the incidence of opportunistic, excessive, and frivolous proceedings, the risk of disruption to business activities and strategic positioning might be reduced. [---]
>
> By limiting the amount of opportunistic, excessive, and frivolous cases put before the Court, and subsequently increasing legal certainty and business confidence, the risk of reputational damage for businesses caused by some lawsuits could also be reduced.[26]

Further, it is stated in the EPRS report that "[t]*he litigation services market could see benefits in terms of a greater balance between claimant rights and the need to*

---

[24]The EPRS report, p. I. As was discussed in Sect. 3.2, due to the definition of TPLF as used in the EPRS report, it is unclear whether portfolio funding (or PLF, as the EPRS report defines it) should be understood to fall within the term TPLF as used throughout the EPRS report. In the above quoted passage, reference must be understood to be made only to frivolous single claims in the first paragraph, as the concept of portfolio funding is not introduced until the second paragraph.

[25]The EPRS report, p. 27.

[26]The EPRS report, p. 29.

restrain opportunistic, excessive, and frivolous litigation."[27] It is also held that the judicial system as such would benefit from regulation: "*By limiting opportunistic, excessive, and frivolous claims that hamper the smooth running of the system, the legislative initiative would contribute to increased efficiency.*"[28]

The perceived risk for frivolous claims as an effect of TPLF is thus at the centre of the EPRS report. As shown above, the language of the summaries and conclusions is broadly drafted and provides the reader with the understanding that TPLF in general has the effect or high risk of leading to more frivolous claims—i.e. abusive claims without any legal merit whatsoever. In the referenced sections, there is no suggestion that the risk of frivolous claims should be understood as limited to the practice of so-called portfolio funding, but as an effect of TPLF in general.

The fact that the perceived risk for frivolous claims, according to the annexed study on which the concluding part of the report relies, is limited to portfolio funding (see below) is entirely suppressed in the summarizing remarks of the report and surface only occasionally in other parts, such as in a matrix on identified risks where it is stated that "[c]*laims cases* [sic] *funded through portfolio TPLF can bring about a large number of excessive and frivolous litigation cases*".[29] This statement will be further dealt with below.

It is thus repeatedly stated throughout the EPRS report that there is a risk for frivolous claims with respect to TPLF in general. Indeed, the word "*frivolous*" in relation to litigation funding occurs not less than 23 times in the EPRS report, spread over 13 different pages.[30] Only on two of these pages is it stated that the risk for frivolous claims is related to portfolio funding.[31] Following this repetitious language, any reader—including the intended reader in the shape of a Member of the European Parliament considering potential policies on TPLF—glancing through the EPRS report without the time to conduct a thorough reading would get the impression that it is a well-established fact that litigation funding either leads to, or has a very high risk of leading to, frivolous claims. However, when one sets out to identify the sources on which the EPRS draws upon to make its conclusions, another picture emerges.

---

[27]The EPRS report, p. 30.

[28]The EPRS report, p. 30.

[29]The EPRS report, p. 18. See also p. 20. With respect to the term "*portfolio TPLF*", it is of some interest since it shows—as argued in Sect. 3.2 above—that the term TPLF as defined in the EPRS report does in fact not cover portfolio funding, but only single claim funding (otherwise, the addition of "*portfolio*" would have been circular). This also shows that the repeated assertions throughout the report that TPLF has a high risk for frivolous claims should be understood as—or intended to be understood as—a reference to single claim funding. It is not clear why the EPRS report does not in this context use the acronym PLF which it—in its attempt to "*clarify some terminology used*" (p. 43) has defined as "*the professional practice of funding a portfolio of disputes for business purposes*" (p. 43).

[30]The EPRS report, pp. I, III, 1, 2, 18, 20, 25, 27, 29, 30, 31, 32, and 33.

[31]The EPRS report, pp. 18 and 20.

4.2 The EPRS Report States That the Risk for Frivolous Single Claims as an Effect of TPLF Is "Extremely Low"

As mentioned above, the analysis and conclusions of the EPRS report builds on the annexed study. Considering the weight that the EPRS report puts on the risk for frivolous claims as an effect of TPLF and the frequent and repetitious, yet broad and vague, language implying such risk, one would of course expect the issue to have been thoroughly researched and dealt with, or at least that the EPRS report would draw upon other previous research on the topic. Against that background, one may be somewhat surprised to learn that the section in the annexed study specifically devoted to frivolous claims (or "*vexatious litigation*"), and on which the above referenced conclusions with respect to policy recommendations is built, reads—in its entirety—as follows:

> 3.3.1 Risk of vexatious litigation
>
> As noted by Lord Jackson,[122 [footnote in original, see below comment]] in TPLF, the risk of vexatious litigation is extremely low with respect to the litigation financing of single cases, as funders tend to filter out unmeritorious individual claims and do not take on the high risk of such cases. However, portfolio financing could allow for some flawed suits to be presented in court, as funders spread the risk on a portfolio basis.[32]

Thus, it is explicitly set out in the research section of the report that the risk for frivolous funded single claims is "*extremely low*" (!). Further, it must be stressed that the above quoted passage, which contains one (1) sentence relating to the alleged fact that portfolio funding (but not single claim funding) could allow for some flawed suits in fact contains the only ground on which the EPRS seems to base its repeated language of the risk for frivolous cases emanating from TPLF and the policy recommendations suggested to deal with such alleged risk.

It should also be noted that there is only one source cited in the referenced section. In contrast to the citation and footnote structure in the rest of the report, the footnote (footnote no. 122, which has not been omitted in the above quotation) is placed directly after the name of the referenced author, rather than after the statement made. Thereby, the reader is led to believe that both statements that follow is supported by the only referenced source. However, that is not the case. To the contrary, what Lord Justice Jackson finds on the referenced page with respect to whether funded claims are meritorious is summarized as follows: "*Third party funding tends to filter out unmeritorious cases, because funders will not take on the risk of such cases. This benefits opposing parties.*"[33] There is no mentioning whatsoever that third party funding—whether on a single or portfolio basis—"*could allow for some flawed suits*".

[32] The EPRS report, p. 74.

[33] https://www.judiciary.uk/wp-content/uploads/JCO/Documents/Reports/jackson-final-report-140110.pdf, p. 117.

Thus, it is from the above unfounded statement that portfolio financing could allow for "*some*" flawed suits, that the EPRS sets out that "[c]*laims cases* [sic] *funded through portfolio TPLF can bring about a large number of excessive and frivolous litigation cases*".[34] It is not clear whether this is an intentional distortion of the (unsupported) view in the research section when copied to the concluding section, or merely an unintentional slippage from "*some*" to "*a large number*" of frivolous claims.

Even if the above one paragraph quote under the heading "*Risk of vexatious litigation*" constitutes the entire analysis section on frivolous claims in the study (!), there is also some mentioning on the issue in the specific section on collective redress. There, the following is set out:

> However, even in the field of collective redress, concerns have been raised with regard to TPLF. In particular, it has been noted that (i) a financial incentive to mass claims might stimulate abusive litigation;[137 [footnote in original, see below comment]] moreover, (ii) the third party intervention may lead to conflicts of interests between the funder and the defendant, or may give the funder a predominant position in case management terms.[35]

It is thus again set out that TPLF might lead to "*abusive litigation*"—now with a footnote added to show the source (footnote 137, not omitted in the above quotation). However, when reviewing the source on which the study relies with respect to the risk for abusive litigation emanating from the funding practice, it turns out that footnote 137—which one expected to form the basis for the alleged finding of abusive litigation—reads, in its entirety, as follows:

> However, in that respect, see I. Tillema (2017), 'Entrepreneurial motives in Dutch collective redress', in W.H. van Boom (ed.), Litigation, Costs, Funding and Behaviour: Implications for the Law, Routledge, p. 222-243. Tillema's research has shown that there is no evidence of a rise in frivolous lodging of collective damages claims.[36]

Thus, it is evident that the EPRS report again contains statements of the risk for frivolous claims without support. To the contrary, the reference to actual research carried out shows the entire opposite finding, i.e. that "*that there is no evidence of a rise in frivolous lodging of collective damages claims.*"

The EPRS report does not present any source whatsoever for its key position that TPLF may lead to frivolous claims. This is remarkable, considering the fact that the alleged risk for frivolous claims and the importance of policies to deal with such risk is at the very foreground of the EPRS report as such. This is even more intriguing considering that the EPRS report—on its face—seems thoroughly well-researched, referencing a considerable number of books and articles on litigation funding, as well as EU regulation and national legislation and case law. It is not a far-reaching conclusion that there may actually not exist any support for the statement.

[34] The EPRS report, p. 18, emphasis added.

[35] The EPRS report, pp. 77–78, emphasis added.

[36] The EPRS report, p. 78, footnote 137, emphasis added.

If one takes a step back and considers the fact that TPLF is a commercial practice where investors make money if, and only if, funded claims are successful in court or are favourably settled, it seems rather counterintuitive that any funder should be willing to back a frivolous claim, i.e. a claim that lacks legal basis or merit, which is worthless and in effect constitutes an abuse or harassment. That a funder only wishes to purse strong cases is in fact also acknowledged in the report, however in a different section:

> According to our qualitative analysis, the elements that are usually examined by the funder in the due diligence phase include the following:
>
> a. [---]
>
> b. Length of the claim and likelihood of success (which must be very high). Funders always carefully assess the strength of the claim, the available evidence and the presence of any counterclaims to calculate the likelihood of the lawsuit being successful; [. . .][37]

Thus, it is set out in the report that according to the qualitative analysis conducted, it was established that in claim due diligence carried out by funders, the likelihood of success "*must be very high*" and that funders "*always carefully assess the strength of the claim*". If this is the finding established through careful analysis, one must ask on what grounds it is repeatedly set forth in the main parts of the EPRS report—as shown above—that frivolous claims by funders is a high risk and that there is a need to put in place policies to deal with such current or future misconduct within the field of TPLF in general, i.e. whether relating to single claim funding, funding of collective redress or portfolio funding.

4.3 The EPRS Report Presents No Support or Argument for the Position That Portfolio Funding May Lead to Frivolous Claims

Further, there is no research or evidence presented in the report to support the alleged claim that portfolio funding should lead to more frivolous cases, let alone a "*large number*" of frivolous cases as alleged in the report. In fact, there is even *no argument* presented as to why that should be the case. It is merely stated in a footnote that "[*p*] *ortfolio litigation practices refer to the funding of a portfolio of disputes. Consisting of funders spreading the risks across a bundle of cases to diversify their investments, the approach has the potential to lead to cases without merit also receiving funding.*"[38] This should not be regarded as an uncontroversial statement.

Some initial remarks may be made with respect to the concept of portfolio funding. In general, portfolios can be based either on (1) the funding of cases emanating from a specific claimant which is a repeat player in litigation and has a

[37] The EPRS report, p. 65, emphasis added.

[38] The EPRS report, p. 20, footnote 46.

large number of cases—which in practice means the big corporates—or on (2) the funding of a specific law firm in return for a share of its success fees on the cases for various clients that it runs on a contingency fee or under a DBA. As to the big corporates with large case loads, one may hesitate to find it conceivable that they would start filing abusive frivolous cases and request that such cases be funded as part of professional funders' portfolio structures.

With respect to law firm portfolio funding, that is the most common form of portfolio funding in the US and UK, where funders are indeed starting to collaborate more closely with law firms and entering into portfolio financing deals with them. However, there is an important difference between the US/UK and the EU litigation services markets, in the sense that EU law firms are generally restricted to work on success fee, even if some exceptions do apply.[39] That means that the most common portfolio structure as used in the US/UK is in principle *not even available* within the EU. This is one of the reasons why the discussions on TPLF held in US/UK will play out differently within the EU and cannot just be imported here without due consideration. The EPRS fails to grasp this hugely important difference. It should also be stressed that in the exceptional cases where law firm portfolio funding could be carried out within the EU, for a frivolous claim to be funded as part of a portfolio, the law firm must first have taken on such success fee case and suggested and agreed that the frivolous claim be filed.

Further, the argument that portfolio funding would lead to frivolous claims presupposes that the funder should no longer set up standard criteria as to which cases that are suitable for funding and that it should take an "anything goes" approach as to the strength of cases in the portfolio. There is no basis for such argument, nor has the report provided any. Even if one—for the sake of argument—were to accept the notion that a portfolio funding structure would allow for some cases which have a higher risk for loss than any of the funders referenced in the study would accept, that could not lead to the conclusion that frivolous claims could be expected. For a funder, nothing could be worse for its business and its reputation than funding frivolous claims, and thus their highest priority is to seek out and fund highly meritorious claims, either on a single claim or portfolio basis. If, again for the sake of argument, one would consider a situation that a funder under a portfolio would also accept some weaker cases to be funded, presumably even below 50%, such as 40% or even 30% likelihood of success, even that would not mean that such claim would be without merit, let alone "frivolous". What such type of high-risk litigation—*nota bene*, beyond any funding criteria risk levels as presented in the EPRS report itself (see Sect. 5.3.2 below)—means in practice is that if such case would be tried before 100 different judges, 40 or 30, respectively, of such judges would provide claimant with full recovery. Of course, that could not be a case entirely without merit, let alone "frivolous". It is not made clear why any funder should like to accept weak claims in its portfolio, and there seems to be no reason why any funder should accept to finance not only a weak case, but a frivolous case,

[39] See, e.g. *Code of Conduct for European Lawyers*, item 3.3, p. 17.

just because it is part of a portfolio. Yet, this is precisely what the EPRS claims in its report.

4.4 Concluding Remarks Regarding the Report's Position on Frivolous Claims

The report's repeated statements that TPLF poses a risk for frivolous claims, i.e. claims which are worthless and in effect constitutes abuse of legal procedure, constitute severe critique of the emerging funding market. Against that background, one would of course expect to find a thorough and well-researched basis for such position. It is therefore intriguing that the report makes such statements without solid support.

To the contrary, the study annexed to the report found that there is an "*extremely low*" risk that single claim funding should lead to frivolous claims. With respect to collective redress, the only source relied on in the report found that "*there is no evidence of a rise in frivolous lodging of collective damages claims.*" As regards portfolio funding, which in contrast to the US/UK (for legislative and Bar rules reasons) is a minor part of the EU TPLF market, there is no referenced support for a position that such practice would lead to a high risk for frivolous claims. Even if—for the sake of argument—the unfounded statement that portfolio funding leads to frivolous claims were true, it cannot be reasonably sustained that TPLF in general should lead to frivolous claims. In fact, the report's concluding statements on the alleged risks for frivolous claims in TPLF can itself be considered a frivolous claim—within the traditional meaning of the term.

5 The Perceived Risk for Conflicts of Interest as an Effect of TPLF

5.1 Introduction

The EPRS report pays close attention to the perceived risk for conflicts of interest with respect to TPLF. It is not explained in the report what is meant by such term, but another department of the European Parliament sets out the following: "*Generally, a conflict of interest can be defined as a conflict between the private interests and the official or professional responsibilities of a person, or a conflict arising when a person holds a private interest that conflicts with the one of his/her employer.*"[40] Further:

[40] The European Parliament's Policy Department for Citizens' Rights and Constitutional Affairs, *The Effectiveness of Conflict of Interest Policies in the EU Member States*, 2020, p. 8. According to

> CoI [i.e. Conflict of Interest] as a legal concept has a long agreed-upon meaning in law used to regulate fiduciaries – individuals entrusted to serve the interest of another party or to serve a designated mission – who are held to the highest legal standards of conduct. Generally, these laws and codes do not permit fiduciaries to promote their own interests or the interests of third parties. Instead, they require fiduciaries to be loyal to the party they serve, to act prudently and diligently, and to account for their conduct.[41]

It is important to note that *conflicting or competing interests* as such are not the same as *a conflict of interest* within the legal meaning of the term, which is underlined by a European Parliament Policy Department as follows: "*In daily life, multiple conflicting interests may pull people in different directions but only when they compromise professional obligations is there a conflict of interest.*"[42] Thus, at the core of the term is the compromise of professional obligations, or the risk that such obligations are compromised. This is sometimes also referred to by the phrase that *one cannot serve two masters*.[43]

In the executive summary of the EPRS report, it is set out that "*funders may* [...] *operate in a conflict of interests with the claimant in managing or settling the case.*"[44] The conflicts identified by the EPRS seem to emanate mainly either from the relationship (1) between the funded party and the funder or (2) between the funder and any other entity or person involved in the proceedings. With respect to the latter situation, the EPRS report finds that "[a]*lthough, in litigation, it is more difficult to imagine cases of a hypothetical conflict of interests with the funder than it is in arbitration, such a possibility cannot be excluded.*"[45] Considering the fact that it according to the EPRS report is difficult to even hypothetically imagine such conflicts with respect to TPLF, it may be presumed that they cannot be of any high risk and therefore should not serve as any important reason for providing policy recommendations on the subject.[46] This paper will therefore deal solely with the

---

Blacks' Law Dictionary, a conflict of interest means the following: "*1. A real or seeming incompatibility between one's private interests and one's public or fiduciary duties. 2. A real or seeming incompatibility between the interests of two of a lawyer's clients, such that the lawyer is disqualified from representing both clients if the dual representation adversely affects either client or if the clients do not consent.*"

[41] The European Parliament's Policy Department for Citizens' Rights and Constitutional Affairs, *The Effectiveness of Conflict of Interest Policies in the EU Member States*, 2020, p. 38.

[42] The European Parliament's Policy Department for Citizens' Rights and Constitutional Affairs, *The Effectiveness of Conflict of Interest Policies in the EU Member States*, 2020, p. 36.

[43] See, e.g., Griffiths-Baker (2002).

[44] The EPRS report, p. I. It is further stated that "[t]*he lawyer might also be in a potential conflict of interests with clients, given that the former usually obtains their fees directly from the litigation funder.*" (Ibid.) Any issue relating to conflicts of interest for a lawyer when representing a client (whether or not such client has entered into a litigation funding deal) is mainly a problem of general character for any legal services provider which is and should be thoroughly dealt with in relevant Bar rules, legislation or soft law applicable to attorneys and will not be further discussed in this paper (as it is not a particular problem relating to TPLF).

[45] The EPRS report, p. 75.

[46] With respect to any conflict of interest for an attorney, please see footnote 44.

report's findings with respect to the first category, i.e. potential conflicts of interest regarding the funded party and the funder.

5.2 *Potential Conflicts of Interest Regarding the Funded Party and the Funder*

According to the report, "[t]*he study has revealed that an attempt made by the funder to influence decisions on procedural strategies, including settlements, might result in a conflict of interests between the claimant and the funder.*"[47] The report's main concern with respect to conflicts of interest emanating from the relationship between the funder and the funded party is thus the potential influence by funders on procedural issues and settlement decisions, which may be to the detriment of the funded party.[48] This is explained as follows:

> A conflict of interests may arise when the funder has an economic interest in accepting the settlement offer to bring a swift end to the proceedings (so as to recover its own investment), while the claimant has an interest in rejecting the offer, as the sum proposed by the opponent is – in the claimant's opinion – not 'satisfactory'. In this respect, it should be noted that many TPLF agreements provide that the funder's remuneration and its reimbursement of the procedural costs must be the first to be paid, pursuant to so-called 'waterfall' provisions. The remainder is then paid to the funded party. Such a situation may induce the claimant to raise the stakes at the expense of the counterparty, or to continue the litigation, which might otherwise have been settled.[49]

It is indeed true that the economic interests of a funded party and the funder, respectively, are not always perfectly aligned with respect to whether a particular settlement should be entered into or not. However, as noted above, competing or conflicting interests may very well exist without any party or person finding itself in a conflict of interest, since such term requires that professional obligations or fiduciary duties are, or risk to be, compromised.

Against that background, it is important to note that a litigation funder in general is not a service provider, but an investor in a certain asset class—a funder has committed capital to a disputing party in return for a share of the recovery. This is acknowledged also in the EPRS report, which states that "*funders do not provider* [sic] *services*...".[50] Thus, even if a funder of course acts under a contractual duty of loyalty as any other party in a business relation, it does not risk serving two masters as an attorney or other professional services provider may do if and when it finds

[47] The EPRS report, p. 87.

[48] The EPRS report, pp. 21 and 87.

[49] The EPRS report, p. 72.

[50] The EPRS report, p. 5, footnote 13. There may exist specific arrangements among some funders that could involve the rendering of services under certain contracts; that would however not be considered the ordinary type of TPLF deal, cf. the definition of TPLF and Third Party Litigation Funder in the EPRS report as discussed above in this paper.

itself to be in a situation of serving clients with competing interests or with interests competing with the attorney's own interest.

It is correct as the EPRS report points out that a funder may potentially have rights under the LFA to affect the strategy and to have a say—or even decision power—on settlement proposals. That is however not always the case. Thus, either (1) the funder has a contractual right to affect the strategy and the level at which the funded party shall accept a settlement, or (2) it does not have any contractual right to do so. Neither of these alternatives lead to a conflict of interest situation, as under scenario (1) the funded party has pre-agreed to and provided the funder with contractual power if and when such very situation occurs, and as under scenario (2) the funders' hands are and should be tied. Since the funder is an investor and not a service provider, it does not represent or act on behalf of the funded party—whatever it can and may do is or should be explicitly set out in the LFA. If the funder has a contractual right to decide, and as it does not have any fiduciary duties, it cannot be correct that the funder is in a conflict of interest within the established meaning of the term (including as understood in the expert report on conflicts of interest by the European Parliament's Department on Constitutional Affairs) if exercising the powers it has bargained for and is entitled to under the LFA. And if the funder has no right to influence decisions, the funder should of course not be able to exercise any powers and the funded party shall do as it pleases without concern to the funder's wishes.[51]

The EPRS report is silent with respect to any legal authority as to why the identified situation should amount to a conflict of interest, particularly with respect to the funding of commercial cases.[52] As regards consumer group actions, the EPRS report refers to Article 10 of Directive 2020/1828, which according to the report "*addresses the problem of conflicts of interest between the claimant and the funder in the field of consumer collective redress.*"[53] What is set out in said Article in this regard is the following:

1. [---]

[51] The funder may of course use other tactics in a settlement situation than as formally agreed under the contract, such as negotiating with the funded party that the funder will lower its profit share if the funded party accepts the settlement. That means that the funded party is presented with a new and better alternative which it may or may not accept.

[52] The EPRS report only refers to the fact that a proposed Directive on common minimum standards of civil procedure in the EU has been suggested to include a provision under which a funder should not be allowed to influence procedural decisions of the funded party: "*Member States shall ensure that in cases where a legal action is funded by a private third party, the private third party shall not: (a) seek to influence procedural decisions of the claimant party, including on settlements*". Article 16, European Parliament resolution of 4 July 2017 with recommendations to the Commission on common minimum standards of civil procedure in the European Union (2015/2084(INL)). Even if no such influence were to be allowed, that does not mean that exercising such influence would constitute a "*conflict of interest*".

[53] The EPRS report, pp. 72 f.

> 2. [. . .] Member States shall in particular ensure that:
>
> (a) the decisions of qualified entities in the context of a representative action, including decisions on settlement, are not unduly influenced by a third party in a manner that would be detrimental to the collective interests of the consumers concerned by the representative action; [---][54]

It does not follow from the Directive that a settlement situation constitutes a conflict of interest for the funder. Further, it does not even follow that a funder may not influence a consumer group's decision on settlement, only that such influence may not be "*unduly*" exercised. Thus, influence from a funder on a consumer settlement decision does not in and of itself imply that a funder should have acted in conflict of interests.

Considering the above analysis, there seem to be no valid argument as to why a funder exercising its rights under a perfectly valid LFA in a settlement situation should be acting in conflict of interest. However, in the EPRS report it is not only stated—without solid support—that such is the case, but even that actions by the funder affecting a settlement scenario amount to "*corrupting justice*" (!):

> Court settlement is one of the most sensitive issues in the relationship between the claimant, his or her lawyer and the funder, in respect of which there is a risk that the latter may attempt to restrict the claimant's freedom in determining the procedural strategy, this way 'corrupting justice'.
>
> In fact, many TPLF model agreements require the funded party to obtain prior consent from the funder for any act of disposal of the claimed right, such as the power to enter into a settlement.[117 [footnote in original, see below comment]55]

It is thus held that any control on the procedural strategy from a funders' side amounts to corruption of justice. That is strong language indeed. Such position may have been influenced by arguments derived from the common law historical doctrines of champerty and maintenance, which arguably have limited relevance in a European Union perspective. The EPRS report does not contain any legal authority or basis as to why parties who are free to contract as they wish and who enter into a financing deal under which a funder has the right to influence a funded party's decisions in relation to an opposite party in a dispute before a court should be considered "*corrupting justice*" under any legislation or case law in any jurisdiction within the European Union. The only cited reference with respect to the above quoted paragraphs on corruption of justice (footnote 117, not omitted from the above quotation) refers to three funding contracts which contain prior consent clauses in settlement discussions, whereafter the following remark is made in the report:

> However, in that respect see Akhmedova v Akhmedov [2020] EWHC 1526 (Fam), para 60. The English court held that "A funder of litigation is not forbidden from having rights of

[54] Directive 2020/1828, Article 10.

[55] The EPRS report, p. 72.

control but is forbidden from having a degree of control which would be likely to undermine or corrupt the process of justice. With respect to settlement, I observe that even if the Wife [the funded party] was required to obtain Burford Capital's consent before settling her enforcement action, that would appear to be a perfectly proper protection for Burford Capital as funder and would not tend to corrupt justice".[56]

Thus, not even in England—where champerty and maintenance were long upheld and still apply to some extent—would a veto right for the funder to refuse the funded party to settle as it wishes constitute corruption of justice.

The position that a funder exercising its contractual rights under an LFA—presumably negotiated by sophisticated counsel representing the funded party—to have a say on settlement discussions should constitute an action amounting to corruption of justice, as set out in the EPRS report, lacks support under current legislation and case law within the EU and may be considered manifestly untrue.[57]

5.3 *Comments on the Example in the EPRS Report Intended to Illustrate a Conflict of Interest Situation with Respect to Settlement*

5.3.1 Initial Remarks

To illustrate the alleged problems and risks occurring in a settlement situation, a practical example has been provided in the EPRS report. Much of the concerns in the report with respect to conflicts of interest in settlement situations indeed seem to stem from the analysis of the following exemplifying scenario, a passage which is hereby quoted *in extenso*:

> Let us illustrate this circumstance with an example: imagine that, during the proceedings, the counterparty offers to pay €100 to the claimant (settlement offer). Alternatively, if the proceedings are continued, the claimant could either win a sum of €200 or lose the case and receive €0. For the sake of simplicity, let us assume that the claimant has the same chance of winning or losing the case (50 % probability of winning and 50 % probability of losing). However, under the waterfall arrangement, €80 must be reimbursed to the funder. Therefore, if the offer is accepted, the claimant would receive €20 (€100 – €80), while the funder would receive €80. If the offer is refused, the expected payoff for the claimant is much higher: 0.5 × (€200 – €80) + 0.5 × (€0) = €60, instead of €20 if the settlement offer is accepted. The situation is completely different for the funder, whose expected payoff would be much lower if the proceedings were to be continued: 0.5 × (€80) + 0.5 × (€0) = €40, instead of €80 if the settlement offer were to be accepted. Therefore, if the decision depends on the claimant exclusively, the settlement offer will not be accepted.[58]

---

[56] The EPRS report, p. 72, footnote 117, emphasis added, square brackets in original.

[57] The statements made are thus in contradiction with the title of the annexed study—*State of play of the EU private litigation funding landscape and the current EU rules applicable to private litigation funding*.

[58] The EPRS report, p. 72.

This example may initially be considered to raise serious doubts as to the functioning of the funding market and the business practices of funders. However, against the background of the findings of the report itself, the presumptions of the alleged illustrative example do not seem to reflect the real world funding situations. This will be discussed below.

5.3.2 Estimated Chance of Success in a Litigation Funding Deal

In the above example, there is a 50% risk that the case will be lost in its entirety. In the EPRS report, the following is set out with respect to the chance of success in a litigation funding deal.

> According to our qualitative analysis, the elements that are usually examined by the funder in the due diligence phase include the following:
>
> a. Value of the claim. [---];
>
> b. Length of the claim and likelihood of success (which must be very high). Funders always carefully assess the strength of the claim, the available evidence and the presence of any counterclaims to calculate the likelihood of the lawsuit being successful;
>
> [---][59]

In a footnote to the above quote, it is also added that "[a]*ccording to our qualitative analysis (interview with three leading funders), some funders finance litigation when the success chance rate is higher than 50 %, others require a success chance rate higher than 70 %, others a 'very high possibility of winning the case'*."[60]

Thus, according to the report itself, the likelihood of success must be very high for a funder to enter into a TPFL deal and there is no data presented whatsoever of any funder entering into deals on a 50% risk of loss.[61] However, such presumption (i.e. a 50/50 case) forms the basis of the example. The claimant in this case should thus be quite pleased to have been able to identify, approach and enter into a funding arrangement with a funder willing to take on higher risk than the rest of the market. Such circumstance would of course affect the pricing of the deal so that the claimant will keep less of the recovery than it would under a normal litigation funding risk scenario (i.e. within the market risk range as presented in the report). It should thus be borne in mind that the alternative scenario presumably would be that claimant had not recovered any amount whatsoever, were it not for this particular high risk funding deal (as it did not have the necessary funds or were too risk averse to file for litigation on such high risk claim). The pricing of the deal will be further commented upon below.

---

[59] The EPRS report, p. 65.

[60] The EPRS report, p. 65, footnote 87.

[61] Cf. that the lowest success chance rate referenced and reported by any funder is "*higher than 50 %*".

5.3.3 The Claimant's Alleged Unwillingness to Accept the Settlement

In the above example, it is concluded that "*if the decision depends on the claimant exclusively, the settlement offer will not be accepted.*" This warrants some further comments.

With respect to the claimant's share of the proceeds, it is set forth that "[i]*f the offer is refused, the expected payoff for the claimant is much higher: 0.5 × (€200 – €80) + 0.5 × (€0) = €60, instead of €20 if the settlement offer is accepted.*" However, claimant cannot "*expect*" a EUR 60 payoff if the case goes to trial, and it is not true that "*the expected payoff for the claimant is much higher*" if the settlement offer is refused. The claimant in the example cannot expect any other result than EUR 120 or EUR 0 (zero) if the offer is refused (the latter provided that the claimant has contracted for a full indemnity for adverse costs from the funder in case of loss; otherwise the claimant would have to make further payment to defendant to cover its costs of proceedings, i.e. ending up in a below EUR 0 negative result).[62] This follows from the fact that the likelihood of success in the example has been set at the same level as for flipping a coin (50% risk of losing the entire case; 50% chance of winning EUR 200). To receive EUR 60 is not even an alternative scenario and can thus not be expected, even if the mathematical *financial value* of the claim under the judgment scenario may be EUR 60.[63]

It is also noted that the EPRS report holds that the claimant would not accept the offer if it was claimant's decision. However, there may be strong reasons to question that assumption, since there is a considerable 50% risk of losing the entire claim and not get a single cent. Therefore, it may in fact be expected that many claimants would prefer the safe EUR 20 rather than to test their luck in a coin tossing probability

[62] It may be presumed that the LFA in the example contains an adverse costs protection clause, as there is no downside risk mentioned for the claimant in respect of a loss (it is only stated than in case of loss, claimant will receive 0 EUR; i.e. there is no mentioning that claimant should also pay the adverse costs and thus have a negative result, which is of course a major factor when considering whether to accept a settlement offer or risk not only the full disputed amount but also having to pay adverse costs). As the loser pays rule with respect to cost of proceedings applies throughout the EU, it is clear that someone has to foot the bill—if there is not a risk for claimant in this respect (which seems to be the case as this significant piece of information is not mentioned in the hypo), that means that claimant has contracted with the funder to do so. Full adverse costs are thus part of the funder's exposure if the case goes to trial, which of course affects the pricing of the deal.

[63] Under the same logic, the funder cannot expect a EUR 40 payoff in the judgment scenario, since it will receive a success fee of EUR 80 (if the case is won) or lose its entire investment *and* have to pay the defendant's adverse costs, which means that under a loss scenario, the funder not only receives EUR 0 (zero), but has a much worse result because it even has to make further payments for adverse costs, resulting in a significant negative result. It is thus not even true that the *financial value* of the claim for the funder in the judgment scenario is EUR 40, but significantly less, taking into account the adverse costs in the loss scenario. Why the EPRS report does not mention the adverse cost issue—one of the most important issues for any serious considerations in a TPLF deal and in a settlement scenario—is not clear. It may have suited the EPRS not to do so.

situation and risking ending up with EUR 0 (zero), as the EPRS report suggest (or even facing full adverse costs, if not indemnified under the LFA).

Further, the whole example builds on the presumption that it is not entirely up to the claimant to decide in this settlement situation, but that the funder also has a say. Thus, as discussed above, this is precisely what the funded party accepted when entering into the funding agreement—a solution that, considering the exceptionally high risk of the funding deal in the example, may have been a pre-supposition for concluding the contract in the first place. It is not even suggested that the funder should be acting in breach of the agreement or in breach of any duty owed to the funded party by exercising the power it has contracted for. Thus, no professional obligations are compromised and there is no conflict of interest within the established meaning of the term.

5.3.4 Remuneration Payable in a Litigation Funding Deal

As regards the remuneration payable in a litigation funding deal in general, the report sets out that "*the recovery percentage of funders, according to the information included in Annex 1, seem to range from 20 % to 50 % of the amount awarded in the case, when the percentage approach is applied.*"[64] The average of such range is thus approximately 35% or about one third of the recovery. According to the findings of the report itself, there is no data suggesting that funders would require that the recovery be split so that the funder should receive 80% of the recovery.[65] Yet, such situation (i.e. a 80/20 recovery split) is what follows under the EPRS report's example, as the funder is said to be paid EUR 80 out of the settlement amount of EUR 100.

However, it is clear that the recovery splitting arrangement under the LFA in the example must be such that the funder's return is based on a multiple approach rather than a percentage approach, as the funder's return is not affected by the level of the recovery amount payable by the opposing party (receiving EUR 80 in both the settlement and in the favourable judgment situation, respectively), whereas the claimant receives EUR 20 in the settlement and EUR 120 in the favourable judgment situation, respectively. The claimant's recovery in the example is thus 600% higher if the case proceeds to a favourable judgment, whereas the funder's recovery from a favourable judgment is 0% higher in relation to what it would receive in a fully secure settlement situation. Thus, in the example the funder's return under the LFA is totally unaffected of whether the case is settled at no risk (0% risk) for the funder at an early stage or tried in court after a long period of time at a very high risk (50%

---

[64] The EPRS report, p. 55.

[65] There may exist individual cases where the funder's remuneration reaches such extraordinary level—that would however only be the case if the claim is not nearly as successful as expected (and provided that the funder has priority for its success fee under the waterfall agreement).

risk) of losing the entire investment *and* having to make further payments for adverse costs (presumably equalling the payments already made).

What is peculiar with the allegedly illustrative example using a multiple approach based LFA with adverse cost protection is that it does not in any way take consideration of the exceptionally high risk of the deal as such, nor the time value of money or the considerably higher risk of a judgment instead of a settlement, even though the report itself sets out in another section that "[t]*he higher the litigation risk and the longer the civil proceedings, the greater the remuneration earned by the funder if the case is won*."[66] The example does not reflect how LFAs are structured.[67]

Since the EPRS provides an example of a multiple based approach LFA (rather than a percentage based LFA), without explicitly stating the level of the success fee multiple, it is at first not clear how to assess the deal. As noted above, the EPRS report has set forth that funders' remuneration under the percentage approach seem to range from 20% to 50%. When it comes to the multiples used in multiple based LFAs, the report notes that "*the Economist reports that 'Funders of a winning suit can expect to double, triple or quadruple their money'*."[68] That means that multiple based LFAs use a 2×, 3× or 4×multiplier when calculating success fee.

Further, the EPRS makes the following remark about the typical level of investment:

> As the remuneration depends on the claimant's recovery by winning the litigation, funders are generally more interested in funding high value claims. Legal scholars have noted that funders usually seek a ratio of between 1 to 10 in terms of the amount of money needed to finance the dispute and the value of the financed claim.[69]

For support of the statement, reference is made to Rowles-Davies' *Third Party Litigation Funding*, where it is actually held that a budget to quantum ratio of one to ten is an industry norm (rather than, as stated in the EPRS report, a ratio somewhere "*between*" one to ten).[70] It is important to note that the ratio refers to the value of the

[66]The EPRS report, p. 46.

[67]Remuneration under LFAs are generally based on either a percentage of the recovery (which may be unaffected as to the fee split as such at time of settlement or trial but where the amounts would be substantially different for both the funded party and the funder, i.e. higher for both if the case succeeds after trial instead of settling), or through a multiple approach, where the funder would be paid a higher amount as time evolves (i.e. later pay-out means higher multiple), but where the level of recovery for the claimant does not affect the remuneration payable to the funder (provided that such remuneration does not exceed the funded party's recovery).

[68]The EPRS report, p. 55, footnote 38.

[69]The EPRS report, p. 46.

[70]The paragraph in Rowles-Davies to which the EPRS report refers reads as follows: "*In most cases, a litigation funder would look to ensure that the ratio of likely quantum of damages to the budget is a minimum of one to four, with most looking at a more likely ratio of one to ten. If the budget to trial for a proposed case is £1m then the likely quantum needs to be a minimum of £10m for a funder to be satisfied that it is a case to fund. Again, this is not a strict rule, but it is, in the author's experience, an industry norm.*" Rowles-Davies (2014), p. 10, para. 1.48.

claim (i.e. not the capital amount claimed as such, but its value—which of course is dependent on the likelihood of success).

If relying on the same data as the EPRS in this respect, knowing that the value of the claim in the example is EUR 100 (since there is a 50% chance of defendant having to pay EUR 200), this means that the investment made by the funder may be presumed to equal EUR 10 (under a one to ten budget to claim value ratio as mentioned in the source referenced in the report).

Using the key figures following from the standard parameters referenced in the EPRS report and its sources, it is now possible to make a few assumptions. If, for the purposes of the analysis, one would accept the above mentioned (1) investment to claim value and (2) success fee multiple, a multiple based LFA would under such presumption mean that a funder would invest one tenth of the claim value and—at the most—be entitled to quadruple that investment in case of a win (i.e. a 4× multiple).

Applying these factors on the EPRS report's own example, that means that the funder in that case should have committed capital in the amount of EUR 10 (one tenth of the claim value of EUR 100), and be entitled to four times that amount if successful. Thus, under the assumptions reported by the EPRS itself, the funder would in case of success receive remuneration in the amount of (EUR 10 (investment amount) × 4 (multiple)) = EUR 40. If the multiple would be based on the lower end spectrum as referenced by the EPRS report, i.e. a 2× multiplier, the remuneration would be EUR 20 (which in fact would also correspond with the lower end spectrum of the percentage approach based model of 20% of the recovery, as reported by the EPRS, if applied under the settlement scenario of EUR 100).

However, in the EPRS report example, the funder receives EUR 80. That means that the funder must have been entitled to a 8× multiple success fee under the LFA, rather than a success fee based on the highest reported market multiple of 4× as referenced in the report. Thus, the remuneration to the funder under the example amounts to 200% of the remuneration that would follow if the EPRS report had created an example using a multiple which in the report has been presented as the highest multiple on the market.

If applying the reported average market practice of a 3× multiple, the remuneration to the funder in the example would instead have amounted to EUR 30 in the settlement scenario. That means that the claimant under the settlement scenario would have received (EUR 100 – EUR 30) = EUR 70, rather than the stated EUR 20. This is also in line with the average remuneration of around one third of the recovery as reported by the EPRS to be payable under a percentage based LFA. However, such example and result may not have suited the conclusions that the EPRS report wished to draw. Instead, the report provided an example which manifestly deviates from the key parameters of the market as they have indeed been presented in the report itself.

5.3.5 Summary Regarding the Settlement Scenario Example

Against the above background, it may be concluded that the EPRS provides an allegedly illustrative example on a hypothetical settlement situation using key parameters which are fundamentally at odds with a real funding situation and the findings of the TPLF market as reported in the study itself. Thus, the example (1) is built on a single claim TPLF deal involving higher risk for the funder than the study has reported that funders on the market are willing to take on, (2) uses a multiple based LFA which takes no consideration of the time value of money or the risk involved in concluding the case through judgment rather than settlement, (3) assumes that any funded party would prefer a 50% risk of no recovery whatsoever rather than to recover 20% of the value of the claim in a safe settlement, (4) does not deal with the significant issue of adverse costs, and (5) provides that the funder's success fee should amount to eight times its investment, whereas the highest multiple reported by the study is four times the investment (with a market range between 2× and 4× the invested amount). By thus skewing the example, the claimant is said to be left with EUR 20 in case of a settlement, whereas the parameters presented elsewhere in the report itself indicates that claimant would rather have the lion's share of the recovery, amounting to EUR 70, in the settlement situation.

One cannot but ask why the EPRS report was drafted so as to present the members of the European Parliament with an example which manifestly deviates from the findings which the EPRS has itself made in its report. It may be no coincidence that the result of the hypo seems to reinforce and underline the concerns of the report about allegedly excessive remuneration and conflicts of interest with respect to TPLF.

5.4 Summary Regarding Conflicts of Interest

In the EPRS report, it is repeatedly emphasised that there is a significant risk for conflicts of interest with respect to TPLF, particularly in settlement situations. However, that position does not take into account the fact that the funder is an investor and not a service provider; it does not represent or act on behalf of the funded party—there is thus no risk for conflict of interest within any established meaning of the term, as the funder's professional obligations are not compromised, and it does not serve two masters. Whatever it can and may do is set out in the LFA, including the reach of its powers—as pre-agreed between the parties—in settlement situations.

Making reference to the section of the EPRS report which contains the above closely commented example, it is set out in the report that it "*has revealed*" that a funder's influence on procedural decisions may result in a conflict of interest.[71]

[71] The EPRS report, p. 87.

However, what has in fact been revealed is that the EPRS has provided an utterly skewed example which does not reflect the data and the information presented elsewhere in the EPRS report itself. The reason behind the flawed example cannot be other than to provide ground for an argument that claimants are at risk if and when entering into litigation funding deals. It is however not clear why the EPRS is so eager to divert the views of the Members of the European Parliament in such direction.

6 Concluding Remarks

TPLF is a rather new and unregulated practice. If it emerges from theoretical or empirical research that the practices of funders harms any of its users—particularly consumers—or that there are risks of any tampering with justice, regulation of the TPLF market should indeed be carried out. However, if and when legislation is proposed, it is of course of utmost importance that any such recommendations are brought forward on solid ground. Reviewing the EPRS report, published by an institution which prides itself of providing the European Parliament with "*objective and authoritative analysis*" for the drawing up of EU law and policy, that seems not to be the case. To the contrary, the EPRS report contains sweeping and misleading statements about TPLF and the practice of funders.

It should be emphasised that the critique in this paper raised against the conclusions presented in the EPRS report does not emanate from or draw upon other sources than the report itself and the sources on which it relies. Carefully analysing the connection between the highly critical conclusions on TPLF that are presented in the EPRS report, and the study and research on which such conclusions are said to be based, this paper has thus identified fundamental slippages and several internal contradictions, inconsistencies, and flaws in the report with respect to (1) the TPLF taxonomy used, (2) the alleged risk for frivolous claims and (3) the alleged risk for conflicts of interest. Regrettably, the Members of the European Parliament must look elsewhere for an objective and authoritative analysis of TPLF before considering which, if any, political policy that should be implemented with respect to the emerging TPLF market.

Online Sources

https://knowledge4policy.ec.europa.eu/organisation/eprs-european-parliament-research-service_en

References

Code of Conduct for European Lawyers, 2006

Committee on Legal Affairs (2022) Report with recommendations to the Ccommission on Responsible private funding of litigation, 2020/2130(INL), 25 July 2022

Directive (EU) 2020/1828 of the European Parliament and of the Council of 25 November 2020 on representative actions for the protection of the collective interests of consumers

European Parliament (2017) Resolution of 4 July 2017 with recommendations to the Commission on common minimum standards of civil procedure in the European Union (2015/2084(INL))

European Parliamentary Research Service (2017) From arbitration to the investment court system (ICS)

European Parliamentary Research Service (2021) Responsible private funding of litigation

Griffiths-Baker JE (2002) Serving two masters: conflicts of interest in the modern law firm. Hart

Jackson LJ (2010) Review of civil litigation costs: final report. The Stationary Office

Report of the ICCA-Queen Mary Task Force on Third-Party Funding in International Arbitration, 2018

Rowles-Davies N (2014) Third party litigation funding. Oxford University Press

Solas GM (2019) Third party funding. Law, economics and policy. Cambridge University Press

The European Parliament's Policy Department for Citizens' Rights and Constitutional Affairs (2020) The effectiveness of conflict of interest policies in the EU Member States

Funding as an Element of Access to Justice in Environmental Protection Cases in Belgium: A Socio-Legal Analysis

Florence Van Durme and Alberto Nicòtina

Contents

Abstract Like many other countries, in the last years Belgium has seen a rise in environmental and climate litigation. At first sight, one could argue that this proves that claimants in environmental and climate cases manage to find their way to court. Following some legislative amendments, the legal standing of litigants acting in the collective interest in Belgium seems to have improved. However, this constitutes only one part of the story, and a closer look at some high-profile environmental and climate cases in Belgium suggests that litigants acting in the collective interest often rely on crowdfunding or other forms of private funding to be able to pay the fees. This chapter investigates whether the legal framework currently in force in Belgium

F. Van Durme and A. Nicòtina (✉)
Government and Law Research Group, University of Antwerp, Antwerp, Belgium
e-mail: Florence.VanDurme@uantwerpen.be; Alberto.Nicotina@uantwerpen.be

E. Storskrubb (ed.), *YSEC Yearbook of Socio-Economic Constitutions 2022*,
YSEC Yearbook of Socio-Economic Constitutions (2023) 2022: 119–146,
https://doi.org/10.1007/16495_2023_46, Published online: 14 April 2023

ensures a satisfactory level of equality when it comes to access to funding for parties acting for the protection of the environment. To establish what a "satisfactory" level of access to justice could be, we rely on the multi-layered understanding of this right as established by the relevant supranational and international legislation and case-law, as well as by the Belgian Constitution as interpreted by the Belgian constitutional court. Through a small selection of cases from Wallonia, Brussels and Flanders and semi-structured interviews with claimants acting for the protection of the environment, we offer an overview of the funding instruments and modalities used in practice to bring environmental protection cases before Belgian courts. Our contribution is meant as an exploratory study into the topic of funding for these types of cases. In doing so, we point out how the legal framework on legal aid (public funding) currently in place in Belgium proves unable to guarantee access to justice in environmental matters, resulting in litigants looking for other, often private, sources.

1 Introduction

Among the many aphorisms attributed to Groucho Marx, there is also one that says: "*there are so many things in life more important than money, but they cost so much!*". Whether or not Groucho Marx has actually ever pronounced these words, this aphorism carries out its task, as it tells a big truth to which both lawyers and activists can relate: justice is important, but it has a cost.

Access to justice has always been a quintessential topic in legal scholarship. In Europe, beyond the single national constitutions, it is enshrined both at the international level—where Articles 6 and 13 of the European Convention on Human Rights (ECHR) recognise the right to a fair trial and the right to an effective remedy respectively—and at the EU level, with Article 67, para. 4 of the Treaty on the Functioning of the European Union (TFEU) providing that "the Union shall facilitate access to justice" and Article 47 of the Charter of Fundamental Rights of the European Union establishing the right to an effective remedy. It pertains indeed to the conditions under which individuals (or groups) can claim their rights before a court. As such, it is a constitutive element of the notion of the rule of law.[1] Yet, it goes with a cost, and although legal systems have sought to take special measures and set up specific procedures to meet the needs of those who do not have enough financial means to assert their rights in a court of law, in many cases access to justice is *de facto* still made impossible or significantly discouraged. Over time, several petitions to the EU Parliament[2] have confirmed that "high or disproportionate amount of legal costs or the absence of legal aid mechanisms may discourage

[1] For a more careful approach to the equation between the concepts of access to justice and rule of law see Lucy (2020), pp. 377–402.

[2] Article 227 TFEU.

citizens from bringing a claim before a court, thus impeding effective access to justice".[3]

This is particularly evident when it comes to the judicial protection of collective interests, among which is the protection of the environment. Access to justice in environmental matters is indeed one of the most debated topics in legal scholarship. It also represents the third pillar of the Aarhus Convention on Access to Information, Public Participation and Access to Justice in Environmental Matters, adopted under the auspices of the United Nations Economic Commission for Europe (UNECE) in 1998 by 45 European States, including the European Union and all its Member States.[4] Our study focuses precisely on this third pillar and the protection of the environment as a collective interest.

1.1 Research Question(s) and Structure of the Study

As the United Nations Economic Commission for Europe (UNECE) recently reported, currently the two most important issues related to access to justice in the context of the Aarhus Convention are "(a) the regulation of the rights of environmental NGOs to seek judicial or administrative remedies in environmental cases ("standing"); and (b) financial barriers".[5]

Accordingly, in this chapter, we analyse these two issues with both a theoretical and an empirical approach. We chose to limit our contribution to the case of Belgium, and the multi-level legal framework applicable to Belgian litigants. Thus, the overall research question we intend to answer in this chapter is *whether the current Belgian legal framework ensures a satisfactory level of equality when it comes to access to funding (and thus to justice) for parties acting for the protection of the environment*. To establish what a "satisfactory" level of access to justice could be, we rely on the multi-layered understanding of this right as established by the relevant supranational and international legislation and case-law, as well as by the Belgian Constitution as interpreted by the Belgian constitutional court.

To this purpose, in the following sections we will first "set the scene" by picturing the broader (legal) context in which Belgian law is situated, and by briefly recalling the main steps that brought the environment to the core of the international legal agenda over the past decades (Sect. 2). Subsequently, we provide a detailed overview of the Belgian legislation on legal standing, and legal and judicial costs (Sect. 3) with specific attention to the practice, the so-called "law in action" (Sect. 4). In the fourth section, we report the insights we gained by conducting semi-structured interviews with four representatives of Belgian environmental NGOs and citizen groups that, over the last few years, have promoted judicial cases aimed at protecting

[3] Rass-Masson and Rouas (2017), p. 10.

[4] See para. 2.

[5] UNECE (2021), p. 45.

the environment. The respondents are members of organisations that meet the criteria specified below in Sect. 1.2 and that are active each in one of the three regions of which Belgium is composed: Brussels-Capital, Flanders and Wallonia.[6]

Several data on the perception of access to justice is already available thanks to the public consultations carried out by public authorities at the regional, national and supranational levels in the framework of the implementation of the Aarhus Convention. On those occasions, citizens and organisations have already highlighted several problems arising out or connected to access to justice in environmental matters. From them, it prominently emerges how Belgian environmental NGOs and active citizens complain about "the high cost associated with initiating legal proceedings, in particular, those related to barristers' fees, which hamper citizens' and associations' access to justice".[7]

Such consultations are however limited to collecting the voices of only a limited public, mostly consisting of highly structured environmental NGOs. Public consultations are indeed often criticized for leaving aside other relevant, less active stakeholders, especially citizens.[8] The originality of our contribution thus lies in gathering the voices of both structured organisations and spontaneous citizen groups, and—most importantly—in shedding light on how they actually fund their judicial and legal fees.

1.2 Methodology and Limitations

From a methodology standpoint, we combine doctrinal legal research with (limited) empirical research. We carried out semi-structured interviews to combine the need for structure and data harmonization with the possibility of letting useful first-hand insights emerge through less formal discussion.[9]

For the past two decades, qualitative methods are not novel anymore in legal research,[10] although certainly, their use is still not as common as it is in social and

[6]In line with the best scientific practices, we proceeded to the pseudonymization of the respondents' names in order to protect them from potential undesired consequences relating to the publication of their organizations' sources of funding. We also recorded the interviews with the sole purpose of keeping track of the respondents' answer. Such recordings have also been pseudonymised and securely kept under password-protected computers for a period of one year after the publication of this study.

[7]Aarhus Convention National Implementation Report of Belgium (2021), p. 3.

[8]Public consultations are indeed seen as a tool of "strategic group politics", understood as a way for public authorities "to regulate their interactions with outside constituencies in a way that fulfils their strategic objectives"—see Peterson (1992), p. 612. On the limitations of the public consultations run by the EU Commission, see also Turtelboom (2019), p. 85; McLaughlin and Greenwood (1995), p. 144.

[9]Roulston and Choi (2018), pp. 233–245.

[10]See Webley (2014).

political sciences.[11] Furthermore, targeting experts as respondents increases the level of complexity of the task, but also the value of the data collected. In our case, a further layer of complexity virtually applies. As Korkea-aho and Leino notice, interviews with legal experts "pose lawyer-specific challenges" relating to "access, confidentiality and control of the research process and data".[12] In our experience, however, the challenge consisted only of a more conscious understanding by respondents of the significance of the data at stake but did not translate into an actual obstacle to the smooth implementation of the study. On the contrary, the involvement of (legal) experts[13] has increased the credibility and specificity of the information collected.[14]

In selecting the respondents, we aimed at interviewing organisations that had recently gone to court or are currently involved in court proceedings. We thus selected four organisations (of different size and organizational structure) active in different regions of Belgium and contacted them through e-mail. All of them replied positively. We interpret this circumstance as positive feedback on the practical relevance of the topic, for both practitioners and academics. Our contribution is meant as an exploratory study into the topic of funding for these types of cases. More research into this topic is of course desirable. In particular, it would be interesting to investigate a bigger sample and how other countries deal with the issue.

Finally, it has to be noted that our findings refer to a small population of four respondents who have promoted high-profile judicial cases over the past few years. This limited number of cases on the one hand prevents us from drawing generalised conclusions, but on the other enables us to pursue the actual aim of this study, which is to open up the way to the academic debate about the funding of access to justice in environmental matters by providing a first overview of the Belgian case both in theory and in practice.

2 Environmental Protection as a Collective Interest and as an Enforceable Right

In several constitutional texts, legislators have sought to include the protection of the environment, starting as early as 1970.[15] In Europe, the most comprehensive international treaty on access to justice in environmental matters is the already recalled 1998 UNECE Aarhus Convention. It is considered "the most far-reaching and

[11] For an overview see Rubin and Rubin (2012) and Bailer (2014).

[12] Korkea-aho and Leino (2019), p. 36.

[13] Not all of the interviewees have had a legal education. They are however familiar with legal proceedings.

[14] See Bogner et al. (2009).

[15] See for instance the 'early' environmental clauses inserted in the constitutions of Switzerland (1971), Greece (1995), Portugal (1976) and Spain (1978).

detailed environmental treaty" in the area of access to justice and represents a source of inspiration for the so-called Escazu Agreement, which replicates the same mechanisms and establishes the same rights and obligations in Latin America.[16]

The Aarhus Convention also represents "one of the most noticeable examples of the so-called 'Europeanisation' of international law"[17] since it has been ratified by both the EU and all its Member States, with the practical effect that it now forms an integral part of the EU legal order. As a consequence, not only the individual Member States but also the EU itself "*can be considered to be in breach of the Convention if its Member States breach the Convention and if the EU has not established a regulatory framework ensuring compliance on the side of the Member States*".[18]

To avoid such a scenario, the EU, at least on paper, has put into place several ad hoc pieces of legislation that nowadays constitute a comprehensive *corpus* aimed at implementing the Convention's provisions in a precise and detailed fashion.[19]

Access to justice represents the third pillar of the Aarhus Convention, and the normative gear enabling the whole mechanism to function. It gives individuals and groups of individuals the right to enforce the Convention's provisions not only before domestic courts but also before the Aarhus Convention Compliance Committee. As Loibl underlines, since Aarhus, "compliance procedures have become a fact in international environmental law",[20] with the practical effect that the principles established by international law provisions can be interpreted and safeguarded not only by domestic courts but also at the international level itself.[21] In the case of the Aarhus Convention, the compliance mechanism is considered one of the most

[16]Regional Agreement on Access to Information, Public Participation and Justice in Environmental Matters in Latin America and the Caribbean Adopted at Escazú, Costa Rica, on 4 March 2018.

[17]As Wouters et al. (2008) put it, "Europeanisation of international law" means that "its application and interpretation by EU Member States is no longer solely a matter for their own constitutional order, but is also governed by EU law". See also Nicòtina (2021), p. 100.

[18]Squintani and Perlaviciute (2020), p. 137.

[19]Regulation (EC) No 1367/2006 of the European Parliament and of the Council of 6 September 2006 on the application of the provisions of the Aarhus Convention on Access to Information, Public Participation in Decision-making and Access to Justice in Environmental Matters to Community institutions and bodies [2006] OJ L264/13; Directive 2003/4/EC of the European Parliament and of the Council of 28 January 2003 on public access to environmental information and repealing Council Directive 90/313/EEC [2003] OJ L41/26; Directive 2003/35/EC of the European Parliament and of the Council of 26 May 2003 providing for public participation in respect of the drawing up of certain plans and programmes relating to the environment and amending with regard to public participation and access to justice Council Directives 85/337/EEC and 96/61/EC—Statement by the Commission[2003]OJ L156/17 and Directive 2004/35/CE of the European Parliament and of the Council of 21 April 2004 on environmental liability with regard to the prevention and remedying of environmental damage [2004] OJ L143/56. When it comes to the implementation of the Convention provisions, this supranational legal framework follows the logic of the "Europeanisation of international law" (see fn 18), meaning that, in practice, it strengthens the homogeneous interpretation and the enforcement of the Convention provisions at the national level.

[20]Loibl (2021), p. 310.

[21]Fitzmaurice (2004).

efficient,[22] with the result that also key issues such as the *locus standi* of environmental NGOs and citizen groups are dealt with (see below).

The aim of this paper is indeed to investigate whether a misalignment between principles and practices exists concerning the Belgian case. Before doing so, in the remainder of this section, we will first analyse the novelty of Article 9 of the Aarhus Convention and the issue of the legal standing of environmental groups at the international and supranational levels.

2.1 The Disruptive Reach of Article 9 of the Aarhus Convention

Article 9 of the Aarhus Convention represents a general innovative clause governing access to environmental justice for the protection of the rights granted by the Convention. It is divided into three paragraphs, each of which addresses a different subject.

Paragraph 1 stipulates the right to appeal a decision regarding a request for access to environmental information to a court or an independent administrative body. It allows enforcing the provisions of Article 4 of the Convention which establishes the right of the public to receive environmental information from public authorities.

Article 9 paragraph 2 refers to public participation in environmental decision-making processes. It ensures that members of the 'public concerned' have access to a review mechanism before a court of law or other independent and impartial body, through which they can contest the substantive and procedural legality of any decision, act, or omission that is subject to the Convention's provisions.

This right to access to a review procedure assumes that the applicant can demonstrate a sufficient interest in getting the review or that the challenged decision, act, or omission has harmed their rights. It also clearly states that NGOs advocating environmental protection and meeting the standards set out in the relevant State law are regarded to have a substantial interest. This has been confirmed by the Aarhus Convention Compliance Committee in a case concerning specifically Belgium.[23]

Contrary to the first two paragraphs, Article 9, para. 3 establishes a general right of the "members of the public" to have access to administrative and judicial procedures to challenge acts and omissions by public authorities. According to Article 2, para. 4 the term 'public' refers to the corresponding category at the national level, so in practice, it is for each State to dictate whether associations, organisations, and groups of individuals are included in this definition. The following para. 5 specifically mentions environmental NGOs but still assigns States the right to identify the requirements that such organisations shall meet. As it has been noticed in

[22] Fasoli and McGlone (2018).

[23] Aarhus Convention Compliance Committee, decision C/2005/11—Belgium, adopted on 16 June 2008.

scholarship, "although the Convention aims to secure a basic recognition of environmental NGOs this does not mean that it aims to harmonize their status amongst the parties of the Convention".[24]

Considering the broad discretion the Convention grants the States parties in this respect, the role of the EU in the interpretation of this provision is crucial.

The EU has implemented Article 9 through Regulation 1367/2006, which however addresses only EU institutions and bodies without affecting national institutions. With the 2011 *Zoskupenie* judgement,[25] the Court of Justice of the EU has answered a request for preliminary ruling coming from the Slovak Supreme Court by establishing that "*a specific issue which has not yet been the subject of EU legislation is part of EU law, where that issue is regulated in agreements concluded by the European Union and the Member State and it concerns a field in large measure covered by it*".[26] At the same time, however, the CJEU has denied that Article 9, para. 3 of the Aarhus Convention has direct effect, since such provision "is subject, in its implementation or effects, to the adoption of a subsequent measure".[27]

2.2 *The Role of Environmental NGOs and Their* Locus Standi *Under EU Law: A Brief Overview*

Despite the Aarhus Convention seeming to point at a greater role for environmental NGOs and citizen groups, the wording of its provisions often grants the contracting parties the opportunity to restrict the scope of application of the Convention's provisions. While the enjoyment of NGOs' rights relating to public participation is virtually full, when it comes to access to justice the issue of NGOs' standing is still one the most controversial both at the national and supranational levels.[28] Nonetheless, according to the EU Commission, "individuals and NGOs play a crucial role in identifying potential breaches of EU law by submitting complaints to administrations or taking cases to court".[29]

In practice, under EU law, access to justice to enforce NGOs' right to access to environmental information is largely unproblematic.

If a request for access to documents made by an NGO is rejected, that same NGO can always challenge the refusal before a court or an administrative body both at the

[24] Van Wolferen and Eliantonio (2020), pp. 154–155.

[25] CJEU, C-240/09, *Lesoochranárske zoskupenie VLK v. Ministerstvo životného prostredia Slovenskej republiky*, Judgment of 8 March 2011, ECLI:EU:C:2011:125.

[26] Ibid. (emphasis added).

[27] Ibid.

[28] Ligugnana (2019).

[29] EU Commission (2020), para. 9, p. 3.

national and supranational levels.[30] By contrast, in all those cases addressing substantive judicial review of EU law, the CJEU used to deny *locus standi* every time an entity fails to demonstrate its "individual concern" which exists "only if the contested act affects them by reason of certain attributes that are peculiar to them; or by reason of circumstances in which they are differentiated from all other persons, and by virtue of these factors distinguishes them individually".[31] In general terms, judicial review of regulatory acts that do not need implementing measures is possible through the general clause laid down in Article 263, para. 4 TFEU.[32] The provision makes a distinction between "individual concern" (as outlined above) and "direct concern". To challenge an EU regulatory act before the CJEU it is sufficient to demonstrate that the contested act is of "direct concern" to the applicant. According to the established case-law of the CJEU such condition is met when the contested measure affects directly the legal situation of the applicant and leaves no discretion in its implementation.[33] However, even in this context, the existence of a "direct concern" by environmental NGOs has proven difficult to demonstrate, as the EU Commission has also acknowledged.[34] Indeed, Article 11 of the so-called "Aarhus Regulation"[35] establishes a set of criteria that organisations must meet "to request internal review to the Community institution or body that has adopted an administrative act under environmental law or, in case of an alleged administrative omission, should have adopted such an act" under Article 10 of the same Regulation. These include: being an independent non-profit-making legal person; having as main objective "the promotion of environmental protection in the context of environmental law"; having existed since more than 2 years; and the subject matter brought before the courts is covered by its objectives and activities.[36]

---

[30]See for instance CJEU, C-57/16 P, ClientEarth v. Commission, ECLI:EU:C:2018:660; CJEU, C-615/13 P, CJEU, ClientEarth and Pesticide Action Network Europe (PAN Europe) v EFSA, ECLI:EU:C:2015:489.

[31]Lycourgos (2021). See for instance GCEU, T-330/18, Carvalho, ECLI:EU: T:2019:324.

[32]According to such provision "any natural or legal person may, under the conditions laid down in the first and second paragraphs, institute proceedings against an act addressed to that person or which is of direct and individual concern to them, and against a regulatory act which is of direct concern to them and does not entail implementing measures".

[33]See CJEU, C-33/14 P, *Mory and Others*, ECLI:EU:C:2015:609; CJEU, C-386/96 P, *Dreyfus*, ECLI:EU:C:1998:193; CJEU, C-622/16 P, *Scuola Elementare Maria Montessori*, ECLI: EU:C:2018:873; CJEU, C-486/01 P, *Front national v Parliament*, ECLI:EU:C:2004:394; C-41/70, *International Fruit Company*, ECLI:EU:C:1971:53; CJEU, C-519/07 P, *Commission v Koninklijke FrieslandCampina*, ECLI:EU:C:2009:556.

[34]See EU Commission (2020).

[35]Regulation (EC) N° 1367/2006 of the European Parliament and of the Council on the application of the provisions of the Aarhus Convention on Access to Information, Public Participation in Decision-making and Access to Justice in Environmental Matters to Union institutions and bodies, OJ L 264, 25.9.2006, p. 13, entered into force on 28 September 2006 and into application on 17 July 2007.

[36]For an overview see Kramer (2015), p. 131.

However, after the EU has been found in breach of the Convention by the Aarhus Convention Compliance Committee,[37] since 2021 a request for internal review can be filed by "other members of the public" if they can demonstrate either an "impairment of their rights" from which they are "directly affected" or "a sufficient public interest" that can be proved by submitting at least 4000 signatures from individuals residing in at least five EU member states.[38]

Considering this scenario, and its recent improvements, arguably the main obstacle to wider access to justice that environmental NGOs face is not much *de jure*, but rather *de facto*, and lies in the incomplete implementation of Article 9, para. 5 of the Aarhus Convention which cites: "to further the effectiveness of the provisions of this article, each Party (. . .) shall consider the establishment of appropriate assistance mechanisms to remove or reduce financial and other barriers to access to justice". In the next section, we deal with how the Belgian legislator has tackled this issue.

3 Access to Justice for the Protection of the Environment as a Collective Interest in Belgium

As explained in the previous section, the Aarhus Convention provides for wide access to justice for all violations of environmental law. If an individual or an association believes that a legal provision relating to the environment has been violated by public authorities or private persons, they have the right to take the matter to court[39] provided sufficient interest in the case, under national standing rules, is shown. In the following sections, we first discuss the requirement of sufficient interest for associations and subsequently for individuals, as inscribed in Belgian law (Sect. 3.1). Subsequently, Sect. 3.2 discusses the costs of legal proceedings in Belgium and the exemptions from these costs. Thereafter, we discuss how the Belgian legislator tries to fulfil the requirements of Article 9, para. 5 of the Aarhus Convention.

[37] Aarhus Convention Compliance Committee decision No. ACCC/C/2008/32 of 17 March 2017.

[38] Article 1 of the Regulation (EU) 2021/1767 of the European Parliament and of the Council of 6 October 2021 amending Regulation (EC) No 1367/2006 on the application of the provisions of the Aarhus Convention on Access to Information, Public Participation in Decision-making and Access to Justice in Environmental Matters to Community institutions and bodies.

[39] As Belgium is a federal state, several authorities are responsible for implementing the Aarhus Convention: the federal authority and the three federal entities (Walloon Region, Brussels-Capital Region and Flemish Community).

3.1 *Protection of Collective Interests: The Necessity of Demonstrating an Interest*

In principle, Belgian law requires the demonstration of an interest as a condition for the admissibility of the appeal/claim.[40] Such interest used to have to be an interest of its own, i.e. a personal and direct interest. Therefore, an *actio popularis* is not possible for those who demonstrate no personal interest of their own.[41] Environmental organisations regularly refer to their specific statutory purpose to demonstrate their interest, and Belgium's highest courts started to accept that this collective interest can meet the requirement of an "interest" as prescribed in the law. The aforementioned Aarhus Convention has had an important influence in this respect. The sub-sections below discuss the requirement of an interest in civil cases, administrative cases and before the Constitutional Court in Belgium.

3.1.1 Administrative Courts and the Interest Requirement

Since administrative decisions, like environment permits,[42] can have an impact on the environment, Belgium's administrative courts, especially the Flemish Council for Permit Disputes[43] and/or the Council of State,[44] play an important role, depending on the content of the case. The procedural rules regarding the demonstration of an interest differ from the rules for civil proceedings and are therefore discussed separately in this section.

As regards the Council of State, proceedings may be initiated by any party which demonstrates a disadvantage or an interest,[45] which should be lawful and legitimate, certain, personal and direct, but also current.[46] It is settled case-law of the Council of State that non-profit associations may take legal action in defence of the purpose or purposes for which they have been established. When a non-profit association, which does not plead its personal interest, acts before the Council of State, it is required (1) that its statutory objective is of a special nature and therefore distinct from the general interest, (2) that it acts in defence of a collective interest, (3) that its statutory objective may be affected by the contested measure, and (4) that it does not

[40] See Article 2, 2°, of the special law of 6 January 1989 on the Constitutional Court, Articles 17 and 18 of the Judicial Code, Article 19 of the coordinated laws on the Council of State and Article 35 of the Decree of 4 April 2014 on the organisation and procedure of some Flemish administrative courts.

[41] Lefranc (2017).

[42] Translation of "Omgevingsvergunning": a unified permit that governs aspects of zoning, environment and exploitation.

[43] Translation of "Raad voor Vergunningsbetwistingen".

[44] Translation of "Raad van State", Belgium's highest administrative court.

[45] Article 19 Laws on the Council of State, coordinated on 12 January 1973.

[46] Baert and Debersaques (1996), p. 203.

appear that that objective is not or is no longer actually pursued.[47] The legislative proposal amending the coordinated laws to the Council of State with a view to grant associations a right of action in defence of collective interests[48] was rejected on 19 March 2019, referring to the existing case-law of the Council. However, it should be stressed that although case-law exists, the interpretation is strict[49] and it is not guaranteed that it is applied uniformly by all chambers of the Council of State.[50] A legislative right of action remains desirable.[51]

As regards the Council for Permit Disputes proceedings may be initiated by persons identified in Article 4.8.11 of the Flemish Zoning Code[52] and Article 105 of the Decree of 25 April 2015 regarding the environment permit. Moreover, the amended Article 35[53] of the Decree of 4 April 2014 on the organisation and procedure of some Flemish administrative courts regulates the need for an interest in the remedy. The amended Article 35, which entered into force on 24 June 2021, stipulates that the violation of a standard or a general principle of law cannot give rise to an annulment if the party that invokes the violation is not prejudiced by the invoked illegality (damage to interests), if the invoked illegality evidently does not serve the protection of the interests of the party invoking it (relativity requirement) or if the party has manifestly failed to invoke the invoked illegality during the administrative procedure (duty of care).

In the preparatory works, the reason for the amendment is explained in light of the relativity requirement. It is stated that scholarship seems unable to draw a common line between the case-law of the Council of State and the Council for Permit Disputes or even speaks of inconsistencies, as regards the theory of the 'interest'.[54]

---

[47] Council of State, General Meeting of the Administrative Jurisdiction Division, Coomans and Others, No 187 998, 17 November 2008, see e.g. Council of State No 240 980, 8 March 2018, Council of State No 241.864, 21 June 2018 and Council of State No 244.351 of 2 May 2019.

[48] Legislative proposal amending the coordinated laws to the Council of State with a view to grant associations a right of action in defence of collective interests, Parliamentary document 2014-201, No 54 0465/004.

[49] See for example Council of State No 232.91, 17 November 2015: The direct nature of the interest means that there must be a direct causal link between the contested decision and the disadvantage suffered by the applicant. The very broad statutory objective of the applicant has not been touched in a sufficiently direct manner to distinguish the harm caused to the applicant from the harm which any unemployed person may suffer as a result of the implementation of the contested decision.

[50] Legislative proposal amending the coordinated laws to the Council of State with a view to grant associations a right of action in defence of collective interests, Parliamentary document 2014-201, No 54 0465/004, p. 9.

[51] Ibid, p. 9.

[52] Translation of "Vlaamse Codex Ruimtelijke Ordening".

[53] Decree of 21 May 2021 amending the Decree of 4 April 2014 on the organisation and procedure of certain Flemish administrative courts as regards the optimisation of procedures.

[54] Document *(Parl. St.)* Flemish Parliament. 19 March 2021 699 (2020–2021)—Nr. 1, Draft decree amending the decree of 4 April 2014 on the organisation and procedure of certain Flemish administrative courts as regards the optimisation of procedures, p. 5; reference is made to Eggermont (2017), Wirtgen (2015), Verhelst (2015) and Schoukens and Woldendorp (2014).

This amendment is not without controversy and authors have noted that it undeniably influences access to justice.[55] The question rises if it was introduced to make a successful appeal for annulment more difficult or to ensure a more streamlined procedure. It is not the first time that the Flemish Government tried to make it more difficult to appeal in urban planning law. The Constitutional Court has intervened several times before invoking precisely the right of access to justice.[56] Likewise, the recent amendment of Article 35 gave rise to actions for annulment before the Constitutional Court. These cases are still pending thus it remains to be seen whether these amendments will stand a test by the Constitutional Court.[57] In this context, we refer to the judgement of the CJEU in the case of *Stichting Varkens in Nood* of 14 January 2021, which could influence the Belgian legal framework since the legal provisions in question are similar.[58] The CJEU came to the conclusion that the obligation for interested parties in Dutch administrative law to have made use of the possibility to express views in the administrative phase, before gaining access to the administrative court, is not in conformity with Article 9 paragraph 2 of the Aarhus Convention.[59] While access to court is expanding in the Netherlands following this judgement,[60] the Belgian legislator has chosen to do the opposite. In our opinion, this CJEU judgement will undoubtedly play a big role in the assessment of the Constitutional Court.

3.1.2 Civil Courts and the Interest Requirement

In Belgium, claims relating to environmental damages are to be brought before ordinary civil courts. This set of courts is vertically structured on three layers: Tribunal of First Instance, Appellate Court and Court of Cassation. Here too, demonstrating an "interest of its own" is crucial for the admissibility of the action on the basis of Article 17, para. 1 of the Judicial Code.[61] The Belgian legislators and courts have long been afraid to recognise the idea that a collective interest could be defended before a court of law. Over time, numerous legislative amendments have been proposed to introduce a collective interest right, but they have never been adopted.[62] Only in 2013, the Court of Cassation established that environmental

[55] Meulebrouck (2021a), p. 8.

[56] Constitutional Court, No. 46/2019, 14 March 2019.

[57] Actions for annulment of Articles 6 and 9 of the Decree of 21 May 2021 amending the Decree of 4 April 2014 have been brought before the Constitutional Court. These cases are numbered 7638, 7644, 7656, 7683, 7698 and 7701 and are still pending.

[58] Jans and Marseille (2010); Meulebrouck (2021b).

[59] CJEU, Case C-826/18, LB, Stichting Varkens in Nood, Stichting Dierenrecht, Stichting Leefbaar Buitengebied tegen college van burgemeester en wethouders van de gemeente Echt-Susteren,- ECLI:EU:C:2021:7, para. 69.

[60] ABRvS 14 april 2021, ECLI:NL:RVS:2021:786; ABRvS 4 mei 2021, ECLI:NL:RVS:2021:953.

[61] Judicial Code of 10 October 1967 (hereafter: "Judicial Code").

[62] Lefranc (2019).

organisations meeting the requirements of the Aarhus Convention enjoy effective access to justice.[63] Following an amendment in 2018,[64] claims by legal persons seeking the protection of human rights or fundamental freedoms recognised in the Constitution and the international instruments binding Belgium are admissible provided that four conditions are met: (1) the statutory purpose of the legal entity is of a special nature, distinct from the pursuit of the general interest, (2) the legal entity pursues this statutory objective in a sustainable and effective manner, (3) the legal entity acts in the context of that statutory purpose, intending to defend an interest that is related to that purpose, and (4) the legal entity pursues with its legal action only a collective interest.

The new provision is "without prejudice to more favourable arrangements deriving from international law that would have a direct impact in Belgium".[65] This means that for environmental organisations, the interest is initially assessed against Article 17, para. 1 Judicial Code, interpreted in accordance with the objectives of the Aarhus Convention and the case-law of the Court of Cassation, which might be more favourable than Article 17, para. 2. Environmental organisations which do not meet the conditions of the Aarhus Convention may, where appropriate, bring an action to defend collective interests in accordance with Article 17, para. 2 Judicial Code, just like other non-environmental organisations meeting the requirements in this Article.[66]

It should be noted that the right of collective action is not an *actio popularis*. The collective action must be instituted to protect the collective interest that the legal person has set as its statutory purpose.[67] This new regime should also not be confused with a class action, such as the collective redress action in the Economic Law Code (for consumers and SMEs), because the concerned legal entities do not act for the collective interests of claimants or members of the legal entity.[68] They act to protect the statutory objective or collective interest pursued by the legal person itself.

These advancements only refer to organisations. Individuals, by contrast, cannot, for the time being, stand up for the collective interest in court. As a consequence, in practice, several legal entities are founded for the sole purpose of protecting a collective interest in court.

---

[63] See Court of Cassation, No P.12.1389.N, 11 June 2013, *Huldenberg*.

[64] The law of 21 December 2018 'containing various provisions on justice' added Article 17 para. 2 to the Judicial Code; Allemeersch and Vandensande (2019).

[65] Explanatory Memorandum, document chamber of representatives (*Memorie van toelichting, Parl.St. Kamer*) 2018–19, nr. 3308/1, pp. 96–100.

[66] Advice Council of State, document chamber of representatives (*Parl.St. Kamer*) 2018–19, nr. 3303/1, p. 215.

[67] Report, document chamber of representatives (*Verslag, Parl.St. Kamer*) 2018–19, nr. 3308/8, 106–110 (statement B. ALLEMEERSCH at the hearing of 6 November 2018).

[68] Lefranc (2019).

3.1.3 The Constitutional Court and the Interest Requirement

Before the Constitutional Court, actions for annulment may be brought, among other things, by any natural or legal person showing, again, an "interest".[69] The established case-law of the Constitutional Court confirms that such a requirement does not undermine the right of associations to take legal actions in defence of their statutory objectives. It requires (1) that its statutory objective is of a special nature and, therefore, distinct from the public interest, (2) that the collective interest is not limited to the individual interests of its members, (3) that the statutory objective may be affected by the contested provisions and (4) that it does not appear that the statutory objective is not or is no longer actually pursued.[70]

3.1.4 Right of Substitution for Citizens

Citizens will usually not fulfil the interest requirement if they would want to start a proceeding in the collective interest. The legal provisions require a personal interest and not a collective interest. Exceptions are only made for organisations, not for citizens. However, this does not mean that individuals can never act for the protection of the environment or climate as a collective interest.

One of the avenues that is open to individuals, is the right of substitution for citizens. This right entails that citizens can take legal action on behalf of a Flemish municipality or Flemish province of which they are an inhabitant.[71] These provisions are intended for cases in which the municipality or province refuses to take action and allows infringements to take place.[72]

The possibility for citizens to take legal action on behalf of the municipality or province received renewed interest following the introduction of the environmental malpractices claim[73] by the Law of 12 January 1993 on a right of action for the protection of the environment. The environmental malpractices claim cannot be initiated by the citizen in his personal name, but only by the municipality, an environmental association, or the king's public prosecutor. The right of substitution was therefore frequently used so that the citizen could bring an environmental malpractices claim on behalf of the municipality.

The Local Government Decree[74] intended to abolish this right of action on behalf of the municipality or province. However, the Constitutional Court judged in its

---

[69] See Article 2, para. 2 of the Special Law of 6 January 1989 on the Constitutional Court.

[70] E.g. Constitutional Court, No 32/1990, No 133/2013, 10 October 2013 and No 53/2019, 4 April 2019.

[71] Article 194 of the Flemish Municipal Decree of 15 July 2005 and Article 187 of the Flemish Provincial Decree of 9 December 2005.

[72] Schaiko (2020).

[73] Translation of "Milieustakingsvordering".

[74] Flemish decree of 22 December 2017 on local government.

judgements of 10 October 2019 that by abolishing the right of action on behalf of the municipality or province, the legislator has significantly reduced the level of protection afforded by the applicable legislation, without any reasons relating to the public interest.[75] This is problematic since Article 23 of the Belgian Constitution contains a standstill obligation that prohibits the competent legislator from decreasing significantly the level of protection offered by the applicable legislation, e.g. for environmental protection, without reasons related to the general interest. The judgment of the Constitutional Court, therefore, in our opinion rightly, revived the right of substitution. In practise, the environmental malpractice claim is often used by activists and citizen collectives without a legal entity, as one of our interviewees pointed out (see below).

3.2 *Overview of Various Costs of Resolving Disputes Within the Formal Judicial Machinery and Exemptions*

As discussed above, the Aarhus Convention requires that procedures be effective, expeditious, equitable and free of charge or inexpensive. It also stipulates that States shall consider the establishment of appropriate assistance mechanisms to remove or reduce financial and other barriers to access to environmental justice.

Court fees are fixed in Belgium. Such costs vary depending on the court before which the proceedings are brought (civil and criminal courts, administrative courts, constitutional court, . . .) and the stage of the proceedings (first instance or appeal).

The costs of legal proceedings before the Belgian civil courts can be high. A litigant has to take into account summons costs,[76] registry[77] and registration fees,[78] the costs, emoluments and salaries for judicial documents, the costs relating to the measures of investigation (witnesses and experts), travel costs, procedural indemnity for the lawyer of the successful party, service costs and, potentially, costs of an

[75] Constitutional Court, No 129/2019 and 131/2019, 10 October 2019.

[76] The rates are determined in the Royal Decree of 30 November 1976 'fixing the rate for bailiffs' deeds in civil and commercial matters and the rate of certain allowances'. A summon usually costs between EUR 200 and EUR 500 per party which must be summoned.

[77] Registry fees consist of fees for register entry, drafting and copy execution and are set out in the Code on Registration, Mortgage and Registry Fees, under Article 268 et seq. As of 1 February 2019 the amount of the registry fee is as follows: Justice of the Peace Court and Police Court—50 EUR, Court of First Instance and Business Court—165 EUR, Court of Appeal—400 EUR, Court of Cassation—650 EUR, Council of State, 200 EUR—Flemish Council for Permit Disputes, 200 EUR (annulment) or 100 EUR (suspension).

[78] Article 1019 Judicial code states that the registration fees classed as legal costs consist of a general fixed fee, specific fixed fees and fees due on judgments leading to conviction, liquidation or collocation of monies or securities. Registration fees can be explained as taxes and are intended as general compensation for services that the court delivers (in addition to the registry fee). A conviction for an amount in excess of EUR 12,500 is subject to a registration fee of 3% to be paid by the losing party, calculated on the amount to which it was convicted.

appeal and/or appeal in cassation.[79] There is no regulation governing lawyers' fees. Lawyers set their fees freely and can negotiate them with their clients. The party who won the proceedings in full can receive a partial reimbursement in the form of the procedural indemnity, though this usually does not come close to covering the actual fees of the lawyer.[80]

In order to guarantee access to justice also to people without sufficient financial means, Belgian legislation foresees the so-called "first-line and second-line legal aid" and an exemption from costs for judicial proceedings in specific cases.

First-line legal aid consists of free legal advice, available to every individual.[81] It is fairly limited in scope and does not include comprehensive advice or in-depth treatment of the issue. The Belgian bar is entrusted with this service, organised in walk-in fashion in courthouses.

If the initial advice indicates that action—it may be a legal letter, a mediation or a legal claim—is relevant or necessary, then support by a lawyer is often appropriate. With second-line legal aid (also called pro deo) the lawyer provides, as for a paying client, full legal advice, assistance and representation, whether in the context of proceedings or not. An individual can apply for second-line legal aid if he or she has insufficient means.[82]

Next to first and second-line legal aid, Belgium also has a system regarding free legal costs for people with limited financial resources.[83]

However, in the context of environmental and climate cases in the collective interest, second-line legal aid will typically not be applicable. Firstly, second-line legal aid is intended for individuals, not for organisations. As seen above, proceedings in the collective interest are mostly initiated by organisations.

It should be also mentioned that some environmental associations are eligible for subsidies, which are however not meant (at least not directly) to support legal actions.[84] There will be no call for new recognitions for the period 2022–2026.

---

[79] Article 1018 Judicial Code.

[80] Article 1022 Judicial Code; Article 66 of the Regent's Decree of 23 August 1948 regulating the administration of justice before the Administrative Jurisdiction Division of the Council of State; Royal Decree of 26 October 2007 setting the rate of the procedural indemnity referred to in Article 1022 of the Judicial Code and fixing the date of entry into force of Articles 1–13 of the Law of 21 April 2007 on the recoverability of lawyers' fees and costs associated with legal assistance; Article 66 of the Regent's Decree of 23 August 1948 regulating the administration of justice before the Administrative Jurisdiction Division of the Council of State. For non-monetised claims, the basic amount is 1440.00 EUR in civil cases and 700 EUR in administrative cases.

[81] Article 508/5 et seq. Judicial Code.

[82] Article 508/7 et seq. Judicial Code.

[83] Article 664 et seq. Judicial Code.

[84] See the Decree of the Flemish Government of 18 December 2015 and the Decree of the Walloon Government of 23 January 2014, both regulating the recognition and subsidising of environmental and nature associations.

The existing framework will be thoroughly evaluated with a view to reforming it before the start of the next grant period 2027–2031.[85]

As a consequence, it does not come as a surprise that organisations active in the field of the environment complain about the high cost associated with initiating legal proceedings and the lack of financial support to carry out their missions of collective interest.[86] It is one of the recurring critiques in the Aarhus Convention National Implementation Report of Belgium, in the context of which environmental organisations complain about high costs of justice and a delay in the implementation of the measures that should provide financial support to the organisations of the third sector.

4 From 'Law in the Books' to 'Law in Action': Do Belgian Organisations Acting in the Collective Interest Find Their Way to Court?

As anticipated in the introduction, to investigate whether a misalignment exists between what the law establishes and the actual legal practice we conducted (limited) empirical legal research. The four organisations that we randomly selected show both similarities and differences in their aims, internal organisation and structure. They are distributed over the three regions that compose Belgium and their size varies significantly: from teams of 10–15 volunteers and organisations with one employee to thousands of members. In this section, we will analyse the results of the interviews by taking into account this difference between big and small organisations, and by focusing on the following three aspects: (a) human and financial resources, (b) legal and judicial costs and (c) the perceived legitimacy of the Belgian legal framework on access to funding as an element of access to environmental justice.

Three out of the four organisations or collectives agreed to be mentioned in this study. These are Klimaatzaak, Grondrecht and Beperk de Straling. As a consequence, In the remainder of this section, these three organisations are named, whereas the other will remain confidential.[87]

---

[85] www.omgeving.vlaanderen.be/erkenning-en-subsidi%C3%ABring-van-milieu-en-natuurverenigingen.

[86] Aarhus Convention National Implementation Report of Belgium (2021)

[87] All interviews were conducted in January–February 2022.

4.1 *Human and Financial Resources*

4.1.1 Structure of the Organisations/Collectives and Aims

The considered population of cases shows a significant variation not only in the size of the organisations or collectives, but also regarding their nature and scope.

Klimaatzaak started with a group of concerned friends. In 2014, 11 concerned citizens decided to take action against the Belgian governments for Belgium's ailing climate policy. They set up a non-profit association (vzw/asbl Klimaatzaak) and started legal proceedings against the competent authorities.[88] Since its establishment, the organisation has grown significantly. As a non-profit organisation, Klimaatzaak has board members. It has one employee on the payroll of the organisation. The organisation invites citizens to become a joint plaintiff or supporter of the case. Joint claimants are legally, as full claimants, involved in the lawsuit (on the same level as the initiators of the lawsuit). They gave a power of attorney to the non-profit association, in consultation with the lawyers, to take all necessary decisions on their behalf as well. However, the non-profit association stipulated that the risk is borne exclusively by the non-profit association, not by the individual joint claimants. Citizens can also become a supporter. Supporters do not join the court case legally but support the climate change case morally. This means the non-profit association takes on all legal costs. More than 67,000 people are now collaborating on the project as a joint plaintiff or supporter. On the 17th of June 2021, The Brussels Court of First Instance has collectively condemned Belgian governments for their negligent climate policies.[89] On the 17th of November 2021, Klimaatzaak decided to appeal the judgement, even though the judgement went against the Belgian governments.[90] Klimaatzaak explains on their website that in the months following the verdict, there was no indication that the Belgian governments were taking the verdict seriously.[91] In court, they ask for binding emission reduction targets to be imposed on the governments, obliging them to do their part to prevent dangerous global warming. The case will be pleaded from 14 September tot 6 October 2023, which is significantly faster than suggested by the Court's average turnaround times. According to Klimaatzaak, this demonstrates the importance of the case.

Beperk de Straling has grown organically. To date, it has no legal entity and it is an informal group represented by a core group of citizens of around 10–15 citizens who volunteer for the cause, backed by a broad support base. Beperk de Straling is a group of citizens who are concerned about the exponential increase in radiation

[88] Klimaatzaak. www.klimaatzaak.eu/en.

[89] Consult the verdict here: Klimaatzaak. www.klimaatzaak.eu/nl/the-case; Auvray et al. (2021).

[90] It is possible to consult the appeal online in French: Klimaatzaak. https://affaireclimat.cdn.prismic.io/affaireclimat/989e74fe-3d01-4cd0-9fff-d8642f974d8a_2021117_Reque%CC%82te+d%27appel_Def+DOCX_00832397+DOCX+-+PDF.pdf.

[91] Klimaatzaak. www.klimaatzaak.eu/nl/the-case.

levels to which the population is exposed.[92] To date, they have initiated four court cases. They have won the first case before the Constitutional Court against the Flemish government regarding smart gas and electricity meters in January 2021.[93] On 20 October 2022, the Constitutional Court dismissed the appeal in the second case, regarding an unclear formulation in the decree concerning the installation of an electronic meter without a communication tool.[94] Two procedures at the Council of State, are still ongoing. They plan to initiate two more court cases before the Constitutional Court.

Grondrecht started as a citizen collective, but became a non-profit association (vzw/asbl Grondrecht) in May 2022. It is a collective of concerned citizens demanding clarity on PFAS pollution in their living environment and its consequences for themselves, their children and grandchildren.[95] The core team consists of around 15 volunteers, backed by a broad support base. They work project-based in smaller groups. They summoned PFOS manufacturer 3M, with around 600 affiliated citizens, they initiated an environmental malpractice claim and became a civil party in a criminal investigation. They recently also started a proceeding before the Council of State.

The last interviewed organisation is a large, established environmental NGO with several employees and volunteers carrying out environmental advocacy for many years.[96]

4.1.2 Financial Resources

Only one out of the four interviewed organisations relies steadily on government funding for most of its activities in the context of framework agreements with the regional government. No government sources of funds are however directly available to initiate court proceedings.

In general, all organisations rely on voluntary donations. All respondents confirmed that financial means are collected through a mix of (or one of) the following: membership fees, donations, organisation of events, and crowdfunding. For the promotion of specific activities, and in particular, for judicial activities, crowdfunding is by far the most used source.

The organisations and collectives differ in crowdfunding strategies. The anonymous NGO relies mainly on membership fees and mobilises its basis through crowdfunding only for specific projects, including lawsuits, dealing with issues that are considered as very important by its community of members. The majority of donations is represented by small donations (within 20 EUR) from individuals.

[92] Beperk de Straling. www.beperkdestraling.org/.

[93] Constitutional Court, No. 5/2021, 14 January 2021.

[94] Constitutional Court, No. 133/2022, 20 October 2022.

[95] Grondrecht. www.grondrecht.eu.

[96] The choice of confidentiality prevents us from disclosing further details.

Klimaatzaak has chosen to implement a system with monthly contributions named "coffee for climate" (3, 5 or 12 EUR/month) on their website, next to the possibility of one-time donations. They work with known financial systems such as Paypal and Mollie. The majority of their funding comes from small amounts donated by a large number of people. Grondrecht works with a paid online open collective fundraising platform. They offer various funding options to the public, including one-time and monthly recurring options, to not miss anything. Individuals can choose to donate to scientific research or the legal fight. Both Klimaatzaak and Grondrecht make extensive use of social media and traditional media to promote their case. Beperk de Straling has a separate bank account number for donations. This account number is mentioned on their website, through social media, in newsletters, at protest actions and door-to-door campaigns. Interested people are free to choose the amount of the donation but Beperk de Straling makes some suggestions. On average people donate around 50 EUR (one-time donations).

All organisations confirm that obtaining the necessary funds is never easy, but to date, they manage to receive the funds necessary to cover the expenses. They agree that in order to receive the necessary funds, name recognition among the wider public is required. When there is less (media) attention on the case, it becomes more difficult to receive the necessary support. Sometimes it is necessary to protest or campaign to get a platform. Klimaatzaak, for example, received considerable media attention when it launched and a lot of known public figures joined the case, increasing its prominence. The case of Grondrecht also appears in the media, especially in the beginning when the PFAS scandal became known to the bigger public. The victory of Beperk de Straling in court did however not generate a lot of media attention. The interviewees explain that they do not find a big platform in mainstream media, their cause seems to be a taboo subject. Radiation can be considered as an environmental pollutant but this is not yet widely seen as such by the public. The fact that they do not appear in mainstream media as much as other organisation, results in less prominence, which can be an obstacle for crowdfunding.

The interviewees also point out that there is great competition on the market. There are of course many good causes and praiseworthy initiatives, not limited to environmental and climate protection initiatives. Grondrecht started looking for other financial sources, especially for their legal proceedings. They joined forces with major environmental organisations such as Greenpeace and Bond Beter Leefmilieu,[97] and share the cost of the legal proceedings. This collaboration is also useful to strengthen their know-how and spread potential risks. Beperk de Straling organises protest actions and movie nights where they also provide the opportunity to make donations. Klimaatzaak supplements its stream of income by for example organising fundraising events, sporting events, donations from philanthropists and collaborations with AS Adventure, an outdoor store. This avenue is however not open to smaller collectives since they lack the capacity to organise such bigger

[97] Bond Beter Leefmilieu unites nature and environmental organisations and strengthens the voice of sustainable leaders in Flanders.

events. All organisations ensure transparency of the received funds on their respective websites.

Several interviewees pointed out that they are mainly concerned with the substantive work and are not necessarily experts in researching other potential funding products that could be available, either on the private market or via subsidies. Additionally, the routes for obtaining subsidies are described as vague and entailing a big administrative burden. Several interviewees mentioned they would be interested in sharing experiences and expertise among various organisations.

4.2 *Locus Standi and Expenses*

4.2.1 Locus Standi

Not all our respondents are established environmental NGOs, as the one that preferred to remain confidential, and in relation to which no standing issue arises. Klimaatzaak is also a non-profit organisation fulfilling the criteria of the Judicial Code as discussed in Sect. 3, and it therefore has *locus standi* in court. The non-profit association was established specifically to initiate the court proceedings. Grondrecht started as a *de facto* collective, but became a non-profit association in May 2022 for liability reasons and because this could have an advantage regarding the locus standi in court. Before becoming a non-profit association, they made use of the right of substitution for citizens (as discussed in Sect. 3) or worked together with associations. They mentioned that working together with others also is an advantage for access to know-how, expertise in communication with policy-makers, spreading risk, sharing funds and carrying the case together. Likewise, Beperk de Straling is a *de facto* collective. Their procedures are initiated by individuals who have a personal interest.

Organisations without legal entity point out that while the environmental malpractice claim is a very useful instrument for them, the detour of bringing the claim on behalf of the municipality is a threshold, which also creates an additional cost.

4.2.2 Cost of the Proceedings (Judicial and Legal Fees) and Other Expenses

The legal costs are in general the biggest expense. As stated on Klimaatzaak's website, all donations are used to finance the association. On the one hand, there are legal costs, such as the lawyers' fees, bailiff fees, file costs, etc. On the other hand, there are the operating costs of the non-profit association: the personnel costs, the costs of maintaining the website, organising events, bilingual communication, etc. Figure 1 shows the division of costs Klimaatzaak incurred during the period

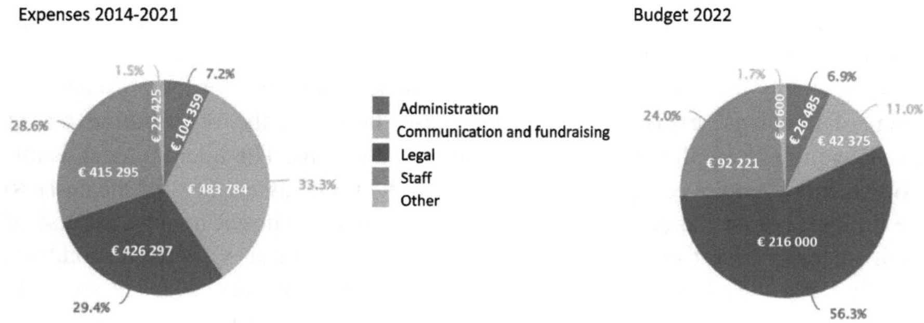

Fig. 1 Klimaatzaak's expenses 2014–2021 and budget 2022. Source: www.klimaatzaak.be

2014–2021. For 2022, the estimated budget foresees 216,000 EUR, out of 383,681 EUR for legal fees.[98]

Compared to general expenses (as represented in Fig. 1) the division of costs relating to the individual court proceedings changes dramatically. Respondents refer that in relation to individual judicial cases 80% of the funds are spent on lawyers' fees. Grondrecht uses donations for scientific research and legal expenses. Since they use an online crowdfunding platform, a small percentage of each donation is going to the open collective, which is transparently communicated to each funder. Grondrecht's expenses can be tracked live on the crowdfunding platform. From January–October 2022, most of the expenses, amounting in total to 44,477.52 EUR, were lawyers' fees. The other costs were limited and included summon costs, scientific research and costs for the establishment of the non-profit organisation.[99] Beperk de Straling uses the donations only for the court proceedings and the cost of its bank account for donations. So far, they have spent 12,471.16 EUR on lawyers' fees for their court cases and 1675.00 EUR as contribution for court cases initiated by another collective with similar aims.[100] All organisations ensure transparency of the expenses on their respective websites.

In all cases, initiating a court proceeding is subject to the availability of money and, given the limited budget, an assessment is made about the opportunity of bringing the case to court. In one case, the anonymous respondent has revealed that such assessment procedure is highly structured and takes into account a number of criteria, including the merit of the case and its mediatic, as well as an evaluation of whether the same objective could be pursued via political advocacy. All organisations indicate that their lawyers make an initial financial assessment for the legal proceedings.

As anticipated in the introduction, the respondents are active members of the interviewed organisations or initiatives. Klimaatzaak has one employee, responsible for the coordination. Grondrecht and Beperk de Straling rely on volunteers. Even

[98] Klimaatzaak. https://www.klimaatzaak.eu/nl/financials.

[99] Grondrecht. https://opencollective.com/pfonds/expenses.

[100] Beperk de Straling. https://www.beperkdestraling.org/ (situation on 31 July 2022).

though some volunteers have legal expertise or are familiar with the laws they engage with, they all rely on hired lawyers for legal expertise regarding their proceedings. Only the interviewed NGO has a structure allowing for the presence of a team of two legal experts. Even in this case, however, the organisation makes extensive use of legal consulting from external law firms. The internal legal teams, volunteers or employees, play a crucial role in the initial assessment of the cases to be brought before the courts. Lawyers are subsequently chosen mainly because of their specific expertise and based on their proposed fees. Various respondents mention that they have very good relations with their lawyers, who are similarly engaged for the cause. They consider themselves close-knit teams with matching aims. One respondent mentioned that the lawyer applied a discounted fee for their case in the collective interest, but only regarding the consultancy activities, litigation fees being fixed.

4.3 Perceived Legitimacy of the Belgian Legal Framework

In our interviews we probed the perception of the interviewed stakeholders regarding the fairness of the Belgian system of access to funding in environmental cases.

The responses we received consistently highlighted the substantive impossibility for common citizens to bring environmental protection cases in the collective interest to court. This is due not only to the aforementioned limitations *de jure*, but also *de facto*: know-how and capacity is needed to have environmental cases in the collective interest declared admissible, and this is in practice out of the reach of most citizens. Additionally, the interviewees express dissatisfaction with the rising political voices to constrain citizens' procedural options, which would not be conducive.

Several organisations pointed out that litigating against a government that is deliberately trying to delay proceedings requires them to obtain more funds. Indeed, governments have used delaying legal tactics in several court proceedings. Moreover, sometimes organisations need to initiate additional proceedings to safeguard their interest in the ongoing proceeding.

Klimaatzaak and Beperk de Straling regret that court victories are not followed by a consequent political reaction, as it happens—they feel—in other countries. Respondents also point out that Belgium's complex state structure is probably not conducive in this respect. Likewise, Beperk de Straling refers to the lack of political reaction and describes their fight as the fight of David against Goliath. There are huge interests at stake—they explain—and it is difficult to challenge everything legally.

For all respondents, the availability of funding is crucial to start a court proceeding. The organisations indicate that more resources for environmental organisations would be healthy for the litigation landscape as this brings debate and discussion into society. The current avenues for legal entities to receive funding (next to crowdfunding) are vague and opaque. It is hard for organisation to find their way and the process entails a considerable administrative burden for which in-house capacity is needed. The biggest hurdle for small organisations is finding funds, especially with lawyers' fees that tend to run up tremendously fast. Representation by a lawyer is however necessary to increase the chances of success of the proceedings. Environmental cases are very complex and the legal details are important. Moreover, the organisations are facing a government that always has lawyers at their disposal.

All respondents agree that legal proceedings are a very important instrument to achieve the objectives of the organisations and associations. Legal proceedings, indeed, pursue a legal goal (a change in the legal system, or the acknowledgment of a right's violation) that is not achievable with other means, not even with massive protest or other forms of advocacy.

5 Conclusions

The overall research question this chapter intended to answer was whether the legal framework implementing the third pillar of the Aarhus Convention in Belgium ensures a satisfactory level of access to funding to promote court actions for the protection of the environment as a collective interest.

To answer such question, we had first to discern what a "satisfactory" level of access to justice could be. Accordingly, we proposed a review of the international and supranational sources of the right of access to justice in environmental matters. Such a review now leads us to conclude that the Aarhus Convention and its Compliance Committee are clear in affirming that citizens and environmental NGOs shall enjoy their right to (be put in the conditions to[101]) file complaints before a court of law or other administrative bodies, without exceptions. But also that, in practice, it is for the States part of the Convention to implement the legal framework on both access to court (legal standing) and access to funding.

The European Union, as a signatory of the Aarhus Convention itself, implemented Article 9 with several pieces of legislation that, however, are confined to the EU institutions without ensuring a broader access to environmental justice at the national level. The case-law of CJEU has evolved positively over the last few years, widening the legal standing of environmental NGOs.

In Belgium, legal standing of environmental organisations and citizen groups has been a controversial issue for many years, but nowadays organisations are mostly entitled to file complaints in the public interest before both administrative and civil courts. Despite the fact that common citizens are still excluded (unless they have a personal direct interest), the possibility for them to "substitute" (see Sect. 3 above) and to organise themselves in groups makes their access to justice "satisfactory" within the meaning above.

[101] We refer here to Article 9, para. 5 of the Aarhus Convention.

What is—in our opinion—still missing in the case of Belgium is a more precise implementation of Article 9, para. 5 of the Aarhus Convention, establishing the duty on contracting States to remove the obstacles that *de facto* undermine the right of citizens and groups to bring environmental protection cases to court. In this respect, our analysis leads us to conclude that access to funding is still not fully satisfactory and could be improved.

Despite this might seem an "academic" conclusion, since the comparison with other contracting States places Belgium among the countries with the highest levels of implementation of the Convention's provisions,[102] the voices of the stakeholders on the field are loud and clear: funding is a key element of access to environmental justice. Its importance in legal scholarship should not be neglected, especially considering the fact that stakeholders usually have to face companies or governments with far more extensive resources. More research into this topic is desirable. In particular, it would be interesting to investigate (1) a bigger sample, including organisations that did not find their way to court (2) how other countries deal with the issue and (3) if the establishment of objective criteria to grant legal aid to collective interest initiatives is feasible.

References

Aarhus Convention National Implementation Report of Belgium (2021) Synthesis report submitted on behalf of the Federal Authority, the Brussels-Capital Region, the Walloon Region and the Flemish Region of the Kingdom of Belgium to the UNECE (2021), p 3. https://www.health.belgium.be/sites/default/files/uploads/fields/fpshealth_theme_file/synthesis_implementation_report_def_clean_1.pdf

Allemeersch B, Vandensande E (2019) Een Gemeenrechtelijk Regime van Vorderingen ter Verdediging van Collectieve Belangen. Rechtskunding Weekblad 32:1242

Auvray F et al (2021) Belgische Klimaatzaak: Enkel(e) Vaststellingen? Juristenkrant 436:6–7

Baert J, Debersaques G (1996) Raad van State Afdeling Administratie, 2. Ontvankelijkheid. die Keure, Brugge

Bailer S (2014) Interviews and surveys in legislative research. In: Martin S et al (eds) The Oxford handbook of legislative studies. Oxford University Press

Beperk de Straling. https://www.beperkdestraling.org

Bogner A et al (2009) Interviewing experts, ECPR research methods

Eggermont F (2017) Rechtsmacht en Belang bij het Middel. Tijdschrift Voor Bestuurswetenschappen en Publiekrecht 2017:380–397

EU Commission (2020) Communication from the Commission to the European Parliament, the Council, the European Economic and Social Committee and the Committee of the Regions: Improving access to justice in environmental matters in the EU and its Member States, COM (2020) 643, Brussels, 14 October 2020

Fasoli E, McGlone A (2018) The non-compliance mechanism under the Aarhus Convention as 'Soft' enforcement of international environmental law: not so soft after all! Netherlands Int Law Rev 65(1):27–53

[102] See UNECE Secretariat, Synthesis Report on the status of implementation of the Convention. https://unece.org/sites/default/files/2021-10/ECE_MP.PP_2021_6_E.pdf.

Fitzmaurice M (2004) The Kyoto Protocol compliance regime and treaty law. Singapore Yearb Int Law 8:23–40

Grondrecht. https://opencollective.com/pfonds/expenses

Grondrecht. www.grondrecht.eu

Jans JH, Marseille AT (2010) The role of NGOs in environmental litigation against public authorities: some observations on judicial review and access to court in the Netherlands. J Environ Law 22:373–390

Klimaatzaak. https://www.klimaatzaak.eu

Korkea-aho E, Leino P (2019) Interviewing lawyers: a critical self-reflection on expert interviews as a method of EU legal research. Eur J Leg Stud 12:17–47

Kramer L (2015) The EU courts and access to environmental justice. In: Boer B (ed) Environmental law dimensions of human rights. Oxford University Press, p 131

Lefranc P (2017) De 'Actio Popularis' ter Bescherming van het Milieu. Wenselijk? Tijdschrift Voor Milieurecht, special edition 27:19–29

Lefranc P (2019) Artikel 17, tweede lid Ger.W.: Hooglied van het Algemeen Collectiefvorderingsrecht voor de Hoven en Rechtbanken of de Zwanenzang van de Eikendael-doctrine. Tijdschrift Voor Milieurecht 3:239–261

Ligugnana G (2019) Environmental NGOs and access to justice: Article 9(3) of the Aarhus Convention and the EU Courts' perspective. In: Recent challenges of public administration, vol 3. Iurisperitus Kiadó, pp 11–38

Loibl G (2021) Compliance procedures and mechanisms. In: Fitzmaurice M et al (eds) Research handbook on international environmental law. Edward Elgar, p 310

Lucy W (2020) Access to justice and the rule of law. Oxf J Leg Stud 40(2):377–402

Lycourgos C (2021) Locus standi of non-governmental organizations in environmental matters under EU law. In: Lycourgos C et al (eds) Access to justice of environmental NGOs: a comparative perspective (EU, France, Cyprus). Friedrich Ebert Stiftung. www.library.fes.de

McLaughlin A, Greenwood J (1995) The management of interest representation the European Union. J Common Mark Stud 33(1):143–156

Meulebrouck M (2021a) Controversiële Decreetswijziging Beperkt Toegang tot de Bestuursrechter in het Omgevingsrecht. Juristenkrant 430:8–11

Meulebrouck M (2021b) Verplichte participatie van de burger in het omgevingsrecht in Nederland en Vlaanderen onder druk ingevolge het arrest Varkens in Nood van het Hof van Justitie: beter voorkomen dan genezen. TMR 6:588–599

Nicòtina A (2021) A procedural idea of environmental democracy. Rev Eur Adminis Law 14:85–106

Peterson M (1992) The presidency and organized interests: White House Patterns of Interest Group Liaison. Am Polit Sci Rev 86(3):612–625

Rass-Masson N, Rouas V (2017) Effective access to justice. Study for the PETI Committee, EU Commission, DG for Internal Policies, Policy Department, PE 596.818, p 10. https://www.europarl.europa.eu/RegData/etudes/STUD/2017/596818/IPOL_STU(2017)596818_EN.pdf

Roulston K, Choi M (2018) Qualitative interviews. In: Flick U (ed) The SAGE handbook of qualitative data collection. SAGE, pp 233–245

Rubin HJ, Rubin IS (2012) Qualitative interviewing. The art of hearing data. SAGE

Schaiko G (2020) Het Substitutierecht van de Burger: Graadmeter van een Democratische Rechtsstaat. Tijdschrift voor Ruimtelijke ordening, Omgeving en Stedenbouw 98:112–119

Schoukens H, Woldendorp H (2014) Juridische Moeilijkheden bij Proactieve Natuurontwikkeling: een Laatste Reddingsboei voor het Polderdorpje Doel? Tijdschrift voor Omgevingsrecht en Omgevingsbeleid 105–106:97–118

Squintani L, Perlaviciute G (2020) Access to public participation: unveiling the mismatch between what law prescribes and what the public wants. In: Peeters M, Eliantonio M (eds) Research handbook on EU environmental law. Edward Elgar, p 137

Turtelboom A (2019) Public consultations – an essential tool for bringing the EU closer to its citizens. Eur Court Auditors J 4:81–86

United Nations Economic Commission for Europe (UNECE) Secretariat (2021) Synthesis report on the status of implementation of the convention, UN ECE/MP.PP/2021/6, para. 189, 191 and 259, p 45

Van Wolferen M, Eliantonio M (2020) Access to justice in environmental matters in the EU: the EU's difficult road towards non-compliance with the Aarhus Convention. In: Peeters M, Eliantonio M (eds) Research handbook on EU environmental law. Edward Elgar, p 154

Verhelst G (2015) Raad voor Vergunningsbetwistingen en Milieuhandhavingscollege krijgen bestuurlijke lus 2.0. Rechtskunding Weekblad 79(24):923–939

Wouters J et al (2008) The Europeanisation of international law: the status of international law in the EU and its Member States. TMC Asser Press

Webley L (2014) Qualitative approaches to empirical legal research. In: Cane P, Kritzer HM (eds) The Oxford handbook of legislative studies. Oxford University Press

Wirtgen A (2015) Het Belang als Ontvankelijkheidsvoorwaarde van het Middel in het Kader van het Beroep tot Nietigverklaring bij de Raad van State. Tijdschrift voor Bestuurswetenschappen en Publiek Recht 3:131–151

Standing, Justiciability, and Burden of Proof in Climate Litigation: Challenges and Proposals

Gianni Ghinelli

Contents

Abstract Climate change impacts fundamental rights with increasing and irreversible effects. Yet, it remains largely unresolved by political action, and tipping points in the climate system are a genuine concern. Citizens are therefore seeking relief in

---

G. Ghinelli (✉)
Department of Legal Studies, University of Bologna, Rimini, Italy
e-mail: gianni.ghinelli2@unibo.it

E. Storskrubb (ed.), *YSEC Yearbook of Socio-Economic Constitutions 2022*,
YSEC Yearbook of Socio-Economic Constitutions (2023) 2022: 147–182,
https://doi.org/10.1007/16495_2023_50, Published online: 4 July 2023

court. However, traditional standing, justiciability, and evidence rules hinder access to climate justice, making it uncertain and potentially expensive for plaintiffs. Many cases have, in fact, been rejected based on procedural grounds. In addition, procedural rules appear to mismatch the fragmented nature of climate change harm. This Chapter argues that the 2020 *Model Statute for Proceedings Challenging Government Failure to Act on Climate Change*, drafted by the International Bar Association, might offer viable solutions for procedural law reform to decrease the hurdles identified for climate justice.

1 Introduction

This Chapter focuses on the procedural law implications of climate litigation.[1] It aims to show that most standing, justiciability, and evidence rules are designed for traditional individual conflicts; they do not fit the features of climate change harm, which is widespread and potentially involves anyone. To set the stage, Sect. 2 sums up the legally relevant features of climate change and why climate change poses an issue of justice. It then explains the reasons that pushed citizen groups to bring court proceedings relying on international climate law. Section 3 highlights the constitutional relevance of climate litigation, regardless of the different aims, legal basis, and jurisdictions. Despite some inevitable differences, all climate litigation potentially involves protecting human rights and the collective interests of younger and future generations.

Section 4 focuses on three main legal obstacles that obstruct access to justice: standing, justiciability, and evidence rules. Section 5 suggests that an adequate set of standing, justiciability, and evidence rules should match the public interest implications of climate litigation. Hence, Sect. 5 presents the proposals made in 2020 by the International Bar Association's Model Statute for Proceedings Challenging Government Failure to Act on Climate Change (Model Statute).[2] Finally, Sect. 6 argues that the Model Statute offers a helpful reference point for procedural reform to better fit the significant wave of public interest litigation seeking to vindicate climate rights.

[1] Estrin (2016).

[2] David Estrin and Baroness Helena Kennedy QC co-chaired the IBA Task Force on Climate Change Justice and Human Rights. The text of the Model Statute and a commentary are available on the IBA's website https://www.ibanet.org/Climate-Change-Model-Statute. On the IBA's climate commitment, see Leslie (2016).

2 The Roots of Climate Litigation

2.1 *Climate Change and Justice*

2.1.1 Background

This Section argues that climate change is a matter of justice and that it is appropriate for national courts to deal with it based on international obligations undertaken by governments. The link between climate change and justice requires an understanding of the relationship between anthropogenic Green House Gases (GHGs), climate change, and its effects on individuals and communities based on the Reports issued by the Intergovernmental Panel on Climate Change (IPCC). The IPCC is the United Nations body that assesses climate science.[3] It releases Assessment Reports and Special Reports on the state of knowledge regarding climate change impacts, risks, and possible solutions for mitigation and adaptation to climate change. Three Working Groups contributed to the Sixth Assessment Report (AR6).

The climate science summarized by the IPCC shows that climate change is a matter of justice for three reasons. First, climate change impacts fundamental rights. Second, climate change exacerbates social inequality. Third, the long-term effects of climate change and "tipping points" put younger and future generations at risk.

2.1.2 Human Rights

Working Group I drafted the report Climate Change 2021: The Physical Science Basis. The report helps understand the link between anthropogenic climate change and human rights. Human activities contribute to global warming and interfere with natural climate fluctuations. Between 1890–1900, human-produced GHGs have been responsible for approximately 1.1 °C of warming. Although the climate has always changed, the rate at which the climate is currently warming is unprecedented. Unless sufficient is action, by 2040, the global average temperature is expected to increase by 1.5 °C above pre-industrial levels.

Working Group II reinforced these conclusions in its Report Climate Change 2022: Impacts, Adaption, and Vulnerability.[4] For the purposes of this Chapter, the core takeaway is that climate change affects our health and safety and will increasingly do so, impacting every aspect of our lives. Hence, climate change can potentially cause mass human rights violations. Furthermore, Working Group II reported that climate change has increasingly contributed to extreme weather events

[3] The IPCC was created in 1988 by the World Meteorological Organization (WMO) and the United Nations Environment Programme (UNEP). It represents 195 countries and aims to provide governments with scientific knowledge for climate policies. It does not research on its own. The IPCC reviews studies conducted all over the world on climate-related matters.

[4] IPCC (2022).

(e.g., heatwaves and wildfires) and slow onset processes (e.g., ocean acidification and sea level rise). Working Group II also stressed that such impacts concern food and water security, urban infrastructure, economic damages, and humanitarian crises. Climate change impacts occur both in developed countries as well as in the Global South.

2.1.3 Inequality

In 2019, the UN Special Rapporteur, Robert Boyd, found that climate change also drives inequality: countries and communities characterized by poverty, political instability, or conflicts have fewer resources to adapt to climate change.[5] Climate change-driven inequality harms both the Global South and less affluent communities in developed countries.[6]

Working Group II identified—with high confidence—global hotspots for human vulnerability: West-, Central- and East Africa, South Asia, Central, and South America, Small Island Developing States, and the Arctic. One of the effects identified is migration.[7] Even within developed countries, some individuals are more vulnerable than others. According to a report by the US Environmental Protection Agency (EPA) released in 2021, socially vulnerable populations are more exposed to climate change and less able to cope. The EPA found that low income, belonging to minority groups, and lack of high school diplomas are the main factors determining how much climate change affects people in the US.[8] A further element concerns the ratio between who bears responsibility for most GHG emissions and who suffers climate change harm. Historically, not all countries have contributed equally to climate change, as developed countries account for most of the emissions. Yet the Global South is disproportionately affected, and indigenous peoples are particularly exposed.[9]

Consequently, climate change reiterates historical and ongoing patterns, such as colonialism. Working Group II stated, "*Across sectors and regions, the most vulnerable people and systems are observed to be disproportionately affected.*"[10] This factual element is legally acknowledged by the principle of "*common but*

[5] See, Boyd (2019). Also, United Nations Environmental Program Report (2015) Climate Change and Human Rights. https://www.unep.org/resources/report/climate-change-and-human-rights.

[6] See Malijean-Dubois (2015). Also, see Diffenbaugh and Burke (2019).

[7] The Italian Supreme Court granted the right to humanitarian protection to a migrant coming from the Niger Delta because it is an area hit by environmental damage and climate change. See Italian Supreme Court (Corte di cassazione), judgment No. 25143 of 2020.

[8] EPA (2021).

[9] Ibid footnote 4, SPM. B.2.1.: "*Loss of ecosystems and their services has cascading and long-term impacts on people globally, especially for Indigenous Peoples and local communities who are directly dependent on ecosystems, to meet basic needs (high confidence)*".

[10] Ibid footnote 4, SPM.B.1.

differentiated responsibilities" enshrined in Articles 3 and 4 of the 1992 UN Framework Convention on Climate Change (UNFCCC).

2.1.4 Future Generations

Future generations will be disproportionally affected by climate change.[11] The AR6 Summary for Policymakers exposes the mismatch between present GHG emissions and the increasing threat posed by climate change. The irreversible effects of emissions will increasingly impair the enjoyment of fundamental rights. As recognized by the German Constitutional Court, present climate policies will affect the fundamental rights of future generations in two separate ways: first, they will be more exposed to risks deriving from climate change, and second, restrictive measures will most probably be introduced to meet the emission targets impacting on individual freedoms.[12]

2.1.5 Conclusion: Climate Change Is a Matter of Justice

In conclusion, climate change is a matter of justice, as it impacts fundamental rights, drives inequality, and due to its long-term effects and the risk posed by "tipping points," it endangers younger and future generations. This Chapter argues that these features—highlighted by IPCC Reports—conflict with the structure of traditional standing, justiciability, and evidence rules, mainly designed for individual disputes. However, before conducting that analysis, it is important to outline the roots of climate litigation—starting from international climate change law.

2.2 *From International Law to National Courts*

Given the implications on justice of climate change and its inherent cross-border features, international law has addressed climate change. The first milestone of climate law is the 1992 UN Framework Convention on Climate Change, which entered into force on 21 March 1994. Under Article 2, the Convention aims to "*achieve (...) stabilization of greenhouse gas concentrations in the atmosphere at a level that would prevent dangerous anthropogenic interference with the climate system*". Article 3(1) acknowledges that not all countries have equal responsibilities. It, therefore, states the principle of "*common but differentiated responsibilities*," which requires developed countries to lead in granting effective mitigation. Article

[11] Sanson and Burke (2020).

[12] *Neubauer* et al. *vs. Germany*, German Constitutional Court (BVerfG), judgment of the First Senate of 24 March 2021, BvR 2656/18 -, paras. 243–245.

7 of the UNFCCC instituted the Conference of the parties for the further implementation and development of the UNFCCC. In 1997 the Kyoto Protocol was signed to operationalize the UNFCCC. It attributed mandatory targets to developed countries and created a market-based mechanism to reduce emissions. It was then updated in 2012 in Doha.

The 2015 Paris Agreement (PA) was signed to hold the global temperature rise to a maximum of 2 °C, preferably to 1.5 °C, above pre-industrial levels. For this purpose, it relies on each country's commitment to the mechanism of Nationally Determined Contributions (NDCs). Thus, the PA does not impose a reduction quota on individual countries. Instead, the common goal of limiting the temperature increase to 1.5 °C requires the engagement of each national government in the procedural mechanism created by the PA. The latest development of international climate law is the 2021 Glasgow Climate Pact,[13] which further implements the PA and commits to a 1.5 °C temperature increase limit. All these legal instruments, developed under the UNFCCC, arguably constitute essential steps forward in the fight against climate change. However, they all share a concerning element: they impose only procedural duties—such as the NDCs—and mere "best efforts" obligations. It is ultimately up to governments to determine their climate ambition.[14]

The lack of coercive legal mechanisms at the international law level and other factors, such as political and practical difficulties in addressing the climate crisis, has contributed to a lack of sufficient climate action. As a result, emissions have been increasing, despite the UNFCCC and the PA.[15] The consequence is the erosion of the so-called "carbon budget," i.e., the emissions allowed before hitting the 1.5 °C temperature increase thresholds that the IPCC considers relatively safe.[16]

In light of the threats of climate change and the failure to reduce emissions through international law, individuals and citizen groups are resorting to litigation to enforce the PA's temperature goals. In addition, shareholders, investors, or private citizens have sued so called carbon majors for damages or to hold their directors accountable on different legal bases. Climate litigation is expanding as leveraging courts seems to be the last resort to enforce the PA[17] This bottom-up approach reflects the failure of the political branches of government to address climate change promptly. It also creates friction between courts and the other branches of the state.[18] The following Section presents the main categories of climate litigation: each type presents specific challenges in establishing standing and justiciability and sustaining the burden of proof.

[13] The Glasgow Climate Pact is the result of 2021 Glasgow Climate Change Conference COP26.

[14] Preston (2020a).

[15] See the World Meteorological Organization (2021) Greenhouse Gas Bulletin No.17: The State of Greenhouse Gases in the Atmosphere Based on Global Observations through 2020.

[16] For a definition of carbon budget, see Matthews et al. (2021).

[17] Wegener (2020).

[18] See Sindico and Mbengue (2021).

3 Litigation Categories

3.1 Classification

Section 3 proposes to organize climate litigation into categories. Based on the remedies and aims sought by the parties, climate litigation can be classified as strategic litigation against governments, strategic litigation against actors in the private sector, and claims seeking damages. Climate litigation can be further divided based on the legal basis for the claims made in such litigation. Accordingly, this Section deals separately with claims that rely on statutory duties under administrative law and those leveraging fundamental rights. The analysis of the latter category is further separated with respect to the specific human rights claimed by plaintiffs and the chosen jurisdiction level. The purpose of this categorization is to assist the later analysis of strategies to overcome the procedural hurdles of standing, justiciability, and the burden of proof.

3.2 Strategic Litigation Against Governments

3.2.1 General

In many countries across the world citizens have resorted court to enforce the international law commitments of their governments. This litigation category is commonly referred to as "strategic."[19] Strategic litigation against governments commonly relies on the UNFCCC and the PA as legal basis. Citizen groups seek judicial orders to reduce national GHG emissions consistent with the PA's 1.5 °C temperature increase limit. The following cases exemplify strategic litigation against governments: *Leghari vs. Federation of Pakistan*[20] (*Leghari*), *Juliana vs. the United States* (*Juliana*),[21] *Urgenda vs. The Netherlands* (*Urgenda*),[22] and *Neubauer and others vs. Germany* (*Neubauer*).[23] This Section will briefly discuss each case to highlight the core features of strategic climate litigation.

[19] Peel and Osofsky (2019).

[20] *Ashgar Leghari* vs. *Federation of Pakistan* (W.P. No. 25501/2015), Lahore High Court Green Bench, Orders of 4 and 14 September 2015.

[21] *Juliana vs. United States*, U.S. District Court for the District of Oregon, case No. 947 F.3d 1159 (9th Cir. 2020).

[22] The case developed over three decisions and ended with the Supreme Court ruling: The Hague District Court 24 June 2015, ECLI:NL:RBDHA:2015:7145. ECLI:NL:RBDHA:2015:7196; The Hague Court of Appeal 9 October 2018, ECLI:NL:GHDHA:2018:2591. ECLI:NL:GHDHA:2018:2610; Supreme Court, 13 January 2020, ECLI:NL:HR:2019:2007. See Spier (2020).

[23] Ibid footnote 12.

3.2.2 Leghari

In *Leghari*, a Pakistani farmer sued the Federation of Pakistan and the local State of Punjab, maintaining that they failed to implement the necessary climate adaptation measures previously identified by these governments in a national adaptation plan.[24] The Lahori High Court held that the government's response to the threat of climate change was delayed and "lethargic" in violation of fundamental rights protected by the Constitution. The remedy provided indicates the "strategic" nature of this case. The Court requested the relevant government ministries to nominate a "focal person" responsible for the plan of implementation and present to the Court a list of actions necessary to implement the plan. To further supervise the progress of the government the Court also created a commission composed of government representatives, NGOs, and experts.

3.2.3 Juliana

Twenty-one young plaintiffs brought the *Juliana* case before the US District Court for the District of Oregon, United States. The claim relied on constitutional rights and the public trust doctrine. They sought an order against the United States government to draft and implement a national plan to phase out fossil fuel emissions and stabilize the climate system. The suit has had a complex and lengthy judicial journey through various levels of court challenges by the US Government and, at one point, by significant carbon emitters, which were given leave to intervene. In 2020, the relief sought was found not redressable by a two-to-one decision of an appellate panel of the Federal Court. The majority took the view that the required supervision activity would have resulted in a violation of the principle of separation of powers. The Court held that the claim lacked redressability—which led to the claim's dismissal for lack of standing under Article 3 of the Constitution. Thus, the case was dismissed. The plaintiffs then sought to amend their claim for relief, and settlement discussions followed, but at present there appears to be no final resolution.

3.2.4 Urgenda

The *Urgenda* case led to a more fortunate outcome. The Urgenda foundation and 886 citizens sued the Dutch Government and maintained that its GHG emission reduction targets were insufficient, resulting in a breach of the civil duty of care owed by the state to the plaintiffs under Dutch tort law. They also argued that such conduct violated the rights to life and private and family life, protected by Articles

---

[24] The 2012 National Climate Change Policy and the Framework for Implementation of Climate Change Policy.

2 and 8 of the European Convention of Human Rights (ECHR), which are directly applicable in the Netherlands. All courts levels rejected the government's objections to the alleged lack of standing and justiciability. Based on human rights obligations and the duty of care, the Supreme Court ordered the Dutch government to reduce national emissions by 25% by 2020 compared to 1990 levels,[25] leaving it to the government's discretion how to achieve such reductions. The strategic ambition of this case stands between *Leghari* and *Juliana*. The plaintiffs obtained a ruling that the government had a duty to reduce national emissions to a greater extent and more urgently. Such a result was unprecedented. However, the plaintiffs did not require, as in *Leghari*, to undertake any supervising activity. Nor did the plaintiffs ask the court, as in *Juliana*, to order the government to restructure the national energy system. In *Urgenda*, plaintiffs only requested an order to reduce emissions, leaving it to the government to make any further assessment on the methods to curb emissions.

3.2.5 Neubauer

In the *Neubauer* case, the German Constitutional Court declared the partial unconstitutionality of the law regulating climate change-related emissions because these provisions did not set sufficient guidelines for the reductions required after 2031 and offloaded the great majority of the necessary cuts after 2030.[26] As a result, according to the Court, the law disproportionately impaired future generations' fundamental rights. This judgment stands out as it acknowledges the irreversible effects of climate tipping points for future generations.

3.2.6 Conclusion

Leghari, *Urgenda*, and *Neubauer* show that strategic litigation against governments may help obtain more climate action. An analysis of all the cases presented above also suggests that plaintiffs should consider the issues of justiciability, redressability, and standing when preparing their request for relief. Balancing the strategic ambitions of the claim with the existing procedural rules has proven crucial. Based on their national law, plaintiffs should seek a type of relief that can be granted in light of the separation of powers principle. Requesting an effective remedy within the framework of the separation of powers principle is essential to reduce the risk of dismissal on procedural grounds.

---

[25] The year 1990 is the benchmark chosen by the UNFCCC for any reduction target. The 25% reduction target is based on the IPCC Climate Change 2007: Synthesis Report. Contribution of Working Groups I, II and III to the Fourth Assessment Report of the Intergovernmental Panel on Climate Change [Core Writing Team, Pachauri, R.K and Reisinger, A. (eds.)]. IPCC, Geneva, Switzerland.

[26] KlimaSchutzGesetz, § 3(1) second sentence and § 4(1), in conjunction with Annex 2.

Even in the face of the climate emergency, courts may—at least in the short term—resist ordering relief against governments on the ground that by such decisions, the judiciary would step into the province of political discretion. However, as shown in *Urgenda*, judges who appreciate the arguments can help shape the relief provided to be effective while staying within the appropriate ambit of judicial responsibilities. If provided by domestic law, the best option is to bring proceedings directly before the Constitutional or Supreme Court to seek a declaration of unconstitutionality of national climate legislation.

3.3 Strategic Litigation Against Actors in the Private Sector

3.3.1 General

While governments have the legal power to impose the reductions required by the PA, the 1.5 °C limit objective could arguably not be reached without the cooperation of the private sector. Certain groups of companies—so-called carbon majors—have more impact than entire countries.[27] If climate action by actors in the private sector is not achieved through compliance with national regulation or by voluntary measures, court action appears to be the last resort for citizens. Strategic litigation against carbon majors aims at curbing emissions in line with the PA. Litigation against the actors in the private sector can be separated into two categories: cases aiming at an order to reduce overall emissions and cases aiming at an order to stop specific development projects deemed incompatible with the objective set out by the PA.

3.3.2 Claims Seeking to Reduce Emissions

The first category is exemplified by *Milieudefensie* et al. *vs. Royal Dutch Shell plc*[28] (*Shell*). In 2021, the Hague District Court ordered Royal Dutch Shell—the holding company of the well-known oil and gas conglomerate—to cut the group's emissions by 45% by the end of 2030 compared to 2019 levels, including Scope 3 emissions meaning those created once the products are sold to consumers. This decision shares one element of commonality with the ruling in Urgenda. The Court made similar use of tort law in combination with the ECHR. In both cases, Dutch courts held that the

---

[27] The Shell group emits more than the entire Netherlands, as ascertained by *Milieudefensie* et al. *vs. Royal Dutch Shell plc*, The Hague District Court. 6 May 2021. ECLI:NL:RBDHA:2021:5339, paragraph 4.4.5.

[28] *Milieudefensie* et al. *vs. Royal Dutch Shell plc*, The Hague District Court. 6 May 2021. ECLI:NL:RBDHA:2021:5339.

tort law principle of *neminem laedere* must be construed in conjunction with the ECHR. In *Shell*, the Court also set a new precedent in finding that the private sector—not just governments—has a duty of care toward citizens regarding carbon emissions. Thus, the Court allowed the extension of strategic litigation to the private sector.

3.3.3 Claims Against Specific Projects

Alternatively, plaintiffs can seek to enforce strategic climate objectives by halting a specific highly emitting development or industrial project through judicial planning decisions. The Australian case, *Gloucester Resources Limited v Minister for Planning*[29] *(Gloucester Resources)*, provides an excellent example of a planning decision involving climate change considerations. This judgment arises from an appeal to the Land and Environment Court of New South Wales by Gloucester Resources Limited (Gloucester), a company operating in the mining business. Gloucester requested the Court to approve its application for the construction of a coalmine following a negative decision by the local government, which was based on the mine's environmental, social, and economic impact. The Court dismissed the appeal finding that, despite climate change's multiple sources, single significant emissions sources are still sufficiently relevant contributors to climate change. Compared to strategic litigation based on human rights and tort law strategic, statutory planning decisions have the substantial advantage of causing less angst for judges or administrative hearing officials. Considering many factors, they often have broad discretion regarding what constitutes good planning. They are also given statutory authority to make a "yes or no" decision regarding the feasibility of a project from a planning perspective. In other words, justiciability is a less relevant issue. Also, planning decisions are easily enforceable, as once a project has been denied, the GHG emissions will not occur.

Conversely, decisions ordering the reduction of future emissions based, for example, on tort law require the defendant to comply with the order and, therefore, implement those actions to modify its corporate climate policy or how it operates its business. The ability to access procedural mechanisms in national law to enforce the order is crucial if there is no voluntary compliance. These concerns do not exist when planning decisions produce the effect of preventing GHG emissions.

---

[29] *Gloucester Resources Limited vs. Minister for Planning*, Land and Environment Court New South Wales, Australia, 8 February 2019. [2019] NSWLEC 7.

3.4 Litigation for Compensatory Damages Against Actors in the Private Sector

Litigation against carbon majors can also aim to recover economic damages caused by climate change harm. Both individuals and municipalities harmed by climate change are seeking damages in Court to provide for costly adaption measures.

In *Luciano Lliuya vs. RWE AG* (*Luciano Lliuya*), a Peruvian farmer filed an action in the German courts against the largest German energy company, seeking an order to pay 0.47% of the financial loss caused by climate change.[30] The claim is based on study concluding that 0.47% of all atmospheric GHG emissions are attributable to RWE AG's activities. The case was initially dismissed based on insufficient proof of causality between RWE AG's emissions and the climate change effects suffered by plaintiff. However, the Court of Appeal established the admissibility of the claim. Hence, the proceeding are currently pending and continue before the first instance court and at the time of writing have entered the evidentiary phase, with the presentation of facts proving the causal link.

In the *City of Charleston vs. Brabham Oil Company Inc.* et al. (*City of Charleston*), the City of Charleston sued fossil fuel companies before the South Carolina Court of Common Pleas, seeking compensatory and punitive damages and disgorgement of profits.[31] The plaintiff argued that climate change produced land and beach erosion, floods, and higher sea levels, causing social and economic harm. Further, the plaintiff maintained that the defendants knowingly deceived consumers about the direct connection between their products and climate change harm, well aware of such risks for over 50 years; also, according to the plaintiffs, the defendants did not pursue less hazardous alternatives. This case was still pending at the time of writing.

The *Luciano Lliuya* and *City of Charleston* cases indicate that litigation may help recover resources needed to adapt and compensate for climate harm. In addition, the fact that plaintiffs claim damages for the infringement of their individual rights, rather than seeking redress for collective interests, helps prevent the objections of lack of standing and justiciability. From the plaintiffs' perspective, the main problem with this litigation category might be proving the causal link between the defendant's conduct and the actual damages under existing evidentiary rules.

[30] *Luciano Lliuya vs. RWE AG*, Landgericht Essen, Case No. 2 O 285/15. See Dellinger (2018).

[31] *City of Charleston vs. Brabham Oil Company Inc.* et al., case No. 2:20-cv-03579-BHH.

3.5 *Claims Based on Statutory Environmental Assessment Law*

3.5.1 General

To date, statutory administrative provisions have primarily been used by plaintiffs in conjunction with the PA to pursue strategic litigation against actors in the private sector in planning and environmental assessment cases. In this context, plaintiffs face the challenge of successfully arguing that, before approving a project, public authorities must consider its climate change impact. This task is facilitated if the national law includes GHGs as relevant criteria. However, the case law shows that most national environmental assessment legislation does not include climate change-specific provisions. Plaintiffs must, therefore, be creative and try to link administrative law with the PA and the UNFCCC. This category of cases is exemplified by the *Gloucester Resources* case mentioned above,[32] *Earthlife Africa Johannesburg vs. Minister of Environmental Affairs and Others*[33] (*Earthlife Africa*), and *Vienna Airport Third Runway*[34] (*Vienna Airport*).

3.5.2 Gloucester Resources

As mentioned above, in *Gloucester Resources*, the Land and Environment Court of New South Wales upheld the local government's decision to deny planning permission for a coal mine based on the overall impact of the mine. However, the Court also considered the expert evidence as to the proposed consequences of GHG emissions that would occur through the use of the coal made available from the new mine on the Australian and NSW carbon budgets. By doing so, the decision provided renewed content to the general clause of public interest long codified in the Australian legal system. The "public interest" notion included the project's impact on the carbon budget. The Court further noted that the evaluation must include Scope 3 emissions—meaning also deriving from the consumption of the final product.

To secure the decision from further appeals, the Court apparently chose a pragmatic approach by relegating such climate change arguments to an ancillary role. While at first, the Court states that, given the obligations deriving from the PA, the emissions of new coal mines are contrary to the "public interest"[35] and that this

[32] Ibid. footnote 28.

[33] *Earthlife Africa Johannesburg vs. Minister of Environmental Affairs and others*, Case no. 65662/16 (2017).

[34] *Third Runway at Vienna International Airport*, Case No. W109 2000179-1/291E, Federal Administrative Court, Austria, 2 Feb. 2017.

[35] Section 4.15(1)(2) of the New South Wales Environmental Planning and Assessment Act 1979 No 203.

sole fact could form the basis for dismissal, the application was then primarily dismissed on the poor environmental, social, and economic impact of the mine.

3.5.3 Earthlife Africa Johannesburg

In *Earthlife Africa*, the plaintiff challenged the government's permit to develop a coal-fired energy plant based in the negative impact of the project on climate change. Although the national statutes did not expressly mention climate change as part of the legal criteria for environmental assessment, the South African High Court held that the Ministry's environmental review was unlawful for not adequality considering the impact on climate change. Further, the Court found that national provisions on environmental assessment require the public authority to evaluate whether highly emitting development projects are compatible with the NDCs and the overall obligations accepted by the government of South Africa in signing the PA.[36]

3.5.4 Vienna Airport

In *Vienna Airport*, the Federal Administrative Court quashed the government's permission to construct a third runway at Vienna Airport in light of obligations under the PA to mitigate climate change. The case revolved around the notion of "public interest" in the context of planning permits and climate change. As a result, Court held that obligations under the PA must be considered by public authorities when issuing permits for development projects that impact on the carbon budget.

This decision was overturned by the Austrian Constitutional Court in 2017. The Constitutional Court held that the lower court had erred in its balancing the climate change and land use concerns with the other public interests at stake in constructing a third runway. Importantly, the Constitutional Court also held that the Kyoto Protocol and PA are sources of international law that cannot directly be applied in the context of planning review decisions. The judgment thus significantly limited the possibility of enforcing climate obligations through administrative review in Austria. However, despite this setback, Vienna Airport still shows that climate obligations are a *potentially* relevant criterion.

3.5.5 Conclusion: The Potential of Environmental Assessment Litigation

Gloucester Resources, *Earthlife Africa*, and *Vienna Airport* show that national law regulating environmental assessment and planning can—and should—be interpreted in a way that considers the impact of a development plan on the carbon budget. If

[36] See *Earthlife Africa*, par. 91.

domestic legislation does not explicitly mention climate change among the relevant factors to consider, it is arguable that public authorities should interpret legal concepts, such as the one of public interest, in such a way as to include climate change.

Leveraging statutory provisions, rather than directly fundamental rights, is a different litigation pathway to pursue the same constitutionally relevant objective. This strategy, however, secures a decision with immediate effects, as the halt of a carbon-intensive project prevents all emissions from occurring. Conversely, in rights-based claims before ordinary courts, plaintiffs must deal with the fact that enforcing the judgment might be difficult as mentioned above.

3.6 Fundamental Rights Litigation

3.6.1 General

In recent years, plaintiffs have increasingly resorted to causes of action based on fundamental rights in litigation against governments and actors in the private sector. Some legal scholars called it a "rights-turn" in climate litigation, following a first wave based on statutory avenues.[37] This shift may reflect a growing realization that anthropogenic climate change involves people and rights—not only the environment.

The following sub-section separates fundamental rights litigation based on legal basis and based on jurisdiction. The separation will help understand the variation in the spectrum of climate litigation; however, the categories not immutable and will sometimes overlap.

3.6.2 Legal Foundations

Plaintiffs seeking judicial redress for fundamental rights rely on legal sources conceived at different times. Some are as old as the 1787 Constitution of the United States; others are the result of the post-Second World War era[38] or are even more recent, such as the 1996 South African Constitution. In Italy and Germany, for example, Constitutions were drafted in the late 1940s but have been amended over time. In 2022, the Italian Parliament introduced a new version of Articles 9 and 41: Article 9 now includes the environment, biodiversity, and ecosystems in the interest

---

[37] Peel and Osofsky (2018).

[38] The United Nations General Assembly adopted the Universal Declaration of Human Rights on December 10, 1948. The Japanese Constitution was promulgated in 1947, the Italian Constitution was enacted in 1948, and the German Basic Law the following year. The ECHR was adopted in 1950.

of future generations, and Article 41 now provides that free enterprise should benefit society, respect the right to health, human dignity, and the environment.[39]

The different historical backgrounds of the legal sources leveraged in climate litigation matters for plaintiffs, as the law crystalizes the social tensions of a specific society at a given time. Similarly, fundamental rights are not immutable—they are constantly confronted with evolving sensitivities and novel threats. Environmental and climate protection are among those new urges seeking legal recognition. However, not all constitutions provide explicit provisions in this regard; once again, plaintiffs' creativity is crucial to successfully anchor climate litigation claims to legal sources conceived in the past. Another relevant issue is the relationship between international and national law. In some jurisdictions, human rights provided by international law apply directly to all citizens. In The Netherlands, for example, individuals can claim ECHR directly before Courts.[40] Conversely, in Italy, the Constitutional Court has held that the provisions of the ECHR are not directly effective.[41]

Considering the diversified legal context of each jurisdiction, human rights-based climate litigation can be divided into three categories: cases based on fundamental rights protecting the individual, claims that rely on the implied existence of a right to a safe climate or the public trust doctrine and claims leveraging provisions that recognize the right to a safe climate. The first category includes those claims based on individual fundamental rights protecting human dignity, life, health, and private property, usually protected under constitutional or treaty provisions. The argument here is that governments, or carbon majors, are contributing to climate change, with their actions or omissions, in a way that harms the Plaintiff's rights.

For example, in *Mathur vs. Ontario*[42] (*Mathur*), the applicants sought declaratory and mandatory orders against the Province of Ontario to set more stringent emission targets and a more ambitious plan for combating climate change over the coming 10 years. In addition, they argued that the government's initiative to repeal the Climate Change Act violated Applicants' rights, protected by sections 7 and 15 of the Canadian Charter of Fundamental Rights.[43] In *Urgenda*, plaintiffs based their claim on Articles 2 and 8 of the ECHR, protecting life and private and family life, and sought an order to reduce Dutch emissions by 40% compared to 1990 levels. Similarly, *Shell* was based on Articles 2 and 8 of the ECHR combined with the Dutch tort law provisions. The argument was that the Shell's GHG emissions, including Scope 3 emissions, violate the duty of care that generally prevents

---

[39] Constitutional Law n. 1, February 11, 2022.

[40] See Nollkaemper (1998).

[41] See the Italian Constitutional Court extensive case law on the indirect effects of the ECHR in the Italian jurisdictions: judgment No. 80 of 2011 and judgments No. 348 and No. 349 of 2007. Conversely, all Courts involved in Urgenda accepted the idea that Articles 2 and 8 ECHR apply directly to Dutch residents.

[42] *Mathur vs. Ontario*, Ontario Superior Court of Justice, case No. 2020 ONSC 6918.

[43] *Canadian Charter of Rights and Freedoms*, s 7, Part 1 of the *Constitution Act*, 1982, being Schedule B to the *Canada Act 1982* (UK), 1982, c 11.

anyone—private or public actor—from harming others. While climate change is one of the factual elements composing the cause of action, in all these cases, the primary objective is protecting the individuals' fundamental rights, not the climate.

In jurisdictions lacking explicit constitutional provisions that establish a right to a safe environment or climate, some plaintiffs have developed arguments based on the implied existence of a right to a safe climate or the public trust doctrine. The common characteristic is the evolving interpretation of existing rights or legal theories to achieve climate protection. The recent Italian case *A Sud* et al. *vs. Italy*[44] (*Giudizio Universale*) is partially based on the implied existence of a right to a safe environment, and the plaintiffs requested the Court to order the government to reduce national emissions according to the PA obligations. In *Juliana*, the plaintiffs argued that the defendants violated their rights to life, freedom, and private property. They also argued that the defendants knowingly endangered the atmosphere, which is a vital component of the public trust. The public trust doctrine roots back to Roman law; it was further developed in the 1970s by prominent legal scholars to protect the natural heritage.[45] Recently, it has been argued that the scope of the public trust doctrine should be extended to the atmosphere, considering that the latter is a public good and respecting certain GHG thresholds responds to the general interest to live in a sustainable climate. *Juliana* is part of a vaster wave of cases named atmospheric trust litigation launched in the US by Our Children Trust.[46]

A third category includes claims that leverage the explicit recognition of a right to a safe environment or climate by constitutions or other legal instruments. In *ENvironnement JEUnesse vs. Procureur General du Canada*[47] (*La Jeunesse*), the plaintiffs alleged the violation of the right to live in a "healthful environment in which biodiversity is preserved" under the explicit provision of Article 46.1 of the Québec Charter of Human Rights and Freedoms.

3.6.3 Jurisdiction Levels

Another relevant factor in assessing strategic climate litigation is the forum available to or chosen by the plaintiffs to hear the case. Cases have generally been adjudicated in three layers of jurisdiction: (i) at national, state or provincial level; (ii) at the constitutional or highest court level; and (iii) at the supra-national or regional level.

First-level court cases: falling under this category are *Leghari*, *Urgenda*, *Juliana*, *Mathur*, and *Giudizio Universale*. In *Leghari*, *Juliana*, and *Mathur*, the cause of action lay directly in constitutional rights, while *Urgenda* and *Giudizio Universale*

---

[44] The ENGO A Sud together with over 200 Plaintiffs filed on 5 June 2021 a lawsuit against the Italian government alleging the violation of fundamental rights including the right to a stable and safe climate.

[45] See Sax (1970).

[46] See Our Children Trust's website via https://www.ourchildrenstrust.org/mission-statement.

[47] *ENvironnement JEUnesse vs. Procureur Général du Canada*, Cour Supérieure, Province de Québec, District de Montréal (Canada), 26 November 2018.

coupled constitutional rights with tort law provisions. The causes of action were all based on fundamental rights, and the relief sought was an order to reduce emissions compatible with the PA to protect the rights to life, health, security of the person, and private property. In Leghari and *Juliana*, plaintiffs requested the drafting of a plan containing sufficiently ambitious climate actions.

Constitutional claims: In the *Neubauer* case, fundamental rights were actioned directly before the German Constitutional Court requesting a declaration of unconstitutionality of the specific national provisions regulating GHG emissions. Resorting to constitutional courts may present a substantial advantage, as it allows for a direct court intervention – modification indeed – on the legal source deemed incompatible with fundamental rights. In addition, such direct access eliminates the delays and costs of several prior lower court hearings.

Supra-national jurisdictions: some important climate-related fundamental rights cases have been brought to supra-national courts and tribunals based on fundamental rights recognized by international or regional instruments. In *Innuit Petition,*[48] plaintiffs resorted to the Inter-American Commission on Human Rights (IACHR) against the United States and Canada for their omissions in preventing climate change. The IACHR rejected the petition due to insufficient information provided to the Commission.

Carvalho and Others vs. Parliament and Council[49] (*People's Case*) provides another example of a fundamental rights-based claim. The plaintiffs were families living across the EU who, for various reasons, alleged to have been harmed in their fundamental rights due to climate change. They sought the annulment of the EU legislative package regulating emissions,[50] under Article 263 of the Treaty on the Functioning of the European Union (TFEU), as well as compensation in kind for breach of non-contractual liability, under Article 340 TFEU. Both actions were based on the violation of fundamental rights threatened by climate change. The claim was first dismissed by the General Court and then appealed to the European Court of Justice (ECJ)[4]. The case was dismissed on procedural grounds for lack of standing. The applicants were found missing sufficient "individual concern" under Article 263(4) TFEU, as shaped by the ECJ judgment *Plaumann*.[51] Despite the right to an effective remedy under Article 47 of the European Charter of Fundamental Rights (EUCFR) and Article 9(2) of the Aarhus Convention, the ECJ held that the plaintiffs lacked standing as they could not show "individual concern" given that anyone is potentially affected by climate change. The result is paradoxical, the wider the effects of a supposedly harmful act, the more restricted the access to justice will be. In action for damages, the plaintiffs sought compensation "in kind" for the

[48] *Sheila Watt-Cloutier, et al. vs. United States*, Inter-American Commission on Human Rights, Petition No. P-1413-05, 16 November 2006.

[49] *Armando Carvalho and Others vs. European Parliament and Council of the European Union,* Court of Justice of the European Union, Case C-565/19 P, 25 March 2021.

[50] Directive (EU) 2018/410, the Regulation (EU) 2018/842, and Regulation (EU) 2018/841.

[51] *Plaumann & Co. v Commission of the European Economic Community*, European Court of Justice, case No. 25-62, ECLI:EU:C:1963:17.

extra-contractual liability of the EU institutions in the form of an order to modify the legislative package. The ECJ noted the equivalence of the two claims and dismissed also the request for compensation.

In *Duharte Agostinho and Others vs. Portugal and Others*[52] (*Duharte Agostinho*), six young Portuguese citizens filed a claim directly with the European Court of Human Rights (ECtHR) against Portugal and 32 other countries. The plaintiffs alleged that the respondents' inaction infringed their fundamental rights. This case is particularly interesting because the plaintiffs skipped their national courts and resorted directly to the ECtHR, despite Article 35(1) of the ECHR requiring the Plaintiffs to have resorted to all available remedies in their respective national jurisdictions. The plaintiffs argued that they could not obtain an effective remedy before a domestic court. In their view, a Portuguese court lacks jurisdiction against other foreign governments; the urgency of the "climate emergency" requires a top-down approach; finally, the plaintiffs do not have the resources to sue all 32 respondents before their national courts. This case takes multi-party cross-border litigation to a new level and raises some serious arguments on the issue of effective judicial remedies.

Comparing national, constitutional, and supra-national courts leads to some considerations. National courts are in general the only judicial resort for claims against actors the private sector, while it might be more effective to pursue strategic ambitions directly before constitutional or international courts. The *Neubauer*, *Inuit Petition*, the *People's Case*, and *Duharte Agostinho* prove that it makes sense for plaintiffs to opt for a top-down approach, which presents substantial procedural effectiveness advantages with respect to the remedy. If plaintiffs reach a positive result, the judgment rendered by constitutional or supra-national courts does not need further enforcement. Constitutional courts can annul unlawful legislative provisions, while international courts can declare that the climate policy of one or even multiple governments violates international law. This is certainly a meaningful advantage considering the need for urgent global action. However, there may still be significant procedural hurdles to bringing cases, as shown in particular by the cases concerning the international level immediately above.

3.7 Conclusion: Enforcing Climate Rights Through Litigation

Section 3 of this Chapter showed that climate litigation responds to an increasing urge for access to justice across countries and social settings. Some plaintiffs bring claims because they see a discrepancy between government policies and the need to tackle climate change decisively.[53] Others are affected individually or want to hold

[52] *Duarte Agostinho and Others v. Portugal and Others* (communicated case), Application No. 39371/20.

[53] See Marx et al. (2017).

the private sector accountable or leverage litigation to push toward a more sustainable society. Personal motives, causes of actions, and court actions are different and fast evolving.

Strategic litigation against governments or actors in the private sector constitutes a way to protect fundamental rights enshrined in constitutions or international charters endangered by climate change. It is also a means, complementary to the political process, to enforce international commitments. Claims seeking monetary damages are also constitutionally relevant as they can help recover financial losses deriving from fundamental rights violations. Both statutory- and fundamental rights-based claims contribute secure the interest of living in a sustainable climate system.

The constitutional relevance of climate litigation arguably requires effective procedural rules that allow plaintiffs to access courts and provide adequate judicial protection to diffuse fundamental rights and interests. However, often plaintiffs must spend time and resources dealing with procedural objections raised by the defendant on the issue of standing and justiciability; they also have a hard time sustaining their burden of proof. The following Section argues that traditional standing, justiciability, and evidence rule constitute serious obstacles to access to justice.

4 Outdated Standing, Justiciability and Evidence Rules

4.1 Introduction

Sections 4.2 and 4.3 explore further cases showing how traditional standing and justiciability rules can hamper plaintiff's access justice climate litigation. Similar complaints face different domestic jurisdictions and procedural rules. Despite national differences, there is an emerging trend across all climate litigation categories and jurisdictions: standing and justiciability are genuine concerns for plaintiffs everywhere as already evidenced by the cases presented above. Many cases are being dismissed on motions to strike before even considering the merits. Other times, defendants leverage the lack of standing or justiciability to appeal up to the highest courts, draining the plaintiff's finances and delaying any decision on the merits.

Standing rules identify who, among the general public, is sufficiently entitled to claim rights and interests. Climate litigation highlights a paradox: the more comprehensive the harm claimed by plaintiffs, the harder it is to pass the standing test. In effect, standing seems to be a difficult hurdle to overcome, especially in strategic litigation, which is oriented at protecting the public interest. The issue of justiciability concerns the fine line between political power and court jurisdiction in matters of public interest. Establishing the limits of the judiciary when plaintiffs seek vindication of fundamental rights and public interests can be particularly difficult in strategic cases as emerged in some of the cases presented above.

If plaintiffs overcome the procedural hurdles of standing and justiciability, the next major obstacle is sustaining the burden of proof. Based on traditional evidence rules, providing sufficient evidence is complex and potentially costly. Before and during the proceedings, plaintiffs spend significant time and financial resources to present and prove facts requiring scientific knowledge and expert witnesses' involvement. Section 4.3 will explore the complexities in proving the burden of proof.

4.2 Standing Rules

In *Verein KlimaSeniorinnen Schweiz vs. Bundesrat* (*KlimaSeniorinnen*),[54] the association KlimaSeniorinnen, representing older ladies, and four individuals, sued the Swiss Federal Government and several agencies.[55] The plaintiffs argued that climate change and heatwaves exposed them to life-threatening health problems. The plaintiffs pointed out that women aged 75 years and over are subject to significantly higher risk during hot summers and are more severely affected than the general public. The measures taken by the Swiss Government were presented as insufficient for protecting the rights to life, foreseen by article 10 of the Swiss Constitution, and to private and family life, under article 8 ECHR. The claim, however, was rejected for lack of standing, as the first and second instance courts held that the plaintiffs were insufficiently affected by climate change.[56]

The plaintiffs further appealed to the Federal Supreme Court, alleging a violation of the right to be heard and maintaining that they should have standing.[57] The Court, however, found that climate change did not affect the plaintiffs with sufficient intensity, as the threshold of 2 °C is not expected to be exceeded before 2040. Therefore, according to the Court, there is still time to prevent climate harm from materializing. Thus, the plaintiffs' rights were not affected with sufficient intensity, and standing was denied. The case has been brought to the ECtHR and is currently

[54] *Verein KlimaSeniorinnen Schweiz vs. Bundesrat*. The case was filed in 2016 and finally decided by the Swiss Supreme Court on 27 November 2018, after two previous decisions that had dismissed the case for lack of standing.

On 26 November 2020, the plaintiffs applied to the ECHR. The case has not been decided yet. On this case, see Bahr et al. (2018).

[55] The defendants are the Federal Council, the Federal Department of the Environment, Transport, Energy and Communications; the Federal Office for the Environment, and the Swiss Federal Office of Energy.

[56] The claim was initially dismissed by the Agency for Transport Energy and Communications, which ruled on behalf of all the Public Authorities addressed, then by the Federal Administrative Court.

[57] The Appellants claimed the violation of Article 29 of the Swiss Constitution and Article 6 ECHR, as the Federal Administrative Court did not fully engage with decisive factual and legal circumstances that would lead to the conclusion that women aged 75, and over, are actually "particularly affected" by climate change and have, therefore, standing.

pending. Whatever the ECtHR will find on this matter, this case in addition to many of the cases already presented above indicates how difficult it is to have strategic claims heard on the merits. The suit was indeed consistently rejected at all levels of the Swiss courts, based on the fact that climate change creates diffuse harm with long-term and progressive effects.

Standing is a serious concern for plaintiffs, even in group litigation in which it poses issues regarding the class definition. A too-broad or narrow class definition faces the risk of dismissal for arbitrariness or lack of sufficient commonality. In the Canadian class action *La Jeunesse*, plaintiffs pleaded that the Canadian government's emission targets are insufficient and therefore violated the class members' rights to life, inviolability, and security, protected under section 7 of the Canadian Charter of Fundamental Rights and section 1 of the Québec Charter. Plaintiffs also claimed that the Canadian government violated the right to a healthful environment in which biodiversity is preserved, foreseen by the Québec Charter.

The Superior Court of Quebéc found the claim justiciable in certain respects. However, the Court did not certify the class action based on the proposed class definition. First, the Court deemed the class definition arbitrary, as it was launched only on behalf of all residents of Quebéc aged under 35 and unreasonably excluded the older population whose rights could also be violated by climate change. Second, the class included all minors residing in the province of Québec; however, minors cannot act in court without their parent's representing them. Third, the Court deemed the class action useless, given that an individual claim would have an *erga omnes* effect reaching the same results as a class action. Following on appeal, the Court of Appeal dismissed the case based on the different justiciability issues. Nonetheless, the first instance decision remains relevant because it proves that the widespread effects of climate change make it hard to establish standing even using the class action device.

In contrast, the plaintiffs were successful and overcame the hurdle of standing in the *Urgenda* case. However, due to the Dutch government's appeals, it took 5 years of litigation, mainly on procedural matters, for the original decision to be conclusively upheld. The Supreme Court found that, under Article 305a of the Dutch Civil Code,[58] the plaintiffs could sue on behalf of all residents in the Netherlands to protect their right to life and private and family life, protected by Articles 2 and 8 ECHR. The decision also noted that Article 305a of the Dutch Civil Code, i.e. the procedural mechanism of a representative action, is well suited for those cases where plaintiffs invoke harm to diffuse interests—such as in environmental matters.[59] Finally, the Court found that standing must also be granted based on the right to an effective remedy under Article 13 ECHR and 9(3) in conjunction with Article

[58] Art. 305a of the Dutch Civil Code grants standing to bring public interest suits to foundations established to protect public interests. See Loth (2016).

[59] ECLI:NL:HR(2019(2007, Hoge Raad, par. 5.9.2.

2(5) of the Aarhus Convention, which guarantees interest groups access to justice in environmental matters.[60]

Cases aimed at recovering damages seem exempt from procedural objections on standing (and justiciability) as plaintiffs claim an individual right, such as in the *Luciano Lliuyac* case, where a Peruvian farmer based his claim on his property rights endangered by a melting glacier lake waters. Even though plaintiffs might also pursue idealistic objectives and symbolic compensations, their claims follow the traditional patterns of individual litigation. Seeking redress for financial losses helps prevent procedural objections on standing and justiciability.

4.3 Justiciability

In *Gloucester Recources*, the mining company objected that the Court could not prohibit the development of the proposed new open-cut coal mine based on the PA provisions. The company argued that, without national provisions banning new coal mines, a policy of "no new coal mines" in Australia, determined by the Court solely based on the PA, would result in a legislative act and a consequent violation of the separation of powers principle.

In *Shell*, the defendant made a similar argument noting that it did not violate any statutory limit nor the European Emission Trading System (ETS).[61] The Court rejected this objection considering that the tort law *neminem laedere* principle is an open norm, which does not require the breach of explicit legal provisions. Unwritten rules of care are sufficient to establish tortious responsibility. The GHGs produced by Shell were therefore deemed unlawful even without any reference to explicit national provisions. The Court added that the EU "cap and trade" ETS system does not limit the Court's ability to evaluate if the overall emissions—including those produced outside the EU –violate the general duty of care under tort law. Combining the PA with the civil law notion of duty of care helped the Court establish that the claim was justiciable.

In *Juliana*, the Court dismissed the case maintaining that the claim was not "redressable," as the remedy sought by the plaintiffs could be enforced without stepping into the political province. Redressability, at its core, involves the separation of powers in the context of judgment's enforcement.[62]

[60] Convention on Access to Information, Public Participation in Decision-Making and Access to Justice in Environmental Matters, 25 June 1998 (Aarhus Convention).

[61] Directive 2003/87/EC of the European Parliament and of the Council of 13 October 2003.

[62] The case is now continuing, as plaintiffs modified the request for relief. It is nonetheless clear how the issue of justiciability posed a significant obstacle, supposedly draining the Plaintiff's resources: The claim was filed in 2015, and the Court has not even heard the merits.

The issue of justiciability was also discussed in *Urgenda* as the Defendant argued that it is up to the government and the Parliament to set Dutch climate policy.[63] The Court managed to overcome the government's objections, finding that in a democratic state, it is the Court's role to protect fundamental rights, even if the government's climate policy allegedly commits the violation. On the other hand, the Court made sure not to overstep into the political sphere and explicitly left it to the government to determine how to achieve the 40% emissions reductions. Also, the ruling clarified that it was not an order to create legislation, as the defendant could choose what tools to use.

The cases mentioned above range across all categories of climate litigation. It seems that the justiciability argument is relevant both in claims against governments and the private sector. However, these two categories develop their objections differently. Companies tend to object that courts cannot find them responsible for excessive emissions or stop their development projects if their activity does not violate explicit national provisions. Some companies also maintain that the PA does not apply to them. In their view, any decision against the private sector based on the PA would be equivalent to introducing new legislative requirements by the Court with the consequential violation of the separation of powers. Governments argue that courts cannot determine climate policy, as climate change involves many wide-ranging policy issues that fall outside the scope of the court's jurisdiction. That line of argument results in holding a position that climate change is subjected only to discretional political power – regardless of fundamental rights.

Conversely, justiciability does not appear to be a problem in claims to recover damages. Claiming damages plaintiffs vindicate individual rights rather than a public interest. Hence, they resort to the traditional function of jurisdictional power without trying to achieve political change in Court. Juxtaposing claims for damages and strategic litigation sheds light on the real issue behind justiciability rules. Traditional procedural rules are rooted in the idea that Courts can only adjudicate individual rights. Climate litigation, however, is, for the most part, public interest litigation. Plaintiffs act on their interests as well as on behalf of others. It could be a local community or the general public. As a result, the legal community must rethink the judiciary's role if it is considered important to extend the access justice to the fragmented interest and rights of a healthy environment and atmosphere.

4.4 Evidence Rules

In strategic cases against governments based on the violation of fundamental rights, plaintiffs must usually quantify the national GHGs emissions and present how such emissions are inconsistent with those allowed by the carbon budget under the

[63] See Loth (2018).

PA. Plaintiffs must then prove the significant threat to fundamental rights, the environment, or the public trust and the causal link between government's inaction, the subsequent emissions, and rights violations. In *Klimaseniorinnen*, the plaintiffs proved with medical records how their health was being affected by heatwaves, while in *Juliana*, each presented and proved how climate change affected their rights. In *Urgenda*, the Supreme Court confirmed the existence of a causal link between the government's regulatory omissions, Dutch GHG emissions, and the threat to fundamental rights.[64]

When the claim is based on tort law, the plaintiffs must usually prove the violation of a duty of care or diligence, hence that the government has knowingly allowed more emissions than those permitted under the PA. The IPCC reports are helpful as the IPCC represents 195 countries, and its reports determine the reduction targets and the different risk scenarios. In *Urgenda*, for example, the Court relied on the 4th Assessment Report, according to which developed countries should have reduced emissions by 25–40% by 2020 compared to 1990. Yet, IPCC reports cannot prove the causal link between GHGs, and the individual plaintiffs involved in the proceedings.

In strategic litigation against actors in the private sector plaintiffs must often quantify the emissions produced by the company, substantiate that such emissions pose a danger to the plaintiffs' rights, and establish a sufficient causal link between the emissions and violation of the relevant rights. In *Shell,* the Court recognized that the Dutch holding company controls over 1100 subsidiaries worldwide and, given its policy-setting role held that it is directly or indirectly responsible for scope 1, 2, and 3 emissions produced by the entire group of companies. The Court also held that the whole group is liable for emissions that exceed those of the Netherlands and, therefore, have substantial effects on global emissions. This allowed the Court to draw a line of causation between the conduct of *Shell* and the adverse effects on climate change for individual plaintiffs. Establishing causation is naturally different in cases aimed at stopping development plans, such as in *Gloucester Resource*. The burden of proof falls on the inconsistency between the specific project and the national carbon budget rather than the threat to the plaintiff's rights.

An additional burden of proof is at hand when the aim is to recover damages, as demonstrated by *Luciano Lliuya*. In such cases, the plaintiffs must prove a personal economic loss, that the company's emissions have contributed to climate change in a non-trivial and quantifiable way, that the damages are a consequence of climate change, and, finally, the percentage of responsibility attributable to the individual defendants for the specific economic damages. In *Luciano Lliuya,* the first instance court rejected the claim based on a lack of sufficient evidence on causation, holding that it is impossible to attribute the alleged damage to RWE AG given the multiple factors that cause climate change. After a successful appeal the matter is now pending as noted above. Nevertheless, the case shows that establishing causality in damages cases can be significant hurdle.

---

[64]Preston (2020b).

Finally, in Native Village of Kivalina vs. ExxonMobil Corp.[65] *(Kivalina)* the inhabitants of the Alaskan village of Kivalina filed a public nuisance claim against ExxonMobil and other companies, seeking damages deriving from the necessity to relocate the village inland due to climate change-induced coastal erosion. Applying the fair traceability test as a threshold for causality, the Court maintained that the plaintiffs failed to demonstrate a substantial likelihood that the defendants' emissions caused the alleged injuries. The Court held that climate change results from numerous emissions sources over the years and could not be traced back to the individual defendants.

Thus, proving the causal link is costly, requiring plaintiffs to spend time and resources on complex matters, expert fees, and possible appeals. It entails long preparation before a case can be brought to Court. For example, effectively using attribution science requires combining legal and scientific expertise from the early stage of a climate case. A recent study analyzed 73 climate litigation cases and proved how there seems to be a disconnect between what up-to-date attribution science can prove and the facts presented to courts or the content of judicial decisions.[66] Given the scientific feasibility of allocating individual responsibilities for climate change-related injuries, it is necessary to present the correct facts scientifically attributable to climate change and submit evidence demonstrating a causal link. Therefore, cooperation between scientists and lawyers is critical.

4.5 Conclusion: Outdated Procedural Rules Entail Longer and More Risky Court Proceedings

As noted above, a common objection of the defendants in strategic litigation is that plaintiffs lack standing and that the subject matter of the litigation is not justiciable. In strategic climate litigation, standing rules appear inadequate because climate change produces diffuse and fragmented harm, which, according to the best available science, is increasing over time. For example, rising sea levels threaten certain coastal areas, and older people are more exposed to heat waves. But it is difficult to establish that all people in those categories, each plaintiff, are or will undoubtedly be affected by climate change-related events. It is even more complex to establish standing when the damage has not occurred yet, and the claim is brought to Court on behalf of future generations.

Justiciability can also be a severe concern for plaintiffs that undertake strategic claims even though an appropriate framing of the relief sought can help overcome such an issue. The justiciability argument is often based on the consideration that any solution to climate change necessarily requires vast political solutions that courts

[65] Native Village of Kivalina vs. ExxonMobil Corp., United States District Court for the Northern District of California, case No. 696 F.3d 849 (9th Cir. 2012).

[66] Stuart-Smith et al. (2021).

cannot adjudicate or micromanage, given the traditional procedural framework in civil law countries. Defendants often also argue that courts lack jurisdiction to enforce an order to reduce emissions. However, in *Leghari* the Lahore Court went as far as creating a commission to supervise the government's actions in compliance with the Court's ruling. So far this is an unprecedented decision, which would be difficult to replicate in civil law legal systems. Even if the plaintiffs do not require the courts' supervision, it is critical to frame the remedy sought considering the limits of domestic court's jurisdiction. *Urgenda* proved that fundamental rights are helpful, as they have historically been a natural limit to governments' discretionary power. Even if solutions applying existing rules are available, standing and justiciability objections make climate litigation longer and more expensive. This is also true if lawyers donate their work hours, as years of litigation to overcome procedural issues are a heavy burden.

Climate litigation reflects a trend that emerged already in the early 1970s when civil procedural law started facing the issue of group- and public-interest litigation addressing environmental, labour and consumer law matters. Mauro Cappelletti explored this topic extensively in his *Access to Justice and the Welfare State* research project.[67] Cappelletti argued that public interest litigation reflects the irresponsiveness of the political branches of government. Hence, courts get involved in legal and social issues, which necessarily require them to get involved in potentially politically relevant matters. At the same time, however, traditional standing and justiciability rules discriminate against diffuse and fragmented interests, as they are designed for individual claims. Courts must construe procedural law in a constitutionally oriented manner; if that does not happen, the danger is that courts cannot address widespread harm with a significant impact on human rights.

A possible solution is to resort directly to constitutional courts if such direct access is available, as in Germany. This way, while it might still be necessary to answer the question of standing, the issue of justiciability can be avoided, as constitutional courts have the power to assess the constitutionality of legislation, including national climate regulation. The further advantage is that no appeal can be filed, with significant savings of resources. Similarly, plaintiffs can potentially resort to supranational courts such as the ECJ, which can directly impact the EU law, or the ECHR, as in the ongoing case *Duharte Agostinho*. However, not all jurisdictions allow such a top-down approach. Furthermore, as a matter of principle, domestic procedural law should evolve so that access to justice is also granted to protect diffuse interests. After all, access to an effective remedy within one's national jurisdiction is a human right, too.

[67] Kötz (1981), p 102.

5 The IBA Model Statute: Ideas for Procedural Law Reform

The previous sections pointed out how climate litigation, in its various forms and aims, is constitutionally relevant and stressed how the issues of standing, justiciability, and burden of proof could often make access to justice uncertain, lengthy, and costly for plaintiffs. This final section introduces the proposals made by the International Bar Association (IBA) in its 2020 Model Statute for Proceedings Challenging Government Failure to Act on Climate Change (the "Model Statute"). The document's wording clarifies that the Model Statute is meant to apply exclusively to climate litigation against governments. However, nothing precludes extending these rules to litigation against actors in the private sector.

The Model Statute is composed of 23 Articles. After defining fundamental notions (Article 1) and the scope of application (Article 2), it then proposes procedural rule reforms on the matters of standing (Articles 4, 5, and 17), rules of evidence (Articles 5–16), remedies and justiciability (Article 18), costs rules (Articles 19–23). In the subsequent section focus is placed on the key proposals on standing, justiciability, and evidence. The IBA proposals on these issues are feasible solutions that the EU, or national legislation, could implement to make climate justice more accessible.

5.1 The IBA Proposals to Overcome the Issue of Standing

The Model Statute impliedly acknowledges that in most jurisdictions standing rules require plaintiffs to be entitled to the rights claimed and, second, show the remedy sought would bring effective benefits. The judicial protection of fragmented interests poses challenges to both issues, as nobody is exclusively entitled to the right to a safe environment, and one single judgment cannot be decisive in fighting climate change.

Article 4 of the Model Statute proposes to adopt "open standing." Anyone may seek a judicial order to curb GHG emissions, even if their individual rights are not infringed, as long as they raise a serious issue. What "serious" means could be subject to debate, but procedural law necessarily requires the use of ample notions. The real benefit of open standing is to undock standing from the current individualistic conceptions of substantive law. Rights entitlement can be individual or shared. Some human rights, such as those concerning the environment and the climate, are necessarily shared. Nobody can seriously claim an exclusive relationship with public goods. Yet procedural law seems to ignore that. The Model Statute, however, pursues a different notion of how the law should regulate climate-related human rights and their judicial protection.

The IBA's proposal finds its roots in legal traditions across the globe. For example, in Canada, in case of environmental harm, Ontario's 1993 Environmental

Bill of Rights[68] allows anyone to bring an action for public nuisance regardless of personal loss or injury. Likewise, in Australia, the New South Wales Environmental Planning and Assessment Act[69] grants access to the Court regardless of the infringement of individual rights. Similar provisions are contained in Michigan's Natural Resources and Environmental Protection Act, the Rules of Procedure for Environmental Cases in the Philippines,[70] and the Ecuadorian Constitution.[71] In light of Article 9(3) of the Aarhus Convention, which requires signatory parties to allow access to justice in environmental matters, it seems plausible that this solution might also be implementable in the EU.

The Model statute also addresses the intergenerational dimension of climate change, allowing plaintiffs to represent future generations. Such a provision would fit the exponential threat to fundamental rights posed by climate change. The recent *Neubauer* and *Mathur* rulings accepted the need to represent in Court's future generations. This provision reflects the idea that climate and environmental rights are shared between the present and future generations.

5.2 The IBA Proposals to Overcome the Issue of Justiciability

Justiciability has proved to be a genuine and potentially costly concern for plaintiffs. In strategic litigation against governments and the private sector any judicial order to reduce GHGs emissions is confronted with the principle of separation of powers. Defendants argue that it is not for the courts to shape climate policy. The Model Statute tackles justiciability from two perspectives.

First, and in principle, Article 18 of the Model Statute proposes a suite of remedial measures allowing courts to issue declaratory relief and order government to reduce emission. While rendering an order against governments is normal in most jurisdictions, an explicit provision allowing a judicial order to curb emissions would simplify the plaintiff's legal arguments on justiciability.

Second, Article 18 enables courts to monitor the government's actions after the issuance of an order. This rule extends the court's jurisdiction beyond the decision providing it with supervising powers over the government. Supervision might be enforced by an order to a public authority to monitor the execution of the order or by a duty to submit reports to the court. This provision relates to the common law notion of "appropriate remedy," which, in some human rights cases, allowed courts to retain jurisdiction over the execution of their orders. In *Leghari*, the Court went as far as creating a commission composed of government officials and NGOs. In the linguistic minority rights case *Doucet-Boudreau vs. Nova Scotia*, the Canadian Supreme

[68] See, par 103(1) of the Ontario's 1993 Environmental Bill of Rights.

[69] See, par 9.45 of the 1979 New South Wales Environmental Planning and Assessment Act.

[70] See Rule 2, § 4 of the Rules of Procedure for Environmental Cases 2010 AM No 09-6-8 SC.

[71] See Article 71 of the 2008 Ecuador's Constitution.

Court held that, based on Section 24 of the Canadian Charter of Fundamental Rights and Freedoms, Canadian judges can require governments to take affirmative actions and to report back on the progress made to rectify a breach of fundamental rights. Considering that Section 24 requires courts to grant an "appropriate remedy," the Supreme Court ruled that it is appropriate for the judiciary to supervise the government's action. In order to do so, the Provincial Government was required to report on the measures taken to ensure the education rights of the French minority.[72] In Environmental matters, the 1993 Ontario Environmental Bill of Rights grants a similar power to Canadian courts, as its §93(1) provides for negotiating a plan of restoration and a duty to report to the court on its implementation.

The Pakistani and Canadian jurisdictions prove that Article 18 of the IBA Model Statute could be implemented in those jurisdictions that recognize broad judicial discretionary power for granting an appropriate remedy. Conversely, Article 18 does not fit well with civil law jurisdictions that are traditionally based on legislative predetermination of subjective rights and remedies. In civil law systems, however, enforcement could be secured through pecuniary penalties for the delay in enforcing a judgment.[73]

5.3 The IBA Proposals on Evidence Rules

Providing sufficient evidence is complex, given the need to present complex facts and scientific knowledge in an accessible way. Especially in claims for damages, proving causation requires skilful use of attribution science to allocate marginal responsibility to significant individual emitters in the face of uncountable GHG sources across space and time.

Article 6 of the Model Statute proposes that courts take judicial notice of the findings contained in IPCC Reports. Thus, plaintiffs could refer to the IPCC Reports to prove the causes and effects of climate change. Article 6 also reverses the burden of proof on defendants concerning the content of IPCC Reports. If adopted, such a provision would greatly unburden the plaintiffs; it might also reduce the plaintiff's submissions in terms of sheer volume.

Article 7 of the Model Statute lists all the various government-produced records on GHG emissions as admissible evidence. In most climate litigation cases, various documents prepared by public agencies are already being used to quantify the emissions for which governments are accountable. Similarly, the same may be foreseen for claims against the private sector, as major companies usually produce

---

[72] Doucet-Boudreau v. Nova Scotia (Minister of Education), 2003 SCC 62 (CanLII), [2003] 3 SCR 3. Full text available here: https://www.canlii.org/en/ca/scc/doc/2003/2003scc62/2003scc62.html.

[73] For example, the French law foresees the *astreintes*. Similar systems are provided by Article 614-bis of the Italian Code of Civil Procedure and by §§ 888 and 889 of the German ZPO and §§ 354 and 355 of the Austrian ZPO.

records of their emissions. Among the list of admissible evidence, Article 7 of the Model Statute mentions peer-reviewed government studies and information deriving from climate models. Such pieces of evidence seem to be already admissible in most jurisdictions if combined with the testimony of expert witnesses. However, the IBA Model Statute proposes to make such government studies acceptable per se and recommends that courts, at their discretion, may regard them as sufficient to adjudicate the relief sought by plaintiffs.

Article 9 proposes to apply the precautionary principle to climate litigation. As a result, Article 9 flips the burden of proof requiring the defendant to prove that its actions do not impact on climate change or that the risk for the plaintiffs is negligible. Article 9 would greatly facilitate plaintiffs, as the lack of complete scientific certainty should arguably not impede a court from granting relief. Article 9 has solid roots in international law and many national jurisdictions. The precautionary principle is a longstanding legal mechanism for environmental protection and is stated by Principle 15 of the 1992 Rio Declaration.[74] Following Article 191 of the Treaty on the Functioning of the European Union, European jurisdictions foresee the same principle in their environmental legislations, such as in Article 301 of the Italian Environmental Code.[75] In Canada, the precautionary principle is recognized by the Canadian Environmental Protection Act,[76] the Canadian Environmental Assessment Act, and in Supreme Court case law.[77]

The Model Statute could also be a game-changer for Plaintiffs based on joint interpretation of standing and evidence provisions. Open standing allows anyone to vindicate the public interest rather than individual rights. Therefore, the burden of proof would only concern the origins and causes of climate change for a geographical area or a specific demographic, regardless of the individual Plaintiffs. The IPCC Reports and government documents extensively prove these matters. Further, the precautionary principle would require the Defendant to prove their actions are harmless. In such a hypothetical regulatory setting, climate justice would be genuinely accessible.

[74] 1992 Rio Declaration on Environment and Development, adopted after the United Nations Conference on Environment and Development, held in Rio De Janairo from 3-14 June 1992.

[75] Art. 301 of the legislative decree 3 April 2006, n. 152.

[76] Canadian Environmental Protection Act, 1999 S.C. 1999, s. 2(1).

[77] *114957 Canada Ltée (Spraytech, Societé d'arrosage) vs. Hudson (Town)*, Supreme Court of Canada, case No. 2001 SCC 40, [2001] 2 SCR 241, at paras 31 and 31. On Canadian environmental law see, Estrin (1993). Also, see Muldoon et al. (2015).

6 Conclusion

In all its forms, climate litigation is a way to enforce human rights enshrined in constitutions and international treaties. While a political solution to climate change is necessary and preferable, courts play a role in mitigating climate injustice. In this scenario, the IBA Model Statue provides feasible model rules on standing, justiciability, and evidence rules that could form the basis for future potential reform. In addition, the Model Statute taps into procedural techniques developed in environmental law across multiple domestic jurisdictions, offering a solid background experience for legislators.

The core takeaway from the IBA experiment is that the global legal community should rethink the role of procedural law in light of the growing need for public interest litigation. Mauro Cappelletti's *Access to Justice* project is still an authoritative reference point.[78] He raised the need to reshape the judiciary's role in constitutional democracies with regard to fragmented interests.[79] Procedural law should free itself from the outdated and narrow conception that limits its function to deal only with individual disputes. While traditional individual claims will remain, the entitlement to some rights is inherently shared among multiple persons. Climate litigation shows that in a dramatic way. Common goods, such as the atmosphere and the environment, cannot be merely individual. Substantive and procedural law should acknowledge and protect fragmented and collective interests to which nobody is entitled exclusively. One way to do that is to reform substantive law by recognizing such emerging rights in constitutions, treaties, and statutory law. At the same time, scholars and legislators should develop new procedural devices geared toward the protection of fragmented interests.

Case Law

114957 *Canada Ltée (Spraytech, Societé d'arrosage) vs. Hudson (Town)*, Supreme Court of Canada, case No. 2001 SCC 40, [2001] 2 SCR 241

Ashgar Leghari vs. *Federation of Pakistan* (WP No. 25501/2015), Lahore High Court Green Bench, Orders of 4 and 14 September 2015.

City of Charleston vs. Brabham Oil Company Inc. et al., case No. 2:20-cv-03579-BHH

Earthlife Africa Johannesburg vs. Minister of Environmental Affairs and others, Case no. 65662/16 (2017).

Environnement Jeunessevs. Procureur Général du Canada, Cour Supérieure, Province de Québec, District de

[78] Kötz (1981). Firenze. See also Cappelletti and Garth (1978), p. 194.

[79] Cartabia (2016).

Gloucester Resources Limited vs. Minister for Planning, Land and Environment Court New South Wales, Australia, 8 February 2019. [2019] NSWLEC 7
Italian Supreme Court (*Corte di cassazione)*, judgment No. 25143 of 2020.
Juliana, US District Court for the District of Oregon, case No. 947 F.3d 1159 (9th Cir. 2020)
Luciano Lliuya vs. RWE AG, Landgericht Essen, Case No. 2 O 285/15
Mathur vs. Ontario, Ontario Superior Court of Justice, case No. 2020 ONSC 6918
Milieudefensie et al. *vs. Royal Dutch Shell plc*, The Hague District Court. 6 May 2021. ECLI:NL:RBDHA:2021:5339., paragraph 4.4.5
Montréal (Canada), 26 November 2018
Native Village of Kivalina vs. ExxonMobil Corp., United States District Court for the Northern District of California, case No. 696 F.3d 849 (9th Cir. 2012).
Neubauer et al. *vs. Germany*, German Constitutional Court (BVerfG), judgment of the First Senate of 24 March 2021, BvR 2656/18 -, paras. 243-245
Plaumann & Co. v Commission of the European Economic Community, European Court of Justice, case No. 25-62, ECLI: E.U.:C:1963:17
Urgenda vs. The Netherlands, Supreme Court of the Netherlands, 13 January 2020, ECLI:NL:HR:2019:2007
Urgenda vs. The Netherlands, The Hague Court of Appeal 9 October 2018, ECLI: NL:GHDHA:2018:2591. ECLI:NL:GHDHA:2018:2610
Urgenda vs. The Netherlands, The Hague District Court 24 June 2015, ECLI:NL: RBDHA:2015:7145. ECLI:NL:RBDHA:2015:7196
Third Runway at Vienna International Airport, Case No. W109 2000179-1/291E, Federal Administrative Court, Austria, 2 February 2017

References

Bahr C, Brunner U, Casper K, Lustig SH (2018) KlimaSeniorinnen: lessons from the Swiss senior women's case for future climate litigation. J Human Rights Environ 9(2):194–221
Cappelletti M, Garth B (1978) Access to justice: the newest wave in the worldwide movement to make rights effective. Buffalo Law Rev 27(2):181–292, 194
Cartabia M (2016) Mauro Cappelletti: one of the precious few of our generation. Int J Const Law 14(2):464–473
Dellinger M (2018) See you in court: around the world in eight climate change lawsuits. William Mary Environ Law Policy Rev 42(2):525–552
Diffenbaugh NS, Burke M (2019) Global warming has increased global economic inequality. Proc Natl Acad Sci U S A 116:9808–9813. https://doi.org/10.1073/pnas.1816020116
Estrin D (1993) Business guide to environmental law. Carswell, Toronto
Estrin D (2016) Limiting Dangerous Climate Change: The Critical Role of Citizen Suits and Domestic Courts—Despite the Paris Agreement. CIGI Papers No. 101. Available via https://www.cigionline.org/publications/limiting-dangerous-climate-change-critical-role-citizen-suits-and-domestic-courts/. Accessed 31 March 2022
Kötz H (1981) Public interest litigation: a comparative survey. In: Cappelletti M (ed) Access to justice and the welfare state, Firenze, pp 85–117
Leslie N (2016) IBA takes leading role in increasing awareness of climate change justice. J Energy Nat Res Law 34(1):7–15

Loth DMA (2018) The civil court as risk regulator: the issue of legitimacy. Eur J Risk Regul 9: 66–78

Loth M (2016) Climate change liability after all: Dutch landmark case. Tilburg Law Rev (Gaunt) 21(1):5–30

Malijean-Dubois S (2015) Climate change litigation. Oxford Public International Law, Oxford

Marx W, Haunschild R, French B et al (2017) Slow reception and under-citedness in climate change research: a case study of Charles David Keeling, discoverer of the risk of global warming. Scientometrics 112:1079–1092

Matthews HD, Tokarska KB, Rogelj J et al (2021) An integrated approach to quantifying uncertainties in the remaining carbon budget. Commun Earth Environ 2:7. https://doi.org/10.1038/s43247-020-00064-9

Muldoon P, Alastair L, Gibson RB, Pickfield P, Williams J (2015) An introduction to environmental law and policy in Canada. Emond Montgomery Publications Limited, Toronto

Nollkaemper A (1998) Judicial application of international environmental law in The Netherlands. Rev Eur Comp Int Environ Law 7(1):40–46

Peel J, Osofsky H (2018) A rights turn in climate change litigation? Transnatl Environ Law 7(1): 37–67. https://doi.org/10.1017/S2047102517000292

Peel J, Osofsky HM (2019) Litigation as a climate regulatory tool. In: Voigt C (ed) International judicial practice on the environment. Questions of Legitimacy. Cambridge

Preston BJ (2020a) The influence of the Paris agreement on climate litigation: legal obligations and norms (part I). J Environ Law 00:3–6

Preston JB (2020b) The influence of the Paris agreement on climate litigation: causation, corporate governance and catalyst (part II). J Environ Law 00:5

Sanson AVS, Burke SEL (2020) Climate change and children: an issue of intergenerational justice. In: Balvin N, Christie D (eds) Children and peace. Peace psychology book series. Springer, Cham, pp 243–259. https://doi.org/10.1007/978-3-030-22176-8_21

Sax J (1970) The public trust doctrine in natural resource law: effective judicial intervention. Mich Law Rev 68(3):471–566. https://doi.org/10.2307/1287556

Sindico F, Mbengue MM (eds) (2021) Comparative climate change litigation: beyond the usual suspects. Springer, Geneva

Spier J (2020) The "strongest" climate ruling yet: the Dutch Supreme Court's Urgenda Judgment. Neth Jud Decis Law Rev 67:319–391

Stuart-Smith RF, Otto FEL, Saad A et al (2021) Filling the evidentiary gap in climate litigation. Nat Clim Change 11:651–655. https://doi.org/10.1038/s41558-021-01086-7

Wegener L (2020) Can the Paris agreement help climate change litigation and vice versa? Transnatl Environ Law 9(1):24

Reports

Boyd R (2019) Report of the Special Rapporteur on the issue of human rights obligations relating to the enjoyment of a safe, clean, healthy and sustainable environment. A/74/161. https://www.ohchr.org/en/special-procedures/sr-environment/safe-climate-report

EPA (2021) Climate Change and Social Vulnerability in the United States: A Focus on Six Impacts. US Environmental Protection Agency, EPA 430-R-21-003. www.epa.gov/cira/social-vulnerability-report

IPCC (2007) Synthesis Report. Contribution of Working Groups I, II and III to the Fourth Assessment Report of the Intergovernmental Panel on Climate Change. In: Core Writing Team, Pachauri, RK, Reisinger A (eds) IPCC, Geneva, Switzerland

IPCC (2022) Climate Change 2022: Impacts, Adaption, and Vulnerability. https://www.ipcc.ch/report/ar6/wg2/downloads/report/IPCC_AR6_WGII_SummaryForPolicymakers.pdf. Accessed 30 March 2023

United Nations Environmental Program Report (2015) Climate Change and Human Rights. https://www.unep.org/resources/report/climate-change-and-human-rights. Accessed 30 March 2023

World Meteorological Organization (2021) Greenhouse Gas Bulletin No.17: The State of Greenhouse Gases in the Atmosphere Based on Global Observations through 2020

Simplification of Procedure

A Realistic (or Unrealistic) Alternative to Lawyer-Conducted Litigation?

Sebastian Wejedal

Contents

Abstract One of the greatest challenges facing courts throughout the world is undoubtedly the growing number of litigants in person; when confronted with the complexity of modern-day legal proceeding, unrepresented litigants are (in)famous for creating havoc. This problem can, however, be viewed from two different

---

S. Wejedal (✉)
Göteborg, Sweden
e-mail: Sebastian.Wejedal@crusner.se

E. Storskrubb (ed.), *YSEC Yearbook of Socio-Economic Constitutions 2022*,
YSEC Yearbook of Socio-Economic Constitutions (2023) 2022: 183–214,
https://doi.org/10.1007/16495_2023_48, Published online: 19 May 2023

perspectives: Some commentators perceive individuals' insufficient litigation skills as the key problem, to be solved by compelling litigants to rely on qualified counsel. Others argue that the level of complexity inherent in court litigation is the real problem, to be solved by simplifying the procedure. Unfortunately, both of these "solutions" create their own problems.

If a procedural system presumes that individuals are represented by counsel, then counsel fees must be alleviated to ensure that anyone can have "access to a lawyer" (and thereby "effective access to court"). Relieving parties of their lawyers' fees will, however, only shift costs from one subject to another. Ultimately, someone must pay. This explains why legislators have instead tried to "simplify the procedure" (thereby reducing the "need for counsel"). However, if individuals are to proceed without counsel, then the court must usually "help" the unrepresented party to conduct his/her case. This is not uncontroversial since it may contradict basic principles of procedural law, by blurring the line between the parties and the court.

In this chapter, the Swedish administrative procedure is used as an example to discuss the problems outlined above: Is simplification of procedure a realistic alternative to lawyer-conducted litigation? Drawing on empirical data regarding litigation outcomes for pro se litigants, this question is answered in the negative.

1 Introduction

> Legal fees rise, legal aid sinks, and LIPs flood the courts.[1]

In many jurisdictions (where legal representation is not mandatory[2]) it has become increasingly common for litigants to represent themselves in court.[3] This tendency towards self-representation can be explained by two distinct but interlinked developments: On the one hand, lawyers' fees are increasing; on the other hand, public spending on legal aid is decreasing. Consequently, a wave of litigants in person (LIP: s) is overflowing the courts.

[1] Sharpe (2016), p. 435.

[2] In this respect, the Swedish system is more reminiscent of common law, rather than civil law, jurisdictions; cf. Assy (2015), p. 1, who concludes that "common law countries regard self-representation as a fundamental right [while] most civil law systems take the oppositive view and impose obligations of legal representation in most proceedings".

[3] See Genn (2015), p. vii, who refers to "an unprecedented growth in self-representation" and, e.g., Zuckerman (2014), p. 355; Moorhead (2003), p. 133; Kramer and Kakiuchi (2015), p. 144; Dyer (2007), p. 718; Swank (2005a) p. 1539; Swank (2005b), p. 376; Zorza (2004), p. 423; Snukals and Sturtvant (2007), p. 93; Engler (1999), p. 1987; Cameron and Kelly (2002), p. 313; Zimerman and Tyler (2010), p. 478; Buhai (2009), p. 983.

1.1 Access to Lawyers (or "Lawyer-Less" Litigation?)

To proceed pro se is—for many reasons—not a walk in the park, especially not for laypersons without adequate legal training.[4] The rise in pro se litigation has therefore been described as "one of the most significant challenges" currently facing courts throughout the world.[5] At least three problems, all of which are well-documented in the scholarship, can be connected to the growing number of unrepresented litigants: (1) a lack of efficiency; (2) a lack of justice; and (3) a lack of equality.[6]

It has been observed that LIP:s are rarely able to comply with the rules of procedure and/or follow instructions from the court. This give rise to delays and—since time is money—increased costs for both counterparties and the court/society at large.[7] However, the damages that litigants in person inflict on themselves (by failing to represent themselves adequately) are even more troublesome. Studies have shown that parties who have access to a lawyer fare better (have higher "success rates", i.e., probability to win) than do unrepresented parties—a statistical finding commonly referred to as "the lawyer advantage".[8] In fact, the differences in outcome are, on an aggregated level, so great that it is safe to assume that a large number of LIP:s are losing cases that are in fact "winnable", simply because they lack access to a lawyer.[9] As Hazel Genn has rightfully stated, it should indeed be considered an injustice "when cases with legal merits are lost for want of representation".[10] Since this deficiency in the administration of justice typically affects only people who cannot afford to hire a lawyer, the problem can, ultimately, be addressed in terms of inequality before the law (or be framed as an access to justice-problem): "poor justice for the poor". To conclude, using the words of Eugene Cerruti:

> An adversarial proceeding cannot proceed as such when the adversaries are not capable of behaving as such. The system simply implodes.[11]

---

[4]For example, Trechsel (2005), pp. 245ff. makes a distinction between technical, psychological, humanitarian, and structural aspects motivating a right to counsel. Regarding the technical aspect, see also Assy (2011), p. 267, who concludes that "[a]dversarial rules of evidence and procedure are designed by and for lawyers and judges, and therefore LIPs are unable to use them properly" and Genn (2015), p. vii., who argues that laypersons "may not understand the law; they may struggle with legal language; they are often baffled by the complexity of the court procedure; and they have difficulties advocating their own cause". These problems are developed in Sect. 5.1 *infra.*

[5]Genn (2015), p. vii. See also Sharpe (2016), p. 435.

[6]Cf. Zuckerman (2014), pp. 355f., who refers to an "efficiency deficit" and a "justice deficit".

[7]It has even been said that LIP:s "obstruct the general administration of justice and impact on other cases in which they are not involved". See Assy (2012), pp. 19f. and 22ff.; cf. Zorza (2009), p. 521.

[8]See Sect. 4 *infra.*

[9]Assy (2015), p. 10; Moorhead (2003), p. 135.

[10]Genn (2015), p. vii.

[11]Cerruti (2009), pp. 962; cf. Assy (2015), p. 12: "Where LIPs are involved, it is particularly clear that the elementary conditions of adversarial adjudication do not obtain." See also, e.g., Assy (2011), p. 269; Assy (2012), pp. 4ff.; Toone (2005), p. 650; Sabeli and Leyton (2000), p. 169.

What is particularly interesting, though, is that the problems associated with pro se-litigation can be regarded from two opposed perspectives, hence, with two different "solutions" in sight: Some hold *LIP:s themselves* responsible for their own failure to litigate effectively, while others blame *the system* for its failure to secure effective access to court for unrepresented parties.[12]

Within the first perspective, individual litigants' insufficient skills is regarded as the key problem, which could (and should) be resolved by *compelling litigants to rely on lawyers* when bringing or defending an action in court. For example, Rabeea Assy argues that cases brought by pro se litigants are "characterized by a fundamental and systematic failure to grasp the process and make arguable applications or present the case according to proper procedure". Since this "systematic failure is typical of LIPs", the problem is, according to Assy, "best prevented by restricting self-representation".[13]

By contrast, the second perspective regards the level of complexity inherent in modern day court systems as the key problem; courts "exist for their users, not the other way round".[14] Accordingly, *simplification of procedure* is instead proposed to make courts accessible to all. In the words of Lord Woolf:

> Only too often the litigant in person is regarded as a problem for judges and for the court system rather than the person for whom the system of justice exists. The true problem is the court system and its procedures which are still too often inaccessible and incomprehensible to ordinary people.[15]

What complicates the matter further is that these opposing "solutions" (i.e., *use of lawyers* versus *user-friendly procedures*) do not nearly solve the complicated issue at hand, since they both give rise to new problems.

If, on the one hand, a procedural system presumes that individuals are represented by lawyers (or at least ought to be) then the costs of such counsel must in some way be alleviated in order to ensure that anyone—not just the rich—can have "access to a lawyer" (and thereby be guaranteed "effective access to court"). A solution that relieves parties of their lawyers' fees will, however, only shift costs from one subject to another (viz., counterparty/third party/state). As the saying goes: Talk is cheap, until lawyers get involved.[16] Ultimately, someone must pay the price.

Since the decline of the welfare state, and in times of economic recession, many modern states are no longer willing (or able) to fund generous legal aid schemes.[17] Instead, legislators have tried to solve the pro se-problem by simplifying the

[12] Cf. Assy (2015), p. 13.

[13] Assy (2015), p. 25.

[14] Woolf (1995), p. 119.

[15] Woolf (1995), p. 119.

[16] For a discussion on what lawyers "bring to the table" (besides costs), see, e.g., Mather (2003), pp. 155ff.

[17] See, e.g., Sorabji (2014), p. 4. Regarding the Nordic/Scandinavian context, see also Halvorsen Rønning (2018), Schoultz (2018), Rissanen (2018), Lemann Kristiansen (2018) and Fjóla Antonsdóttir (2018) as well as Wejedal (2022a) and Johnsen (2022).

procedure, thereby reducing the "need for counsel" (and, hence, the need to provide state-funded legal aid). This solution has also, in theory, been accepted by the European Court of Human Rights (ECtHR) as compliant with the fair trial rights under Article 6 of the European Convention on Human Rights (ECHR), at least in cases regarding civil rights and obligations.[18] In the seminal judgment on (civil) legal aid, *Airey v. Ireland,* the Court made the following statement:

> [W]hilst Article 6 guarantees to litigants an effective right of access to the courts . . . it leaves to the State a free choice of the means to be used towards this end. The institution of a legal aid scheme . . . constitutes one of those means but there are others such as, for example, a simplification of procedure.[19]

In other words, the goal is fixed: individuals must be provided effective access to court. However, there are two alternative routes (a and b) to get there: If legal proceedings are complex, then the ECtHR has ruled that (a) *legal aid must be made available,* at least for indigent litigants, who otherwise could not afford to hire necessary legal representation.[20] If states do not want (or cannot afford) a comprehensive legal aid scheme, then (b) the *procedure must instead be simplified* to such an extent, that laypersons can conduct their own case effectively. In theory, this might seem reasonable. In practice, however, the whole idea of "simplification" is not nearly as simple as it sounds.

If individuals, on the other hand, are to represent themselves, then the court must usually—in some shape or form—help unrepresented parties to conduct their case adequately, e.g. through so-called "active case management".[21] Having judges "lean over the bench" in order to secure effective access to court is not, however, uncontroversial, since it may contradict other fundamental principles of procedural law.[22] For example, both the principle of adversarialism and the principle of impartiality require a clear division of the respective roles of the parties (arguing the case) and the court (deciding the case, preferably at arm's length from the

[18] For disputes regarding civil rights and obligations, there is no explicit right to legal aid under the civil head of article 6. However, the ECtHR has on many occasions concluded that such a right is implicit to article 6 § 1, either to secure effective access to court or a fair trial, in particular "equality of arms" between the parties.

[19] *Airey v. Ireland,* app. no. 6289/73, § 26. The same clarification was made in *Steel & Morris v. the United Kingdom,* app. no. 68416/01, § 60.

[20] Recent case law from the ECtHR also show that a right to get counsel fees reimbursed through cost shifting rules too can be derived from article 6 § 1, at least in cases regarding civil rights and obligations. See *Stankiewicz v. Poland*, app. no. 46917/99, *Černius and Rinkevičius v. Lithuania,* app. nos. 73579/17 and 14620/18 and *Zustović v. Croatia,* app. no. 27903/15.

[21] There are, of course, several ways to "help" unrepresented litigants/"facilitate" the procedure. For example, Albrecht et al. (2003), p. 16 mention "easy-to-use forms; simplified instructions; printed and online information about substantive and procedural law; and direct assistance from court staff". See also Zuckerman (2014), p. 355, who makes a distinction between "out-of-court assistance" and "in-court-assistance"; cf. Genn (2013).

[22] The benefits of judicial passivity are well framed by Assy (2015), pp. 95ff.

parties).[23] Expecting an overly active court may, in other words, obscure the boundaries laid down for the various actors in adversarial litigation.[24] Accordingly, many have argued that "lawyer-less litigation" is impractical, or at least inappropriate, and its implementation has therefore faced severe criticism.[25] Bluntly put: you are (as a judge faced with a pro se-litigant) "damned if you do, damned if you don't". Or more eloquently framed by John Sorabji:

> In the absence of lawyers, the court is faced with a dilemma: either take on the lawyers' role in addition to its adjudicatory role or, potentially, fail to discharge its duty as a court of law to provide a fair trial.[26]

To summarize the problem outlined in this section, it might be fruitful to compare the courts with a complex machine of some sort. For example, flying an aircraft is not an easy task. Consequently, not everyone is equipped to do so, at least not without adequate training. This problem could—hypothetically—be resolved either (a) by requiring people to *hire trained pilots* to maneuver the plane, or (b) by *reducing the complexity* of the aircraft. However, hiring pilots is not a feasible alternative for people with limited means (unless, of course, someone else is willing to pay for poor peoples' airplane tickets). Nor can we simplify the aircraft by removing, its wings, rudder and engine, and still expect it to fly (at some point, the airplane will simply cease to be an airplane).[27] This catch-22, which is analogous for the court system, forms the starting point for the present chapter.

1.2 Aim and Outline

The aim of this chapter is to contribute to the ongoing discussion regarding "simplification of procedure" as a realistic (or rather unrealistic?) alternative to

---

[23] Zuckerman (2014), pp. 357ff. (especially at p. 372: "The paradoxical truth is that in order to maintain an unbiased decision making process, the parties must not rely on the decision maker to develop their respective positions but must each have their own champion unburdened by responsibility to the opponent beyond ethical obligations of propriety and fair play."). See, however, Lucy (2005), discussing "procedural impartiality" (especially at p. 22: "If legal representation is available only to those who can afford to pay, and if it is true that legal representation significantly influences disputants' likelihood of success, then those who cannot pay are undoubtedly disadvantaged in the adjudicative process.").

[24] As Fuller has put it: "If it is true that a man in his time must play many parts, it is scarcely given to him to play them all at once." See Fuller (1978), pp. 383; cf. Assy (2015), pp. 95ff.; Albrecht et al. (2003), pp. 16; Goldschmidt (2002), pp. 37ff.

[25] See, e.g., Swank (2005a), p. 1539, who argues that "the fundamental notions of fairness and justice for all demand a preservation of the traditional rules and roles", and Zuckerman (2014).

[26] Sorabji (2015), p. 165.

[27] Cf. Sorabji (2021), pp. 221ff., who concludes that a civil justice system "where lawyers are designed-out of the system is one that would design-out the very features that render a civil justice system one that is committed to securing, and forms part of a constitutional system committed to, the rule of law".

lawyer-conducted litigation. To discuss this theme, I will use the Swedish administrative court procedure as a telling example. For this example to be illustrative also for non-Swedish readers, some introductory clarifications are necessary.

Access to justice-problems are often framed as being either *civil* or *criminal* in nature; securing *civil justice* is something distinct from safeguarding *criminal justice*.[28] This separation can, for example, be found in human rights treaties such as Article 6 of the ECHR and is echoed in the constitutional call for a "Civil Gideon" within the U.S. context. Globally, The World Justice Project (WJP) also uses this distinction in its *Rule of Law Index*.[29]

In this chapter, I will focus primarily on access to civil justice in Sweden. According to the WJP index, civil justice (factor 7) measures "whether ordinary people can resolve their grievances peacefully and effectively through the civil justice system". For this assessment, questions regarding "accessibility and affordability" are at the core (subfactor 7.1).

As of the latest report, Sweden is ranked fourth across 140 countries in terms of overall rule of law performance, out ranked only by our neighboring Scandinavian countries (Denmark, Norway and Finland). Does this mean that civil justice is both accessible and affordable? To answer this question, it is important to note that Sweden (unlike Denmark and Norway, but just like Finland) has two different categories of courts: general courts (*allmänna domstolar*) and administrative courts (*förvaltningsdomstolar*), both of which form three-tier systems, with first instance courts, courts of appeal and a supreme court on top of each pyramid. When discussing civil justice, the general courts are usually in focus, which is natural since they decide civil law disputes. However, many issues regarding basic civil rights, as well as legal disputes regarding basic human needs,[30] are decided by the often-overlooked administrative courts.[31]

In administrative cases, state-funded legal aid is almost never granted because the procedure is considered "simple"—even for laypersons. In addition, cases decided by the administrative courts are not covered by private legal expense insurances (LEI:s). As cherry on the top, a so-called no-way cost-shifting rule (i.e., the "American Rule") is applied between the parties. Hence, the lack of legal aid, as well as other mechanisms that allow reimbursement of lawyers' fees, force private parties to conduct their own litigation against a public agency, acting as counterparty in a procedure which, in essence, is adversarial. The imbalance that is created between

[28] Robinson (1996), p. 202: "every society sufficiently developed to have a formal legal system uses the criminal-civil distinction as an organizing principle". See also Pleasence and Balmer (2018), pp. 256f.

[29] See https://worldjusticeproject.org.

[30] Cf. Pleasence et al. (2004), p. 1 who state that "the infrastructure of civil justice today plays an important role in realising social justice", and Buck et al. (2005). Regarding the connection between, on the one hand, "knowledge of rights and its relationship with an individual's capacity to 'self-help' and 'self-represent' when faced with a civil justice problem" and, on the other hand, social inclusion/exclusion, see also Denvir et al. (2013) and Balmer et al. (2010).

[31] Cf. Smith (2022) and Lemann Kristiansen (2022) regarding Norway and Denmark.

the parties—an individual, without legal assistance, on one side of the abyss, and a state or municipal agency on the other—has not been considered problematic by the Swedish legislator. In this chapter, I will argue to the contrary.

In the following sections, I will first give a brief *background*, outlining the Swedish court system as well as the basic rules governing legal representation (Sect. 2). In the subsequent section, I will develop how *lawyers' fees* are handled under Swedish law, with a comparison between the general courts and the administrative courts (Sect. 3). Thereafter, I will present some recent empirical data on *lawyer advantage* in the Swedish administrative procedure which—in my opinion—contradict the notion of a "simple" procedure in which individuals are able to conduct their own case effectively (Sect. 4). Finally, I will discuss the results and offer some concluding remarks, arguing that the sporadic help from a judge can never fully compensate for the lack of qualified counsel—not even in "simplified procedures" (Sect. 5).

2 Background

2.1 The Swedish Court System

As already stated, the general courts and the administrative courts constitute the backbone of the Swedish court system.[32] The general courts (consisting of 48 *tingsrätter,* six *hovrätter* and one *Högsta domstol*) has a general competence to decide disputes under both civil law and criminal law. The procedure before the general courts is governed by the Code of Judicial Procedure (*rättegångsbalken* [1942:740], RB). In the year of 2022, the general courts of first instance decided 81,325 civil cases and 122,733 criminal cases.[33]

The administrative courts (consisting of 12 *förvaltningsrätter,* four *kammarrätter* and one *Högsta förvaltningsdomstol*) handle a wide range of administrative law disputes pursuant to the Administrative Court Procedure Act (*förvaltningsprocesslagen* [1971:291], FPL). In the year of 2022, the administrative courts of first instance decided 108,386 administrative cases.[34] Since four of the administrative courts of first instance also function as Migration courts, the overall caseload is about 150,000–200,000 cases per year.[35]

Most of the disputes brought before the administrative courts are initiated by private parties (individuals or corporations) appealing various administrative

[32] There are also a few specialized courts, such as the Labor court and four Migration courts.

[33] See the annual rapport of the Swedish Court Administration (2022), p. 20.

[34] See the annual rapport of the Swedish Court Administration (2022), p. 45.

[35] During 2022, the Migration courts decided 49,265 cases, see the annual rapport of the Swedish Court Administration (2022), p. 45.

decisions made by state or municipal agencies.[36] When such decisions are appealed to an administrative court, the decision-making authority automatically receives standing as counterparty to the private party, creating an adversarial set-up.[37] As party to the dispute, the authority normally requests that its decision be upheld by the court, whereas the private party usually argues that the appealed decision should either be changed in some way, or quashed.

The procedures before the general and administrative courts show both differences and similarities. For example, the Code of Judicial Procedure is based on the principle of orality,[38] with the trial strongly centred around a main (oral) hearing,[39] whereas the Administrative Court Procedure Act prescribes a written procedure, with oral hearings held only exceptionally. However, the division of responsibilities between the court and the parties is quite similar; both procedures are adversarial in their fundamental structure, albeit with some "inquisitorial features", as will soon be elaborated.

2.2 *The "Right" to Counsel: Effective or Illusory?*

Under Swedish procedural law, a party to a dispute—be it civil, criminal, or administrative—is always at liberty (but never obliged) to hire an attorney to conduct his/her case.[40] In this narrow sense, there is an unconditional "right to counsel" (but also a right to proceed without counsel) both before the general courts and the administrative courts. Yet, in reality, this "right" is of course conditional, since hiring a lawyer is always associated with a cost.[41] Given that it is a well-known fact that many—if not most—private litigants will not be able to obtain counsel if counsel fees are not in some way alleviated, a "right to counsel" in a more practical sense must also take into account if and how lawyers' fees can be reimbursed. In this regard, the general courts and the administrative courts are best described as each other's direct opposites.

In cases decided by the general courts, the Swedish legislator has acknowledged that individual parties do need a lawyer to conduct their case effectively. Therefore, there are several overlapping rules and regimes through which individuals can

[36] If, for example, the Swedish Social Insurance Agency has rejected an application for occupational injury compensation, or the Swedish Migration Board has rejected an application for asylum, the individual can appeal the decision to an administrative court and request that the court grant compensation/asylum, while the agency (now acting as counterparty in the procedure) usually argues for its decision to be upheld by the court.

[37] See FPL § 7 a.

[38] See, for example, RB ch. 43 § 5 and ch. 46 § 5.

[39] RB ch. 17 § 2 and ch. 30 § 2.

[40] See RB ch. 12 §§ 1 and 22, ch. 21 § 3; cf. FPL § 48.

[41] Apart, off course, from such cases where a lawyer accepts a case *pro bono* (i.e., without compensation).

receive compensation for their legal fees, including counsel fees. In cases decided by the administrative courts, the legislator has taken the opposite position; individuals are *not* considered to need legal assistance and can therefore *not* get their legal fees reimbursed—not even if they win—since the procedure is considered "simple".

2.3 The Concept of "Simplified Procedures"

In the scholarship, "simplified procedures" have been defined as

> ... court procedures that are distinguished from fully equipped ordinary civil procedures by curtailing or omitting certain procedural steps. In most jurisdictions, they are considered a response to the need for inexpensive and quick procedures, in particular in simple and small matters.[42]

Sweden, like most developed countries,[43] has a simplified small claims track as part of our civil procedure, primarily designed to resolve consumer disputes/disputes regarding small claims (<26,250 SEK) both faster and cheaper than a full-blown civil lawsuit.[44] However, we *also* have our administrative procedure, which *in its entirety* is considered simple. Although some administrative cases might indeed be characterised as "simple and small", I would argue that many cases are not.

The administrative courts handle more than 500 different categories of administrative law disputes concerning, e.g., *social insurance* (disputes with the Swedish Social Insurance Agency in matters relating to, e.g., sickness, disability or parental benefits and occupational injury compensation), *welfare benefits* (disputes with the social welfare services of a municipality regarding, e.g., social allowance), *taxes* (disputes with the Swedish Tax Agency regarding, e.g., income, wealth or property tax and decisions regarding VAT), *migration* (decisions made by the Swedish Migration Board regarding, e.g., refusal of entry, deportation and nationality), *compulsory care* (regarding children, substance abusers and the mentally ill), *public procurement*, different kinds of *permits* and *licenses*, etc. Given this multitude of different case types, it is somewhat surprising that *all of them*—regardless of the circumstances of each case—are considered sufficiently "simple" for laypersons to handle without access to qualified counsel.[45]

---

[42] Kramer and Kakiuchi (2015), pp. 139f. Regarding the use of standard forms to simplify cross-border litigation within the European Union, see Hoevenaars and Kramer (2022), p. 515.

[43] For comparison, see for example Voet (2015), Brosh (2015), Sugiyama (2015), Gomez and Gomez (2015), Silver and Farrow (2015), Gidi and Zaneti (2015), Astrup Hjort (2022) and Wallerman Ghavanini (2022) regarding simplified small claims (civil) procedures in Belgium, Israel, Japan, the United States, Canada, Brazil, Norway and Sweden.

[44] See RB ch. 1 § 3 d regarding so-called "förenklade tvistemål".

[45] With only three exceptions: cases concerning tax, migration and involuntary care, see footnote 59 and Sect. 3.2.2 *infra*.

To justify the position that private parties have no need for legal representation in their disputes with state/municipal agencies, the legislator has emphasized the following three ("simplifying") characteristics: Firstly, as described above, the administrative procedure is in essence a *written* procedure,[46] which is considered more lenient for private parties (compared to a trial centred around an oral hearing). Secondly, the procedure is *informal* in the sense that the court—when rendering its judgment—is not strictly bound the actions of the parties (neither by the claims put forward, nor by the legal grounds invoked).[47] Thirdly, although the parties bare the primary responsibility for presenting evidence to the court, the judge has a secondary (or subsidiary) mandate to engage in active case management[48] (*materiell processledning*) in order to obtain necessary evidence.[49] The million-dollar question, then, is whether (or not) these ("quasi-inquisitorial"[50]) characteristics are sufficient to make legal representation superfluous. I will return to this question in Sect. 4. Before that, I will develop how counsel fees are handled before Swedish courts. Since the focus of this chapter is on civil justice (or at least "non-criminal justice"[51]), I will leave the criminal procedure out of the picture.

Above all, I am interested in identifying types of proceedings where individual parties, who are engaged in a legal dispute against either another private party or a state/municipal counterparty, can *never get their fees reimbursed*—neither through legal aid/legal expense insurances, nor by cost-shifting rules—compelling them to represent themselves.

3 Lawyers' Fees

Hypothetically, a party to a dispute can shift his/her lawyers' fees onto one of the following subjects: (1) the *opposing party*, through cost-shifting rules which allow the winner to wholly or partly recover his/her litigation costs from the loser (party funding); (2) the *state*, through a state-funded legal aid scheme (public funding); or

[46] FPL § 9.

[47] FPL §§ 29–30.

[48] Regarding the term "case management", see Sorabji (2018) with a comprehensive comparative analysis of active case management in Austria, Australia, Brazil, Canada, Chile, England and Wales, France, Germany, Hong Kong, Italy, the Netherlands, Norway, Poland, Singapore and the United States. See also Andrews (2014) and Resnik (1982). Regarding active judicial assistance more generally, see Assy (2015), pp. 108ff. and Beka (2018).

[49] See FPL § 8: "The court shall ensure that the case is investigated according to what its nature requires. Through questions and observations, the court shall work to ensure that the parties remedy ambiguities and incompleteness in their statements." [my translation]

[50] Sorabji (2015), p. 165.

[51] Compare the list of non-criminal so-called "justiciable problems" (i.e., problems "which raise civil legal issues") in Pleasence et al. (2013), p. 20, many of which would be characterized and handled as administrative disputes in Sweden. See also Pleasence and Balmer (2012).

(3) a *third-party*, in Sweden usually a private insurance provider, through a legal expense insurance scheme (third-party funding).[52] In the following subsections, I will do a brief inventory of these legal frameworks.

3.1 Cost-Shifting

In this section, I will examine the allocation of counsel fees *between parties* through cost-shifting rules. In my opinion, it is fruitful to systematize such rules as a scale, ranging from black to white, with a grayscale between the two poles.[53] On one end of this spectrum, we find the so-called "English Rule" (a.k.a. the "loser pays-principle"). According to this rule, the losing party is forced to bear his/her own legal expenses, as well as the winning party's expenses ("two-way cost-shifting", in Swedish *principen om full kostnadstäckning*). On the other end of the spectrum, we find the "American Rule", which compels each party to bear their respective legal expenses regardless of the outcome of the litigation ("no-way cost-shifting", in Swedish *kvittningsprincipen*).

Between these two extremes, there are several conceivable intermediate solutions, for example rules allowing costs to be shifted only from a winning plaintiff to a losing defendant ("pro-plaintiff rules") or vice versa ("pro-defendant rules") or, alternatively, only from presumably weaker to stronger parties, e.g., from consumers to businesses, but not the other way around ("one-way cost-shifting"). Finally, both two-way and one-way cost-shifting rules can be combined with other limitations. For example, in the Swedish small claims-procedure, costs are allocated according to the loser pays principle, but there is a cap on lawyers' fees, limiting the amount that can be recovered from the losing party.[54]

Using this scale-metaphor, it can be concluded that the Code of Judicial Procedure and the Administrative Court Procedure Act, as mentioned above, are more or less each other's opposites. In the general courts, the main rule is that a winning litigant will get his/her costs reimbursed (according to the English Rule), whereas private parties in administrative proceedings will have to bear their own costs regardless of the outcome (i.e., the American Rule applies).

---

[52] Costs, or—more accurately—risks, can also be shifted from the client to his/her own lawyer, by conditional/contingent fee agreements. Such arrangements are, however, very uncommon in Sweden.

[53] Regarding cost shifting under Swedish law, see Wejedal (2017), pp. 109ff.

[54] See RB ch. 18 § 8 a.

3.1.1 Two-Way Cost-Shifting in Civil Proceedings

Chapter 18 § 1 of the Code of Judicial Procedure stipulates that a losing party in a civil law dispute shall bear the counterparty's legal fees (including counsel fees).[55] In other words, for civil procedure, a two-way cost-shifting rule is applied between the parties. This rule has been justified with reference to the *purpose of civil litigation* which, according to the preparatory works, is to provide "legal protection" to the winning party. This purpose would not be adequately safeguarded, if the winning party were not able to get his/her costs for bringing or defending a legal action reimbursed.[56] Therefore, counsel fees in civil cases are allocated according to the loser pays-principle, except for a small number of cases covered by special exceptions.[57]

3.1.2 No-Way Cost-Shifting in Administrative Proceedings

In contrast to the Code of Judicial Procedure, the Administrative Court Procedure Act does not contain any rules concerning counsel fees, and in the absence of fee shifting rules, Swedish administrative courts have considered themselves precluded from allowing prevailing individual parties to recover their legal costs. [58] In other words, an uncodified no-way cost-shifting rule is applied as a compulsory rule, leaving no margin of discretion—not even in the most objectionable of situations.[59]

---

[55]In Swedish criminal proceedings, as in civil litigation, legal fees are today distributed according to the outcome of the case, see RB ch. 31 §§ 1–2.

[56]See SOU 1938:44 p. 231, SOU 1926:33 p. 208 and Bellander (2017).

[57]A few exceptions are foreseen from the general rule in the Code of Judicial Procedure, precluding or limiting cost shifting in certain types of proceedings, e.g., in cases concerning labor law, discrimination law, family/children's law (regarding custody/residence/visitation), as well as in small claims-disputes.

[58]The Swedish Supreme Court has found that the right to a fair trial may be breached if a private party, who has won a case against a state agency, cannot recover his/her counsel fees, see NJA 2015 s. 374, NJA 2020 s. 908, NJA 2021 s. 235 and Wejedal (2020–2021). The Swedish Supreme Administrative Court has not come to the same conclusion regarding no-way cost shifting in the administrative procedure, see e.g., RÅ 2006 ref. 89, RÅ 2009 not. 202, HFD 2020 not. 47 and HFD 2022 ref. 10. I have criticized this case law from the Supreme Administrative Court in Wejedal (2021, 2022b, 2023).

[59]From this general no-way rule, precluding cost shifting, the Swedish administrative procedure contains only one exception: tax proceedings. The Swedish Tax Procedures Act (*skatteförfarandelagen* [2011:1244], SFL) specifically provides that individual parties in need of legal representation can indeed recover their counsel fees if, for example, their substantive claims are wholly or partially granted by the court, see SFL ch. 43 § 1. This rule has, in the preparatory works, been justified by the need to safeguard individuals' legal certainty in various ways, insofar that it has been considered vital that taxpayers are not deterred from engaging legal counsel, when necessary, see prop. 1988/89:126 p. 7 and prop. 1993/94:151 p. 133. It is not clear, however, why this consideration is assigned such importance in tax law proceedings, but not in other administrative law proceedings, such as social insurance and welfare proceedings concerning basic needs.

In the preparatory works, the legislator has justified this rule by taking the position that individuals are *not in need of legal assistance*, and that there is consequently *no need for cost-shifting rules*.[60]

In sum, we can conclude that individual parties can never, in administrative proceedings, recover their counsel fees from their counterparty; this being the case irrespective of the circumstances and substantive outcome of the case. The fact that administrative courts have not considered themselves mandated to order cost shifting (without a statutory rule allowing them to do so) has resulted in the unconditional application of the (non-codified) rule of no-way cost-shifting. This constitutes a significant difference vis-à-vis the cost shifting rules applied in civil (and criminal) proceedings.

3.2 Legal Aid (and Legal Expense Insurances)

The Swedish legal aid system can be divided into four separate—but interlinked—frameworks:

- The Legal Aid Act (*rättshjälpslagen* [1996:1619], RhjL) has, at the outset, a general scope of application. Under this regime, a party to a dispute can be assigned a state-funded "legal aid counsel" in any court proceeding not explicitly excluded in the law. In practice, however, legal aid counsels are mainly appointed in civil proceedings.
- The Code of Judicial Procedure contains specific provisions regarding state-funded "public defence counsels" in section 21. Such a counsel can, in theory, be appointed for the defendant in all criminal cases.
- The Act concerning Counsel for the Injured Party (*lagen* [1988:609] *om målsägandebiträde*, LMB), contains specific provisions giving the victim of a crime a right to a state-funded so-called "counsel for the injured party", in most criminal cases.
- The Act concerning Public Counsel (*lagen* [1996:1620] *om offentligt biträde,* LOB) contains specific provisions giving the private party a right to a state-funded so-called "public counsel" in a few categories of administrative cases.[61]

These four regimes have some common features, but also important differences, in particular regarding the conditions for granting legal aid.

The Legal Aid Act is best understood as a "minimum standard". As such, the law contains the most restrictive framework,[62] since the granting of legal aid is subject to

[60] See, e.g., SOU 1971:76 pp. 71f.

[61] These four frameworks are elaborated in Wejedal (2017), pp. 269ff.

[62] The first legislation providing free legal assistance to the poor was introduced into Swedish law in 1919. The current Legal Aid Act was enacted in 1996, through prop. 1996/97:9 and replaced the former act of 1972. The purpose of this reform was to cut public spending on legal aid, by

two general conditions: (1) a "means test" (or "income ceiling"); and (2) a "needs test" (or requirement of "necessity").[63]

According to the *means test*, legal aid may only be granted to applicants whose financial base does not exceed 260,000 SEK.[64] This condition must be understood in relation to the general income level in Sweden; for the fiscal year of 2021, the average annual income was approximately 445,200 SEK.[65] Hence, the majority of the population has too high earnings to qualify for legal aid; the income ceiling excludes even low income-earners, who could never afford to hire a lawyer by their own means.[66]

For persons who pass the means test, the *needs test* applies.[67] According to this test, legal aid may only be granted if the applicant "needs" legal assistance, and this need cannot be met by any other mechanism than state-funded legal aid, such as a LEI[68] (or even active case management from the court[69]).

The restrictive application of The Legal Aid Act is compensated in two ways: In (most) *civil cases*, on the one hand, legal costs are usually, to some extent, covered by LEI:s. For *criminal* and *administrative* cases, on the other hand, three complementary state-funded mechanisms have been introduced into Swedish law, as listed

---

(1) creating a more restrictive framework; (2) introducing a "legal aid fee"; and (3) making the state funded legal aid scheme secondary (or "subsidiary") to LEI:s. Regarding the Swedish legal aid system, see Wejedal (2017), pp. 278ff., Wejedal (2022a) and, with a Nordic comparison, Barlow (2019).

[63] See RhjL §§ 6–7. In fact, there are three general conditions; according to RhjL § 8, there is also a "test of reasonableness", i.e., legal aid is refused if it is not considered *reasonable* for the state to contribute to the costs.

[64] RhjL § 6. The financial base includes annual income with regard to maintenance obligations, assets and debts, see RhjL § 38.

[65] Statistics Sweden, average income 2021.

[66] See SOU 2014:86 p. 16. In this state report, it was suggested that the income ceiling should be raised to 400,000 SEK, which would make 80% of the population eligible for legal aid. However, no such change has been made by the legislator. This is remarkable, given that the ceiling has not been raised since 1999, see Wejedal (2022a).

[67] RhjL § 7.

[68] In Swedish, *rättsskydd* (as opposed to state-funded legal aid, *rättshjälp*). Such insurances are included as a mandatory part in every home insurance and cover most civil disputes. If the applicant has (or should have had) a LEI that covers the legal dispute in question, legal aid cannot be granted, see RhjL § 9. This means that the public legal aid scheme is activated *only in such cases that cannot be covered by a private insurance*. By this construction, Sweden has managed to shift the costs for providing legal aid, from the state budget to private insurance companies/holders. Whether this "privatization" of the (civil) legal aid—which followed from the enactment of the 1996 Legal Aid Act—was "good" or "bad", is a topic for discussion in the scholarship. See, e.g., the contributions in Hammerslev and Halvorsen Rønning (2018).

[69] Active case management is considered to "simplify" the procedure and is therefore seen as an alternative to providing legal aid. By this logic, legal aid is normally refused in administrative procedure, see Sect. 3.2.2 *infra*.

above.[70] These three frameworks (RB, LMB and LOB) have a narrower scope of application, but are more generous (than RhjL), since they do not contain a means test (i.e., legal aid can be granted regardless of the income of the party). However, the right to state-funded counsel is still subject to a needs test.[71]

The relationship between the four regimes that—taken together—constitute the Swedish legal aid system (viz. RhjL, RB, LMB and LOB), is best understood with regard to the Swedish division between general courts and administrative courts. I will therefore develop the conditions under which legal aid is granted in civil proceedings as compared to administrative proceedings in the two subsequent sections.[72]

3.2.1 Legal Aid (and LEI:s) in Civil Proceedings

Since there are no other public legal aid schemes that cover civil law disputes, state-funded legal aid in civil procedure can only be granted under the conditions laid down in the Legal Aid Act. This means that civil legal aid can only be granted (1) for a limited number of people (viz. persons with very low income, or no income at all); and (2) in a limited number of civil cases (viz. cases that are not "insurable").

However, most swedes have a home insurance (including a LEI) that covers most categories of civil disputes. Hence, the restrictive application of the Legal Aid Act is mitigated in civil proceedings by the wide existence of LEI:s. These insurances contain provisions that are sometimes criticised, but overall, they provide sufficient protection for such disputes not exempted by the insurance policies.[73]

3.2.2 Legal Aid (and Public Counsel) in Administrative Proceedings

In administrative cases, a legal aid counsel can—in theory—be appointed to the private party, since administrative cases are not formally exempted from the scope of application of the Legal Aid Act. In practice, however, applications for legal aid filed under the Legal Aid Act are never granted. In the preparatory works to the Legal Aid

[70] If legal aid can be granted under one of these supplementary public schemes, the Legal Aid Act is not applicable.

[71] The only exception from the requirement of necessity is found in the criminal procedure, where the right to public defence counsel is sometimes—but not always—unconditional (or "absolute").

[72] In criminal proceedings, both the defendant and the injured party can be granted legal aid according to the more generous rules laid down either in the Code of Judicial Procedure or in the Act concerning Counsel for the Injured Party.

[73] Two common categories of civil cases that cannot be covered by LEI:s are small claims-disputes and many family law disputes. However, for legal aid to be granted in these categories of cases, there must be "special reasons" motivating a need for legal assistance in the particular case, according to RhjL § 11 (i.e., legal aid is normally refused). Since these categories of cases are also exempted from the LEI:s, private parties are often forced to conduct their own litigation.

Act, the legislator considered, with reference to the far-reaching "investigative powers" of administrative courts (i.e. the courts mandate to engage in active case management) that there is rarely any need for legal counsel in administrative proceedings.[74] Because of this statement, courts tend to refuse granting legal aid.

However, in some administrative cases, a so-called public counsel can instead be appointed, according to the more generous rules laid down in the Act concerning Public Counsel.[75] As opposed to the general system of public defence counsels and public counsels for injured parties in the criminal procedure, public counsels can only be appointed in a narrow category of administrative cases, namely those concerning compulsory care and migration.[76] In the remaining (circa 500) categories of administrative cases, there is no possibility to be granted a public counsel.

3.3 Lawyer-Less Litigation Before the Administrative Courts

In this section, we have concluded that a no-way cost-shifting rule is applied between the parties in Swedish administrative procedure; even if the private party is successful, his/her legal fees cannot be recovered from the public counterparty. We also established that legal aid is in practice never granted under the Legal Aid Act in administrative cases, due to the restrictive application of the needs test, and that the more generous Act concerning Public Counsel is only applicable in a small number of administrative cases (i.e., in cases concerning involuntary institutional care and migration). Since administrative cases are also generally exempted from Swedish LEI:s,[77] we can conclude that there *are no rules or regimes whatsoever* through which individuals can get reimbursement for lawyers' fees incurred before the administrative courts. As a result, private parties have no choice but to conduct

---

[74] See prop. 1996/97:9 p. 115; cf. footnotes 48–49 *supra*.

[75] See LOB § 1. This act was introduced in 1996 through prop. 1996/97:9. However, equivalent rules regarding public counsels existed long before that; the oldest system can be traced back to 1914, when aliens risking expulsion were first granted a right to state-funded counsel. Since then, the system has been gradually expanded to include other administrative cases which are highly intrusive, i.e., cases concerning compulsory care.

[76] See the Care of Young Persons Act (*lagen* [1990:52] *med särskilda bestämmelser om vård av unga*, LVU) § 39, the Care of Abusers Act (*lagen* [1988:870] *om vård av missbrukare i vissa fall*, LVM) § 42, the Compulsory Psychiatric Care Act (*lagen* [1991:1128] *om psykiatrisk tvångsvård*, LPT) § 38 a and the Aliens Act (*utlänningslagen* [2005:716], UtlL) ch. 18 § 1. However, in the few categories of cases that fall within the scope of application of the Act concerning Public Counsel, legal aid is granted according to a very generous framework. Firstly, the appointment of public counsels is not subject to a means test. Secondly, the needs test is more or less constructed as a presumption that works in favour of the private party, i.e., legal aid is only refused when it is clear that the party does not need legal assistance. Hence, persons risking involuntary care or expulsion de facto always have access to a lawyer.

[77] Standard insurance clauses will grant legal assistance only for civil litigation before the general courts, precluding legal assistance in administrative proceedings.

their own litigation in almost every administrative dispute, regarding, e.g., taxes, social security, welfare benefits, permits, etcetera.

The fact that private parties are forced to proceed pro se in disputes with state and municipal agencies is legitimized with reference to the "simplified" nature of administrative proceedings. According to the Swedish legislator, there is no need for legal counsel in administrative cases and, consequently, private parties have no corresponding need to get their counsel fees reimbursed. In the following section, I will challenge this notion.

4 Lawyer Advantage

In a recent study, Rebecka Lorentzon, Louise Holm and myself have examined if there is a statistical lawyer advantage in Swedish administrative proceedings.[78] In contrast to the common notion that individual parties can effectively present their own case, our study showed that lawyer-represented parties enjoyed significantly higher success rates than unrepresented parties. In fact, the calculated advantage of having access to a qualified counsel, compared to not having a counsel (measured as odds ratios, *OR*[79]) was even higher in our study than what has been previously reported in some meta-studies regarding success rates for represented/unrepresented litigants in the U.K. and U.S. This is quite remarkable, since Anglo-American litigation is usually considered to be "more adversarial" in its structure—and hence more challenging for pro se-litigants—than continental and Scandinavian court procedure.[80] In the following sub-sections, I will give a brief account of our findings, building on Marc Galanter's party capability theory.

4.1 The Sailor and the Shark

In his classic article *Why the "Haves" Come Out Ahead*, Galanter introduced a typology of different categories of parties, based on their Interactions with the court system:

> [S]ome of the actors in the society have many occasions to utilize the courts (in the broad sense) to make (or defend) claims; others do so only rarely. We might divide our actors into those claimants who have only occasional recourse to the courts (one-shotters or OS) and repeat players (RP) who are engaged in many similar litigations over time.[81]

[78] Lorentzon et al. (2022).

[79] $OR > 1.0$ indicate that lawyer-represented parties tend to have better outcomes (in terms of likelihood of winning their cases) than do unrepresented people, on average.

[80] Cf. Assy (2015), p. 1.

[81] Galanter (1974a), p. 97. See also Galanter (1974b), pp. 347ff.; McCormick (1993), pp. 523ff.

Repeat players, on the one hand, are typically resourceful subjects ("haves"), e.g. state or municipal agencies, as well as larger corporations and organizations. One-shotters, on the other hand, are usually low-resource subjects ("have-nots"), such as private individuals or smaller companies.[82] Based on this distinction, Galanter concluded that RP:s enjoy several qualitative and quantitative advantages over OS:s, which are likely to influence the outcome of a legal procedure to the benefit of the former. Galanter's own parable is illustrative:

> Basically, this distinction is between the casual participant for whom the game is an emergency and the party who is equipped to do it as part of his routine activity. The sailor overboard and the shark are both swimmers, but only one is in the swimming business.[83]

The assumption that certain categories of parties, for various reasons, are better equipped to handle the court system than other categories of parties, is usually referred to as "the party capability theory" (or "the resource inequality theory").[84] A large number of empirical studies have confirmed this theory,[85] demonstrating that repeat players and one-shotters have different success rates in court proceedings.[86] In nuce, research show that it is much more likely for an RP to come out as the winning party in a dispute against an OS, than for the outcome to be the opposite.[87] This statistical pattern is even more clear, when the repeat player is a state or municipal agency, and the one-shotter is an individual.[88]

Statistics gathered from the Swedish Court Administration show that only approximately 10% of the decisions appealed by a private party to an administrative

[82]Cf. McCormick (1993), p. 525, who defines repeat players as "organizations whose activities frequently and routinely involve litigation", while one-shotters are "individuals whose involvement with the courts is rare, sporadic and frequently involuntary".

[83]Galanter (1974b), p. 363; cf. McCormick (1993), p. 524.

[84]Galanter (1974b), p. 360; cf. Haynie (1994), p. 753.

[85]See McCormick (1993), pp. 523ff. and the contributions in Kritzer and Silbey (2003).

[86]Cf. Epp (1999), pp. 1090f., who concludes that "[t]he relative success of a repeat player has been borne out in a large body of empirical research", that "individuals fare relatively poorly against organizational and governmental litigants" and that these conclusions belong to "one of the most consistently observed and remarkably stable patterns of observations in Law and Society research".

[87]See, for example, Wheeler et al. (1987), Atkins (1991), Songer and Sheehan (1992), Blomgren Bingham (1997), McGuire (1998) Songer et al. (1999), Kinsey and Stalans (1999) Farole (1999), Dotan (1999), Songer et al. (2000), Cohen and Spitzer (2000), and Kong-Pin et al. (2014); cf. Haynie (1994), Sheehan et al. (1992), Smyth (2000) and Kopczynski (2008). Regarding alternative dispute resolution (ADR), see also Menkel-Meadow (1999).

[88]See, e.g., Dotan (1999), p. 1075, who concludes that "public agencies are, in fact, the most successful litigant in almost all the surveys that studied outcomes in litigation" and Kritzer (2003), p. 351: "While there are some specific types of exceptions, the advantage to government greatly exceeds that of the other set of 'haves', business or corporations. Moreover, in cases pitting one level of government against another level of government, the higher level of government, in whose courts the case is typically decided, has an advantage." See also Risenfors et al. (2020), confirming the same pattern in Swedish administrative procedure (*infra* footnote 92).

Table 1 Overall success rates in Swedish administrative procedure

Case category	The appealed decision was changed by the court (%)	The appealed decision was upheld by the court (%)
Tax	13.9	86.1
Social insurance	15.7	84.3
Welfare benefits	11.4	88.6
Compulsory care, children	3.1	96.9
Compulsory care, addicts	0.4	99.6
Compulsory care, mentally ill	0.5	99.5
Public procurement	0.8	99.2

court are changed (wholly or partially[89]) by the court, indicating (at least some) "success" for the private party. This means that in circa 90% of the cases decided by administrative courts of first instance, the court upholds (i.e., confirms) the appealed decision, without any change at all, giving the public party a "complete success". In fact, in some categories of cases, the numbers are even more skewed to the advantage of the public party, as the examples in Table 1 illustrates.[90]

Since private parties in administrative cases are usually one-shotters, whereas their public (state or municipal) counterparty can often be regarded as a repeat player, the statistics presented in Table 1—showing remarkable success rates for public parties in Swedish administrative procedure[91]—are in line with the existing literature on varying party capabilities and their effect on case outcomes.[92]

[89] If a decision is changed only partially, then both parties have "won" in part (i.e., both parties are partially winners/losers).

[90] The statistics presented in Table 1 was received upon request from the Swedish Court Administration, using the search tool "SIV – måluppföljning". The numbers were collected from the system 28/10/2021.

[91] It should be noted that the second column (appealed decisions "changed by the court") includes two categories of cases: Here, we find cases where the court completely agreed with the private party's claims and changed the decision accordingly, resulting in a "complete success" for the private party. However, this column also includes such cases where the court only *partially* agreed with the private party, giving both parties a "partial success". In the third column (appealed decisions "upheld by the court"), we find such cases where the court did not make any change in the decision, resulting in a "complete success" for the public party.

[92] As indicated in footnote 88 *supra,* this pattern has been confirmed in socio-legal research. For example, in Risenfors et al. (2020), we could show that state agencies had highest "success rates", followed by municipal agencies, followed by corporations, followed by individuals. When these categories of parties appealed a verdict from an administrative court of first instance (*förvaltningsrätt*) to an administrative court of appeal (*kammarrätt*), state agencies were granted leave to appeal in 78% of the cases, municipal agencies in 51% of the cases, corporations in 21% of the cases, whereas individuals were only granted leave to appeal in 8% of the cases (*ibid.* p. 294).

4.2 Levelling the Playing Field

At least qualified counsels (typically lawyers) can themselves be described as repeat players, since they possess both the theoretical skill-set necessary to prepare and argue a case effectively, and—with accumulated time spent in court—practical hands-on experience. Based on Galanter's research, several follow-up studies have accordingly examined if and how having access to a lawyer affects weaker parties' success rates in court proceedings.

The empirical question asked in the body of research regarding lawyer advantage is quite straightforward: Can access to a lawyer somehow "level the playing field", i.e., create some sort of balance between otherwise imbalanced parties, by improving the weaker party's prospects of success? In several studies, this question has been answered in the affirmative—not just in formal and highly adversarial settings, but also in informal and "simplified" procedures, where private parties are presumed to appear pro se.[93]

In short, it has been proven that parties who have access to counsel have a statistical advantage (i.e., higher success rates), compared to parties who proceed without counsel. Unfortunately, it is not possible to account for all such studies here.[94] Instead, I will use three meta-studies conducted by Rebecca Sandefur, to summarize some of the existing knowledge.

> In the first study, *Effects of Representation on Trial and Hearing Outcomes in Two Common Law Countries* (2005), Sandefur concluded that "lawyer representation is usually positively related to case outcomes: on average, parties with lawyers increase their odds of winning by 72% over parties who represent themselves." In the present study, the highest observed lawyer advantage was almost 4-fold ($OR = 3.92$), meaning that parties with lawyers increased their odds of winning by 392% compared to parties who represented themselves.[95]

> The subsequent study, *The Impact of Counsel: An Analysis of Empirical Evidence* (2010) gave similar results. Sandefur concluded that "lawyer-represented people are more likely to win than are unrepresented people in every study". However, "though this difference consistently indicates that lawyer-represented parties enjoy better outcomes than do unrepresented parties, just how much better varies considerably across studies—from a study where lawyer-represented people are 19% more likely to win than unrepresented people, to studies where lawyer-represented people are three or four times more likely to win, to a study which finds that lawyer-represented people are almost fourteen times (*odds ratio* = 13.79) more likely to win than are unrepresented people".[96]

> The final study, *Elements of Professional Expertise: Understanding Relational and Substantive Expertise through Lawyers' Impact* (2015), differed somewhat from the two

[93] See, for example, Lewis (2007) and Genn and Genn (1989).

[94] However, a few examples could be mentioned: Scherer (2006), Lederman and Hrung (2006), Moorhead and Sefton (2005), Murphy (2003), Hannaford-Agor and Mott (2003), Dewar et al. (2000), Gunn (1995), Bezdek (1992), and Mosier and Soble (1973); cf. Williams (2011) and Engler (2010). See also the two randomized trial studies conducted by Pleasence and Balmer (2007) and Seron et al. (2001).

[95] Sandefur (2005), p. 15.

[96] Sandefur (2010), p. 69.

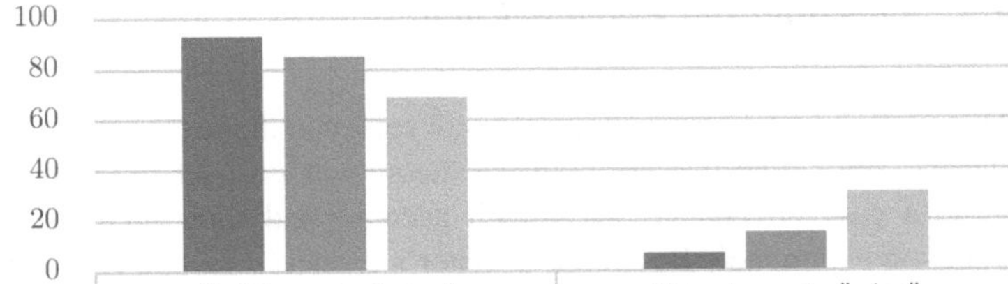

	Public party "wins"	Private party "wins"
No counsel	93	7
Unqualified counsel	85	15
Qualified counsel	69	31

Fig. 1 Success rates in Swedish administrative procedure when private parties lack/have access to legal representation

> previous studies, since it made a distinction between lawyer representation, representation by a non-lawyer advocate (NLA) and no representation at all. Sandefur concluded that "the effect of lawyers on case outcomes is to increase the likelihood of winning by about 540 percent (*OR* = 5.4), on average". Sandefur could also show that having access to a qualified counsel increased the chances of winning more than having access to an unqualified counsel.[97]

In our above mentioned study, titled *Ombudsfördel i förvaltningsmål* ("Lawyer Advantage in administrative cases"), we have examined if a lawyer advantage could be statistically proven in the Swedish administrative procedure. We selected three very different categories of administrative cases, regarding taxes, public procurement, and the right to have a personal "care assistant" (the latter being a social security benefit, that can be granted people with very severe physical or mental disabilities[98]). In each category, we collected, coded, and analysed about 1200 cases (i.e., our study contained approximately 3600 cases in total). Among other variables, we took into account *who won the case*, excluding such cases where both parties had "partial success". Then, we coded if the private party *had access to a counsel*, and if so, whether the counsel was *qualified* (had some sort of legal qualifications) or was *unqualified* (usually a family member). The overall success rates (in percent) for these three categories of private parties (viz. "no counsel", "unqualified counsel", and "qualified counsel") are summarised in Fig. 1.[99]

[97] Sandefur (2015), pp. 921f.: "Under the assumption that representation is exogenous to the probability of winning, replacing NLAs with lawyers would raise the chance of winning by an average of 40 percent (*OR* = 1.4)."

[98] According to the Act concerning Support and Service for Persons with Certain Functional Impairments (*lagen* [1993:387] *om stöd och service till vissa funktionshindrade*, LSS).

[99] Lorentzon et al. (2022), p. 85.

If the numbers in Fig. 1 are instead presented as *odds ratios*, having access to a *qualified counsel* in Swedish administrative procedure increased the odds of winning the case by roughly 600% ($OR = 6.08$), if compared to having *no counsel at all.*[100]

5 Discussion and Conclusions

As noted in the broader discussion regarding (lack of) "access to justice" in modern societies, people in general have great difficulty in both identifying and vindicating their legal rights.[101] When a layperson is forced to go to court, the challenge becomes even greater, since the party must now deal with two different legal frameworks at the same time: on the one hand, the substantive law (governing the underlying legal dispute/relationship); on the other hand, the procedural law (governing the legal procedure).[102] In other words, a court procedure *as such* will inevitably add an additional layer of complexity to an already complex legal situation.

5.1 Debunking the Myth of "Simplified Procedures"

A trial is, both literally and figuratively, a *procedure,* a *process,* a *proceeding,* i.e., a course, a passage, a sequence of events—it is a movement in time and space, taking the parties from point a to point b. This means that the trial necessitates *actions* to move forward. Every act (claim, petition or motion made, ground or evidence invoked, etcetera), as well every failure to act, have consequences. In this sense, a trial can be compared to a walk along a dangerous path, or "a perilous journey", to quote Stephan Trechsel:

> Regularly, it leads to crossroads, where decisions have to be taken. Failure to act decisively lead to the definite forfeiture of a right. The wrong decision may cause irreparable damage. Reliable knowledge of law and practice is required in order to assess the consequences of such decisions.[103]

Regarding the (in)ability of LIP:s to walk this road, Kim Williams made the following conclusion in his literature review:

> [M]ost research suggested that litigants in person may experience a number of problems, which in turn impact on the court. For instance, the research pointed to problems with

[100] Lorentzon et al. (2022), p. 85, footnote 113.

[101] See, e.g., Currie (2009); Sandefur (2009), p. ixf; Albiston and Sandefur (2013), pp. 103f. See also Cappelletti and Garth (1981) and Rhode (2004).

[102] Cf. Zuckerman (2013), p. 3.30: "Court proceedings are of necessity regulated by rules for without rules there can be no system of justice, only anarchy and arbitrariness."

[103] Trechsel (2005), p. 245.

> understanding evidential requirements, difficulties with forms, and identifying facts relevant to the case. A number of sources also pointed out that litigants in person may have difficulty understanding the nature of proceedings, were often overwhelmed by the procedural and oral demands of the courtroom and had difficulty explaining the details of their case.[104]

Several studies have shown that this conclusion holds true even for such "simplified" (or "informal") procedures, in which individuals are presumed to conduct their own case. For example, in a study regarding small claims-procedure in the U.K., Paul Lewis found that litigants in person experienced "difficulty in adducing adequate evidence" and suffered "detriment as a result". Hence, the author concluded that his study supported "the findings of researchers who have shown that both difficulty and detriment can occur even in informal legal procedures where self-representation is encouraged or expected".[105] In another study, regarding informal tribunal-hearings (also in the U.K.), Hazel Genn and Yvette Genn concluded that their data "demonstrated conclusively that, the presence of a representative significantly increases the probability that social security appellants, appellants before immigration adjudicators, industrial tribunal applicants and patients detained in mental hospitals will succeed with their cases at tribunal hearings".[106] As I have shown above, with reference to my own research, our findings regarding Swedish administrative procedure are the same.

5.2 *There Is No Such Thing as a Free Lunch*

With this contribution to the Yearbook of Socio-Economic Constitutions, my aim has been to challenge the narrative that public spending on legal aid can be cut, simply by "simplifying" legal procedure. The following conclusion, drawn by Genn and Genn, is—in my opinion—analogous for the Swedish administrative courts:

> [N]o matter how well-intentioned tribunals might be, it was impossible to compensate for lack of representation. [. . .] Tribunals cannot spend the time necessary to elicit relevant information from the undifferentiated stream of information in which most appellants and applicants present their stories. Nor can they always know, in advance of hearing the evidence, what questions should be asked.[107]

Access to justice refers to the fundamental notion that all people—even disadvantaged groups in society—should enjoy effective legal protection, ultimately through the courts. The principal aim of the access to justice-movement has been to identify, and try to overcome, so-called "access barriers", i.e., different legal and practical

[104] Williams (2011), p. 5. See also, e.g., Lewis (2007), pp. 32ff.; Langan (2005), p. 843; Sales et al. (1993), pp. 569f.; Genn and Genn (1989), p. 244; Moorhead and Sefton (2005), pp. 153ff.; Hannaford-Agor and Mott (2003), p. 163.

[105] Lewis (2007), p. 46.

[106] Genn and Genn (1989), p. 107.

[107] Genn and Genn (1989), p. 215.

obstacles that make it difficult, or even impossible, for the general public to turn to the courts in order to vindicate their rights. One of these barriers is legal fees in general, and counsel fees in particular—nota bene—if, and only if, the procedure *has been designed in such a way that individuals need to engage a lawyer to effectively bring (or defend) an action in court.*

This approach to counsel fees draws upon the wider definition of "access to court" as it has been developed in the case-law of the ECtHR. In several cases, the ECtHR has concluded that law—substantive as well as procedural—is a rather complicated matter, which is often unintelligible for laypersons.[108] Although the Court has accepted "simplification of procedure" as a theoretical alternative to providing legal aid, empirical research clearly show that this is not working in practice. Consequently, many self-represented litigants are not accorded effective access to court—contrary to the requirements of Article 6 ECHR—simply because they lack the skills necessary to present their case properly.

In Sweden, the right to counsel is unconditional, in the sense that a party to a dispute is always free to hire a lawyer. Yet, since lawyers' fees are not reimbursed in the administrative procedure, this right—that is theoretically bestowed on all—is in practice denied many by the realities of economics. Considering the imbalance between the private party (who is often in a vulnerable position) and his/her public counterparty (a state or municipal agency), it can indeed be questioned whether individuals are guaranteed effective access to court and a fair trial—especially equality of arms. Statistics from the Swedish Court Administration show that private parties lose over 90% of the cases brought before the administrative courts (in some case categories over 99%). Our empirical data corroborate these figures, but also demonstrate that individuals have much greater prospects for success if they enjoy legal representation.

In sum, it may seem as we are trapped between Scylla and Charybdis: If simplification is not a feasible alternative (and market solutions, such as LEI, are not in place) then—according to the case law of the ECtHR—we have no other alternative than to make lawyers available through legal aid and/or cost-shifting rules. However, this conclusion may be easier to digest, if securing access to civil justice (through effective access to court) is not considered yet another "welfare program" (or a "public service"), but rather as a core function of government.[109] In the words of Richard Sanders: "If it is a legitimate role of the government to build courthouses and hire judges, is it not only a difference in degree, not kind, to assure

[108] See, e.g., *Pishchalnikov v. Russia*, app. no. 7025/04, § 84; cf. Trechsel (2005), p. 245.

[109] See Clarke and Sorabji (2009), p. 39, who argue that the civil justice system "is at the heart of the State in exactly the same way as Parliament, which is to say the legislature, and the Government, which is to say the Executive, are both at the heart of the State. The legislature, executive and justice systems, which in this context encompass the courts and the judiciary, are equal, independent and essential limbs of the State and particularly a State committed to democracy and the rule of law. Absent any one of these limbs a State cannot truly be democratic and properly committed to the rule of law."

litigants adequate representation so they may properly present their case when they go to court?”[110]

Legal Statues

The Act concerning Counsel for the Injured Party, (*lagen* [1988:609] *om målsägandebiträde*)
The Act concerning Public Counsel (*lagen* [1996:1620] *om offentligt bitrade*)
The Act concerning Support and Service for Persons with Certain Functional Impairments (*lagen* [1993:387] *om stöd och service till vissa funktionshindrade*)
The Administrative Court Procedure Act (*förvaltningsprocesslagen* [1971:291])
The Aliens Act (*utlänningslagen* [2005:716])
The Care of Abusers Act (*lagen* [1988:870] *om vård av missbrukare i vissa fall*)
The Care of Young Persons Act (*lagen* [1990:52] *med särskilda bestämmelser om vård av unga*)
The Code of Judicial Procedure (*rättegångsbalken* [1942:740])
The Compulsory Psychiatric Care Act (*lagen* [1991:1128] *om psykiatrisk tvångsvård*)
The Legal Aid Act (*rättshjälpslagen* [1996:1619])
The Tax Procedures Act (*skatteförfarandelagen* [2011:1244])
The Young Offenders Act (*lagen* [1964:167] *med särskilda bestämmelser om unga lagöverträdare*)

Government Bills

Prop. 2000/01:79, Stöd till brottsoffer
Prop. 1996/97:9, Ny rättshjälpslag
Prop. 1993/94:151, Rättssäkerhet vid beskattningen
Prop. 1993/94:26, Om utvidgad rätt till målsägandebiträde, m.m.
Prop. 1989/90:158, Om utvidgad rätt till målsägandebiträde, m.m.
Prop. 1988/89:126, Om ersättning för kostnader i ärenden och mål om skatt, m.m.
Prop. 1987/88:107, Om målsägandebiträde
Prop. 1983/84:23, Om rätten till offentlig försvarare
Prop. 1972:4, Förslag till rättshjälpslag, m.m.

[110] Sanders (1999); cf. Zuckerman (1999), p. 9, concluding that access to justice is “a fundamental civic or constitutional right recognized by all civilized societies”.

Official Reports of the Swedish Government

SOU 2014:86, Rättvisans pris
SOU 1971:76, Offentligt biträde och kostnadsersättning i förvaltningsärenden
SOU 1938:44, Förslag till rättegångsbalk – motiv, m.m.
SOU 1926:33, Angående rättegångsväsendets ombildning – rättegången i tvistemål
SOU 1926:32, Angående rättegångsväsendets ombildning – rättegången i brottmål

Case Law: The European Court of Human Rights

Airey v. Ireland, app. no. 6289/73, 9/10/1979.
Černius and Rinkevičius v. Lithuania, app. nos. 73579/17 and 14620/18, 18/06/2020
Pishchalnikov v. Russia, app. no. 7025/04, 24/09/2009
Stankiewicz v. Poland, app. no. 46917/99, 06/04/2006
Quaranta v. Switzerland, app. no. 12744/87, 24/05/1991
Steel & Morris v. the United Kingdom, app. no. 68416/01, 15/02/2005
Zustović v. Croatia, app. no. 27903/15, 22/04/2021

Case Law: The Supreme Court of Sweden

NJA 2021 s. 235
NJA 2020 s. 908
NJA 2015 s. 374

Case Law: The Supreme Administrative Court of Sweden

HFD 2021 ref. 36
HFD 2020 not. 47
RÅ 2009 not. 202
RÅ 2006 ref. 89

Other Sources

Swedish Court Administration [*Domstolsverket*], Annual rapport 2022. https://www.domstol.se/globalassets/filer/gemensamt-innehall/styrning-och-riktlinjer/arsredovisning/arsredovisning_2022_sverigesdomstolar.pdf. Accessed 19/03/2023.

Statistics Sweden [*Statistiska Centralbyrån*], Average income 2021. https://www.scb.se/hitta-statistik/sverige-i-siffror/utbildning-jobb-och-pengar/medelloner-i-sverige. Accessed 19/03/2023.

References

Albiston C, Sandefur R (2013) Expanding the empirical study of access to justice. Wisconsin Law Rev 2013:101–120

Albrecht R, Greacen M, Hough B, Zorza R (2003) Judicial techniques for cases involving self-represented litigants. Judges' J 42:16–48

Andrews N (2014) Case management and procedural discipline in England & Wales: fundamentals of an essential new technique. In: van Rhee C, Yulin F (eds) Civil litigation in China and Europe: Ius gentium: comparative perspectives on law and justice. Dordrecht, pp 335–347

Assy R (2011) Revisiting the right to self-representation. Civil Justice Q 30:267–282

Assy R (2012) Revisiting the right to self-representation. Oxford Leg Res Papers 2:1–25

Assy R (2015) Injustice in person: the right to self-representation. Oxford University Press, Oxford

Astrup Hjort M (2022) Norsk småkravsprocess og access to justice. In: Wallerman Ghavanini A, Wejedal S (eds) Access to justice i Skandinavien. Santérus Academic Press, Stockholm, pp 211–234

Atkins B (1991) Party capability theory as explanation for intervention behavior in the English Court of Appeal. Am J Polit Sci 35:881–903

Balmer N, Buck A, Patel A, Denvir C, Pleasence P (2010) Knowledge, capability and the experience of rights problems. Public Legal Education Network, London

Barlow A (2019) The machinery of legal aid: a critical comparison, from a public law perspective, of the United Kingdom, the Republic of Ireland and the Nordic countries. Åbo Akademi University Press, Åbo

Beka A (2018) The active role of courts in consumer litigation: applying EU law of the national courts' own motion. Intersentia, Cambridge

Bellander H (2017) Rättegångskostnader – om kostnadsbördan i dispositiva tvistemål. Iustus, Uppsala

Bezdek B (1992) Silence in the court: participation and subordination of poor tenants' voices in legal process. Hofstra Law Rev 20:533–608

Blomgren Bingham L (1997) Employment arbitration: the repeat player effect. Employee Rights Employment Policy J 1:189–220

Brosh E (2015) Cutting corners or enhancing efficiency: simplified procedures and the Israeli quest to speed up justice. Erasmus Law Rev 8:185–200

Buck A, Balmer N, Pleasence P (2005) Social exclusion and civil law: experience of civil justice problems among vulnerable groups. Soc Policy Adm 39:302–322

Buhai S (2009) Access to justice for unrepresented litigants: a comparative perspective. Loyola L A Law Rev 42:979–1020

Cameron C, Kelly E (2002) Litigants in person in civil proceedings. Hong Kong Law J 32:313–342

Cappelletti M, Garth B (1981) Access to justice and the welfare state: an introduction. In: Cappelletti M (ed) Access to justice and the welfare state. Alphen aan den Rijn, Sijthoff, pp 1–24

Cerruti E (2009) Self-representation in the international arena: striking a false right of spectacle. Georgetown J Int Law 40:919–984

Clarke A, Sorabji J (2009) The importance of civil justice. Bracton Law J 41:32–43

Cohen L, Spitzer M (2000) The government litigant advantage: implications for the law. Florida State Univ Law Rev 28:391–425

Currie A (2009) The legal problems of everyday life. In: Sandefur R (ed) Access to justice. Emerald Group, Bingley, pp 1–41

Denvir C, Balmer N, Pleasence P (2013) When legal rights are not a reality: do individuals know their rights and how can we tell? J Soc Welfare Family Law 35:139–160
Dewar J, Smith B, Banks C (2000) Litigants in person in the Family Court of Australia. Report to the Family Court of Australia, research report no. 20:2000
Dotan Y (1999) Do the "haves" still come out ahead? Resource inequalities in ideological courts: the case of the Israeli High Court of Justice. Law Soc Rev 33:1059–1080
Dyer C (2007) The Queen of Chula Vista: stories of self-represented litigants and a call for using cognitive linguistics to work with them. Law Library J 99:717–756
Engler R (1999) And justice for all – including the unrepresented poor: revisiting the roles of the judges, mediators, and clerks. Fordham Law Rev 67:1987–2070
Engler R (2010) Connecting self-representation to Civil Gideon: what existing data reveal about when counsel is most needed. Fordham Urban Law J 37:37–92
Epp C (1999) The two motifs of "why the 'haves' come out ahead" and its heirs. Law Soc Rev 33: 1089–1098
Farole D (1999) Reexamining litigant success in State Supreme Court. Law Soc Rev 33:1043–1058
Fjóla Antonsdóttir H (2018) Legal aid in Iceland. In: Hammerslev O, Halvorsen Rønning O (eds) Outsourcing legal aid in the Nordic Welfare States. Palgrave Macmillan/Springer, Cham, pp 125–146
Fuller L (1978) The forms and limits of adjudication. Harv Law Rev 92:353–409
Galanter M (1974a) Why the "haves" come out ahead: speculations on the limits of legal change. Law Soc Rev 9:95–160
Galanter M (1974b) Explaining litigation. Law Soc Rev 9:347–368
Genn H (2013) Do-it-yourself law: access to justice and the challenge of self-representation. Civil Justice Q 32:411–444
Genn H (2015) Foreword. In: Assy R (ed) Injustice in person: the right to self-representation. Oxford University Press, Oxford, pp vii–viii
Genn H, Genn Y (1989) The effectiveness of representation at tribunals. Report to the Lord Chancellor, Lord Chancellor's Department
Gidi A, Zaneti H (2015) Brazilian civil procedure in the age of austerity. Erasmus Law Rev 8:245–257
Goldschmidt J (2002) The pro se litigant's struggle for access to justice: meeting the challenge of bench and bar resistance. Family Court Rev 40:36–62
Gomez M, Gomez J (2015) A view from the sky: general overview about civil litigation in the United States with reference to the relief in small and simple matters. Erasmus Law Rev 8:225–231
Gunn S (1995) Eviction defense for poor tenants: costly compassion or justice served? Yale Law Policy Rev 13:385–428
Halvorsen Rønning O (2018) Legal aid in Norway. In: Hammerslev O, Halvorsen Rønning O (eds) Outsourcing legal aid in the Nordic Welfare States. Palgrave Macmillan/Springer, Cham, pp 15–41
Hammerslev O, Halvorsen Rønning O (eds) (2018) Outsourcing legal aid in the Nordic Welfare States. Palgrave Macmillan/Springer, Cham
Hannaford-Agor P, Mott N (2003) Research on self-represented litigation: preliminary results and methodological considerations. Justice Syst J 24:163–181
Haynie S (1994) Inequalities and litigation outcomes in the Philippine Supreme Court. J Polit 56: 752–772
Hoevenaars J, Kramer X (2022) Improving access to information in European Civil Justice: a mission (im)possible? In: von Hein J, Kruger T (eds) Informed choices in cross-border enforcement, the European state of the art and future perspectives. Intersentia, Cambridge, pp 503–525
Johnsen J (2022) Offentlig rettshjelp og tilgang til rettshåndheving. In: Wallerman Ghavanini A, Wejedal S (eds) Access to justice i Skandinavien. Santérus Academic Press, Stockholm, pp 137–164

Kinsey K, Stalans L (1999) Which “haves” come out ahead and why? Cultural capital and legal mobilization in frontline law enforcement. Law Soc Rev 33:993–1024
Kong-Pin C, Kuo-Chang H, Chang-Ching L (2014) Party capability versus court preference: why do the “haves” come out ahead? J Law Econ Organ 31:93–126
Kopczynski M (2008) The haves coming out behind: Galanter’s theory tested on the WTO Dispute Settlement System. Asper Rev Int Bus Trade Law 25:25–50
Kramer X, Kakiuchi S (2015) Austerity in civil procedure and the role of simplified procedures. Erasmus Law Rev 8:139–146
Kritzer H (2003) The Government Gorilla – why does government come out ahead in appellate courts? In: Kritzer H, Silbey S (eds) In litigation: do the haves still come out ahead? Stanford University Press, Stanford, pp 342–370
Kritzer H, Silbey S (eds) (2003) In litigation: do the haves still come out ahead? Stanford University Press, Stanford
Langan AM (2005) Threatening the balance of the scales of justice: unrepresented litigants in the family courts of Ontario. Queen’s Law J 30:825–862
Lederman L, Hrung W (2006) Do attorneys do their clients justice – an empirical study of lawyers’ effects on tax court litigation outcomes. Wake Forest Law Rev 41:1235–1296
Lemann Kristiansen B (2018) Legal aid in Denmark. In: Hammerslev O, Halvorsen Rønning O (eds) Outsourcing legal aid in the Nordic Welfare States. Palgrave Macmillan/Springer, Cham, pp 99–124
Lemann Kristiansen B (2022) Access to justice i forvaltningssager i Danmark. In: Wallerman Ghavanini A, Wejedal S (eds) Access to justice i Skandinavien. Santérus Academic Press, Stockholm, pp 59–82
Lewis P (2007) Litigants in person and their difficulties in adducing evidence: a study of small claims in an English County Court. Int J Evid Proof 11:24–48
Lorentzon R, Holm L, Wejedal S (2022) Ombudsfördel i förvaltningsmål – ett empiriskt bidrag till teorin om “lawyer advantage”. Förvaltningsrättslig Tidskrift 1:47–93
Lucy W (2005) The possibility of impartiality. Oxf J Leg Stud 25:3–32
Mather L (2003) Changing patterns of legal representation in divorce: from lawyers to pro se. J Law Soc 30:137–155
McCormick P (1993) Party capability theory and appellate success in the Supreme Court of Canada, 1949–1992. Can J Polit Sci 26:52–3540
McGuire K (1998) Explaining executive success on the U.S. Supreme Court. Polit Res Q 51:505–526
Menkel-Meadow C (1999) Do the “haves” come out ahead in alternative judicial systems? – repeat players in ADR. Ohio State J Dispute Resolution 19:19–61
Moorhead R (2003) Access or aggravation? Litigants in person, McKenzie Friends and Lay representation. Civil Justice Q 22:133–155
Moorhead R, Sefton M (2005) Litigants in person – unrepresented litigants in first instance proceedings. Cardiff University, DCA Research Series 2/05, Cardiff
Mosier M, Soble R (1973) Modern legislation, metropolitan court, miniscule results: a study of Detroit’s Landlord-Tenant Court. Univ Mich J Law Reform 7:8–70
Murphy J (2003) Engaging with the state: the growing reliance on lawyers and judges to protect battered women. Am Univ J Gender Soc Policy Law 11:499–521
Pleasence P, Balmer N (2007) Changing fortunes: results from a randomized trial of the offer of debt advice in England and Wales. J Empir Leg Stud 4:651–673
Pleasence P, Balmer N (2012) Caught in the middle: justiciable problems and the use of lawyers’. In: Trebilcock M, Duggan A, Sossin L (eds) Middle income access to justice. University of Toronto Press, Toronto, pp 27–54
Pleasence P, Balmer N (2018) Measuring the accessibility and equality of civil justice. Hague J Rule Law 10:255–294

Pleasence P, Buck A, Balmer A, O'Grady A, Genn H, Smith M (2004) Causes of action: civil law and social justice. The Final Report of the First LSRC Survey of Justiciable Problem, Legal Service Commission
Pleasence P, Balmer N, Sandefur R (2013) Paths to justice: a past, present and future roadmap. Report prepared under a grant from the Nuffield Foundation (AJU/39100)
Resnik J (1982) Managerial judges. Harv Law Rev 96:374–448
Rhode D (2004) Access to justice. Oxford University Press, Oxford
Risenfors A, Holm L, Wejedal S (2020) Vem får prövningstillstånd i kammarrätt? Ett empiriskt bidrag till teorin om "party capability". Förvaltningsrättslig Tidskrift 2:261–304
Rissanen A (2018) Legal aid in Finland. In: Hammerslev O, Halvorsen Rønning O (eds) Outsourcing legal aid in the Nordic Welfare States. Palgrave Macmillan/Springer, Cham, pp 77–97
Robinson P (1996) The criminal-civil distinction and the utility of desert. Boston Univ Law Rev 76: 201–214
Sabeli M, Leyton S (2000) Train wrecks and freeway crashes – an argument for fairness and against self representation in the criminal justice system. J Crim Law Criminol 91:161–236
Sales B, Beck C, Haan R (1993) Is self-representation a reasonable alternative to attorney representation in divorce cases? Saint Louis Univ Law J 37:553–606
Sandefur R (2005) Effects of representation on trial and hearing outcomes in two common law countries. In: Paper prepared for presentation at the meetings of the Research Committee on the Sociology of Law of the International Sociological Association
Sandefur R (2009) Access to justice: classical approaches and new directions. In: Sandefur R (ed) Access to justice. Emerald Group Publishing, Bingley, pp ix–xvii
Sandefur R (2010) The impact of counsel: an analysis of empirical evidence. Seattle J Soc Justice 9: 51–95
Sandefur R (2015) Elements of professional expertise: understanding relational and substantive expertise through lawyers' impact. Am Sociol Rev 80:909–933
Sanders R (1999) "Access to Justice": a noble principle in beggar's rags. In: Access to justice conference, 25–27 June 1999, Washington State
Scherer A (2006) Why people who face losing their homes in legal proceedings must have a right to counsel. Cardozo Public Law Policy Ethics J 3:699–732
Schoultz I (2018) Legal aid in Sweden. In: Hammerslev O, Halvorsen Rønning O (eds) Outsourcing legal aid in the Nordic Welfare States. Palgrave Macmillan/Springer, Cham, pp 43–76
Seron C, Frankel M, Van Ryzin G, Kovath J (2001) The impact of legal counsel on outcomes for poor tenants in New York City's Housing Court: results of a randomized experiment. Law Soc Rev 35:419–434
Sharpe R (2016) Injustice in person: the right to self-representation, by Assy, R [Oxford University Press, Oxford, 2015]. Camb Law J 75:435–437
Sheehan R, Mishler W, Songer D (1992) Ideology, status, and the differential success of direct parties before the Supreme Court. Am Polit Sci Rev 86:464–471
Silver J, Farrow T (2015) Canadian civil justice: relief in small and simple matters in an age of efficiency. Erasmus Law Rev 8:232–244
Smith E (2022) I Norge avgøres forvaltningsrettslige saker (stort sett) utenfor domstol. In: Wallerman Ghavanini A, Wejedal S (eds) Access to justice i Skandinavien. Santérus Academic Press, Stockholm, pp 35–58
Smyth R (2000) The "haves" and the "have nots": an empirical study of the rational actor and party capability hypotheses in the High Court 1948–99. Aust J Polit Sci 35:255–274
Snukals B, Sturtvant G (2007) Pro se litigation: best practices from a judge's perspective. Univ Richmond Law Rev 42:93–105
Songer D, Sheehan R (1992) Who wins on appeal? Upperdogs and underdogs in the United States Courts of Appeals. Am J Polit Sci 36:235–258

Songer D, Sheehan R, Haire S (1999) Do the "Haves" come out ahead over time? Applying Galanter's Framework to decisions of the U.S. Courts of Appeals 1925–1988. Law Soc Rev 33:811–832

Songer D, Kuersten A, Kaheny E (2000) Why the haves don't always come out ahead: repeat players meet amici curiae for the disadvantaged. Polit Res Q 53:537–556

Sorabji J (2014) The crisis of legal aid and alternative solutions. In: Effective access to justice, International Association of Procedural Law Seoul Conference 2014, pp 1–28

Sorabji J (2015) Austerity's effect on English Civil Justice. Erasmus Law Rev 8:159–173

Sorabji J (2018) Managing claims. Peking Univ Law J 6:179–235

Sorabji J (2021) Justice without lawyers. In: Kramer X, Biard A, Hoevenaars J, Themeli E (eds) New pathways to civil justice in Europe. Springer, Cham, pp 221–242

Sugiyama E (2015) Simplified civil procedure in Japan. Erasmus Law Rev 8:201–209

Swank D (2005a) In defense of rules and roles: the need to curb extreme forms of pro se assistance and accommodation in litigation. Am Univ Law Rev 54:1537–1594

Swank D (2005b) The pro se phenomenon. Brigham Young Univ J Public Law 19:373–386

Toone R (2005) The incoherence of defendant autonomy. N C Law Rev 83:621–666

Trechsel S (2005) Human rights in criminal proceedings. Oxford University Press, Oxford

Voet S (2015) Relief in small and simple matters in Belgium. Erasmus Law Rev 8:147–158

Wallerman Ghavanini A (2022) Access to justice för de små anspråken i den svenska civilprocessen. In: Wallerman Ghavanini A, Wejedal S (eds) Access to justice i Skandinavien. Santérus Academic Press, Stockholm, pp 137–164

Wejedal S (2017) Rätten till biträde – om biträdeskostnaders hantering vid svenska domstolar. University of Gothenburg

Wejedal S (2020–2021) Från Bolesławiec till Borås – om statens kostnadsansvar i domstolsärenden. Juridisk Tidskrift 3:726–744

Wejedal S (2021) Rättegångskostnaderna och den rättvisa rättegången – fyller RF tomrummet i FPL? Förvaltningsrättslig Tidskrift 3:515–546

Wejedal S (2022a) Rättshjälp i förvaltningsmål – två utvecklingslinjer i svensk rätt. In: Wallerman Ghavanini A, Wejedal S (eds) Access to justice i Skandinavien. Santérus Academic Press, Stockholm, pp 109–136

Wejedal S (2022b) Vingklippta domstolar? En kommentar till HFD 2022 ref. 10. Förvaltningsrättslig Tidskrift 3:471–496

Wejedal S (2023) "Finn fem fel" — några (sista) reflektioner med anledning av HFD 2022 ref. 10. Svensk Juristtidning 3:174–198

Wheeler S, Cartwright B, Kagan R, Friedman L (1987) Do the "Haves" come out ahead? Winning and losing in the state supreme courts 1870–1970. Law Soc Rev 21:403–445

Williams K (2011) Litigants in person: a literature review. Minist Justice Res Summ 2:2011

Woolf H (1995) Access to justice. Interim Report to the Lord Chancellor on the Civil Justice System in England & Wales, Lord Chancellor's Department

Zimerman N, Tyler T (2010) Between access to counsel and access to justice: a psychological perspective. Fordham Urban Law J 37:473–507

Zorza R (2004) The disconnect between the requirements of judicial neutrality and those of the appearance of neutrality when parties appear pro se: causes, solutions, recommendations, and implications. Georgetown J Leg Ethics 17:423–454

Zorza R (2009) An overview of self-represented litigation innovation, its impact, and an approach for the future: an invitation to dialogue. Family Law Q 43:519–544

Zuckerman A (1999) Justice in crisis: comparative dimensions of civil procedure. In: Zuckerman A, Chiarloni S, Gottwald P (eds) Justice in crisis: comparative dimensions of civil procedure. Oxford University Press, Oxford, pp 3–52

Zuckerman A (2013) Civil procedure: principles of practice. Sweet & Maxwell, London

Zuckerman A (2014) No justice without lawyers – the myth of inquisitorial solution. Civil Justice Q 33:355–374

"Equality of Legal Protection": On the Constitutional Derivation of the Right to Legal Aid in Administrative Proceedings and Its Effects on Legal Persons

Nils Schaks

Contents

Abstract This article addresses the question of where in German constitutional law the entitlement to legal aid is rooted and what effects this has on the entitlement to legal aid for legal persons. After a brief review of the rather inconsistent case law from the German Constitutional Court, the weaknesses of its approach are elaborated. This article then argues that, for administrative proceedings, the right to legal aid follows from the fundamental right which guarantees legal recourse (Article 19 [4] sentence 1 of German Basic Law [Grundgesetz or GG]). Legal aid is—in contrast to the prevailing view in German jurisprudence and scholarly literature—not anchored in the constitutional principles of social welfare, equality under the law, or the general principle of the rule of law.

This has a direct effect on legal persons' right to legal aid; contrary to the general opinion, they may also have a right to legal aid on constitutional grounds. While

N. Schaks (✉)
University of Mannheim, Mannheim, Germany
e-mail: nils.schaks@uni-mannheim.de

E. Storskrubb (ed.), *YSEC Yearbook of Socio-Economic Constitutions 2022*,
YSEC Yearbook of Socio-Economic Constitutions (2023) 2022: 215–244,
https://doi.org/10.1007/16495_2023_45, Published online: 28 March 2023

statutory law grants legal persons a right to legal aid, it does so only if additional requirements are met. One significant restriction is the requirement that the legal action not be contrary to the "public interest". It is precisely this additional requirement, which moreover dates back to a "law" passed in 1933 by the national socialist government, that makes individual legal protection for legal persons dependent on the interest of the public or third parties. This is an unnecessary burden and therefore unconstitutional.

1 The Constitutional "Equality of Legal Protection"

According to the prevailing opinion in German jurisprudence and scholarly literature, the Basic Law requires that in court proceedings the position of a less well-off person be at least largely aligned with that of a wealthier person. This is described using the term "equality of legal protection"[1] and is predominantly derived from the general fundamental right to equality (Article 3 [1] GG—"allgemeiner Gleichheitssatz") in conjunction with the general principle of the rule of law (Article 20 [3] GG—"Rechtsstaatsprinzip"), and partly also in conjunction with Article 20 (1) GG (the welfare state principle—"Sozialstaatsprinzip") or Article 19 (4) sentence 1 GG (the guarantee of legal recourse—"Rechtsweggarantie"). Furthermore, legal aid is predominantly regarded as a "welfare state benefit",[2] sometimes referred to as a "benefit of state welfare",[3] "social assistance in the field of administration of justice",[4] or a "special form of social assistance".[5]

The research question is whether legal persons also have a constitutional right to legal aid, and to what extent. This will be addressed in the following in three steps: Firstly, the legal aid situation for natural and legal persons will be presented. Secondly, the constitutional basis of the right to legal aid will be examined. Thirdly, the concrete effects of the constitutional foundation on the legal aid system for legal persons under statutory law will be discussed.

---

[1] German Constitutional Court Decisions 9, 124; 10, 264/270; 22, 83/86; 51, 295/302; 63, 380/394; 67, 245/248; 78, 104/117 et seq.; 81, 347/356 et seq.; 122, 39/49 et seq.; German Constitutional Court Chamber Decisions 9, 123/126; Ernst (2021), Article 19, marginal number 157; Huber (2018), Article 19, marginal number 464; Jarass (2022), Article 3, marginal number 85 et seq.; Peters and Altwicker (2022), chapter 21, marginal number 196.

[2] Gottwald (2004), p. 308; Rosenberg et al. (2018), § 87, marginal number 1. Similarly, see Riese (2022), § 166, marginal number 5.

[3] An earlier verdict: German Constitutional Court Decisions 9, 256/258; 35, 348/355.

[4] German Federal Supreme Court, NJW 2009, 3658/3659. An earlier verdict is in the German Constitutional Court Decisions 78, 104/113.

[5] See also Munich Administrative Court, decision of 27 July 2017—15 C 14.2047, BeckRS 2017, 121559, marginal number 11; Scholz (1995), p. 726.

Although this paper focuses on German law, the topic is of interest on the European level as well, as the decisions of the European Court of Justice (ECJ) and the European Court of Human Rights (ECtHR) demonstrate.[6] Legal aid for legal entities is also contested in other European states such as Austria and Switzerland. There is a clash between an emphasis on welfare state approaches to justifying legal aid and rule-of-law approaches, with the former tending to exclude legal persons.[7] The argument will be that the entitlement to legal aid for administrative proceedings is anchored in Article 19 (4) sentence 1 GG, which is a fundamental right to which legal persons are entitled. As a result, this would lead to a broader interpretation of the legal aid provisions for legal persons, because § 116 sentence 1 no. 2 of the Code of German Civil Procedure ("Zivilprozessordnung"—ZPO) with its additional requirements (public interest) is unconstitutional.

2 Legal Aid According to the Statutory Provisions

Litigation can be costly. Under German law, the losing party is required to pay not only its own legal fees, but those of the opponent and the court costs as well. The court costs must even be paid in advance. To compensate for the hardships to parties seeking legal protection, legal aid was introduced. Upon application, legal aid can be granted to a party "who, according to his or her personal and economic circumstances, cannot afford the costs of litigation, or can afford them only in part or only in instalments" "if the intended legal action or legal defence offers sufficient prospect of success and does not appear to be reckless", § 114 (1) sentence 1 ZPO. §§ 115–127 ZPO contain further stipulations regarding the prerequisites, procedure, and effects of the grant. As a result, the indigent party does not have to pay court costs or the costs of his or her own legal representation, or at most is only obligated to pay proportionately in instalments. These provisions of the ZPO are also referred to *inter alia* in the public law procedural rules in § 166 (I) sentence 1 of the German Code of Administrative Court Proceedings ("Verwaltungsgerichtsordnung"—VwGO). Thus, the ZPO's rules on legal aid also apply to public law procedural codes.

In the following, this article focuses on administrative proceedings under the VwGO,[8] for two reasons: First, a representative of the state is directly involved in these proceedings as a party. Second, the Basic Law contains a specific fundamental right that guarantees access to court in the event of a possible violation of rights by

[6] See Sect. 4.2.2 below.

[7] See Swiss Federal Supreme Court, BGE 88, II, 386/389 and Austrian Constitutional Court, reference VfGH, G26/10–11, order of 5 October 2011, paras. 45 et seq., https://www.vfgh.gv.at/downloads/VfGH_G_26-10_VH.pdf, 2.11.2022.

[8] To facilitate the flow of reading, the following does not cite the provision referenced, § 166 (1) sentence 1 of the German Code of Administrative Court Proceedings (VwGO); rather, the ZPO is cited directly.

public authorities, the fundamental right of legal recourse (Article 19 [4] sentence 1 GG). This fundamental right is not directly applicable in legal disputes between two private persons, which requires administrative and civil proceedings to be analysed separately.

2.1 Legal Aid for Natural Persons

A central prerequisite and reason for the granting of legal aid is indigence. Legal defence or action should not be impossible due to insufficient financial means. The needy person should be put on an equal footing with a person of means, which is why the term "equality of legal protection[9]" is used.[10] If we regard natural persons alone, this argument seems conclusive at first, even though legal aid provisions existed long before the Basic Law enshrined the welfare state principle in 1949.[11]

2.2 Legal Aid for Legal Persons as an Exception

There are doubts about the view just outlined, not only because legal aid existed even before 1877, when it was uniformly codified in the ZPO for the whole of what was then the German Empire.[12] Inconsistencies also become apparent when legal persons are included in the analysis. Since 1933, legal persons have been entitled to legal aid. However, according to § 116 sentence 1 no. 2 ZPO, which applies today, this requires—in addition to the general requirements for legal aid to which natural persons are also subject (sufficient prospect of success and lack of recklessness)—that (1) the legal person or association capable of acting as a party (hereinafter abbreviated to "legal persons"[13]) is established in Germany, in another member state of the European Union, or in another state party to the Agreement on the European Economic Area and is domiciled there, (2) that the costs can neither be met by it nor by the parties economically affected by the subject matter of the dispute, and (3) that the failure to pursue or defend the legal action would be contrary to the public

---

[9]The term predates the Basic Law and was used in the German Empire, when there was no equivalent to Article 3 (1) GG or Article 19 (4) sentence 1 GG; see, for example, Hahn (1880), p. 206, which refers to the "necessity of equal legal protection for rich and poor".

[10]German Constitutional Court Decisions 22, 83/87 et seq.

[11]The explanatory memorandum to the original "Civilprozessordnung" speaks of "law for the poor" or "poor law" ("Armenrecht", today's legal aid) as the extension of Roman and canonical law and states that "law for the poor" is a traditional and generally applicable procedural law; see Hahn (1880), pp. 206 et seq. See also the essay by Linde (1833), pp. 51 et seq.

[12]Legal aid for natural persons can be traced back to Roman and Canonical Law; see Sect. 4.2.3 below.

[13]This is different in Switzerland; see Baldegger (2017), pp. 594–600; Tuchschmid (2006), p. 50.

interest. The latter requirement of fulfilling the public interest does not apply to natural persons, only to legal persons. This shows that according to the legislative conception, legal persons do not deserve support in litigation to the same extent as natural persons. It is exactly this requirement that will be described as unconstitutional because it is not a necessary step to prevent abuse of legal aid and it contradicts the idea of individual legal protection.

In a decision dated 1973, the German Constitutional Court expressly deemed this less favourable treatment of legal persons compared to natural persons in what was then § 114 (4) ZPO[14] (the precursor of the current § 116 ZPO) to be constitutional.[15] Both then and now, it was and is required, among other things, that "the failure to pursue or defend the law be contrary to the public interest" for a legal person to be granted legal aid.[16] The German Constitutional Court assumes that legal aid is only constitutionally required for natural persons, not for legal persons.[17] It is the principle of the welfare state that requires the legislature to ensure that the less wealthy party is also able to assert his or her interests in the legal dispute in a manner that complies with the principle of equality. The "caring" character of legal aid and its constitutional justification derived from the principle of the welfare state, however, do not apply to legal persons. The principle of the social or welfare state serves first and foremost to preserve and safeguard human dignity, the supreme principle of the constitution. The state is required by the principle of social solidarity to intervene effectively when people are struggling to have decent lives.[18]

It is clear from the above that the constitutional source of the entitlement to legal aid can have concrete effects on the granting of legal aid to legal persons. However, the view that legal persons do not have to be granted legal aid on constitutional grounds has met with reservations. In 1990, the German Constitutional Court has modified its case law on the constitutional roots of legal aid, and has exchanged the former welfare state foundation for a rule-of-law foundation.[19] But if the basis of legal aid is no longer human dignity and the principle of the welfare state, which indeed apply only to natural persons, then the question arises to what extent the exclusion of legal persons from legal aid can still be justified. Legal persons are

[14]The provision corresponded to the original version dated 1933 and read: "A domestic legal person may be granted assistance for the poor if the prerequisites specified in paragraph 1 are met, if the funds required to conduct the lawsuit can neither be raised by the legal person nor by the economic participants in the lawsuit, and the failure to pursue or defend the law would be contrary to the public interest".

[15]German Constitutional Court Decisions 35, 348/354 et seq. On the version at that time, see the account by Meents (1975), pp. 150–152.

[16]German Constitutional Court Decisions 35, 348/357 et seq.

[17]German Constitutional Court Decisions 35, 348/357. See also Baldegger (2017), pp. 573 et seq., 622, 655, who interprets the German Constitutional Court's case law in such a way that the court categorically excludes a constitutional right to legal aid for legal persons.

[18]German Constitutional Court Decisions 35, 348/355 et seq.

[19]German Constitutional Court Decisions 81, 347/356 et seq. However, this exchange was later relativised, cf. German Constitutional Court Decisions 122, 39/48–50; see Sect. 3.2 below.

clearly not excluded from the rule of law. However, this discrepancy has not been further investigated since then. Therefore, the German Constitutional Court's jurisprudence is not very consistent[20] and merits re-examining.

3 Constitutional Foundation of Legal Aid According to Case Law and Literature

After an overview of the German Constitutional Court's current case law (Sect. 3.1), its development, which has not been straightforward, will be traced (Sect. 3.2). Most of the literature agrees with the German Constitutional Court's case law, rarely accentuating different aspects, and will therefore not be addressed on its own.

3.1 Core Statements from the German Constitutional Court's Case Law on Legal Aid

There is no general constitutional entitlement to freedom from costs under the principle of judicial legal protection.[21] Rather, a party's contribution to the costs of a lawsuit is constitutional, even if it is an impediment to legal protection. The aim of the parties' contributions is to prevent abuse,[22] what is known as "frivolous litigation".[23] However, since cost-bearing leads to hardship for financially weaker litigants, the Basic Law requires that in the implementation of legal protection, the situation of the impecunious party must be largely brought into line with that of the well-off party. It is a central aspect of the general principle of the rule of law to prevent the arbitrary and excessively forceful enforcement of legal claims. If the parties involved are referred to the courts, this also means that the state must set up courts and ensure that everyone has open access to them in a fundamentally equal manner. Otherwise, for a part of the population, the formally existing possibility of

[20] See Bork (2016), before § 114, marginal numbers 8, 11, § 116, marginal number 24; Möbius (2014), pp. 218 et seq.; Neumann and Schaks (2018), § 166, marginal numbers 11 et seq.; Riese (2022), § 166, marginal number 5 and Sect. 3.2 below; Schweigler (2017), pp. 314 et seq. believes that it is worth a separate analysis to examine whether and which conclusions could be drawn from the German Constitutional Court's divergent approaches to reasoning.

[21] German Constitutional Court Decisions 10, 264/268; 18, 302/303 et seq.; 78, 104/117; 80, 103/107 et seq.; 85, 337/346; 92, 122/124; 133, 1/28 et seq.; Scholz (1995), pp. 726 et seq.

[22] This was already the case specifically regarding the law on the poor at the time, in the explanatory memorandum to the German Code of Civil Procedure of 1877, printed in Hahn (1880), p. 207.

[23] German Constitutional Court Decisions 50, 217/230 et seq.; Schenke (1999), p. 170.

obtaining legal protection would in fact be non-existent due to a lack of financial means.[24]

Contribution to the costs, at least where proceedings are unsuccessful (§ 154 (1) VwGO[25]), represents a risk for the party seeking legal protection, which in general is intended to dissuade too-frequent recourse to the justice system. Where this incentive is void because there is no financial risk associated in case of legal aid, the provisions regarding sufficient prospects of success[26] and the lack of recklessness are intended as a corrective to prevent potential abuse.[27]

3.2 *Developments in the German Constitutional Court's Case Law Regarding the Constitutional Basis of the Entitlement to Legal Aid*

Although these statements by the German Constitutional Court are generally accepted, their derivation from the constitution is unclear.[28] For this reason, no constitutional provisions were cited in the previous section. This is because the German Constitutional Court has at different times taken varied approaches to justifying statements that are identical in content.[29] Even though it is often said that the German Constitutional Court has changed in 1990 its reasoning for the anchoring of the entitlement to legal aid,[30] in reality the course of jurisprudence has been much more fluctuating and even inconsistent. In more than 70 years of jurisprudence, the German Constitutional Court has based the right to legal aid on the fact that the Federal Republic of Germany is a social and democratic

[24] German Constitutional Court Decisions 9, 124/131 et seq.; 10, 264/268 et seq.; 78, 104/117 et seq.; 81, 347/356 et seq.; German Constitutional Court Chamber, NJW 1997, 2103/2104; German Constitutional Court Chamber, order dated 14 February 2017—reference 1 BvR 2507/16, paragraphs 12 et seq.

[25] Regarding this, see Neumann and Schaks (2018), § 154, marginal numbers 20–42.

[26] Constitutional according to the German Constitutional Court Decisions 7, 53/55 et seq.; 9, 256/257 et seq.; 10, 264/268 et seq.; 81, 347/357; 92, 122/124; 122, 39/49; German Constitutional Court Chamber Decisions, NJW 2010, 1657; NJW 2013, 1727/728; decision dated 14 February 2017—reference 1 BvR 2507/16, paragraphs 13 et seq., BeckRS 2017, 103367; Schenke (1999), pp. 170 et seq.

[27] More stringent criteria for the prospects of success—for reasons of cost reduction—in part six, chapter I, § 11 of the third decree of the Reichspräsident to safeguard the economy and finances and to counteract political protests, dated 6 October 1931, RGBl. I, p. 563. Criticism in Meents (1975), pp. 63–77, 356–358.

[28] Cf. Huber (2018), Article 19, marginal number 464.

[29] See also Henke (2010), pp. 194 et seq.; Bergner and Pernice (2011), pp. 242–244; Schweigler (2017), pp. 314 et seq.

[30] German Constitutional Court Decisions 81, 347 et seq.

constitutional state according to Article 20 (1) and (3) GG.[31] It has expressly rejected the right to a lawful judge (Article 103 (1) GG—"Recht auf den gesetzlichen Richter")[32] as the source of the right to legal aid, but it has also at times rooted the right to legal aid in this very same provision.[33] Recourse has been made to Article 3 (1) GG[34] (the fundamental right to equality) as well as to Article 3 (1) GG in conjunction with the social duty of the state (Article 20 [1] GG).[35] Later, the German Constitutional Court decided that the right to legal aid is anchored in Article 3 (1) GG in conjunction with the principle of the rule of law.[36] However, years later, in a decision on the principle of legal aid equality in the non-judicial sphere (pre-trial counselling), the German Constitutional Court again referred to the welfare state principle.[37] The supposed change to the rule-of-law principle is thus called into question and the constitutional source of the entitlement to legal aid is obscured rather than illuminated.

3.3 Interim Conclusion

The German Constitutional Court's case law, which is largely accepted by the literature, is inconsistent regarding the citation of the constitutional foundation of legal aid. However, the question of the constitutional foundation of legal aid is not merely a question of the correct citation; it can also have quite considerable practical legal implications, as an analysis of legal aid for legal persons demonstrates. Furthermore, the constitutional standards of review also vary between the individual provisions of the Basic Law.[38]

It is reasonable to assume that, due to the pre-constitutional roots of legal aid and the importance of legal aid, particularly in private law disputes,[39] the legal remedy guarantee in Article 19 (4) sentence 1 GG was not initially considered at all and another provision, namely Article 3 (1) GG, was chosen. It is possible that the invocation of Article 3 (1) GG was not finally overcome because statutory law

[31] German Constitutional Court Decisions 1, 109.

[32] German Constitutional Court, decision of 6 March 1953—reference 1 BvR 392/51, reprinted in Meents (1975), pp. 383 et seq.

[33] German Constitutional Court Decisions 7, 53/56–58. Regarding this, see also German Constitutional Court Decisions 9, 254 et seq.

[34] German Constitutional Court, decision of 6 March 1953—reference 1 BvR 392/51, reprinted in Meents (1975), pp. 383 et seq.; German Constitutional Court Decisions 2, 336/340 et seq.

[35] German Constitutional Court Decisions 9, 124/131; 22, 83/86; 35, 348 et seq.; 51, 295/302; 54, 251/273; 56, 139/143; 63, 380/394 et seq.; 78, 104/108–110.

[36] German Constitutional Court Decisions 81, 347/356.

[37] German Constitutional Court Decisions 122, 39/48 et seq.

[38] Regarding this, see Bork's concern (2016), before § 114, marginal number 8.

[39] A fully developed administrative jurisdiction did not emerge in Germany until the Basic Law came into force.

formulates uniform standards for the granting of legal aid in all branches of the courts (including the German Code of Administrative Court Proceedings), since all codes of procedure refer to §§ 114 et seq. ZPO.

4 Article 19 (4) Sentence 1 of the Basic Law as the Sole Constitutional Anchor of the Entitlement to Legal Aid in Administrative Proceedings

Legal aid law could be more closely reconciled with constitutional values and requirements if the entitlement to legal aid were anchored solely in the fundamental right enshrined in Article 19 (4) sentence 1 GG, the guarantee of legal recourse.[40] This would both avoid the weaknesses of the previous approach (see Sect. 4.1) and be compatible with Article 19 (4) sentence 1 GG as well as with the Basic Law in general (see Sect. 4.2).

4.1 Weakness of the Traditional Approach

The traditional approach fails to recognise that the granting of legal protection is to be understood in terms of access to justice (not in terms of equality law; see Sect. 4.1.1) and that legal persons are dependent on legal protection in the same way as natural persons (Sect. 4.1.2), which is why the predominant view can only be explained by path dependencies; however, it cannot be sufficiently justified dogmatically.

4.1.1 Misguided Invocation of the Law of Equality Instead of the Necessary Invocation of the Law of Benefits

Article 19 (4) sentence 1 GG is intended to grant effective, i.e. actually achievable, legal protection.[41] This provision obliges the legislature, from an objective legal point of view, to provide for access to court in such a way that it is not unreasonably impeded or prevented for the person seeking legal protection.[42] An unreasonable impediment would exist, however, if legal protection were to fail due to the citizen's

---

[40] See also Huber (2018), Article 19, marginal number 464; Nickel (2016), p. 1979.

[41] German Constitutional Court Decisions 138, 33/39 et seq.; Ernst (2021), Article 19, marginal number 144; Huber (2018), Article 19, marginal numbers 333, 354 with further references from the case law of the German Constitutional Court; Schmidt-Jortzig (1994), p. 2569.

[42] German Constitutional Court Decisions 116, 69/88 with further references; 122, 39/49; Huber (2018), Article 19, marginal number 461.

lack of financial resources.[43] The point is that legal recourse must be actually, not only theoretically, accessible and thus effective.[44]

Moreover, Article 19 (4) sentence 1 GG grants the individual a subjective legal right of access to court and a review of the decisions of state authority in fact and in law.[45] Article 19 (4) sentence 1 GG is an individual fundamental right, a subjective right to legal protection.[46] "It focuses on the individual person and the protection of the legal positions associated with his or her person. This objective is paramount for Article 19 (4)."[47] Accordingly, Article 19 (4) sentence 1 GG is intended to grant individual legal protection that is as complete as possible.[48] This requires that procedural law be formulated in such a way that individuals have actual, effective access to court—irrespective of income and assets. Legal persons are not excluded from this, however, as the word "individual person" in the preceding quotation might suggest. Rather, this statement merely refers to the foundational provision of Article 19 (4) sentence 1 GG. The same commentary explicitly states that Article 19 (4) sentence 1 GG also applies to legal persons.[49]

Dogmatics on the dimensions of fundamental rights were naturally less advanced at the beginning of the German Constitutional Court's judicial activity than they are today. If one assumes that the granting of legal protection is first and foremost a state benefit,[50] a derivation in terms of *benefit law* ("Leistungsrecht") based on Article 19 (4) sentence 1 GG is more convincing than one in terms of *equality law* ("Gleichheitsrecht") based on Article 3 (1) GG. The fact that legal aid is a benefit is also in line with the overwhelmingly prevalent view in literature and case law, because here legal aid is regarded precisely as a state social benefit.[51] Admittedly, Article 3 (1) GG is often used—for lack of better options—as a vehicle to grant equal access to a state benefit under public law.[52] However, such a derivation is not

---

[43] German Constitutional Court Decisions 11, 139/143; 54, 39/41.

[44] German Constitutional Court Decisions 35, 348/355, 362.

[45] German Constitutional Court Decisions 15, 275/282; 103, 142/156; 129, 1/20; 149, 407/413.

[46] German Federal Administrative Court Decisions 101, 73/82; German Federal Administrative Court, NVwZ 2012, 567/568; Ibler (2022), Article 19 (4), marginal number 108; Schmidt-Aßmann (2022), Article 19 (4), marginal numbers 7 et seq.

[47] Schmidt-Aßmann (2022), Article 19 (4), marginal number 8.

[48] German Constitutional Court Decisions 8, 274/326; 30 (dissenting opinion Geller, von Schlabrendorff, Rupp), 1/41; 101, 106/122 et seq.; 103, 142/156; Schmidt-Aßmann (2022), Article 19 (4), marginal number 11.

[49] Schmidt-Aßmann (2022), Article 19 (4), marginal number 43a.

[50] Thus, *inter alia*, German Constitutional Court Decisions 101, 106/123; Voßkuhle (1993), p. 314. Others cite Article 19 (4) sentence 1 GG as providing for a right to benefits, for example Ibler (2022), Article 19 (4), marginal numbers 43–46; Jarass (2022), Article 19, marginal number 37; Sobota (1997), p. 203.

[51] See the references in footnotes 2, 3, 4, and 5 as well as the Hamburg Superior Administrative Court decision of 30 June 2021—6. See 19/21, BeckRS 2021, 18458, marginal number 7: "The granting of legal aid ultimately constitutes a granting of benefits [. . .]".

[52] The precedent-setting decision in German Constitutional Court Decisions 33, 303/331 et seq.

necessary if the constitution itself originally grants a benefit in a more specific way, which is true of Article 19 (4) sentence 1 GG. In today's dogmatics, the benefit aspect of Article 19 (4) sentence 1 GG is not only accepted,[53] but is even considered to take priority[54] or to be exclusive.[55]

Finally, "equal" access to court does not necessarily correspond to the will of the party seeking legal protection. It is a matter of *actual* and *effective access* to the courts, not equal access, and actual and effective access is not necessarily identical to equal access. This becomes particularly clear when even a wealthy party cannot afford legal protection. This is typically the case where large amounts are in dispute, because court and legal costs increase with the value of the dispute. In such cases, even well-off parties can receive legal aid, although they are far from receiving social welfare. Equal, but equally insufficient access is not what the constitution is intended to grant. Rather, legal protection as a whole should be as *complete* as possible,[56] including in terms of the beneficiaries.

4.1.2 Ignoring the Legal Person's Reliance on Legal Protection

Moreover, the legal protection sought by the legal person can only be granted by the state due to the state's monopoly on the use of force, so that legal persons are also dependent on the courts.[57] This is all the more the case since in administrative proceedings the state confronts the legal person in three different ways: as an opposing party, as a judge of the legal aid application, as the holder of the monopoly on the use of force, which has also enacted the rules governing the costs of litigation. It cannot be argued against this that legal persons are only created by law and are therefore subordinate to law, so that legal persons do not have to be granted legal protection.[58] It is true that legal entities are artificial creations of purpose and that the purposes pursued may not always be particularly honourable, such as the limitation of possible liability or tax optimisation. For this reason, it is entirely appropriate to treat legal entities and natural persons differently to balance out the risk of abuse by legal persons.

But prevention of abuse is already ensured in other ways by procedural law. This is because before legal aid is granted, the parties economically affected by the

[53] German Constitutional Court Decisions 101, 106/123; Ibler (2022), Article 19 (4), marginal number 43; Schenke (2020), Article 19 (4), marginal number 159; Schmidt-Aßmann (2022), Article 19 (4), marginal number 7 ("*status positivus*"); Voßkuhle (1993), p. 314.

[54] Gaier (2011), p. 385; Jarass (2022), Article 19, marginal number 37; Schenke (2009), § 78, marginal number 6; Schulze-Fielitz (2013), Article 19 (4), marginal number 84; Huber (2018), Article 19, marginal number 374, refers to a "*right of participation* vis-à-vis the state in the provision of judicial procedures for the enforcement of rights".

[55] Epping (2021), marginal number 916; Sachs (2021), Article 19, paragraph 12.

[56] Constitutional Court Decisions 8, 274/326; 54, 39/40 et seq.; 101, 106/122 et seq.

[57] This also applies to the ECHR, cf. Diggelmann and Altwicker (2012), p. 781.

[58] However, see Möbius (2014), pp. 257, 290.

subject matter of the dispute must prove that they are unable to bear the costs of the litigation of "their" legal person. This is a requirement that only exists for legal persons. Moreover, reckless lawsuits or those with no prospect of success are not funded in any case. It is therefore too far-reaching to deny legal aid to legal entities in general because of the risk of abuse, even if abuse is already prevented by other regulations.

The state's monopoly on the use of force has its counterpart in the citizens' duty to keep the peace,[59] which also applies to legal persons. The binding settlement of disputes must therefore be carried out before the courts, because justice on one's own behalf is prohibited: "Along with the elementary duties of the state to protect, the granting of justice as a state duty and individual right is the reverse side of the state's monopoly on the use of force, the civil duty to preserve the peace, and the prohibition of self-justice."[60] This is also emphasised by the German Constitutional Court in its case law, which stated early on that it is a central aspect of the rule of law to fundamentally prevent the arbitrary enforcement of legal claims by force. Therefore, the parties involved are referred to the courts, which at the same time requires that the state must establish courts and grant access to them to everyone in a fundamentally equal manner.[61] This applies to natural and legal persons alike. As a consequence, a legal person can only defend its rights in a court proceeding which must be accessible, even if the legal person and the parties economically affected by the subject matter of the dispute do not have the necessary financial means.

4.2 Derivation from Article 19 (4) Sentence 1 GG

The derivation from Article 3 (1) of the GG, especially in conjunction with Article 20 (1) GG (principle of the welfare state) thus has weaknesses. If the right to legal aid is derived from Article 19 (4) sentence 1 GG, according to the thesis set forth here, these difficulties do not arise. Therefore, Article 19 (4) sentence 1 GG is *sedes materiae* for the entitlement to legal aid. The viability of this argument will be tested in the following by interpreting Article 19 (4) sentence 1 GG using the classical methods.

Of the constituent elements of Article 19 (4) sentence 1 GG ("someone", "the authority of the state", "violation of his or her rights", "legal recourse" and "is

---

[59] Huber (2021), § 6, marginal number 51; Ibler (2022), Article 19 (4), marginal number 360; Meents (1975), p. 351 with numerous references to earlier case law and literature in footnote 2; Voßkuhle (1993), pp. 5 et seq. For basic information on the monopoly on the use of force see Grimm (2006), pp. 18–38; Klein (2018), "Gewaltmonopol"; Klein (2010), pp. 635–656; Möllers (2006), pp. 804–807.

[60] Schmidt-Aßmann (2022), Article 19 (4), marginal number 16 with further references. See also German Constitutional Court Decisions 122, 39/49; Baur (1954), pp. 396 et seq.; Möbius (2014), p. 219.

[61] See also German Constitutional Court Decisions 35, 348/354 et seq.

accessible"), only the terms "someone" and "is accessible" require interpretation in the present context.

4.2.1 Wording: Actual Accessibility of the Legal Process

Interpretation according to wording, also called grammatical interpretation, requires the "meaning of an expression or a combination of words in the general usage of language or, if such can be ascertained, in the particular usage of language by the speakers in question, here in the law concerned."[62] Even if the wording—especially in the Basic Law with its succinct use of language[63]—is often ambiguous, interpretation is required,[64] which must begin with the wording.[65]

Legal recourse means "access to the courts".[66] This access must be open. It cannot be concluded from the term "open" that this applies only to certain cases or persons or groups of persons. On the contrary, it can be concluded that access to the courts is open to all persons in general and is not limited to certain groups of persons; rather, it is independent of personal characteristics in fact, and not merely theoretically.[67] This is confirmed by the use of the indicative: legal recourse *is* open. This also applies to domestic legal persons under private law, since they can also invoke Article 19 (4) sentence 1 GG based on Article 19 (3) GG.

The aim is effective access to court, which can be jeopardised not only where legal obstacles exist, but also in the case of factual obstacles (excessive legal costs). Regarding the question of what prospects of success must be assumed in any main proceedings for legal aid to be granted, the German Constitutional Court has always emphasised that the legal aid procedure is not intended to grant legal protection itself, merely to allow access to it.[68] This follows even from the decisions and writings arguing in favour of the welfare state.[69] In other contexts, the Federal Constitutional Court has warned that the guarantee of legal recourse could be rendered meaningless by an overly strict interpretation of the requirements of

---

[62] Larenz (1991), p. 320. See also Sodan (2010), p. 22.

[63] Cf. German Constitutional Court Decisions 62, 1/45; 79, 127/143; Böckenförde (1974), p. 1529; Bryde (1982), pp. 89–93; Horn (2015), p. 11.

[64] Cf. Puppe (2023), p. 129. Similarly, see Larenz (1991), pp. 320 et seq.; Zippelius (2012), p. 79.

[65] Larenz (1991), pp. 320, 343; Rüthers et al. (2022), marginal number 731; Sodan and Ziekow (2020), § 2, marginal number 6.

[66] Bleckmann (1997), § 39, marginal number 11. Similarly, see Möbius (2014), p. 219: "Access to the courts".

[67] Cf. Bleckmann (1997), § 39, marginal number 11; Schmidt-Jortzig (1994), p. 2569.

[68] German Constitutional Court Decisions 81, 347/357 et seq.; German Constitutional Court Chamber Decisions, FamRZ 2009, 1654; NJW 2013, 1727/1728.

[69] German Constitutional Court Decisions 35, 348/355: "...are actually prevented from pursuing or defending their rights in court ..." and "...could jeopardise the legal protection of the impecunious party in general ..."; Schweigler (2017), p. 315.

procedure:[70] Access to the courts may not be made unduly difficult.[71] This is also confirmed by the purpose of legal aid, because it "is intended to prevent a party from being prevented from seeking justice in court solely for economic reasons."[72] "Economic reasons" in this sense, however, can be manifold. They also include the case in which a party who is itself wealthy can at most pay the costs in instalments because a large amount is in dispute. However, "economic reasons" are not limited to the case in which the party is entitled to social assistance.

As an interim conclusion following the grammatical interpretation, we can state that the "accessibility of the legal process" as defined by Article 19 (4) sentence 1 GG is to be understood broadly and does not exclude actual accessibility for legal persons as well.

4.2.2 Systematics: Subjective Right to Legal Protection as a State Benefit

The context of meaning in which the provision to be interpreted is situated is also important for determining its content.[73] The statement to be interpreted is not considered in isolation, but in its interaction with other statements.[74] Four postulates apply: freedom from contradiction, non-redundancy, completeness, and systematic order;[75] of these, non-redundancy and systematic order will play a special role here.

Special Status of Article 19 (4) Sentence 1 GG Compared to Article 20 (3) GG From a systematic point of view, Article 19 (4) sentence 1 GG is to be regarded as the more specific provision[76] in comparison to Article 20 (3) GG regarding legal aid in administrative court proceedings.

Special Status of Article 19 (4) Sentence 1 GG Compared to Article 20 (1) GG The relationship between Article 19 (4) sentence 1 GG and the welfare state principle in Article 20 (1) GG is less obvious. Admittedly, in 1990 the German

[70] German Constitutional Court Decisions 78, 88/98 et seq.; 96, 27/39.

[71] German Constitutional Court Chamber Decisions, NJW 2016, 44/45 with further references.

[72] German Constitutional Court Decisions 92, 122/124. Similarly, "making legal protection accessible", Behn (1992), p. 1.

[73] Larenz (1991), p. 324.

[74] Puppe (2023), p. 141; Rüthers et al. (2022), marginal number 744.

[75] Puppe (2023), pp. 141 et seq.

[76] This is the general view; see German Constitutional Court Decisions 13, 153/161; 35, 382/401; 50, 1/3; 81, 347/356; Ernst (2021), Article 19, marginal number 157; Huber (2018), Article 19, marginal numbers 353–358, 462 et seq.; Ibler (2022), Article 19 (4), marginal numbers 235 et seq., 360, 362; Meents (1975), p. 362; Schenke (2020), Article 19 (4), marginal number 283; Schenke (2009), § 78, marginal number 1; Schmidt-Jortzig (1994), p. 2569; Sobota (1997), pp. 188 et seq., 202, et seq., 255, 257.

Constitutional Court initially abandoned this provision as the basis of the claim to legal aid. One could conclude from this that the welfare state principle is insignificant in legal aid. But this would be a purely formal argument and would not in itself offer any guarantee of correctness (why should the legal basis first mentioned not have been the correct one after all?) Moreover, even after 1990, Article 20 (1) GG (the welfare state principle) repeatedly found its way into decisions on legal aid by the German Constitutional Court,[77] which has contributed to the unclear legal situation.

Article 20 (1) GG contains the obligation to "provide for a just social order",[78] *inter alia* by protecting "weaker persons".[79] If persons in need require judicial legal protection to safeguard their rights, it could be argued that the state must make this legal protection accessible to them despite their lack of financial means, especially if the state regulations regarding mandatory legal representation and advance payment of court costs impede access to legal protection. But even if court costs are not charged and legal representation is not mandatory, the state's monopoly on the use of force means that legal recourse must be possible and that it is generally easier for a wealthy person to take advantage of it than for a less wealthy person. The welfare state therefore does not seem implausible as the foundation for legal aid. The fact that Article 28 (1) GG refers to the rule of law within the welfare state, i.e. combines both principles ("social rule of law"—"sozialer Rechtsstaat"), and that in the case of legal aid the rule of law and the welfare state principle lead to the same result, has an obscuring effect: The rule of law requires access to courts, and the purpose of the welfare state is to compensate for the disadvantages of weaker persons. The legal comparison also shows that welfare state motives are associated with legal aid or the free administration of justice (Swiss terminology).[80] However, since the different constitutional provisions under consideration each have different effects on legal aid for legal persons, a clear allocation must be made.

The fact that predominantly less well-off persons benefit from legal aid does not contradict the anchoring of legal aid in Article 19 (4) sentence 1 GG, because this provision also takes social aspects into account.[81] Even if the principles of the welfare state and the rule of law are not identical, they can nevertheless lead to the same result in concrete questions. But not everything that happens to be compatible with the welfare state principle is necessarily a "social benefit" or even "social assistance". This is also supported by the fact that the literature on social law rarely addresses legal aid, which would be expected if legal aid were subject to "social

---

[77] German Constitutional Court Decisions 122, 39 et seq.; German Constitutional Court Chamber Decisions, NVwZ 2005, 323; NJW 2018, 449/450.

[78] German Constitutional Court Decisions 94, 241/263; 97, 169/185; 110, 412/445.

[79] German Constitutional Court Decisions 26, 16/37; 35, 202/236; 45, 376/387 et seq.; 89, 214/232; 100, 271/284; 103, 197/221.

[80] Swiss Federal Supreme Court, BGE 88, II, 386/389.

[81] Schmidt-Aßmann (2022), Article 19 (4), marginal number 35.

law". Legal aid is "part of litigation and costs law",[82] not social welfare law. Even wealthy persons who are far from being entitled to social assistance can be "needy" as defined by the ZPO if a large amount is in dispute, thus also entailing high probable legal costs. Furthermore, the provisions in the procedural codes are based on the legislative powers laid forth in Article 74 (1) No. 1 of the Basic Law ("the judicial procedure"), not Article 74 (1) No. 7 of the Basic Law ("the public welfare").

The following is probably true: Access to court is primarily anchored in the guarantee of legal recourse as a specific expression of the rule of law, because it is granted not only to persons in need, but to all others as well. Therefore, the "guarantee of justice" is primarily based upon the general rule of law, even if it may *also* receive support from the welfare state principle.

Therefore, at least for legal aid in administrative proceedings, we will have to assume that Article 19 (4) sentence 1 GG should be granted special status compared to Article 20 (1) GG: It is not merely objective law constituting primarily a formative mandate to the legislature and is therefore more specific in its granting of rights; above all, its content comes closer to addressing access to court. As a result, the principle of the welfare state is also too broad and too indeterminate, so that a requirement to "grant social benefits to a certain extent" cannot regularly be inferred from it.[83]

Special Status of Article 19 (4) Sentence 1 GG Compared to Article 3 (1) GG
Access to court is originally seen as a benefit, and this benefit aspect is described in Article 19 (4) sentence 1 GG in a very specific way. This makes recourse to Article 3 (1) GG obsolete (avoidance of redundancy in the context of systematic interpretation[84]). Moreover, effective access to court does not amount to the equality of two individuals or groups; rather, it means *every* person being *generally* allowed to effectively seek legal protection.

Finally, the German Constitutional Court has ruled that "fee regulations may, in addition to covering costs, also aim to counteract the frivolous or even abusive filing of appeals, for example by defining minimum fees" or by "encouraging citizens to carefully examine whether they have reason to make use of an appeal".[85] However, because of Article 19 (4) sentence 1 GG, this should not make legal protection unreasonably difficult and it should not lead to legal protection being made available "primarily based on financial means".[86]

In another decision, in which both Article 3 (1) and Article 19 (4) sentence 1 GG were challenged, the German Constitutional Court found the failure to grant legal aid to be incompatible with Article 19 (4) sentence 1 GG and explicitly left the

[82] Willenbruch (1977), p. 33. See also Eichenhofer (2021), marginal number 3.

[83] Schmidt-Aßmann (2022), Article 19 (4), marginal number 3 with reference to German Constitutional Court Decisions 110, 412/445 and Grzeszick (2022), Article 20 VIII, marginal number 19.

[84] Cf. Puppe (2023), pp. 141 et seq.

[85] German Constitutional Court Decisions 50, 217/230 et seq.

[86] German Constitutional Court Decisions 50, 217/231.

examination of the principle of equality aside.[87] Article 19 (4) sentence 1 GG thus contains the more precise and concrete standards that take precedence over the general Article 3 (1) GG and determine its assessment.

No Exclusion of Legal Persons Based on Article 19 (3) GG

However, it is questionable whether something different may or even must apply to legal persons here. This is because, even if Article 19 (4) sentence 1 GG were principally the correct basis for the granting of legal aid, this does not mean per se that this must also apply *in full* to legal persons; rather, the requirements of Article 19 (3) GG, which deals with the scope of fundamental rights' protection for legal persons, must be met. Since Article 19 (3) GG only grants protection of fundamental rights to legal persons where the fundamental rights are by their nature applicable to legal persons, Article 19 (3) GG could leave room for a different or stricter interpretation.

If it is recognised that legal persons can invoke Article 19 (4) sentence 1 GG, then the only question that arises is whether legal aid, as part of Article 19 (4) sentence 1 GG, is by its nature inapplicable to legal persons. However, statutory law itself, which also grants legal aid to legal persons in individual cases, evidently contradicts this. Legal aid is therefore applicable to legal persons in a practicable manner and is not excluded by its very nature.

Moreover, legal aid is not to be understood as a social benefit to secure one's livelihood;[88] in most cases, it merely represents the reversal of a deliberate impediment to access to court in certain cases and is intended to ensure the provision of “legal protection”.

The only argument against legal aid for legal persons is that legal persons have been artificially created and may involve structuring possibilities which are not relevant to natural persons. This could lead to an abuse of these structuring possibilities to the detriment of the public, which would have to bear the costs. As seen above, this objection is justified in principle, as legal entities without assets have sometimes been used to avoid parties being held responsible under public law. But this risk can be counteracted by properly addressing the other requirements for granting legal aid to legal persons. In particular, the requirement that even those affected by the economic outcome of the case be unable to afford legal costs should be sufficient to prevent abuse, especially[89] since the party applying for legal aid must prove this.[90] Additionally, the legal person also has to prove sufficient prospect of success and the lack of recklessness. Legal persons are therefore participants in legal transactions to the same extent as natural persons.[91]

---

[87] German Constitutional Court Decisions 78, 88/99 et seq.

[88] German Constitutional Court Decisions 78, 104/121 et seq.; Willenbruch (1977), pp. 33–35.

[89] Bork (2016), § 116, marginal number 24.

[90] Superior Administrative Court of Saxony, NVwZ-RR 2016, 120.

[91] This is very clear, although with regard to civil proceedings and Article 6 ECHR; see Diggelmann and Altwicker (2012), p. 784.

Perspective Under European Law

The fundamental rights in the Charter of Fundamental Rights (CFR) are part of the national legal order and must therefore be considered. In a decision dated 2010, the European Court of Justice (ECJ) stated with regard to the German regulation of legal aid that the national court needed to assess whether the conditions for granting legal aid to legal persons limited the right of access to court unlawfully, but the ECJ did not assume that the German provisions or their application would per se be in violation of Article 47 CFR.[92] However, it should be pointed out that according to Article 47(3) CFR, legal aid is granted to *all* persons who do not have sufficient resources where such aid is necessary to ensure effective access to the justice system, and that this also includes legal persons.[93] In this decision, the ECJ also drew attention to the fact that the right to seek effective remedy before a court, which is granted in Article 47(3) CFR, is not addressed in Title IV of the Charter ["Solidarity"] but is contained in its Title VI ("Judicial Rights"), which enshrines further procedural principles that apply to both natural and legal persons.[94] From this, the ECJ concludes that "this right is not primarily designed as social assistance".[95] Overall, the ECJ appears to be sceptical of the narrow German interpretation. This is a position that is in line with the interpretation of German law propagated here.

The case law of the European Court of Human Rights (ECtHR) regarding the granting of justice pursuant to Article 6 of the European Convention on Human Rights (ECHR) is also relevant to the question at hand. Admittedly, the ECtHR so far has not objected to the German provisions on legal aid, either regarding natural persons[96] or legal persons.[97] In other proceedings, however, the ECtHR has made statements that make the German provisions appear to contradict the Convention in part. Article 6(1) ECHR grants access to court,[98] albeit not fully, due to its limitation to "civil rights and obligations". Nevertheless, it states that the concept of the rule of law, which is essentially expressed in the right to judicial protection, demands

[92] CJEU, Case C-279/09, 22 December 2010, DEB Deutsche Energiehandels- und Beratungsgesellschaft mbH/Deutschland, ECLI:EU:C:2010:811, paras. 59–62 et seq.

[93] CJEU, Case C-279/09, 22 December 2010, DEB Deutsche Energiehandels- und Beratungsgesellschaft mbH/Deutschland, ECLI:EU:C:2010:811, paras. 39 et seq., 52, 59.

[94] CJEU, Case C-279/09, 22 December 2010, DEB Deutsche Energiehandels- und Beratungsgesellschaft mbH/Deutschland, ECLI:EU:C:2010:811, paras. 40 et seq.

[95] CJEU, Case C-279/09, 22 December 2010, DEB Deutsche Energiehandels- und Beratungsgesellschaft mbH/Deutschland, ECLI:EU:C:2010:811, para. 41.

[96] See ECtHR: *Dietrich Eckart v. Germany*, no. 23947/03, § 1, 10 April 2007. (See http://hudoc.echr.coe.int/eng?i=001-80354); ECtHR: *Claus und Heike Herma v. Germany*, no. 54193/07, 8 December 2009. (See https://hudoc.echr.coe.int/eng?i=001-96483).

[97] ECtHR: *Granos Organicos Nacionales S.A. v. Germany*, no. 19508/07, 22 March 2012. (See https://hudoc.echr.coe.int/eng?i=001-109807).

[98] ECtHR: *Golder v. The United Kingdom*, no. 4451/70, paras. 33–36, 21 February 1975. (See http://hudoc.echr.coe.int/eng?i=001-57496); ECtHR: *Stankov v. Bulgaria*, no. 68490/01, para. 50, 12 July 2007. (See http://hudoc.echr.coe.int/eng?i=001-81606); ECtHR: *Georgel and Georgeta Stoicescu v. Romania*, no. 9718/03, para. 68, 26 July 2011. (See http://hudoc.echr.coe.int/eng?i=001-105820).

comprehensive legal protection; in this context, legal aid is also discussed.[99] This includes bringing litigation[100] as well as challenging encroachments on subjective rights.[101] Legal persons may also invoke this right.[102] The right to benefits under Article 6(1) ECHR may be restricted, e.g. by stipulations regarding costs,[103] but only in pursuit of a legitimate purpose and only in compliance with the principle of proportionality.[104] With regard to legal persons having fewer rights, this legitimate purpose cannot be based on the "legal person" characteristic, as this characteristic constitutes the differentiation criterion. However, the differentiation criterion itself is neither grounds for nor a justification as to whether or why a differentiation may be drawn.[105] Accordingly, it would have to be considered disproportionate under the ECHR if the risk of abuse of legal aid for legal persons were to be counteracted not only by subsidiarity (the costs being unaffordable even to the economically affected parties), but by imposing the public interest requirement as well. Both the obligation to bear expenses and the obligation to take out loans, both of which presumably affect legal persons, have been classified by the ECtHR as unrealistic and disproportionate.[106] This shows that the requirements set by the ECHR for the granting of legal aid are less stringent than those of the German ZPO in its predominant interpretation in case law and literature. The approach proposed here avoids violations of European law to a greater extent than the previous view.

If we view the legal protection guarantee in Article 19 (4) sentence 1 GG as the source of the entitlement to legal aid, we have identified a parallelism with European law (Article 6 ECHR, Article 47 [3] CFR), where legal aid is derived from specific human rights and not from the welfare state. The European requirements seem to favour granting legal aid to legal persons to a greater extent than has so far been the case under German law.

Systematic Conclusions Regarding Legal Aid in Administrative Proceedings

The systematic interpretation, taking the stipulations of European law into account, has shown that Article 19 (4) sentence 1 GG is more specific than the general principle of the rule of law (Article 20 [3] GG) and the welfare state principle (Article 20 [1] GG) as well. The values expressed in Article 19 (4) sentence 1 GG

---

[99] Diggelmann and Altwicker (2012), pp. 782 et seq.

[100] ECtHR: *Kübler v. Germany*, no. 37215/06, 13 January 2011, para. 44 with further references. (See https://hudoc.echr.coe.int/eng?i=001-102811).

[101] ECtHR: *Georgel and Georgeta Stoicescu v. Romania*, no. 9718/03, para. 74, 26 July 2011. (See http://hudoc.echr.coe.int/eng?i=001-105820).

[102] ECtHR: *Teltronic-CATV v. Poland*, no. 48140/99, paras. 51 et seq., 10 January 2006. (See http://hudoc.echr.coe.int/eng?i=001-71946); Diggelmann and Altwicker (2012), p. 784.

[103] Diggelmann and Altwicker (2012), p. 783.

[104] ECtHR: *Stankov v. Bulgaria*, no. 68490/01, para. 55 with further references, 12 July 2007. (See http://hudoc.echr.coe.int/eng?i=001-81606).

[105] Diggelmann and Altwicker (2012), p. 784.

[106] ECtHR: *Teltronic-CATV v. Poland*, no. 48140/99, paras. 54–59, 10 January 2006. (See http://hudoc.echr.coe.int/eng?i=001-71946).

also prevail in the context of a possible test of equality pursuant to Article 3 (1) GG. Moreover, legal persons are not excluded from the entitlement to legal aid under Article 19 (4) sentence 1 GG based on Article 19 (3) GG. This confirms the result of the grammatical interpretation above.

4.2.3 Historical Interpretation: Legal Aid as an Imperative Under the Rule of Law

Historical interpretation addresses the origin of the provision in question. It can refer both to the genesis of the provision[107] and to the history of dogma.[108] For this purpose, documents from the time of the provision's origin, such as the grounds for the law,[109] and legal traditions predating the law may be informative.

The subject of interpretation here is first of all Article 19 (4) sentence 1 GG, which has no comparable constitutional precursor in the Weimar Constitution or other earlier constitutions at the federal level.[110] In addition, we can include the early institution of legal aid in our analysis.[111] A historical interpretation underlines the fact that, firstly, legal aid is primarily based on the rule of law and, secondly, that legal persons are not excluded from it.

Legal Aid in the Tradition of the Rule of Law

Legal aid was viewed in the context of the court system, not based on the welfare state principle as—later—formulated by the Basic Law.[112] This applied overall to legal aid law, which was formulated in the ZPO as early as 1877[113] for the entirety of the German Empire. The ZPO was intended to advance the standardisation of law after the founding of the German Reich,[114] and included legal aid. Legal aid was regarded at that time as "traditional and generally applicable *procedural law*",[115] not as *social law*. However, it was also stated that "state welfare" was to be limited to "granting Germans the possibility of legal prosecution and legal defence before the German courts in the event of their poverty."[116] And further: "The exemption of

[107] Larenz (1991), p. 330.

[108] Sodan and Ziekow (2020), § 2, marginal number 8.

[109] Larenz (1991), p. 330.

[110] Article 107 of the Weimar Constitution was formulated much more weakly; see Schenke (2020), Article 19 (4), marginal numbers 126–131, 134, 136.

[111] On the history of legal aid, see, among others, Gogolin (2015), pp. 37–93; Humborg (2000); Linde (1833), pp. 51 et seq.; Meents (1975), pp. 31–78; Schott (1900), pp. 1–30; specifically with regard to legal persons, see Willenbruch (1977), pp. 16–20.

[112] See also Möbius (2014), p. 234.

[113] Code of Civil Procedure of 30 January 1877, RGBl. p. 83.

[114] Hahn (1880), p. 113.

[115] Hahn (1880), pp. 206 et seq.—emphasis added.

[116] Hahn (1880), p. 207.

poor litigants from costs follows from the necessity of equal legal protection for the rich and the poor".[117] *Fritz Baur* would later characterise this as a "social act".[118]

Equality and welfare are indeed addressed here, which could *prima facie* be an argument for an anchoring in equality law and/or the welfare state. However, we must avoid the misjudgement that a principle of equality such as that contained in the current Article 3 (1) GG and a welfare state principle did not exist in the Constitution of 1871. The quoted wording "equal legal protection" and "state welfare" must not be equated with today's principle of equality or the welfare state principle. The wording of the explanatory memorandum is to be interpreted in such a way that *all* persons, regardless of their financial circumstances, are to be granted legal protection in the same manner. This follows from the very concept of justice and the law.[119] Finally, the ZPO was based on the legislative powers stipulated in Article 4 No. 13 of the 1871 Constitution of the German Empire ("Reichsverfassung 1871") which dealt with judicial proceedings,[120] which is also against the welfare state provision as a basis. Thus, in a dissertation dated 1900, it is stated with regard to legal aid in the ZPO: "It [legal aid] even amounts to an institution of the greatest practical importance for the administration of justice. In it the fundamental principle of procedural law as a whole, the duty of the state to grant legal protection to its citizens, appears in concrete form."[121] Here it becomes particularly clear that the aim is legal protection for each individual, not the equalisation of the legal status of different groups. In this case the aim is not the equality of two individuals or groups; rather, it is the *generality of* legal protection. Legal protection, which is ultimately based on the idea of justice, must be independent of the financial situation of those seeking legal protection, if the idea of justice itself is to be upheld. The fact that "poor law" ("Armenrecht"—the term at that time for legal aid) was not treated as "social law",[122] as would have been expected in view of the conceptual overlap, could also be interpreted in this way.

This does not mean that social aspects were irrelevant, but legal aid was considered to be part of procedural law and not general social assistance. Even if the objectives of Article 19 (4) sentence 1 GG (guarantee of legal recourse) and Article 20 (1) GG (principle of the welfare state) are not mutually exclusive, the historical interpretation confirms the special status of the guarantee of legal recourse that we systematically identified above.

Legal Aid for Legal Persons in Historical Perspective

Historically, legal aid for legal persons in Germany is relatively new—at least in comparison to legal aid for natural persons. While legal aid for natural persons can

---

[117] Hahn (1880), p. 206.

[118] Baur (1972), p. 75. Agreement by Rehbinder (1976), p. 395.

[119] Willenbruch (1977), pp. 28 et seq.

[120] Hahn (1880), p. 113.

[121] Schott (1900), p. V.

[122] Breithaupt (1915).

be traced back to Roman and Canonical Law,[123] legal aid for legal persons in Germany can only be traced back to the nineteenth century and existed then only at the level of the individual states.[124] However, provisions along this line remained isolated and were short-lived.[125] The ZPO of 1877 left the question of legal aid for legal persons in limbo.[126] At least the possibility of legal aid for legal persons was taken into account here, and legal aid and legal persons were not considered incompatible. Nevertheless, case law assumed that only natural persons, not legal persons, could be granted legal aid.[127]

After groundwork was laid during the Weimar Republic,[128] an explicit provision regarding legal aid for legal persons was enacted for the first time in 1933[129] at the Reich level with the Act Amending Proceedings in Civil Law Disputes of 27 October (§ 114 (4) ZPO).[130] This was a "law" passed by the national socialist government, which derived its "legislative powers" from the infamous so-called Enabling Act, adopted on 24 March 1933.[131] The following grounds for the "law" were given in the Imperial Gazette ("Reichsanzeiger"):

> The 'public interest' in para. 4 involves cases in which the legal person, e.g. a municipality or a charitable foundation, would be prevented from fulfilling its tasks serving the public if it were not able to conduct the legal dispute in question. However, it may also be the case that the existence of an enterprise depends on the proceedings being conducted, and the preservation of this enterprise is in the public interest because of the large number of workers it employs. Finally, there are cases in which it is a question of defending important patents vis-à-vis foreign countries and similar entities.[132]

Today's interpretation of the current § 116 ZPO relies significantly on this reasoning. It is quite common for legal aid to be denied to a legal person on the grounds that the public interest is not affected, because too few employees are involved or for other reasons.[133] This seems very questionable since the legal situation was very different in 1933—to say the least. This is all the more true in view of the preamble to

[123] Hahn (1880), pp. 206 et seq.

[124] See Willenbruch (1977), p. 17.

[125] See Willenbruch (1977), p. 17.

[126] "The Code of Procedure does not determine to what extent legal persons' right to exemption from fees is to be recognised", Hahn (1880), p. 207.

[127] RGZ 112, 107/108. See also German Constitutional Court Decisions 35, 348/353 and the references in Schott (1900), p. 52 with footnote 2, including evidence for the opposite position, and in Willenbruch (1977), p. 16 with footnote 16.

[128] See § 117 ZPO in: "Entwurf einer Zivilprozeßordnung" (1931), published by the Reichsjustizministerium, pp. 29 et seq., 274, 296 et seq. and, regarding this, Willenbruch (1977), pp. 18–20.

[129] RGBl. I, p. 780.

[130] For details on the history of its development, see Willenbruch (1977), pp. 16–20.

[131] RGBl. I, p. 141.

[132] RAnz. 1933, No. 257, p. 2.

[133] German Federal Supreme Court, ZInsO 2022, 143/144.

Article 1 of the Act Amending the Procedure in Civil Law Disputes of 27 October 1933, which stated:

> The parties and their representatives must be aware that the administration of justice does not serve them alone; it also and primarily upholds the legal security of the people as a whole.[134]

Comparable passages can be found elsewhere, in which the individual law perspective is subordinated to the—supposed—public welfare. Since fundamental rights were suspended in 1933, it was possible to completely disregard individual interests. Under the Basic Law, however, such an argument must be ruled out: Individuals do not exist for the sake of the state and their rights and interests should not be dependent on their usefulness to the common good.[135] However, this makes the (overly) restrictive interpretation of the German legal aid system increasingly questionable.

Historical Conclusions Regarding Legal Aid

It is in doubt whether clear conclusions may be reached regarding the constitutional root of the right to legal aid in legal history. During the process of constitutional drafting, it can be assumed that legal aid was intended to allow impecunious persons access to court and that legal persons could also be beneficiaries of legal aid. With the Basic Law not only enshrining the welfare state principle for the first time (in Article 20 (1) GG) as a constitutional principle, but featuring the guarantee of legal recourse in Article 19 (4) sentence 1 GG as the "crowning glory"[136] of the rule of law (Article 20 (3) GG) as well as the principle of equality (Article 3 (1) GG), several possibilities exist for the derivation of the right to legal aid from constitutional law; however, there was no explicit discussion of which grounds existed for legal aid. Nevertheless, with regard to Article 19 (4) sentence 1 GG, there is a reference to the opinion of Richard Thoma, a member of the "Parlamentarische Rat" (Parliamentary Council, the constituent assembly in 1948/1949) according to which the principles of the rule of law require that everyone be able to defend themselves against real or alleged unlawful acts by appealing to independent courts.[137] Heinrich von Brentano, also a member of the "Parlamentarische Rat", emphasised that legal recourse must be available in all circumstances.[138] This is still not very conclusive. A perusal of the Parliamentary Council's materials and minutes[139] is no more

[134] RGBl. I, p. 780.

[135] Regarding this, see Kunig and Kotzur (2021), Article 1, marginal number 3.

[136] For proofs thereof, see Schenke (1999), p. 153.

[137] Matz (2010), p. 184.

[138] Matz (2010), p. 185.

[139] Der Parlamentarische Rat 1948–1949, files and records in 14 volumes, ed. by the German Bundestag and the Federal Archives.

illuminating.[140] Since—as far as we can determine—legal aid was not discussed in the Parliamentary Council, no valid historical conclusions can be drawn. However, in terms of the history of dogma, there is no reason to view the right to legal aid as being rooted in the welfare state principle. In any case, this does not call into question the results of the grammatical and systematic interpretations.

It also becomes clear, however, that essential ideas explicitly expressed in the law and the grounds for it when legal aid for legal persons was introduced in 1933 contradict the concepts of the Basic Law and can no longer be used to evaluate the legal aid question.

4.2.4 Teleological Interpretation: Actual Enforcement of Individual Rights Vis-à-Vis the State

The interpretation based on the meaning and purpose of a provision, the teleological interpretation, examines the intended aim of the provision. According to the traditional perspective, a provision is to be interpreted in such a way that its purpose or purposes are brought to light as far as possible.[141] In doing so, it must be considered that a provision usually does not explicitly reveal its purpose; rather, this must be determined in an initial step. This in turn requires the application of methods of interpretation.[142]

In the case of Article 19 (4) sentence 1 GG, however, there is agreement on the *ratio legis*. The purpose of Article 19 (4) sentence 1 GG is to safeguard substantive rights procedurally in that they can be sued for by the individual.[143] They do not merely exist; they can also be enforced vis-à-vis the state in a legally binding manner in court proceedings. "Anything else would be a hollow construct existing merely on paper, a purely Platonic pretence, a 'pattern without value'."[144] In this broadside against state authority, however, there are no fundamental differences between legal and natural persons that could provide grounds for legal persons not needing legal

[140] A search of the PDF files of the volumes available electronically (except for volumes 5/II and 13/II) for the term "Armenrecht" ("poor law", the term used for legal aid at the time) did not yield any hits. Nor do the keyword indexes of the volumes overall contain the main keyword "Armenrecht".

[141] Larenz (1991), p. 332.

[142] Müller and Christensen (2013), marginal number 364. See also Hesse (1999), marginal number 68; Rüthers et al. (2022), marginal numbers 725–729; Sodan (1987), pp. 514 et seq.

[143] Schenke (2009), § 78, marginal numbers 1 et seq. Referring solely to substantive fundamental rights, Dr Süsterhenn in the 32nd session of the Committee on Fundamental Questions of the Parliamentary Council on 11 January 1949, reprinted in: Pikart and Werner (1993), p. 927; Pestalozza (1999), pp. 140 et seq.

[144] Schmidt-Jortzig (1994), p. 2571.

protection against state authority:[145] Legal persons are created in accordance with the law, they enjoy substantive rights which are furthermore constitutionally protected by fundamental rights. Still, representatives of the state may infringe upon the rights of legal persons in such a way that legal action becomes necessary. Even if legal persons have no body or psyche which can be harmed, they do have other rights that the state may not violate and which are constitutionally protected. The purpose of legal aid in administrative proceedings is to "prevent a party from being prevented from seeking justice in court against the state merely for economic reasons."[146] To argue otherwise would be to allow the state, which is also a party to the administrative proceedings, to deny legal protection to legal persons.

Only the danger that legal entities without assets could be used as special-purpose entities to outsource a litigation risk is a possible reason for more restrictive rules. However, this danger is neutralised by the stipulations regarding sufficient prospects of success, lack of recklessness and, in particular, the primary allocation of aid to economically affected parties (§ 114 (1) sentence 1, § 116 sentence 1 no. 2 ZPO), so that there is no need for a further category of restrictions.

4.2.5 Interim Conclusion: Anchoring Legal Aid in Article 19 (4) Sentence 1 GG

While the historical interpretation leads to the conclusion, at least in terms of the history of dogma, that legal aid is to be classified in terms of the rule of law and not in terms of the welfare state, the legislative history does not allow for any reliable conclusions. However, the wording, the system, and the meaning and purpose all favour the anchoring of the entitlement to legal aid in Article 19 (4) sentence 1 GG and not in the more general principles of the rule of law or the welfare state based on Article 3 (1) GG.

5 Implications for Legal Aid for Legal Persons and Final Conclusion

Thus, if the fundamental right enshrined in Article 19 (4) sentence 1 GG (guarantee of legal recourse) is the source of the entitlement to legal aid, legal aid for legal persons can no longer be excluded. The classification of legal aid as a social benefit

[145] Willenbruch (1977), pp. 28 et seq. points out that neither substantive law nor civil procedure distinguishes between natural and legal persons in principle and that, with the exception of unique structures, they enjoy the same rights and the same legal protection.

[146] German Constitutional Court Decisions 92, 122/124. Similarly, "making legal protection accessible", Behn (1992), p. 1 (heading under a.).

or even social assistance available solely to natural persons is thus also subject to considerable objections.

Although statutory law in principle provides for legal persons' entitlement to legal aid, it sets different criteria for natural and legal persons. Legal persons have the additional burden of proving "public interest" in the process, which is also interpreted extremely narrowly. However, this is incompatible with Article 19 (4) sentence 1 of the GG, which defines effective access to court as a fundamental individual right. The only legal grounds for the unequal treatment of natural persons and legal entities are the risk of abuse, which is associated with the arbitrary creation of legal entities without assets at the expense of the public. Although this is a recognisable differentiation criterion, the current law reduces the risk of abuse with the prerequisites of "sufficient prospects of success" and "lack of recklessness". Above all, however, the requirement that the "parties economically affected by the subject matter of the litigation" be unable to afford the costs of the litigation (§ 116 sentence 1 no. 2 ZPO) is an appropriate bar, ensuring that no legal entity without assets is utilised to reduce the risk of costs.[147] Thus, the German Federal Supreme Court (Bundesgerichtshof—BGH) correctly decided in 1954 (albeit limiting its decision to a single case of a general partnership, "offene Handelsgesellschaft") that the prerequisite of ensuring the "public interest" was irrelevant, because otherwise certain persons would never benefit from legal aid.[148] Only legal persons that are large enough to have an impact on the general public due to the number of their employees or creditors ("too big to fail") can claim that the lack of legal aid is against the public interest. This does not seem to be a sensible interpretation of the law, especially for a legal system based on individual rights protection.

The additional "public interest" prerequisite required for legal persons to receive legal aid not only makes little sense; it is also unnecessary based on the principle of proportionality. The other requirements are sufficient to ensure that the right to legal aid cannot generally be abused. At the very least, it would be unreasonable to make the individual legal protection rights of legal persons dependent on the existence of a broader general interest in the proceedings. The person seeking legal protection would then be dependent on the interests of third parties. This is not compatible with the concept of individual legal protection. The "public interest" requirement is an irrelevant concept in the system of fundamental rights protection under the Basic Law, one which can only be explained in terms of its historical origin, and which can no longer be legitimised in terms of constitutional law.

Therefore, even in the event of the partial invalidity of § 116 sentence 1 no. 2 ZPO, there is no reason to fear that the risk of litigation and costs will be transferred to financially weak legal persons and thus, in the end, to the general public, if and to the extent that the other prerequisites for legal aid (indigence of the persons behind the legal person, sufficient prospects of success, lack of recklessness) are interpreted and

[147] For more details on this, see Meents (1975), pp. 365–367. Even more far-reaching, because in favour of completely equal treatment, are the arguments of Willenbruch (1977), p. 93.

[148] German Federal Supreme Court, NJW 1954, 1933.

applied in light of this concern. Moreover, it is incumbent on the party applying for legal aid to convince the court that the requirements are met. § 116 sentence 1 no. 2 ZPO is unconstitutional in this respect. Even if we do not accept this line of argument, a broad (to say the least) interpretation of § 116 sentence 1 no. 2 ZPO, one in conformity with the constitution and orientated towards Article 19 (4) sentence 1 GG, would be necessary to counteract the inconsistencies when recourse is made to the "grounds for the law" of 1933.

References

Baldegger M (2017) Menschenrechtsschutz für juristische Personen in Deutschland, der Schweiz und den Vereinigten Staaten. Duncker & Humblot, Berlin

Baur F (1954) Der Anspruch auf rechtliches Gehör. AcP 153:393–412

Baur F (1972) Armenrecht und Rechtsschutzversicherung. JZ 1972:75–78

Behn M (1992) Die verfassungsrechtliche Rechtsschutzgleichheit - Das Bundesverfassungsgericht und die Beurteilung der "hinreichenden Aussicht auf Erfolg" iSd § 114 S. 1 ZPO - Teil II. SozVers 1992:1–8

Bergner I, Pernice C (2011) Die Rechtsprechung des Bundesverfassungsgerichts zum Anspruch auf Rechtsschutz- und Rechtswahrnehmungsgleichheit. In: Emmenegger S, Wiedmann A (eds) Linien der Rechtsprechung des Bundesverfassungsgerichts, vol II. De Gruyter, Berlin, pp 241–270

Bleckmann A (1997) Staatsrecht II - Die Grundrechte, 4th edn. Heymanns, Köln

Böckenförde EW (1974) Grundrechtstheorie und Grundrechtsinterpretation. NJW 1974:1529–1538

Bork R (2016) In: Stein F, Jonas M (eds) ZPO, vol II, 23rd edn. Mohr Siebeck, Tübingen

Breithaupt GW (1915) Das öffentliche Armenrecht in Preußen und dem Reich. Laupp, Gomaringen

Bryde BO (1982) Verfassungsentwicklung. Nomos, Baden-Baden

Deutscher Bundestag, Bundesarchiv (eds) (1975–2009) Der Parlamentarische Rat 1848-1949, 14 volumes. De Gruyter, Berlin

Diggelmann O, Altwicker T (2012) Finanzielle Gerichtszugangsschranken in Zivilprozessen im Licht von Artikel 6 Abs. 1 EMRK, DÖV, 781–788

Eichenhofer E (2021) Sozialrecht, 12th edn. Mohr Siebeck, Tübingen

Epping V (2021) Grundrechte, 9th edn. Springer, Berlin

Ernst C (2021) In: von Münch I, Kunig P (eds) GG, vol I, 7th edn. C.H. Beck, München

Gaier R (2011) Verfassungsrechtliche Vorgaben für die Zulassung der Berufung im Verwaltungsstreitverfahren. NVwZ 2011:385–390

Gogolin M (2015) Die deutsche Rechtskostenhilfe im Umbruch. Duncker & Humblot, Berlin

Gottwald P (2004) Von den Schwierigkeiten der Rechtsverfolgung einer "armen" Prozesspartei. In: Schilken E et al (eds) Festschrift für Walter Gerhardt zum 70. Geburtstag, pp 307–319

Grimm D (2006) Das staatliche Gewaltmonopol. In: Anders F, Gilcher-Holtey I (eds) Herausforderungen des staatlichen Gewaltmonopols: Recht und politisch motivierte Gewalt am Ende des 20. Jahrhunderts, Campus, Frankfurt, pp 18–38

Grzeszick B (2022) In: Dürig G, Herzog R, Scholz R (eds) Grundgesetz, 98th edn. C.H. Beck, München

Hahn K (1880) Die gesammten Materialien zur Civilprozessordnung, vol I. Decker, Berlin

Henke A (2010) Verfassungsrechtliche Anforderungen an fachgerichtliche Prozesskostenhilfeentscheidungen. ZZP 123:193–228

Hesse K (1999) Grundzüge des Verfassungsrechts der Bundesrepublik Deutschland, 20th edn. C.F. Müller, Heidelberg

Horn D (2015) Vom Staat der Demokratie. Schöningh, Paderborn

Huber PM (2018) In: von Mangoldt H et al (eds) GG, vol I, 7th edn. C.H. Beck, München
Huber PM (2021) In: Herdegen M et al (eds) Handbuch des Verfassungsrechts. C.H. Beck, München
Humborg M (2000) Das Armenrecht von der Zeit der Kammergerichtsordnungen bis heute. Dissertation, University of Münster
Ibler M (2022) In: Friauf W, Höfling KH (eds) Berliner Kommentar zum Grundgesetz. Erich Schmidt Verlag, Berlin
Jarass HD (2022) In: Jarass HD, Pieroth B (eds) Grundgesetz, 17th edn. C.H. Beck, München
Klein E (2010) Staatliches Gewaltmonopol. In: Depenheuer O, Grabenwarter C (eds) Verfassungstheorie. Mohr Siebeck, Tübingen
Klein E (2018) In: Görres-Gesellschaft (ed) Staatslexikon, vol II, 8th edn. Herder, Freiburg
Kunig P, Kotzur M (2021) In: von Münch I, Kunig P (eds) GG, vol I, 7th edn. C.H. Beck, München
Larenz K (1991) Methodenlehre der Rechtswissenschaft, 6th edn. Springer, Berlin
Linde (1833) Bemerkungen über die Zweckmäßigkeit der in Deutschland geltenden Grundsätze über das Armenrecht im Prozesse. AcP 16:51–83
Matz W (2010) In: Häberle P (ed) Entstehungsgeschichte der Artikel des Grundgesetzes - Jahrbuch des öffentlichen Rechts der Gegenwart, vol I, 2nd edn. Mohr Siebeck, Tübingen
Meents F (1975) Das Armenrecht im sozialen Rechtsstaat des Grundgesetzes. Dissertation, University of Bonn
Möbius S (2014) Das Prinzip der Rechtsschutzgleichheit im Recht der Rechtskostenhilfe. Mohr Siebeck, Tübingen
Möllers C (2006) Gewaltmonopol. In: Heun W (ed) Evangelisches Staatslexikon. Kohlhammer, Stuttgart, pp 804–807
Müller F, Christensen R (2013) Juristische Methodik, vol I, 11th edn. Duncker & Humblot, Berlin
Neumann W, Schaks N (2018) In: Sodan H, Ziekow J (eds) VwGO, 5th edn. Nomos, Baden-Baden
Nickel M (2016) Pkh-Antragsstellung - (k)ein Buch mit sieben Siegeln. NJW 2016:853–856
Pestalozza C (1999) Artikel 19 IV GG - nur eine Garantie des Fachgerichtsweges gegen die Verletzung von Bundesgrundrechten i.S. der Art. 1-17 GG. NVwZ 1999:140–142
Peters A, Altwicker T (2022) In: Dörr O et al (eds) EMRK/GG Konkordanzkommentar, vol II, 3rd edn. Mohr Siebeck, Tübingen
Pikart E, Werner W (1993) Der Parlamentarische Rat 1948-1949, Akten und Protokolle, vol 5/I. Harald Boldt, Boppard am Rhein
Puppe I (2023) Kleine Schule des juristischen Denkens, 5th edn. Vandenhoeck & Ruprecht, Göttingen
Rehbinder M (1976) Die Kosten der Rechtsverfolgung als Zugangsbarriere der Rechtspflege. In: Rehbinder M (ed) Zur Soziologie des Gerichtsverfahrens - Jahrbuch für Rechtssoziologie und Rechtstheorie, vol IV. Westdeutscher Verlag, Opladen, pp 395–414
Riese K (2022) In: Schoch F, Schneider JP (eds) VwGO, 42nd edn. C.H. Beck, München
Rosenberg L et al (2018) Zivilprozessrecht, 18th edn. C.H. Beck, München
Rüthers B et al (2022) Rechtstheorie, 12th edn. C.H. Beck, München
Sachs M (2021) In: Sachs M (ed) Grundgesetz, 9th edn. C.H. Beck, München
Schenke WR (1999) Die Rechtsschutzgarantie des Artikel 19 IV GG im Spiegel der Rechtsprechung des Bundesverfassungsgerichts. In: Wolter F et al (eds) Einwirkungen der Grundrechte auf das Zivilrecht, Öffentliche Recht und Strafrecht. C.F. Müller, Heidelberg, pp 153–186
Schenke WR (2009) In: Merten D, Papier JP (eds) Handbuch der Grundrechte, vol III. C.F. Müller, Heidelberg
Schenke WR (2020) In: Kahl W et al (eds) Bonner Kommentar zum Grundgesetz, 207th edn. C.F. Müller, Heidelberg
Schmidt-Aßmann E (2022) In: Dürig G, Herzog R, Scholz R (eds) Grundgesetz, 98th edn. C.H. Beck, München
Schmidt-Jortzig E (1994) Effektiver Rechtsschutz als Kernstück des Rechtsstaatsprinzips nach dem Grundgesetz. NJW 1994:2569–2573

Scholz R (1995) Justizgewährleistung und wirtschaftliche Leistungsfähigkeit. In: Gedächtnisschrift für Eberhard Grabitz. C.H. Beck, München, pp 725–745
Schott R (1900) Das Armenrecht der deutschen Civilprozeßordnung. Fischer, Jena
Schulze-Fielitz H (2013) In: Dreier (ed) GG, vol I, 3rd edn. Mohr Siebeck, Tübingen
Schweigler D (2017) Materiell-rechtliche Implikationen der Rechtsschutzgleichheit und des effektiven sozialen Rechtsschutzes. SGb 2017:314–318
Sobota K (1997) Das Prinzip Rechtsstaat. Mohr Siebeck, Tübingen
Sodan H (1987) Kollegiale Funktionsträger als Verfassungsproblem. Hermann Luchterhand, München
Sodan H (2010) Das Verbot kollektiven Verzichts auf die vertragsärztliche Zulassung als Verfassungsproblem. Duncker & Humblot, Berlin
Sodan H, Ziekow J (2020) Grundkurs Öffentliches Recht, 9th edn. C.H. Beck, München
Tuchschmid M (2006) Unentgeltliche Rechtspflege für juristische Personen? SJZ 2006:49 et seq.
Voßkuhle A (1993) Rechtsschutz gegen den Richter. C.H. Beck, München
Willenbruch K (1977) Das Armenrecht der juristischen Personen. Duncker & Humblot, Berlin
Zippelius R (2012) Das Wesen des Rechts, 6th edn. Kohlhammer, Stuttgart

Procedural Contracts About the Costs of Civil Litigation: A Brazilian View in Comparative Perspective

Antonio Cabral

Contents

Abstract The chapter tackles the problem of the funding of civil justice determined by contractual clauses. All around the globe, parties to a contract in general have been negotiating about procedure, something once envisaged only for arbitration, but now a growing trend also for court litigation. "Contract procedure", "procedural contracts" or "procedural agreements" have been frequently used also as a tool to define the costs distribution between the parties, shifting or modifying statutory provisions, assigning or selling claims, and inserting third parties into the equation of

A. Cabral (✉)
University of Rio de Janeiro, Rio de Janeiro, Brazil
e-mail: antoniocabral@uerj.br

E. Storskrubb (ed.), *YSEC Yearbook of Socio-Economic Constitutions 2022*,
YSEC Yearbook of Socio-Economic Constitutions (2023) 2022: 245–266,
https://doi.org/10.1007/16495_2023_53, Published online: 18 July 2023

the conflict by way of appointing them as responsible for the costs associated with judicial procedures (litigation expenses insurance and third party funding). The chapter wishes to highlight the varied possibilities for agreements to transfer costs of civil litigation available in the Brazilian legal system from a comparative perspective, and analyze some of the main related issues, such as the potential conflicts of interest, duties of information and disclosure, the risk of "shadow litigants" controlling the claims, and the normative effects that are expected to derive from the interaction of third parties with both the parties and the court.

1 Introduction: The Growing Contractualisation of Civil Litigation

The possibilities for the parties to modify by contract the formalities of court litigation procedures is a very controversial issue, mainly because of the tradition that sees litigation as an activity embedded with strong public interests. This orthodox approach used to restrict party autonomy in civil procedure, preventing them from deviating from statutory provisions. However, over the past two decades, there has been a growing tendency in many jurisdictions to allow the parties to enter into "procedural agreements" or "procedural contracts", i.e. contracts to shape the formalities of court procedures, something once envisaged only for arbitration, but now a visible trend also for civil litigation.[1]

Procedural contracts have been frequently used in many legal systems also as a tool to define the cost distribution between the parties, shifting or modifying statutory provisions, assigning or selling claims, and inserting third parties into the equation by way of appointing them as responsible for the economic burdens associated to judicial procedures (either by way of litigation expenses insurance or by third party funding contracts). Because procedural contracts are well developed in Brazilian law, this chapter wishes to tackle, from a Brazilian and comparative perspective, some of the issues involved in this movement of allowing the litigants to exert control over the costs of court proceedings by way of contracts and agreements, and some of the related problems and potential impacts that this type of agreement might have over relevant third party and public interests.

[1] Cabral (2019), pp. 363f; Nylund and Cabral (2023), part 1.

2 Which Are the "Costs of Civil Litigation"?

But what does the expression "costs of civil litigation" actually mean? In Brazilian law, by the expression "costs of civil litigation" usually refers to taxes, judicial fees and honoraries payed to public bodies or to certain professionals (experts, lawyers etc.) that perform duties related to dispute resolution.[2]

Judicial taxes are to be payed to the judiciary and will be directed to the public treasury. They are associated with specific judicial services and therefore are to be payed by the parties, the ones that burden the judicial system with a lawsuit.[3] These taxes are regulated by the courts (established in tables that are regularly edited and published) and usually correspond to a proportional sum calculated based on the value of the claim(s) (parties have to indicate value of their claims in their opening motions, and this indication may be contested by the opposing party and is controlled by the judge).[4] They are usually charged for the purpose of sustaining judiciary facilities and services, and are supposed to account for all the expenses of the justice system, which entail the fixed cost that the state has for maintaining structures (court buildings, for instance) and organizing services (including nowadays IT hardware and software for online platforms), plus expenses for payment of salaries for judges and staff (clerks, bailiffs and civil servants in general).

Apart from taxes, parties are also burdened by other types of expenses, variable sums of money they sometimes have to pay depending on the procedural legal acts they intend to perform. One of those is a form of fee charged by notary services (extra-judicial facilities regulated by the judiciary), whenever these services have to perform registrations, notifications or other type of documentation in deeds. Those fees are payed directly to the notary.[5] On top of that, litigation expenses entail also honorary fees paid by the parties for the performance of legal services by various professionals involved in litigation, such as travel expenses for witnesses or the fees and honoraries of experts and technical assistants (article 84 of the Code of Civil Procedure or CPC).[6]

A relevant element of the litigation costs are the lawyers' fees, that can be established by a contract between the party and the attorney (fee agreements). But in Brazil, litigation attorneys are also entitled to an additional sum determined by the judicial sentence in favor of the winning party (so-called "*honorários*

---

[2] Abreu (2003), pp. 66–67; Dinamarco (2009), pp. 651–653; Greco (2011), pp. 363–365.

[3] In case law, *Supremo Tribunal Federal* (Supreme Court or STF)—ADI n° 1.145/PB, 03/10/2002; ADI n° 1.772 (MC)/MG, 04/15/1998; ADI n° 1378 (MC)/ES, 11/30/1995; RE n° 116.208/MG, 04/20/1990. Superior Court of Justice (or STJ)—REsp n° 830511/SP, 09/28/2010. In legal literature, see Cunha (2013), p. 128; Cahali (2011), p. 284.

[4] In Brazil, these specific taxes which are payed by the parties are not enough to account for all the amount of funds necessary to maintain de functioning of judiciary. So revenue coming from other types of taxes (like income tax) are relocated to pay for a part of the costs of the judicial system.

[5] Cunha (2013), p. 128.

[6] STJ—REsp 611.645/SE, 04/10/2007. See Theodoro Jr. (2014), p. 118.

sucumbenciais", or "defeat-based honorary fees", because they have to be paid for by the defeated party). Therefore attorneys can collect honorary fees due to contract (regardless of the outcome, whether their client was victorious or not) and yet another sum determined in the final judgment on the merits, and those two remunerations are independent from one another.[7]

It is important to recall that Brazil is aligned with legal systems of the Roman-Germanic tradition, in which the law usually attributes responsibility to pay for litigation costs based on the "causality rule", according to which the economic costs should be borne by the party that caused litigation by not complying with substantive law provisions (articles 82 §2° and 85, CPC).[8] Therefore, the defeated party bears the duty of paying for the full costs of the winning party (*victus victori in expensis condemnatus est*), which will be reimbursed by the defeated party when litigation ends. If the claim is accepted or rejected partially, there must be a proportional split of the duty to pay for the costs between the parties (articles 86 and 87, CPC).[9] Nevertheless, the costs of litigation also encompass sanctions for behaviour in bad faith,[10] which can be imposed on the litigants regardless of the merits of the claim, i.e. independently of the outcome or if they are victorious or not.

In cases of vulnerable litigants that are unable to pay for the litigation costs because of their economic situation (usually very poor people), the law establishes their right to legal assistance provided by public defenders, that are attorneys payed by the state to represent their interests in court. There are several legal aid rules exempting those litigants from paying taxes, expenses and professional fees (article 98, CPC). It is also important to highlight that, in Brazilian law, some proceedings are almost entirely free of charge for the parties. This is the case in small

[7] A curious aspect of the Brazilian legislation is that the Lawyers Statute provides that lawyers' fees are entitlements of the lawyers themselves, not of the winning party (art.23 of Statute n.8.906/1994; art.85 §14 of the Code of Civil Procedure). Therefore if they are not spontaneously payed by the defeated party, the attorneys themselves should seek enforcement. In case law see STJ—REsp 948.492/ES, 12/01/2011. In my opinion, this model makes litigation costs higher and provokes an unbalance in the system. The honorary fees established by the judicial sentence should be an entitlement of the parties, to reimburse themselves of the expenses that they might have payed to their attorney's according to the contractual fee agreement. The statutory framework impedes the parties to receive full indemnization for what they have spent in a judicial lawsuit.

[8] In contrast to the common law tradition, in which each party will pay for their lawyers' fees. In Brazil, the control of causality is totally objective, and will attribute litigation costs regardless of intention. Exceptions are the costs of collective actions, which are only charged from exponential plantiffs if proven that they filed the lawsuit in bad faith (art.87 of Consumer Protection Code; art.18 of Statute n° 7.347/85 of Collective Redress).

[9] Regarding attorney fees, the reimbursement encompasses only the sum determined by the court, and not the amount regulated in the defeated party's contractual fee agreement with his/her lawyer. Therefore, as a consequence from the defeat, there is no obligation for the defeated party to pay the winning party's attorney directly.

[10] STJ—REsp n° 366.005/RS, 12/172002.

claims courts, which will only charge the parties for taxes and fees if the litigant appeals the final sentence of first instance.[11]

The major problem of the rules on the distribution of litigation costs depicted earlier is that they focus on expenses that are to be payed once the claim has been filed, and fail to account for the costs related to the preparation of the case prior to the filing of a legal proceeding, such as expenses related to negotiation and mediation procedures, expert opinions issued prior to the lawsuit, etc. None of those costs are normally referred to as "litigation costs" by the Brazilian legal literature. In other legal systems, however, those expenses are frequently included in the calculus of what is understood by "litigation costs" in a wider sense.[12]

3 Procedural Agreements that Shape the Formalities of Court Procedures

3.1 The Contractual Nature of Procedural Agreements on the Costs of Litigation

As highlighted before, many jurisdictions have been moving towards the contractualisation of civil litigation, enabling the parties to change the default set out in statute and determine many of the rules of court procedure. In a comparative perspective, one of the most prominent examples of jurisdictions that have taken an attitude favourable to party autonomy is the Brazilian legal system, in which procedural contracts are not only detailed in many specific procedural norms, but are also allowed in general terms in two statutory provisions that empower the parties to contract about procedure (articles 190 and 200 of the CPC, enacted in 2015).[13] These provisions open the system to procedural contracts that are not expressly provided for in a statute, i.e. even if the legislator did not regulate a certain kind of agreement, the parties can nevertheless stipulate changes in the proceeding to

[11]This is regulated by Statutes n° 9.099/95 and 12.153/09 for State jurisdiction, and Staute n° 10.259/01 in federal jurisdiction.

[12]See Kapeliuk and Klement (2013), p. 1486.

[13]The unofficial English translation of these rules is: "Art. 190. When the claim deals with substantive legal rights that permit the resolution of the dispute by party autonomy, the competent parties can lawfully stipulate changes in the procedure to adapt it to the specific characteristics of the claim, and can also agree upon their procedural rights, burdens, powers, and obligations, before or during the proceedings. Sole paragraph. Whether *ex officio* or upon request, the judge shall control the validity of the agreements set forth in this article, denying their application only in the case of nullity or inclusion of unconscionable terms in adhesion contracts or in cases where any of the parties is in a manifest position of weakness".

"Art. 200. The acts of the parties consisting of unilateral or bilateral declarations of will shall immediately produce the constitution, modification or extinction of procedural rights. Sole paragraph. The discontinuance of a lawsuit shall only produce effects once it has been ratified by the court."

adapt it to their needs. According to art. 190 and 200, unless there is a clear public or third party interest involved, party autonomy determines the rules of the procedure, and procedural agreements are binding and enforceable by courts. If there are no grounds for invalidity, judges cannot refuse to apply contractual provisions regulating the procedure (*in dubio pro libertate*).[14]

Following this trend, procedural agreements on the costs of litigation have been widely admitted in the Brazilian legal system, and the underlying rationale comes from arguments that might be similar to other jurisdictions.[15] Firstly, agreements related to the costs of litigation have a contractual nature, so the principles of contract law apply.[16] Moreover, when it comes to contracting about litigation costs, usually there is no public interest involved. Many agreements produce effects and impacts exclusively upon the contracting parties, and if most of the costs of litigation are borne by the parties themselves, who voluntarily choose to bring their cases to court and are able, in most civil cases, to withdraw the claim and waive the substantive rights in dispute, it would be inconsistent with the freedom of contract and party autonomy to prohibit the litigants from agreeing upon any issue related to the costs of litigation. In cases where no public or third party interests are at play and the parties request the enforcement by the court of the cost allocation or shifting established in their agreement, the judge must apply the rules distributing costs as determined by the parties, because the contractual norm overrides the statutory provisions.

Sometimes, however, a few procedural contracts can impact on public or third parties' interests. One could think of budgetary concerns that might impede parties from altering or re-distributing litigation costs if that would implicate a shift from what is previously established in statutory law due to risks for the public expenditure for maintaining the regular functioning of judiciary services. But a procedural contract cannot produce effects to the detriment of the public policy goals of structuring the justice system. Such contractual stipulations would only create obligations between the contracting parties, and would not be opposable to the judiciary. The state has the right to require payment of taxes and fees and has a legitimate interest that the due amount is cashed in favor of the treasury to be added as revenue to the public budget. If this sum is split between the parties (and not be payed by the defeated litigant) is simply not relevant for the state. If the winning party has a contractual obligation to pay for the litigation costs regardless of the outcome, and does not pay due to financial difficulties or insolvency, the state can

[14] Cabral (2016), pp. 144f, 253f; Cabral (2019), p. 379.

[15] However, at least when one thinks about the expenses of the judicial procedures after the filing of the lawsuit, the cost of procedures in Brazil is relatively low if compared to other legal systems, and maybe this was the reason why those types of contracts on litigation costs have not been developed in practice until very recently.

[16] Cabral (2016), p. 55.

collect that amount from the defeated party anyway, since the agreement between them is not opposable to the judiciary (as a third party).[17]

3.2 *Advantages: Predictability and Anticipation of Litigation Costs*

Whenever assessing strategically if it might be convenient to sue or settle from a cost-benefit perspective, litigants take all possible litigation costs into account, especially because in low-value claims, the projected win of a small amount of money might indicate little or no recovery of losses when all the judicial and extra-judicial costs are deducted.

In any case, there remains to a great extent a certain degree of unpredictability for example with respect to the length and duration of proceedings, the potential necessity of evidence, the amount of remuneration of lawyers (which sometimes are payed as *pro labore* on monthly instalments but can also be payed in proportion to the number of motions, applications etc. drafted by the attorneys and their staff—appeals, counterclaims etc.—and/or depending on the value of condemnation in the final judicial sentence). Therefore, there is a great deal of uncertainty in relation to the costs of litigation, and these factors of unpredictability can make it difficult or virtually impossible to anticipate how much parties will spend on a lawsuit in court, considering pre-judicial, filing, pre-trial, trial, appeals and enforcement stages. There are variations in intensity and approach in different legal systems, but in some way calculating how much a lawsuit will cost is a relatively unpredictable task in many jurisdictions.[18]

With all that in mind, a reasonable and comprehensible interest emerges for the litigants to define precisely and *ex ante* the burdens of litigation costs, and this can be operationalised in practice by entering into a procedural contract. A contractually-negotiated procedure can indeed provide a more accurate cost-benefit analysis and contribute to more legal security and legal certainty, reducing unpredictability regarding the expenses.[19] And as we shall see below, procedural agreements allow the parties not only to shift and adapt the statutory rules splitting the costs among themselves, but also to transfer these costs to willing third parties. The contractual modifications of costs reduces risks and allows better planning of litigation strategies.

---

[17] In more analitical terms, the agreement exists and is entirely valid between the parties, but it is partially unenforceable and non opposable to third parties.

[18] See in Germany Riehl (2003), pp. 44f, 59f, 75f; Wehling (2009), pp. 57f.

[19] Cabral (2018a), pp. 70–72.

3.3 *Formal Requirements: Who Are the Parties to the Agreement?*

In Brazil, agreements on costs are usually required to be in written form. They can be entered into prior to filing the lawsuit (either as an autonomous agreement or as clauses inserted in a contract) or incidentally to a pending judicial procedure.[20] If an agreement is made after filing, there is no deadline within which it has to be presented to the judge, but it is likely to be disclosed when the parties settle (as expressly provided for in article 90 §2° of the Brazilian CPC), and is usually invoked when parties ask the court to enforce the distribution of costs according to the contract.

As to the parties, one should remember that the contracting parties may not coincide with the parties who are formally present in the relevant court proceedings. It is possible to draw a distinction between procedural agreements on the distribution of costs between the litigants, which are also parties of a judicial procedure (plaintiff and defendant), on one side, and procedural contracts between a party to the lawsuit and his/her insurer, lawyer, financier etc., on the other side (see further below regarding the possible types of agreements).

Agreements between the parties to the dispute, who are also the persons appearing in court litigation as plaintiffs and defendants are easier to study and tend to be less disturbing in practice because they usually deal with waivable rights. However, several people/entities who are parties to a dispute can be grouped into different sides of the lawsuit, and when there is joinder of parties, despite their goal in defeating the opposing parties, it is not rare that even those on the same side have divergent interests among them. Therefore, sometimes some of the litigants might not agree to the terms of a procedural contract negotiated with other co-litigants on the same side of the court procedure (other co-plaintiffs or other co-defendants), and if they do not consent the contract is not binding and enforceable with respect to them, only to the assenting parties.

But there is a second group of procedural agreements, that of contracts between one of the parties in court litigation with a third party to the lawsuit. As we shall see, banks, credit and other financial institutions can take over the costs of litigation by way of procedural agreements. Those entities that absorb through contract the costs of one of the litigating parties can be commercial enterprises, associations or syndicates, acting in favour of their shareholders, associates or sindicalised members.[21] This kind of procedural contract raises more problematic issues, which will be dealt with in further parts of this article.

[20] Cabral (2016), pp. 75f.

[21] In Brazil, it is not unsual that judges', police officers' or public prosecutors' associations maintain funds to finance the legal expenses with lawyers in the eventuality that one of their associates suffers a lawsuit for liability due to behaviour in the exercise of their office.

3.4 Subject-Matter: Taxes, Public Fees, Expenses with Experts and Witnesses, Attorney Fees

A comparative analysis of the possible subject-matter of procedural agreements on costs shows that these contracts can cover whatever expenses are included in the concept of "litigation costs". Even with considerable variations in each legal system, most types of fees and expenses (whether involving lawyers, experts etc.) can be the subject-matter of contractual stipulations.[22] Of course the people entitled to the respective amount must be parties to the contract, even if they are not formally parties to the respective court procedure (it is important to highlight once again that parties to a procedural agreement are not always parties to the lawsuit that the contractual provisions are supposed to regulate). Thus, when a sum of money is due to be paid to persons other than the parties (experts, lawyers etc.), the entitled people must be a party to the agreement. The litigants themselves cannot dispose of the rights of others,[23] and such stipulations would not be enforceable or opposable in relation to third parties.[24]

With respect to the judiciary taxes, since they represent revenue that must be paid for the benefit of the state, the parties' agreements can mention them, but in order for those contracts to be binding upon the administration, the tax authorities or court administrators have to consent. Private agreements on taxes are valid only between those who have signed the agreement and manifested their assent.[25] They are not opposable and do not produce effects to the detriment of the treasury (who is a third party to the agreement).[26]

Attorney's fees can be negotiated and are waivable, but the attorneys have to be a party to the contract if any obligations are to be effective against them. Via agreement it is possible to regulate the responsibility for payment. Parties can stipulate that one of the them will fully pay for honorary fees of the adversary's lawyers, or that each one will cover the expenses of their own attorneys, regardless of the final result (waiving therefore the causality standard). In jurisdictions in which the court sets an additional sum payable to the winner's lawyer in the final ruling, parties (and their attorneys) can establish parameters to be considered by the court to determine the due amount.

---

[22] In Brazil, the Superior Court of Justice has ruled on this: STJ—AgRg no Ag n° 462.952/MG, 04/03/2003.

[23] Theodoro Jr. (2014), p. 129.

[24] In case law it is quite frequent to find rulings in this sense regarding contracts that were signed between the parties with no consent from their lawyers. STJ—AgRg no REsp 1.008.025-AL, 02/17/2009; AgRg no REsp 1.247.115-MG, 02/07/2012; REsp 1.068.355-PR, 10/15/2013. But if the lawyers participate, the agreement is valid. See Cabral (2016), pp. 219f; Cunha (2013), pp. 159–160.

[25] In Brazil this is regulated by article 123 of the Tax Code.

[26] Cabral (2018a), p. 76.

3.5 *Agreements on Fines and Indemnization for Damages due to Bad Faith*

Another debated issue is the possibility for the parties, by way of a procedural agreement, to eliminate fines, sanctions and other coercive measures of monetary nature, exempting themselves from paying those sums of money. Fines are usually understood as punishments, imposed by punitive orders to reprimand procedural behaviour that is deemed to be against bad faith or contrary to the principle of cooperation between the parties and the court. They are also used to put pressure on one of the litigants to comply with court rulings. In some jurisdictions, cost shifting orders can also be used as incentive or coercion to force a party to adhere to a certain behaviour during court proceedings. These measures are not solely instrumental to the effectiveness of substantive law, but are sometimes related to the public interest of an ethical and collaborative use of judicial resources,[27] and this is the reason why judges can impose fines and monetary sanctions of their own motion (*ex officio*). In the Brazilian legal system, this is reinforced by articles 5 and 6 of the CPC, which provide for the principles of good faith and collaboration.

In light of these public interests, it is questionable if parties are able to negotiate about fines. A unified approach in comparative law is not probable and the outcome depends on the normative framework of each legal system, but some parameters can nevertheless be suggested. If the fine or monetary sanction can be imposed *ex officio* by the court and will be directed to the public treasury, this probably indicates that there are public interests involved, and so procedural agreements on fines are to be considered invalid. Such punishments have no connection with the substantive law, since the winning party (who is proclaimed entitled to the disputed legal rights) can also be punished for misconduct or improper behaviour. This is the case in Brazil with penalties for bad faith conduct (article 77, CPC).[28]

On the other hand, if fines (whether coercive or punitive) must be payed in favour of the opposing party (like those in article 96, CPC), these rules seem to be functionally instrumental to substantive law provisions, and should be waivable as such.[29] Indeed, every coercive court order to pressure the litigant to comply is waivable if dependent on parties' request (the ones that cannot be imposed of the judge's own motion). In these cases, the prohibition of *ex officio* court rulings points to underlying private interests, to which procedural party autonomy is logically connected. At the end of day, such judicially-ordered fines are in the realm of the

[27] Marinoni (2006), p. 179.

[28] Cunha (2013), p. 171. In case law, see STJ—REsp n° 770.753/RS, 02/27/2007; AgRg no REsp 796255/RS, 11/13/2006; REsp 831784/RS, 11/07/2006; AgRg no REsp 853990/RS, published on 10/16/2006. However, exceptions exist in Brazilian statutory law. For example, the fine for filing in bad faith an expedite documental action ("*ação monitória*"), whenever imposed upon the plaintiff, will be collected in favor of the defendant (art.700 §10 of CPC).

[29] In legal literature, Barbosa Moreira (1980), p. 38; Talamini (2001), pp. 248–257. In case law, see STJ—REsp n° 1.006.473/PR, 05/08/2012.

parties' disposable rights, since they can waive them or choose not to collect them by simply not requesting the fines or not applying for their enforcement.[30]

4 Types of Procedural Agreements on Costs

4.1 Distribution and Reimbursement Clauses Among the Parties to the Dispute

Procedural contracts on the costs of litigation can take several forms. I do not intend to exhaust the topic, but some of the most common agreements in comparative perspective should briefly be presented. As mentioned above, procedural contracts on the costs of litigation can involve solely the parties to the dispute. They can agree to a mutuality rule, equally dividing the financial costs (and risks) of a future lawsuit, or distributing those costs as they wish, for instance taking on the responsibility of bearing a percentage of what the other contracting party was sentenced to pay.[31]

The parties can also stipulate reimbursement clauses, with obligations for the debtor to pay a global sum as recovery for the previous payment of court taxes, expenses and lawyers' fees. These clauses can also establish a periodic payment in instalments, which is especially important when a longer litigation proceeding is foreseen.

4.2 Transfer of Costs to Third Parties: Benefits for Repeat-Players and One-Shooters

Procedural agreements also allow parties to transfer, in part or in total, the costs and risks of litigation to third parties.[32] These third parties do not formally participate in the judicial procedure but will be parties to the contract. Such practice emerged years ago with the first forms of legal expenses insurance,[33] and later developed into several formats, becoming a reality all over the globe not only in arbitration, where it has been used for long time,[34] but also in litigation.[35]

[30] Cabral (2018a), pp. 78–80.

[31] Cabral (2018b), pp. 54–55.

[32] Bydlinski (1992), pp. 109–110, 133f; Pardau (2012), p. 66.

[33] Kilian (1998), p. 23; Faure and De Mot (2012), p. 10.

[34] Sahani (2016), p. 397; Faure and De Mot (2012), p. 17; Nieuwveld and Shannon (2012), p. 4.

[35] Dimde (2003), p. 91; Kilian (2003), p. 32; Cox (1990), pp. 159f; Pardau (2012), pp. 69f; Abrams and Chen (2013), p. 1080 and note 20; Goral (2005), pp. 109f; Steinitz (2011), pp. 1286–1292; Faure and De Mot (2012), pp. 18–19; Samra (2016), pp. 2307f; Martin (1999), pp. 58f; Richmond (2005), pp. 652–660; D'Alessandro (2018), pp. 57f.

The benefits of transferring the costs of litigation to third parties are multiple. For repeat-players, it increases predictability and reduces the risk of liability generated by losses in judicial processes.[36] On the one-shooters side, especially poor and vulnerable litigants, this kind of agreement promotes access to justice, making claims that are more complex and valuable viable for people that might not be able to bear the litigation costs in the long run. Therefore, procedural agreements on costs can contribute to the equality of arms and the balance of powers among litigants.[37]

Another advantage of this kind of negotiation is that the party to the agreement becomes a risk-neutral litigant,[38] with a stronger bargaining power in negotiation proceedings. Indeed, by transferring the costs to a third party, the litigant signals to their opposing parties not only absence of fear of court adjudication,[39] but also the capability to engage and absorb complex litigation hardships in long-lasting proceedings, displaying less intention to accept sub-optimal settlement proposals out of despair or hurry.[40]

4.2.1 Pactum de palmario *or* pactum de quota litis*: The Attorney as Funder*

Single individuals can act as funders of litigation, especially lawyers, depending on how their honorary payments are established in a fee agreement. For this purpose it is quite frequent to use of the well-known *pactum de palmario* or *pactum de quota litis*, also called contingency fee agreement, a contract by which the retribution for the lawyer's work is calculated as a percentage of the value to be collected by the client (the party) should she be the winner (*quota pars litis*).[41] Many legal systems allow parties and attorneys to establish outcome-related fees. It is a usual feature of common law jurisdictions, but it is permissible in some civil law countries.[42] Contingency fee agreements are a rudimentary form of litigation financing, since the lawyer and her/his constituent become "partners" in relation to the outcome.

[36] Qiao (2010), pp. 1f; Heyes and Rickman (2004), p. 107; Sahani (2016), p. 396. There are also benefits in terms of the accuracy of accountant records that predict future losses. By transfering the costs, the procedural agreement could prevent that the company would be impeded to engage in M&A transactions or launch an IPO in stock market. See Abreu (2015), p. 175; Kirstein (2000), pp. 251–252; Rickman and Gray (1995), pp. 302–325; Steinitz (2011), p. 1276; Sahani (2016), p. 395; Abrams and Chen (2013), pp. 1077–1079.

[37] Steinitz (2011), pp. 1271–1272, 1303f; Goral (2005), p. 100; Pardau (2012), p. 68.

[38] On this topic, see Van Velthoven and Van Wijck (2001), p. 393; Heyes and Rickman (2004), pp. 109f; Abrams and Chen (2013), p. 1077.

[39] Kirstein (2000), pp. 251–261.

[40] Heyes and Rickman (2004), pp. 114–117; Steinitz (2011), p. 1302.

[41] On this subject, in comparative perspective, see Fernhout (2009), p. 14.

[42] In Brazil, this is a very common practice among attorneys, and has been ruled as permissible by the Superior Court of Justice: STJ—REsp n. 805.919/MG, 10/13/2015.

4.2.2 Legal Expenses Insurance

Another means to transfer the costs of litigation to third parties is a contract for legal expenses insurance. This kind of contract represents an insurance against damages, by which the insurance company absorbs the risks of defeat in a future court litigation. Therefore these agreements usually involve lawsuits that were not yet brought before the courts.[43] Certainly the content of the insurance policy varies depending on the will of the parties, but this type of insurance often covers all litigation costs (either judicial or extra-judicial, as those related to the preparation of the claim).[44]

The Brazilian Code of Civil Procedure of 2015 provides for specific uses for legal expenses insurance. Article 848, sole paragraph of the CPC, for example, allows the attachment of goods in enforcement proceedings to be substituted by an insurance. The insured parties can avoid thereby acts of constraint over their assets (seizure, attachment, deposit etc.).[45] However, statutory law requires that the insured value be no less than the total amount of the debt added 30% on top of it.

A relevant provision in this context is that of article 835 §2°, CPC. Following the tradition of civil law jurisdictions, Brazilian law provides for a list of preferences for attachment, by which some types of goods are to be attached prior to others (for instance, movable goods prior to immovable assets). The law provides that the value of legal expenses insurance is to be considered equivalent to money, the first preferred asset in that list. However, in Brazil there is no "after the event legal expenses insurance", since the costs covered by the policy have to be precisely determined in advance. Most insurance contracts have a fixed term after which the insurance company does not bear any obligation of paying for the litigation expenses. Judges have to be aware, therefore, not to accept, as substitutes for attachment, insurance policies that are in imminent risk of expiring.

A very controversial issue in comparative perspective is the effect of legal expenses insurance in the choice of the lawyer and the autonomy given to the party's attorney to make strategic moves during litigation.[46] In Brazil, we understand that parties should be free to choose their attorney, even in light of a valid insurance contract between them. Once chosen by the party, the lawyer is independent from the insurance company.[47]

[43] In comparative perspective, see Wehling (2009), pp. 82f, 168; Hess (2008), pp. 196–197; Gräfe (2010), pp. 924f; Altenkirch (2013), pp. 1f; Fernhout (2009), pp. 21–22; Prais (1995), pp. 431–446.

[44] Article 779 of the Brazilian Civil Code provides that the default coverage (the "insurance risk") relates not only to the original event, but also to all the damages that arise from the same chain of events.

[45] Melo (2011), pp. 105–109. The matter is also regulated by the *Superintendência de Seguros Privados* (SUSEP), the governmental agency that oversees the insurance market.

[46] On that debate in comparative perspective, see Henssler (1999), pp. 3f; Cadiet (2002), p. 330.

[47] Since legal opinion n° 24161/2006, issued by SUSEP (the governmental regulator of insurance), insurance companies cannot offer attorney services to their clients. This practice was considered

4.2.3 Third-Party Litigation Funding

Another form of litigation financing by third parties are the contracts of litigation funding, procedural agreements by which an investor, financer or funder that is not a party to the lawsuit takes over the costs of litigation (judicial taxes, fees, expenses in general, including lawyers' and experts' honoraries), and in return will collect a certain amount if the financed party's claim succeeds.[48] The sum to be collected by the investor can be a percentage of the damages set in the judicial sentence (frequent when the plaintiff is financed) or a pre-determined amount, more suitable to the cases in which the defendants are the ones seeking financing.[49] In Brazil there are a few companies that constituted funds with the sole purpose of financing litigation and arbitration procedures.[50] In the normative framework of the Brazilian legal system, which encompasses a general clause on procedural contracts (article 190 of the CPC), there seems to be no legal obstacle for the development of such agreements.[51]

Whereas insurance is a contract for risk-transfer, third-party funding is an agreement that creates a partnership towards the victory of the investee, fostering cooperation for an optimal result.[52] Therefore, a more intense limitation of the expenses that are to be covered and payed for by the funder is frequent. Differently from what happens with the insurance for legal expenses, third-party funding usually covers only fees, taxes and honoraries related to the procedural activities of the professionals involved, but not the reimbursement of the sum imposed as a condemnation for damages.[53] On the other hand, because of the partnership that forms between the party and the investor, Brazilian law admits a greater influence to be exerted by the financer on the choices of the disputant (investee) during a litigation. Indeed, parties can loose in part their control over the procedure. For such purposes, so called "performance clauses" are frequently drafted in these type of agreements, i.e. clauses that establish duties of diligence for the party in conducting the proceedings, and can lead to liability if the party to the procedure acts with negligence or fails to inform the

illicit in light of art.3° §2° of the Bar Association Statute, as well as able to generate conflicts of interest between the lawyer and the parties.

48 Third-party litigation funding is very common in arbitration, and has quickly gained importance in litigation, in both common law and civil law jurisdictions. See in comparative perspective, Saraiva (2019), pp. 71f; Pinsolle (2013), pp. 399–416; Mulheron and Cashman (2008), p. 312; Schaner and Appleman (2012), pp. 175–187; Eversberg (2010), pp. 962f; Dethloff (2000), pp. 2225f; Frechen and Kochheim (2004), pp. 1213f; Wegmüller (2013), pp. 235f.

49 Samra (2016), pp. 2299f.

50 Beraldo (2014), p. 145; Abreu (2015), pp. 171, 174f.

51 Cabral (2018b), p. 64.

52 Temer (2020), pp. 359–384. In comparative perspective, Müller-Güldemeister and Rollmann (1999), p. 3540.

53 Samra (2016), p. 2302; Richmond (2005), p. 650; Faure and De Mot (2012), p. 16; Pardau (2012), p. 66; Sahani (2016), pp. 392, 400. This type of procedural contract should not be confused with a loan either. The investee is not obligated to return what the investor has spent and lost. See Skiba and Xiao (2017), pp. 119, 126.

funder of relevant facts and crucial strategic options. Such contracts often impose a duty of disclosure of all relevant information to the investor with respect to the case, the available evidence and other circumstances, not only at the moment of signing the agreement, but also during the whole course of the procedure.[54] Waivers and other acts of disposition are usually valid only if agreed both by the party and the funder. Although not necessary, sometimes financers require consulting with their staff prior to crucial stages. In this context, the litigant's attorney might not be fully independent to define strategy regarding motions, applications, appeals, statements, testimonies etc. This constantly brings up conflicts of interest.

In agreements of this kind, it is also frequent that the parties include a non-disclosure clause, obligating them to keep to the existence of the funding contract confidential, refraining from revealing it to anyone in or out of court. But confidentiality with respect to the terms of the third-party funding contract is a very controversial issue. Some scholars defend the existence of duty to disclose in court that a valid agreement was entered into by one of the parties and the financer. Arguably, such disclosure would also be paramount to reveal conflicts of interest and even to permit an accurate analysis of potential cases of judicial disqualification. Judges can only recuse themselves if they know who is involved and whose interests and rights are in play. There are also public interests that speak for disclosing the terms of the third-party funding contract. Moreover, information is usually beneficial for both parties. Knowing your adversary's risk aversion, for instance, is of utmost importance in settlement negotiations. On the other side, the non-financed party should not bear harmful effects that a contract between the opposing party and the investor might have on its litigation procedure. Therefore, disclosing the existence and the terms of the contract would be consistent with the principle of cooperation. Others argue, to the contrary, that the very knowledge of the agreement could unduly influence judges, who might set the sums to be paid for in terms of fees and honoraries higher knowing that a big company is behind the curtains and will support the expenditure of such an amount. So revealing that funding exists could prove to be worse for the litigation, causing biased and distorted decisions about the costs. Up-until this point, there is no norm in Brazilian law regulating the issue, and how the courts will rule on this matter still remains to be seen.

Another relevant discussion in respect to parties' agreements on costs concerns the consequences of the behaviour of the investor that takes on a leading role in litigation. In Brazil, legal literature uses the "control of litigation standard" to verify who is acting as a *de facto* party to the dispute (even if not formally present in court), and therefore who should suffer the effects of having acted as such. For instance, claim preclusions and punishments for bad-faith behaviour could be imposed on the financer whenever these funders hire and instruct the party's lawyers and make strategic choices during litigation (what to argue, when to file a motion or

[54] This is a rather debated issue among Brazilian legal scholars, since there is no express regulation. And it seems to be more room for secrecy in arbitration than in litigation. See Mannheimer et al. (2020), p. 6.

application, if, when and how to appeal, etc.).[55] By doing so, they are indeed participating in the procedure and having their day in court, and therefore should submit to the same legal consequences as the formal parties would face. Acting as a *de facto party* to the dispute would also oblige the financer to cover the costs of a successful counterpart.

This interpretation is necessary to avoid the so called "shadow litigants", true participants to a court procedure that hide in "backstage interactions" without presenting themselves formally as a party, in order to exclude themselves from litigation costs, to avoid monetary penalties, or to prevent issue or claim preclusion in future lawsuits due to previous engagement in a judicial context in the latter procedure (in which they were funders but a de facto party).

5 Limits of Procedural Agreements on the Costs of Litigation

5.1 Relativity of Procedural Contracts

As contracts in general, a contract can generate rights and obligations only in favour, or to the detriment, of the contracting parties. Hence, nobody can dispose of the rights of third parties.[56] If parties wish to regulate other people's interests via contract, the respective clauses are to be considered invalid and non-enforceable with respect to such third parties. Furthermore, whenever there is a joinder of parties, the agreement signed by some of them is not binding on the others. These contractual clauses would be relatively unopposable with respect to the non-consenting third parties to the agreement.

5.2 Validity of Uneven Allocation of Costs: Exceptions for Vulnerable and Weaker Litigants

The extensive permission to negotiate about procedure has limitations in Brazil expressly provided for in statutory law, and one of the grounds for invalidity of a procedural contract is the "manifest situation of vulnerability" of one of the parties to

[55] This could apply for insurance companies, depending on the powers that the contract gives them to control the litigation strategies. The Brazilian Civil Code (articles 771 and 787 § 3) provides that the insurance company has to be notified of the lawsuit, and legal scholars have been arguing that this invite to participate would atract the application of claim preclusion and res iudicata rules if the insurance company willingly and strategically adopts a "wait and see" attitude. About this issue, see Cabral (2018b), pp. 65–72; Temer (2020), pp. 359–384.

[56] Cabral (2016), pp. 269f.

the agreement (article 190, sole paragraph, of CPC). However, there is no principle that would require an even distribution of litigation costs. As explained earlier, legal aid rules and the possibility of being represented by public defenders are forms of balancing the economical inequality between the parties. Therefore the rules that allocate litigation costs are not a mechanism for implementing procedural equality. Therefore, arguing that any uneven stipulation on costs is unfair and invalid would be inconsistent with the causality rule (the defeated party pays for all the costs), according to which litigation costs naturally impact on the parties differently. On the contrary, the parties' autonomy to determine the allocation of costs is valid, enforceable by the courts (*in dubio pro libertate*), even if the negotiations result in an unequal division of the costs.

Exceptions are the cases involving vulnerable or weaker litigants, where a shift in litigation costs could result in such an intense burden that might reduce fundamental procedural guarantees to a point in which the litigant cannot defend herself appropriately. Whenever parties invoke an agreement in court that contains such a contractual modification creating an impediment (or unsurmountable obstacle) to the vulnerable litigants to defend their legal rights in court, judges can pronounce it void.[57] As a general criterion, it is important to verify if the shift in the distribution scheme can reduce or intensify the impact of litigation costs upon vulnerable litigants. If the agreement results in a format of costs allocation that is *disfavourable* to the weaker litigant, it can be considered invalid (article 190, sole paragraph, CPC). But if this shift *favours* the poorest litigant, it cannot be deemed void solely on those grounds. For the same reasons, procedural agreements that intend to deviate from statutory rules of legal aid are to be pronounced invalid.[58]

6 Conclusive Remarks

Party autonomy to shape the formalities of court litigation has been a growing trend in many jurisdictions. Following this tendency, litigants now enter into contracts on the costs of litigation, stipulating clauses to modify, shift or reallocate the expenses among them, or even transfer those costs to consenting third parties. Procedural contracts on costs are now a reality not only for arbitration, but also for court litigation, and in the past year the interest of lawyers, academics and enterprises for this kind of negotiation has been augmenting in an exponential manner.[59]

[57] I have used this parameter of the practical elimination of a fundamental guarantee of civil litigation in Cabral (2016), p. 337.

[58] Cabral (2016), pp. 327f.

[59] Mannheimer et al. (2020), pp. 1f. As technology advances, and other forms of loans and even crowdfunding allow parties to raise funds over the internet, other types of litigation financing have been discussed among legal scholars (Becker et al. (2022), pp. 1–4). One of those is the so-called "initial litigation offerings", a worldwide search for funding through intermediaries (start-ups) that gather funding from investors spread out in several different places, with promise to proportionately

Contractually modifying statutory default rules related to litigation costs is indeed very useful, especially because it increases predictability and produces important gains in terms of equality and access to justice. However, there are also downsides and concerns about due information and disclosure, possible conflicts of interest, and negative effects upon third parties.

It is up to legal scholars to investigate the several varieties of procedural agreements on costs, suggesting parameters for control and tests to control their validity and enforceability, considering among other factors the potential damages they could cause to weaker litigants, and ultimately also the consequences that the contractual clauses could have on public budget and expenditure, which is crucial for court administration.

Case Law

Supremo Tribunal Federal *(Supreme Court or STF)*

RE n° 116.208/MG, decided on 04/20/1990
ADI n° 1378 (MC)/ES, decided on 11/30/1995
ADI n° 1.772 (MC)/MG, decided on 04/15/1998
ADI n° 1.145/PB, decided on 03/10/2002

Superior Tribunal de Justiça *(Superior Court of Justice or STJ)*

REsp 611.645/SE, decided on 04/10/2007
REsp n° 366.005/RS, decided on 12/17/2002
AgRg no Ag n° 462.952/MG, decided on 04/03/2003
AgRg no REsp 853990/RS, published on 10/16/2006
REsp 831784/RS, decided on 11/07/2006
AgRg no REsp 796255/RS, decided on 11/13/2006
REsp n° 770.753/RS, decided on 02/27/2007
AgRg no REsp 1.008.025-AL, decided on 02/17/2009
REsp n° 830511/SP, decided on 09/28/2010
REsp 948.492/ES, decided 12/01/2011

share the profits, should the claimant be victorious. Payment is to be made through the so called NFTs (non fungible tokens), a type of crypto currency. However, this kind of funding has not yet been seen in practice in Brazil.

AgRg no REsp 1.247.115-MG, decided on 02/07/2012
REsp n° 1.006.473/PR, decided on 05/08/2012
REsp 1.068.355-PR, decided on 10/15/2013
REsp n. 805.919/MG, decided on 10/13/2015

References

Abrams DS, Chen DL (2013) A market for justice: a first empirical look at third party litigation funding. Univ Pa J Bus Law 15:1075–1109

Abreu F (2003) O custo financeiro do processo. RT 818:65–71

Abreu R (2015) Igualdade e processo: posições processuais equilibradas e unidade do direito. RT, São Paulo

Altenkirch M (2013) Die Sicherheitsleistung für die Prozesskosten: Ein Vergleich des deutschen und englischen Zivilprozessrechts und ein Vorschlag für das Schiedsverfahrensrecht. Sellier, München

Barbosa Moreira JC (1980) A tutela específica do credor nas obrigações negativas. In: Temas de Direito Processual – 2ª série. Saraiva, São Paulo

Becker D, Rocha P, Marçal F (2022) Initial litigation offerings e o financiamento de litígios por NFTs. https://www.jota.info/opiniao-e-analise/artigos/initial-litigation-offerings-financiamento-litigios-nfts-20022022. Accessed 26 Feb 2022

Beraldo L (2014) Curso de Arbitragem. Atlas, São Paulo

Bydlinski M (1992) Kostenersatz im Zivilprozeß. Manz, Wien

Cabral A (2016) Convenções processuais. Juspodivm, Salvador

Cabral A (2018a) Convenções sobre o custo da litigância (I): admissibilidade, objeto e limites. RePro 276:61–89

Cabral A (2018b) Convenções sobre o custo da litigância (II): Introdução ao seguro e ao financiamento processuais. RePro 277:47–78

Cabral A (2019) Designing procedure by contract: litigation agreements in contemporary civil procedure. IJPL 9:363–380

Cadiet L (2002) L'économie des conventions relatives à la solution des litiges. In: Deffains B (ed) L'analyse économique du droit dans les pays de droit civil. Cujas, Paris

Cahali Y (2011) Honorários advocatícios, 4th edn. RT, São Paulo

Cox DC (1990) Lawsuit syndication: an investment opportunity in legal grievances. St Louis Univ Law J 35:153f

Cunha LJ (2013) A Fazenda Pública em Juízo, 11th edn. Dialética, São Paulo

D'Alessandro E (2018) Third party litigation financing in Italy. ZZP 23:53–67

Dethloff N (2000) Verträge zur Prozessfinanzierung gegen Erfolgsbeteiligung. NJW 31:2225f

Dimde M (2003) Rechtsschutzzugang und Prozessfinanzierung im Zivilprozess: Eine ökonomische Analyse des Rechts. BW, Berlin

Dinamarco C (2009) Instituições de direito processual civil, vol 2, 6th edn. Malheiros, São Paulo

Eversberg A (2010) Prozessfinanzierung für den Versicherungsprozess. In: Veith J, Gräfe J (eds) Der Versicherungsprozess, 2nd edn. Beck, München

Faure M, De Mot J (2012) Comparing third party financing of litigation and legal expenses insurance. J Law Econ Policy 8(3)

Fernhout F (2009) Outcome-related fee agreements in Europe and Hong Kong. In: Uzelac A, Van Rhee CH (eds) Access to justice and the judiciary: towards new European standards of affordability, quality and efficiency of civil adjudication. Intersentia, Antwerp

Frechen F, Kochheim ML (2004) Fremdfinanzierung von Prozessen gegen Erfolgsbeteiligung. NJW 57(17)

Goral R (2005) Justice dealers: the ecosystem of American litigation finance. SJLBF 21

Gräfe J (2010) Der Versicherungsprozess, 2nd edn. Beck, München
Greco L (2011) Instituições de Processo Civil, vol 1, 3rd edn. Forense, Rio de Janeiro
Henssler M (1999) Rechtsschutzversicherungen und Rechtsverfolgungskosten. ZgV 88:3–21
Hess B (2008) EU trends in access to justice. In: Van Rhee CH, Uzelac A (eds) Civil Justice between efficiency and quality: from ius commune to the CEPEJ. Intersentia, Antwerp
Heyes A, Rickman N (2004) Legal expenses insurance, risk aversion and litigation. IRLE 24:107–119
Kapeliuk D, Klement A (2013) Changing the litigation game: an ex ante perspective on contractualized procedures. Tex Law Rev 91(6):1475–1494
Kilian M (1998) Determinanten des europäischen Rechtsschutzversicherungsmaktes. ZgV 88:23f
Kilian M (2003) Alternatives to public provision: the role of legal expenses insurance in broadening access to justice – the German experience. J Law Soc 30(1):31–48
Kirstein R (2000) Risk neutrality and strategic insurance. In: Geneva papers on risk and insurance: issues and practice 25(2)
Mannheimer S, Monteiro AL, Martins I (2020) Arbitragem, Third-party funding e a proteção dos documentos enviados pela parte financiada ao financiador. RArb 67:143–160
Marinoni LG (2006) Tutela inibitória (individual e coletiva), 4th edn. RT, São Paulo
Martin SL (1999) Financing plaintiffs' lawsuits: an increasingly popular (and legal) business. Univ Mich J Law Reform 33:57f
Melo G (2011) Seguro garantia judicial: aspectos processuais e materiais de uma figura ainda desconhecida. RePro 36(201)
Mulheron R, Cashman P (2008) Third party funding of litigation: a changing landscape. Civil Just Q 27(3):312–341
Müller-Güldemeister L, Rollmann C (1999) Die Prozessfinanzierung der Foris AG ist keine Versicherung. NJW: 3540f
Nieuwveld LB, Shannon V (2012) Third-party funding in international arbitration. Wolters Kluwer, The Hague
Nylund A, Cabral A (2023) Contractualisation of civil litigation. Intersentia, Cambrigde
Pardau SL (2012) Alternative litigation funding: perils and opportunities. U C Davis Bus Law J 12: 65f
Pinsolle P (2013) Third party funding and security for costs. Cahiers de L'arbitrage 2:399–416
Prais V (1995) Legal expenses insurance. In: Zuckerman A, Cranston R (eds) Reform of civil procedure: essays on "access to justice". University Press, Oxford, pp 431–446
Qiao Y (2010) Legal expenses insurance and settlement. AJLE 1(1). https://doi.org/10.2202/2154-4611.1003
Richmond DR (2005) Other people's money: the ethics of litigation funding. Mercer Law Rev 56: 649f
Rickman N, Gray A (1995) The role of legal expenses insurance in securing access to the market for legal services. In: Zuckerman A, Cranston R (eds) Reform of civil procedure: essays on "access to justice". University Press, Oxford
Riehl J (2003) Prozesskosten und die Innanspruchnahme der Rechtspflege: Eine ökonomische Analyse des Rechtsverhaltens. Wiku, Berlin
Sahani VS (2016) Judging third-party funding. U C L A Law Rev 63:388f
Samra E (2016) The business of defense: defense-side litigation financing. Univ Chic Law Rev 83(4):2299–2341
Saraiva M (2019) O financiamento por terceiros na arbitragem e o acesso à justiça. Lumen Juris, Rio de Janeiro
Schaner LS, Appleman TG (2012) Third-party funding in the United States. RArb 32
Skiba PM, Xiao J (2017) Consumer litigation funding: just another form of payday lending? Law Contemp Prob 80(3):117–145
Steinitz M (2011) Whose claim is this anyway? Third-party litigation funding. Minn Law Rev 95: 1268–1338
Talamini E (2001) Tutela relativa aos deveres de fazer e de não fazer. RT, São Paulo

Temer S (2020) Financiamento de Litígios por 'Terceiros' (ou '*Third-Party' funding*): o nanciador é um sujeito processual? Notas sobre a participação não aparente. RePro 309:359–384
Theodoro H Jr (2014) Curso de Direito Processual Civil, vol 1, 55th edn. Forense, Rio de Janeiro
Van Velthoven B, Van Wijck P (2001) Legal cost insurance and social welfare. Econ Lett 72(3): 387–396
Wegmüller M (2013) Prozessfinanzierung in der Schweiz: Bestandesaufnahme und Ausblick. HAVE - Haftung und Versicherung 3:235–245
Wehling M (2009) Finanzierung von Zivilverfahren. Kovač, Hamburg

Court Pays Enforcement Costs? Funding of Enforcement Proceedings in China

Zhixun Cao

Contents

Abstract Funding a civil procedure is of great importance, and funding of enforcement proceedings concerns socio-economic constitutions in different countries. A balance between the input of public resources of the state and the costs borne by the parties should be accomplished. Rules for litigation costs could serve as the basis for the rules for enforcement costs. Litigation costs paid by a party concerned to the court shall include case-filing fees, application fees and other expenses. The case-filing fee shall be prepaid by the plaintiff. Merely the litigation costs incurred in courts are recoverable from the losing party while attorney fees are not eligible for cost-shifting. In contrast, the enforcement application fee need not to be prepaid, which means that the ordinary operation of enforcement proceedings is promoted and financially supported by the courts. However, the enforcement creditor still

Z. Cao (✉)
Law School, Peking University, Beijing, People's Republic of China
e-mail: pkuhector@pku.edu.cn

E. Storskrubb (ed.), *YSEC Yearbook of Socio-Economic Constitutions 2022*,
YSEC Yearbook of Socio-Economic Constitutions (2023) 2022: 267–290,
https://doi.org/10.1007/16495_2023_52, Published online: 18 July 2023

ought to pay the fees for judicial identification and assessment in advance which are then recoverable after the successful enforcement proceedings. Since there is no issue of costs prepaying, there is no need to prepare any cost-shifting rule hereby, and the attorney fees are also not recoverable. As the situation in civil proceedings, the allocation of enforcement costs between the state court and the enforcement creditor is related to the efforts of the court during enforcement proceedings. Although the "court pays" principle is prevailing, there are still doubts based on the interests of general tax-payers. Instead, there are recently public enforcement service paid by the creditor and privatized enforcement systems.

1 Introduction

Funding a civil procedure is of great importance. From the perspective of comparative civil procedure and the practice of civil justice in specific jurisdictions, there are between the court and parties various elements to be considered. In a broader sense, the issue of litigation costs is related to costs which are necessary for administrating the court system, the public and private costs paid by the parties, and the costs for legal aids which ought to be provided by the state.[1] It is argued that "in civil and commercial matters where money is usually the primary object, the financial burden of litigation may well be the single most important consideration in deciding whether to fight in court"[2]. Moreover, the third party funding attracts more and more attention in the area of dispute resolution recently.[3] The same observation applies to the funding of the following enforcement procedure which represents one crucial, although not essential, stage of the civil procedure. Among others, enforcement proceedings could be interpreted as an issue of public management.[4]

Both issues of funding litigation or enforcement proceedings concern socio-economic constitutions in different countries and regions. The allocation of litigation costs does not merely refer to the monetary payment and its division between different actors to civil proceedings, but also has its roots in the general design of civil procedure in distinct jurisdictions. Then it is noticeable that the public resources needed by the judiciary may differ according to whether the judges or the parties play the crucial role in promoting the proceedings further.[5] In other words, which should be the prevailing principle of civil procedure, the party-oriented principle or the court-oriented principle, makes a difference for the issue of costs as well.

[1] Wang (2016), p. 93.
[2] Reimann (2012), p. 4.
[3] E.g. Zhang (2021).
[4] Kennett (2021).
[5] Fu (2001), pp. 245–255.

Accordingly, the cost-shifting rules may be prepared differently since the constitution of costs should be changed item by item.

Indeed, functions and institutions of adjudication and enforcement in civil justice are considered to be separated comparatively[6] and especially in China[7]. However, their main purpose is the same and that is to promote civil justice in national context as a whole. To achieve this purpose, the attitude of gazing outward is always of great use for any specific jurisdiction.[8] Nothing special should apply to the political vision of the Community of Shared Future for Mankind or the development pattern of domestic and international economic cycles suggested by the Chinese government. Enforcement proceedings are now supposed to be taken more seriously[9] rather than as 'a relatively neglected subject'.[10] That is why we now need to have 'Principles of Effective Enforcement' project[11] of the International Institute for the Unification of Private Laws (hereinafter as UNIDROIT) and the segment 14 on enforcement law of the *Compendium of Comparative Civil Justice* organized by Max Planck Institute Luxembourg for Procedural Law and International Association of Procedural Law. The allocation of costs occurred during enforcement proceedings is among the issues which determine the quality and efficiency of the proceedings substantially. More generally, it is emphasized by Yulin Fu on the public interest litigation in China that '[t]he rules on costs and their distribution, the risk of losing the case, as well as the corresponding legal culture, directly affect the motivation of interested persons and entities to bring collective actions'.[12] The same observation should apply to the costs issue in ordinary civil proceedings.

Principally, this contribution concerns the fact that the court, as the public organ monopolizing the power of enforcement in China, is responsible for administrating enforcement proceedings and paying for the various enforcement measures in advance. It is even more noticeable when the full liquidation of the debtor in enforcement proceedings, which is considered as the ordinary destiny of all enforcement cases, could not be accomplished. In such cases, the refund from the debtor to be enforced could not be expected partially or entirely. It means that the state and the general tax-payers have to pay for the service which is merely beneficial for the specific enforcement creditor. This situation relates to the understanding of enforcement proceedings in China and accordingly, provides a strong incentive to the state and individual enforcement courts to search for any enforceable assets of the debtor.[13] Yet, for the sake of extending judicial resources and the efficiency of the proceedings, there could be some enforcement party who would be encouraged by

[6]Hess (2010), p. 46.

[7]Cao (2021c), pp. 116–121.

[8]Especially for the U.S. and China, Woo (2018).

[9]Levy (2017).

[10]Van Rhee and Uzelac (2010), p. xxi.

[11]Stürner (2016), pp. 6–7. On its background and the on-going development, UNIDROIT (2021).

[12]Fu (2021), p. 399.

[13]Cao (2022a). Comparative discussion, Deguchi (2022).

the state to undertake the costs of specific enforcement measures. Accordingly, we may argue that the Chinese enforcement system is partly privatizing right now. In this sense, a balance between the input of public resources of the state and the costs borne by the parties should be accomplished, while especially the shift of costs towards the parties should never harm the parties' access to justice.[14]

2 Rules for Litigation Costs as the Basis for Rules for Enforcement Costs

2.1 Essential Legal Backgrounds Under Chinese Law

To begin with, this contribution has to introduce the Chinese civil justice system[15] in general. Before the newest revision of the Civil Procedure Law (hereinafter as CPL) statute, which was published at the end of 2021 and becomes effective on Jan. 1, 2022, there are previously five versions of the statute which were released subsequently in 1982 (although with a more temporary nature), 1991, 2007, 2012 and 2017.[16] Besides the statute, the Supreme People's Court (hereinafter as SPC) also promulgates judicial interpretations and other judicial instruments, which should merely interpret the statutes but rather are in practice *de facto* laws as well. For instance, there is in the area of civil procedure one "Interpretation of the SPC on the Application of the Civil Procedure Law of the P.R.C. of 2022" (hereinafter as ICPL)[17] which covers every corner of the civil justice with more detailed legal norms. If judges could not find clear rules in the statute, they could then rely on the judicial interpretations in order to make a civil judgment, even considering that these interpretations could sometimes develop the law by themselves. In the area of enforcement law, there are numerous judicial interpretations on various issues of enforcement proceedings. At the end of 2020, many judicial interpretations were revised or even partially deleted due to the Chinese Civil Code,[18] but substantial new

[14] Wang (2016), pp. 94–100.

[15] Fu and Meng (2016).

[16] Without further specification, the CPL is cited in its current version of 2021.

[17] Judicial Interpretation No. 11 [2022] of the SPC. In the scope of this contribution, neither this new document nor the Judicial Interpretation No. 21 [2020] of the SPC, which reflects the progress due to the birth of Civil Code in 2020, modified the related articles of the previous version of this judicial interpretation (Judicial Interpretation No. 5 [2015] of the SPC).

[18] In the area of civil procedure law and the related enforcement law, there are two separate compiled judicial interpretations updating the current ones, namely Decision of the SPC to Amend Eighteen Judicial Interpretations in Area of Enforcement Including the Provisions of the SPC on Several Issues Concerning People's Courts' Impoundment of Goods Transported by Railway, Judicial Interpretation No. 21 [2020] of the SPC; Decision of the SPC to Amend Nineteen Judicial Interpretations in Area of Civil Procedure Including the Provisions of the SPC about Several Issues Concerning the Civil Mediation Work of the People's Court, Judicial Interpretation No. 20 [2020] of the SPC.

rules are rarely visible. While we are looking forward to the proposed brand-new Civil Enforcement Law in 2023, which must be eligible for the solution of many problems, the difficulties in practice are still a very hot topic in China.

Next, it is necessary for this contribution to report the fundamental rules on litigation costs. The only nationwide rule in this field is the "Measures for the Payment of Litigation Costs"[19] (hereinafter Measures Costs), which were adopted by the State Council in December 2006 and came into force on April 1, 2007.[20] Unfortunately, no new revision of such rules has been proposed, while the practical need for a new instrument is very high. This situation could be attributed to the fact that Measures Costs is the product of the State Council which is supposed to initiate a new round of revision. However, the State Council is supposed to deal with almost everything in an administrative state, it may feel hard to find the time and resources to promote the overhaul of the existing regime of litigation costs. For the operation of a gigantic state like China, it is obvious that there is always something more crucial than the costs of judicial affairs. And the issue of litigation costs is also more urgent for other key players in the field, such as the judiciary and the practicing lawyers, than for the State Council. As a result, the Measures Costs is hoped to be modernized but we just do not know when and how. In such occasions, the current rules ought to be respected in this contribution.

When it comes to the role of litigation costs within civil procedure, the payment of litigation costs in advance could be constructed as one of the elements of case-filing examination under both the tradition of German-Japanese civil law system and Chinese law (Article 121 paragraph 1 of the CPL, Article 20 paragraph 1 sentence 1 and Article 22 paragraph 1 of the Measures Costs; corresponding to Article 12 paragraph 1 and Article 22 paragraph 1 of the German Court Costs Act [21]). Article 20 paragraph 1 of the Measures Costs states that the case-filing fee shall be prepaid by the plaintiff, the third party who incorporates an independent claim against both plaintiff and defendant of the current case, or the appellant of the case. Where the defendant files a counterclaim, and is required by the Measures Costs to pay the case-filing fee, the fee shall be prepaid by the defendant as well. But for the cases claiming labor remuneration, no case-filing fee needs to be prepaid. And Article 22 paragraph 1 and paragraph 2 of the Measures Costs stipulate that the plaintiff and the appellant of the disputed case shall pay the respective fees within 7 days as of the next day following receipt of the people's court's notice on payment of litigation costs or as of the day when the appellant submits its appeal. After all, since the payment of litigation costs is as introduced essential for the commencement of civil litigation in general, its calculation may affect the plaintiff's right of action and access to justice.

[19]Order of the State Council, No. 481.

[20]In fact, Measures Costs concerns both the civil and commercial cases and the administrative cases. But for the purpose of this contribution, only the rules for civil and commercial cases are to be discussed hereinafter. And previously, there were in this field two judicial interpretations published by the SPC in 1989 and 1999 which are now void.

[21]Rosenberg et al. (2018), §§ 83 Rn. 10, 96 Rn. 4, 129 Rn. 3.

2.2 Constitutions of Litigation Costs

As a general principle, Article 6 of the Measures Costs makes clear that the litigation costs paid by a party concerned to the people's court shall include: (1) case-filing fees; (2) application fees; and (3) the traffic expenses, accommodation expenses, living expenses, and subsidies for missed work, which are incurred by witnesses, expert identifiers, interpreters and adjustment makers for their appearing in the court's hearings as prescribed.[22] Based on comparative observations completed for the XVIIIth World Congress of Comparative Law organized by International Academy of Comparative Law in 2010, court fees in China are comparatively quite high.[23]

Concretely speaking, according to Article 7 of the Measures Costs, the case-filing fee covers the fees for the plaintiff or appellant of different instances of civil proceedings to initiate those proceedings. And normally, the parties do not need to pay for the trial supervision proceedings[24] which have been successfully accepted by the competent court. The supervision court has to, as a last resort, overrule a final judgment due to the serious errors in the judgment. The erroneous final judgment should not have been given at the first place and therefore, the costs for retrial proceedings to correct it could not be attributed to any private party.[25] As of the calculation of the case-filing fees within the appellate and trial supervision proceedings, Article 17 of the Measures Costs states that whoever appeals in a property

[22] Article 11 paragraph 1 of the Measures Costs says that these expenses shall be charged by the court on behalf of persons who have the aforementioned substantive claims at the statutory rates. Similarly, the party who makes photocopies of the archival materials and legal documents of the case shall pay the actual cost of production to the court (Article 11 paragraph 2).

[23] Reimann (2012), p. 24.

[24] Trial supervision proceedings are to some extent of Chinese characteristics. It has historical roots in the laws of the former Soviet Union. These proceedings are by their nature not a ordinary remedy for parties, like the first (e.g. *Berufung*) and second (e.g. *Revision*, *Cassation*) appeals of the competent courts, but indeed a special/extraordinary remedy. This special remedy ought to be limited to specific types of cases since the res judicata effect of the final judgment would be attacked accordingly. It is then necessary to first have the application for trial supervision reviewed by a special retrial examination procedure, before the case could go into the substantial retrial proceedings. Nevertheless, there are certainly cases which on whichever grounds shall be rectified, and there would be retrial proceedings of the same case accordingly. As a result, the same issue of paying litigation costs is to be introduced by this contribution.

[25] Yet, Article 9 of the Measures Costs mentions two exceptions for this special remedy and in such cases the parties have to pay the litigation costs. It happens when the retrial proceedings are commenced due to some new evidence, which is enough to reverse the original decision or when the party who has successfully commenced the retrial proceedings has previously not filed an ordinary appeal for the decision of the first instance. Following the understanding of trial supervision proceedings, the reason for having these two special rules is very simply. In such cases, the previous instance courts have done nothing wrong in their own proceedings. Rather, to be liable for the costs is the party who discovers some new evidence or even decides not to make use of the ordinary appellate proceedings. Therefore, the general principle should apply and the party, not the court, should pay the litigation costs.

case shall pay the case-filling fee at the amount in the appellate claim for relief on the part which he is dissatisfied with the judgment of the first instance. Similarly, Article 19 of the Measures Costs supplements that the case-filling fee of trial supervision proceedings, if necessary according to Article 9 of the Measures Costs, is also to be determined considering the dissatisfied amount of monetary interests against the operative part of the final judgment.

Moreover, as an exceptional rule, no case-filing fee needs to be paid for the non-contentious cases which are listed by the CPL itself such as declaring the legal incapacity or the death of a person, the first-instance or appellate cases which have been dismissed on procedural grounds and the appeals which are brought by the parties who dissatisfy with the appealable procedural decisions of the court (Article 8 of the Measures Costs). In other words, it means that the parties do not need to pay for the proceedings when there is no substantial adversary hearing and adjudication on the case.

The application fees embrace various situations when there is no judgment to be made. According to Article 10 of the Measures Costs, there are application fees e.g. for the commencement of enforcement proceedings with a valid enforcement title, for taking preservation measures such as seizure and injunctions, for bankruptcy cases, and for the acknowledgement and enforcement of any foreign judgments or foreign arbitral awards.

Excluded from the litigation fees are the expenses which should be directly paid to the competent persons. Article 12 paragraph 1 of the Measures Costs regulates explicitly that these expenses are the ones to be lawfully borne by the party during the litigation due to judicial identification, announcement, survey, interpretation, assessment, auction, selling-off, warehousing, custody, transport, ship supervision, etc. Based on the principle that the party who applies for the aforementioned service shall bear the expenses, the court shall allocate the relevant duty of payment. Then the responsible party shall directly pay the expenses to the relevant institution or entity. Accordingly, the court will order either party to bear such costs to when rendering the final judgment. As a result, if the applicant of these measures wins the case in the end, the opposing party ought to refund the expenses prepaid.

Respectively, these expenses differ from the traffic expenses of the litigation participants for their appearing in the court's hearings as Article 6 item 3 of the Measures Costs regulates in the general principle. Moreover, no fees are allowed when the translation or interpretation for the language commonly used by the local ethnicity is provided during the court's hearings. Since according to Article 11 paragraph 1 of the CPL statute, citizens of all ethnical groups in China shall have the right to use their native spoken and written languages in civil proceedings, this special rule written in Article 12 paragraph 2 of the Measures Costs is necessary. Only with this procedural safeguard, the access to justice could be secured for anyone all over the country. However, it means that the court should pay for these fees since the translation or interpretation is not *pro bono* service at all.

Moreover, special rules for reducing the litigation costs are provided to attract the parties to take desirable steps for a better administration of civil proceedings. There are three norms in the Measures Costs which target at reducing the ordinary rate to a half. Regulated are the situations where the proceedings are terminated by way of mediation or withdrawal of the lawsuit by the plaintiff (Article 15 of the Measures Costs), where a simplified procedure has been adopted (Article 16 of the Measures Costs)[26] and where either a defendant files a counterclaim or a third person brings an independent claim into the current litigation and the people's court decides to consolidate either claim into the current case (Article 18 of the Measures Costs). Meanwhile, Article 206 of the ICPL stipulates that where a people's court decides to reduce by half the case acceptance fee, the case-filling fee may be so reduced only once.

2.3 *Rates of Litigation Costs*

The Measures Costs provides specific rules for the calculation of litigation costs. According to its Article 13 paragraph 1, the case-filling fees shall be paid separately at the following rates.

2.3.1 Property Cases

To begin with, Article 13 paragraph 1 item 1 of the Measures Costs stipulates the rates for the so-called property cases. Their case-filling fees are decided by the amount of the subject matter which shall be calculated by adding up to the amounts within the following rate brackets. To sum up, different parts of the total amount of the subject matter ought to lead to different rates of litigation costs.[27] We could figure out the basic methods adopted by these rules in this way, whereas the accurate calculation itself is a little bit complicated. For many young practitioners, such calculation could be the first barrier in their way to be a real lawyer.

[26] In this respect, the evaluation of the magnitude of litigation costs could be accomplished according to the nature of cases regarding the amount of money at stake. Reimann (2012), pp. 33–35.

[27] To clarify the delicate rules for international audience, the details of the rules are listed as follows. 1. for the part of not more than 10,000 Yuan, 50 Yuan shall be paid for each case; 2. for the part of more than 10,000 Yuan up to 100,000 Yuan, the fee shall be paid at the rate of 2.5%; 3. for the part of more than 100,000 Yuan up to 200,000 Yuan, the fee shall be paid at the rate of 2%; 4. for the part of more than 200,000 Yuan up to 500,000 Yuan, the fee shall be paid at the rate of 1.5%; 5. for the part of more than 500,000 Yuan up to 1 million Yuan, the fee shall be paid at the rate of 1%; 6. for the part of more than 1 million Yuan up to 2 million Yuan, the fee shall be paid at the rate of 0.9%; 7. for the part of more than 2 million Yuan up to 5 million Yuan, the fee shall be paid at the rate of 0.8%; 8. for the part of more than 5 million Yuan up to 10 million Yuan, the fee shall be paid at the rate of 0.7%; 9. for the part of more than 10 million Yuan up to 20 million Yuan, the fee shall be paid at the rate of 0.6%; 10. for the part of more than 20 million Yuan, the fee shall be paid at the rate of 0.5%.

It is of practical importance together with academic interests to compare the costs of state courts with private dispute resolution mechanisms. It could be argued that the arbitration fees of China International Economic and Trade Arbitration Commission (hereinafter CIETAC),[28] one of the leading commercial arbitration institutions, could be cheaper than the court fees when it comes to commercial cases which refer to a great amount of money in dispute. Moreover, CIETAC and other online arbitral proceedings in China provide special fee charts that are slightly lower than the standard charges.[29]

2.3.2 Non-property Cases

Then, Article 13 paragraph 1 item 2 of the Measures Costs determinates the rates for the so-called non-property cases. Their respective case-filling fees shall be paid at the following rates. For each divorce case, first, 50 Yuan up to 300 Yuan shall be paid. If the partition of the couple's property is involved, and the total amount of properties does not exceed 200,000 Yuan, no additional fee shall be paid; for the part more than 200,000 Yuan, the fee shall be paid at the rate of 0.5%. Second, for each case on infringement of the right to name, the right to portrait, the right to reputation, the right to honor or other right to personality, 100 Yuan up to 500 Yuan shall be paid. If damages are claimed, and the compensation amount is not more than 50,000 Yuan, no additional fee shall be paid; for the part of more than 50,000 Yuan up to 100,000 Yuan, the fee shall be paid at the rate of 1%; for the part of more than 100,000 Yuan, the fee shall be paid at the rate of 0.5%. Third, for each other non-property case, 50 Yuan up to 100 Yuan shall be paid.

Based on these rules, the term of non-property cases is rather ambiguous. The rules themselves acknowledge that there could be some issue of property concerned even in such cases. We may presume that the legislator's intention is merely that the cases listed in Article 13 paragraph 1 item 2 of the Measures Costs are supposed to be treated differently than those in Article 13 paragraph 1 item 1 of the Measures Costs. Besides, it is previously disputed whether declaratory claims (*Feststellungsklage*) belong to the property cases or non-property ones. The declaratory judgments are able to declare the existence of legal effect, while they will not affect the legal relationship directly (in the sense of *Gestaltungsklage*) or demand the debtors performing their duties (in the sense of *Leistungsklage*). Indeed, besides the confirmation of the entitlement of a claimant, the payment from the debtor to the creditor is also included in the judgment for performance. However, it is not hard to understand even without such demand for payment, the declaration itself refers still

[28] E.g. CIETAC, Schedule of Fees, http://www.cietac.org/index.php?m=Page&a=index&id=191&l=en.

[29] E.g. CIETAC, Fee Schedule, http://www.cietac.org/index.php?m=Article&a=show&id=2773&l=en.

to the so-called property cases as well. Whether there is a demand for payment should make no difference in determining the nature of these cases regarding litigation costs.

2.3.3 Other Cases

Article 13 paragraph 1 item 3-5 of the Measures Costs covers other types of cases as well. For instance, for civil cases on intellectual property right, if there is no disputed amount, 500 Yuan up to 1000 Yuan shall be paid; if there is any disputed amount or price, the fee shall be paid at the rate for property cases. For labor dispute cases, 10 Yuan shall be paid. There are also rules for administrative cases and for cases where the objection to the jurisdiction of the court over the case has been rejected. Due to the subject of this contribution, the rules for the latter two types of cases will not be introduced.

Moreover, according to Article 13 paragraph 2 of the Measures Costs, it is to be noticed that the people's government of each province may, in light of the local actual situation, formulate specific rates within the range prescribed in Article 13 paragraph 1 of the Measures Costs. Mentioned in this rule are the non-property cases, intellectual property right cases and the cases relating to failed jurisdictional objections.

2.4 *Cost-Shifting Rules*

Cost-shifting refers to the internal transfer of the costs from the winner to loser in individual civil proceedings. Although the difference between the so-called American cost-shifting rule and the English one is deemed as one of the remarkable issues in the field of litigation costs, "such a dichotomy is hopelessly simplistic as well as virtually useless".[30] It is said that in England, considering the varied practice in different tracks, a victorious party should recover its costs from the opponent in principle, in order to deter spurious claims and defences and to indemnify the winning party in litigation results. A further distinction between standard and indemnity cost could be made regarding the determining the scope of cost-shifting, while such cost-shifting could also be one-way and therefore in favor of the plaintiff in certain types of cases.[31] In contrast, the American rule prefers generally to the presumption that each party bears its own attorney's fees whereas the taxable costs

[30] Reimann (2012), p. 9.

[31] Zuckerman (2021), Ch. 28; Andrews (2019), Ch. 18.

other than attorney's fees are recoverable. In this way, American intends not to "make plaintiffs too timid to attempt to vindicate their rights".[32]

In China, normally it is merely possible to recover the litigation costs incurred in courts from the losing party. The attorney fees are not eligible for shifting according to the final results of the case. We may conclude that the American rule also exists in China. On the other hand, there could be special arrangement for cost-shifting under certain substantive legal rules. For instance, in public interest litigations, the costs of plaintiff's inspection, appraisal charges, reasonable legal fees and other reasonable expenses should be compensated by the losing defendant.[33] In cases regarding intellectual property rights, the attorney fees are understood as "reasonable expenses paid by the right-holder for preventing the torts" (e.g. Article 54 paragraph 3 of the Copyright Law) which are therefore a part of the substantive legal compensation.

3 Rules for Enforcement Costs Taken by State Courts

3.1 General Allocation of Enforcement Costs

Partially speaking for a Chinese exceptionalism[34], the enforcement organ is fundamentally liable for enforcement costs at the very beginning of enforcement proceedings in China. In contrast to the aforementioned case-filing fees which ought to be prepaid by the plaintiff in general, the application fee for enforcement proceedings is stipulated differently. The general rule is provided by Article 20 paragraph 2 of the Measures Costs, which says that the application fee shall be prepaid by the applicant just like the case-filing fees. And Article 22 paragraph 3 of the Measures Costs states further that the application fee shall be prepaid by the applicant when the applicant files the application or within the time limit specified by the people's court. However, the specific application fees of enforcement proceedings and bankruptcy cases shall not be prepaid by the applicant. Rather, as exceptional rules, the enforcement application fee shall be paid after the enforcement, and the bankruptcy application fee shall be paid after the liquidation.

In other words, there is in the field of enforcement law a "court pays" principle. The ordinary operation of enforcement proceedings, namely the commencement and termination of the proceedings as well as the discovery, taking control and selling off of the enforceable assets,[35] is promoted and financially supported by the courts. The same applies for taking direct measures to locate the assets of the debtor such as using the online enforcement inquiry and control system or issuing search orders, for

[32] Freer (2017), pp. 8–11.

[33] Fu (2021), pp. 389–390.

[34] Comparing the notorious "American exceptionalism", Chase (2005), pp. 47–71; Marcus (2005).

[35] For the whole process of the Chinese enforcement proceedings, Cao (2021a), pp. 30–38.

taking indirect measures to force the debtor to submit assets such as making the debtor to perform its duty to report the assets, summon the debtor or other relevant persons, and for taking indirect measures to deter the debtor from hiding any assets which among others rely on the well-established credit management network or the restriction of the unnecessary expense of the debtors.[36]

It may look different for observers from other jurisdictions. This situation could be attributed to the arrangement of the Chinese enforcement organ and the jurisdictional rules. It is noted that in China, only people's courts, which also make the final judgment in the first place, have the functional jurisdiction over the enforcement issues regarding civil and commercial matters. Considering that there are enforcement models which consist of fragmented or diffused enforcement organs,[37] Chinese legal system has chosen for the model of a single competent enforcement organ.[38] For other cases whose enforcement titles are not final judgments, it is still the relevant court that has jurisdiction. And since the state is the one behind all courts in China, "court pays" principle could also be understood as "state pays" principle. This principle focuses more on the relationship between the state and the ordinary citizen who could participate in individual enforcement cases as enforcement creditors and debtors.

3.2 *Constitutions of Enforcement Costs*

Similar to Article 6 of the Measures Costs for case-filling fees, Article 10 of the Measures Costs refers to the payment of application fees. The applicable types of cases are listed as followed: (1) Applying for the enforcement of a legally effective judgment, ruling or a mediation-based consent judgment made by the people's court, an arbitral award or mediation-based consent arbitral award made by the arbitration institution, or an authentic instrument confirming the existence of debt with enforcement force provided by the public notarial institution; (2) Applying for taking preservation measures (in the sense of interim measures) which consist of seizure, impoundment and freezing; (3) Applying for a non-contentious order for payment which is the result of a summary procedure for debt collection and substantially follows the German model of German counterpart of *Mahnbescheid*; (4) Applying for issuing a public summon which aims to publicize a public notice for urging and asserting claims in case that a commercial check was stolen; (5) Applying for revoking an arbitral award or for confirming the effectiveness of an arbitration agreement; (6) Applying for bankruptcy; (7) Applying for maritime injunctions, the general average adjustment, the establishment of a limitation fund for maritime

[36] Cao (2022a).

[37] The situation in Germany, Brox and Walker (2018), Rn. 11–16; Baur et al. (2006), Rn. 6.47–6.52.

[38] Cao (2021c), pp. 107–109.

claims, the maritime credit registration, or the summon of priority claims to the ship; and (8) Applying for acknowledging and enforcing the judgment or ruling of a foreign court or the award of a foreign arbitration institution.

Coming back to the topic of this contribution, it is noted that enforcement costs are *per se* a part of the application fees under Chinese law. The other types of costs, as the rest of the application fees, could also be classified as litigation costs in a broader sense. These two approaches to interpreting litigation costs, either in a narrower (merely Article 6-9 of the Measures Costs for case-filling fees) or broader sense (Article 6-9 plus Article 10 item 2-8 of the Measures Costs), are more or less a problem of definition which could be left alone. While having the general picture of application fees in mind, this contribution will focus on the enforcement costs themselves and the procedural treatment of them.

As the aforementioned litigation expenses which are incurred outside the court and should be directly paid to the relevant persons, such as the fees for judicial identification and assessment, similar costs incurred during enforcement proceedings follow the same rule. It means that the enforcement creditor ought to pay the costs to the relevant entities in advance and then be refunded when enforcement proceedings are partially or entirely of success. The assessment plays an even more crucial role in enforcement proceedings compared to during court hearings, since before the auction of seized assets of the debtor, the value of these assets mostly needs to be evaluated properly. The assessment costs could be classified as the litigation costs in a broader sense and the enforcement court has its duty to facilitate the related activities. For instance, Article 487 of the ICPL states that where on-site inspection and survey are required for auction assessment, the people's court shall order the enforcement debtor and the person obliged to assist to cooperate. If these persons refuse to cooperate, the people's court may conduct compulsory enforcement.

In 2018, the SPC even released a specialized judicial interpretation called Provisions of the SPC on Several Issues concerning the Determination of the Reference Prices for Disposition of Property by the People's Courts.[39] Its Article 2 states that to determine the reference price for disposition of property, a people's court may adopt methods such as bargaining by parties, targeted inquiry to specific qualified institutions, online inquiry to a group of potential qualified institutions, and designated assessment, and so forth. As of the designated assessment, its Article 15 paragraph 1 says that the SPC shall establish a list of judicial assessment institutions according to the professional field of assessment and the practicing scope of the assessment institutions. And Article 16 regulates the relevant procedure of selection. It states that the people's court shall notify the two parties of selecting three assessment institutions and the order of them, which are to be decided either by stipulation between the parties or a random lottery. Lastly, its Article 33 paragraph 1 repeats the general principle that the online inquiry fees and the entrusted assessment fees shall

[39] Judicial Interpretation No. 15 [2018] of the SPC.

be prepaid by the enforcement applicant in advance and be assumed by the person subject to enforcement later.[40]

3.3 *Rates of Enforcement Costs*

3.3.1 General Rules for Ordinary Cases

Besides case-filling fees in accordance with the aforementioned Article 13 of the Measures Costs, Chinese law also regulates application fees with Article 14 of the Measures Costs which stipulates rates for various proceedings. As a result, a difference between case-filing fees and application fees has been drawn.

It comes to the enforcement costs in Article 14 item 1 (1)(2) of the Measures Costs at first. When lawfully applying to the people's court for the enforcement of enforcement titles such as a final judgment, a final arbitral award or a consent judgment of the court or of an arbitration institution, the party concerned shall pay the fee at the following rates. If there is no enforceable amount, 50 Yuan up to 500 Yuan shall be paid for each case. If the enforceable amount is not more than 10,000 Yuan, 50 Yuan shall be paid for each case; for the part of more than 10,000 Yuan up to 500,000 Yuan, the fee shall be paid at the rate of 1.5%; for the part of more than 500,000 Yuan up to 5 million Yuan, the fee shall be paid at the rate of 1%; for the part of more than 5 million Yuan up to 10 million Yuan, the fee shall be paid at the rate of 0.5%; for the part of more than 10 million Yuan, the fee shall be paid at the rate of 0.1%.

3.3.2 Special Rules for Representative Actions

There is a special rule for the cases of representative actions, namely the Chinese solution for the issue of class action. Article 57 of the current CPL establishes a specialized procedure for the situation where the subject matters of claims are of the same category and the parties on one side of the claims are numerous. This procedure is to be applied normally when multiple plaintiffs bring lawsuits against the same defendant demanding for damages due to a mass tort incident. It refers to the so-called representative litigation which is by its nature an opt-in procedure.[41] According to Article 57 paragraph 1 of the CPL, the people's court may issue a public notice, stating the particulars and claims of the case and informing the right-

[40] And Article 33 paragraph 2 of the same judicial interpretation adds that where an enforcement applicant prepays the online inquiry fees or entrusted assessment fees in advance by signing an insurance contract, the insurer shall issue a letter of guarantee to the people's court. The letter of guarantee shall specify that the insurer paid the relevant fees since the enforcement creditor has not prepaid the fees and other information, and attach the relevant evidence.

[41] For the details of such procedure, Fu (2021), pp. 372–378.

holders to participate in the case to register their rights with the people's court within a fixed period of time. Moreover, Article 57 paragraph 4 of the CPL states that in such cases, the judgments rendered by the people's court shall be valid for all those who have registered their rights with the court. Such judgments shall apply to those who have not registered their rights but have initiated legal proceedings during period of limitation of the statute.

To facilitate such proceedings, Article 14, item 1 (3) of the Measures Costs makes it clear that if a prospective plaintiff who conforms to such representative action procedure but has not been registered brings a lawsuit with the people's court, such plaintiff shall pay the application fee at the aforementioned rate rather than the case-filling fee. This special rule of costs could be constructed as some preferential treatment for the prospective plaintiffs of a representative action.

3.3.3 Similar Rules for Other Application Fees

Apart from rates for enforcement costs, other types of costs have been considered by Article 14 item 2-7 of the Measures Costs as well. These rules refer to the aforementioned applicable cases of application fees. For instance, Article 14 item 2 of the Measures Costs refers to the costs for preservation measures, the party concerned shall pay the fee at the following rates in view of the value of the actually preserved property. If the property amount is not more than 1,000 Yuan or does not involve any property amount, 30 Yuan shall be paid for each case; for the part of more than 1,000 Yuan up to 100,000 Yuan, the fee shall be paid at the rate of 1%; for the part of more than 100,000 Yuan, the fee shall be paid at the rate of 0.5%. However, the expenses paid by the party concerned in applying for the preservation measure shall not exceed 5,000 Yuan. Additionally, other applicable cases are also covered by these rules, most of which have fixed rates.

3.4 Cost-Shifting Rules

Unlike the situation regarding litigation costs, since the enforcement creditor does not need to prepay the costs of courts, there is no issue of cost-shifting for these costs. When it comes to the attorney fees, in practice, there is rare case where the application for cost-shifting will be granted. It means that if the enforcement creditor hires its lawyer or even private detectives to dig out the assets of its debtor, the court will not make use of the enforced assets to compensate the expenses of the enforcement creditor. And whether in the end, the enforcement creditor needs to pay the attorney the contingency fees, if any, depends on the final results of the individual enforcement. In contrast, we may remember that as mentioned, the costs for assessment may be recovered in a successful enforcement case.

4 Re-allocation of Enforcement Costs in Recent Years

4.1 Logic of Costs Allocation and Recent Trend

4.1.1 Relationship Between Costs Allocation and Efforts of Enforcement Courts

Since we are mainly discussing the allocation of procedural costs between the state court and private parties, which may be changed due to the changes of other crucial factors, we may also turn to the similar situation regarding litigation costs. It has been observed that there could be a dramatic change when Chinese civil procedure moved from the supra-inquisitorial model towards the party-dominating model back in 1990s. From then on, Chinese judges were no more expected to devote themselves to the fact-finding of individual cases via investigating the alleged facts of parties aggressively. Rather, they intended to let the parties to shoulder the risks of losing the case according to rules on burden of proof. In other words, judges were taking relatively passive role in managing the proceedings before them. Since the efforts of judges could be understood as one of the major reasons for calculating litigation costs from the side of the judiciary,[42] there was a movement from the public costs to the private costs within the total of litigation costs. It will be then the parties who should invest more in their attorneys to win the case finally.[43]

Similar observation appears in the field of enforcement law. When it comes to the enforcement of e.g. a final judgment, it means that the judgment debtor does not voluntarily perform its duty. Then, on behalf of the judgment creditor, the statutory enforcement organ should instead force the debtor to do so (indirect measures) or even makes the operative part of the final judgment fulfilled via its own efforts (direct measures). These efforts will give rise to additional costs. Respectively, as mentioned previously, the creditor does not have to pay the enforcement costs in advance according to the "state pays" principle. It could be understood as the logical result of the court's duty to realize its final judgment and then accordingly the confirmed substantive rights of the creditor. In general, the Chinese court plays an all-inclusive role in discovering debtor's assets.[44]

As an illustration, in 2017, the SPC released a judicial interpretation called Provisions of the SPC on Issues concerning Property Investigation during Enforcement in Civil Procedures (hereinafter Provisions Investigation 2017)[45]. Among others, Article 1 of the Provisions Investigation 2017 confirms explicitly that the creditor shall provide clues to the property of the judgment debtor; the judgment

[42] Reimann (2012), p. 24.

[43] Fu (2001), pp. 264–268.

[44] Cao (2022a).

[45] Judicial Interpretation No. 8 [2017] of the SPC. In the scope of this contribution, the related articles of this judicial interpretation were not modified by the new Judicial Interpretation No. 21 [2021] of the SPC.

debtor shall truthfully report its property; and the enforcement court shall investigate through the online enforcement inquiry and control system and adopt other investigative methods if necessary. And complying with Article 249 paragraph 1 sentence 1 of the CPL together with Article 483 of the ICPL, the enforcement court is supposed to discover the personal identity and property of the judgment debtor through the online enforcement inquiry and control system[46] and by means such as on-site investigation.

In such cases, one of the political plans in China, which is against the difficulty in enforcement proceedings, is to be taken into account. It shows that China does take enforcement proceedings very seriously, so spending more money on it is for the state unproblematic. Generally speaking, it is said that the enforcement of a final judgment in China was of great difficulty for a long period of time.[47] In this respect, this practical hardship is to be attributed not only to the tricky enforcement debtors themselves,[48] but also due to the local protectionism of the local governments.[49] Recently, the related situation is better off.[50] Especially since 2014, among various judicial reforms,[51] the governing Communist Party of China (CPC) intends to improve its enforcement mechanism in its political agenda[52] and under this framework, the SPC has resolved a great amount of long-lasting problems. In March 2019, the SPC declared that its three-year campaign against the difficulty in enforcement was basically successful (as solved)[53] and "a long-term effective system that solves the difficult problems of enforcement" needed to be further developed.[54]

4.1.2 Doubt on the "Court Pays" Principle and New Development

The current rules also mean that if enforcement proceedings are not successful, the responsible enforcement organ should take the financial loss. In such cases, the enforcement organ, which is in pursuit of the fulfilment of enforcement titles, shares mutual interests with the enforcement creditor who also intends to achieve the results of liquidation. And the enforcement organ in China, as a public organ, still has to prove its own value in realizing the substantive rights determined in e.g. final judgments. As a result, courts are supposed to improve the percentage of fulfilled

[46] Other perspectives regarding e-justice, Cao (2021b); Cao (2022b).

[47] On the situation more than 25 years ago, Clarke (1996).

[48] Generally Kennett (2003), p. 106.

[49] Wang (2008), pp. 657–659; Peerenboom (2001), pp. 276–279.

[50] Peerenboom and He (2009), pp. 14–15; He (2009).

[51] Generally Fu and Cao (2012).

[52] The key document is the Decision of the Central Committee of the Communist Party of China (CCCPC) on Several Major Issues Concerning the Comprehensive Promotion of the Rule of Law which was adopted in the fourth plenary session of the 18th CCCPC.

[53] Zhou (2019).

[54] SPC of PRC (2019), p. 35. In detail, Cao (2021a), pp. 27–30.

debt in the entire to-be-enforced amount of debt.[55] Yet, some may argue that it is the taxpayer as a whole which is paying the costs under the current system. Therefore, the current rule ought to be overturned.[56] In other words, enforcement proceedings are in fact for the interests of the enforcement creditor in a specific case rather than the general tax-payers. Accordingly, the individual persons who win their cases in the state civil proceedings are taking advantage of enforcement proceedings.

In recent years, the situation has changed partially. The campaign of Chinese authority against the difficulty during enforcement is still ongoing. However, in many occasions, it is the enforcement creditor who needs now to pay some necessary items during enforcement proceedings in advance. These items are not constructed as some default steps to be taken by the enforcement court *sua sponte*. Rather, the enforcement creditor has its choice while without payment these measures will not be taken. Such possibility of taking these additional measures does not affect the judicial duty to discover the debtor's assets, whereas it does make a difference regarding the practical chance of finding those assets in the end. Since all Chinese courts have limited resources but always increasing caseload of all kinds, the individual enforcement court could merely be too busy to push some enforcement cases forward. Naturally, the creditor will then consider what it could contribute for the sake of its own interests in enforcing the substantive judgment. We may argue that the enforcement creditor is now not merely applicant for assistance from the state, but rather a wingman who is to facilitate enforcement proceedings as well. In this respect, some examples of the enforcement service which are to be paid now by the creditor are advantageous for our observations in this contribution.

4.2 Public Enforcement Service Paid by the Creditor

4.2.1 Entrusting an Audit to Audit the Judgment Debtor

Besides the assessment during enforcement proceedings which are to be paid by the parties rather than the court, the enforcement creditor ought to pay the fee for entrusting an audit to audit the financial situation of the enforcement debtor in advance and then the enforcement creditor could be refunded later. In this respect, Article 17 Provisions Investigation 2017 states that the creditor may file a written application for entrusting an audit institution to audit the judgment debtor. After the receipt of the filing, the court has ten days to make its decision. Then it is up to the enforcement court to determine whether to permit the application under following preconditions: 1) the judgment debtor should be a legal person or an unincorporated

[55] Cao (2021c), pp. 121–122.

[56] The critical viewpoint taking this arrangement as "free lunch", Lei (2016).

organization[57]; 2) the debtor fails to fulfil the finally decided obligations; 3) the behavior of the debtor meets one of the following patterns: either refusing to report or falsely reporting its property, concealing, transferring its property or otherwise evading its debts, or that any of its shareholders or investors have stated false capital contribution to the legal entity or have fraudulently withdrawn the capital contributed from the legal entity.

Upon approval of the court, a randomly selected audit institution will begin to examine the necessary materials which shall be submitted by the debtor voluntarily. Otherwise, these materials will be collected by the court during its mandatory search measures (Article 18 Provisions Investigation 2017). The applying creditor should bear the costs of auditing in advance, while the final allocation of costs depends on whether the circumstances of refusing to report or falsely reporting and evading the debts have been proved (Article 20 Provisions Investigation 2017). In other words, the cost-shift in favor of the enforcement creditor is merely available when the suggested audit is proven as reasonable.

4.2.2 Advertising the Enforcement Creditor's Offer of Reward

At the same time, the enforcement creditor has the option to apply the court for advertising its offer of reward for locating any enforceable property. Article 21 of the Provisions Investigation 2017 provides the necessary items of this offer, namely the amount or the calculation basis of the reward, the commitment to willingly paying the reward when the obligations are satisfied wholly or partially because of any unknown property clues, and the methods of advertising offers of reward. Within ten days of receipt of the application, the court shall make its decision. This offer should be broadcasted publicly (Article 22 of the Provisions Investigation 2017). When someone appears with clues, the court shall register the identity of the relevant person and the clues (Article 23 of the Provisions Investigation 2017). After confirming that the clues could contribute to the fulfilment of the enforcement debt, the court shall deliver the reward. The reward shall be deducted from enforcement receivable acquired due to the clues, or alternatively, be paid separately by the creditor (Article 24 of the Provisions Investigation 2017). In practice, some relevant insurance products are provided as well. Normally, it means the enforcement creditor has merely to pay 10% of the prospective reward.

[57]Only the term of unincorporated organization, instead of "other organizations" in the original version, is revised by the Judicial Interpretation No. 21 [2020] of the SPC. In the scope of this contribution, the other related articles of the Provisions Investigation 2017 were not modified.

4.3 *Privatized Enforcement Systems Adopted by the Creditor*

4.3.1 Private Solutions for the Enforcement Funding

To avoid 'run into dead-ends'[58] during enforcement proceedings, the enforcement creditor may hire its representing lawyers who will have to work as a sort of private detectives using all available public and private data platforms to collect financial information of the enforcement debtor. Various registration systems supported by governmental branches are accessible, and customized information service is provided by private companies.[59] Even American-style 'private firms offering post-judgment collection services'[60] are possible as well. All the related costs should be taken by the creditor itself and there is no possibility of cost-shifting.

Alternatively, the enforcement creditor may stipulate with its lawyers to have contingency fee agreement which could be in the name of a special bonus according to percentage of the fulfilled obligation in the total substantive rights recorded in the operative part of the enforcement title. In such occasions, the representing lawyers, which are of course not necessarily to be the ones representing the case during court hearings, will ordinarily request a relatively small amount of money to be the preliminary honorarium to cover the necessary costs incurred during the property investigation and assessment. It is noticeable that the globally intensely discussed third-party funding is not yet popular.

On the other hand, when the creditor has tried its best to contribute to the success of enforcement proceedings, the creditor may begin to doubt whether the enforcement officers within the enforcement court are doing their job properly. If the property discovery is for instance unfortunately unsuccessful, Chinese courts are to explain what it is and why it is so. From the perspective of ordinary citizens, there could be some strong challenge to the authority of the judicial branch. According to the *prima facie* evidence that Chinese judges tend to misuse their power, the enforcement officer has to prove its innocence.

4.3.2 More Private Efforts Within Temporarily Terminated Proceedings

Besides, the primary responsibility of the enforcement court may have been changed, if the court decides to terminate the current enforcement proceedings temporarily, in which no property is to be enforced. In such occasions, in accordance with Article 517 paragraph 1 of the ICPL, the court will declare a failure of enforcement, but will not terminate the proceedings wholly. It means that the enforcement costs will be dramatically shifted to the side of enforcement creditor.

[58] Peerenboom (2001), p. 292.
[59] Cao (2021c), pp. 112–113.
[60] Pajic (2010), p. 245.

This is a special treatment of the enforcement case which has its roots in Chinese practice rather than any lessons following the comparative experience.

Concretely speaking, after the enforcement court has tried its best to search for debtor's assets, it is then to a great extent released from its statutory duty to find out the assets. But there are still some measures for courts to take to a limited extent. In such case, Article 9 paragraph 2 of the Provisions on Strictly Regulating the Termination of the Enforcement Procedure (for Trial Implementation) (hereinafter Provisions Termination 2016)[61] adds a periodic duty of investigation by the enforcement court. It says that within five years after the termination of the current enforcement proceedings (meaning temporary termination), the enforcement court shall investigate the property of the judgment debtor through its internet-based system for assets inquiry and control every six months. Inquiry results shall be informed to the enforcement creditor. And Article 10 of the Provisions Termination 2016 emphasizes that on the motion of creditor or *ex officio*, the enforcement court may take control of the debtor's assets immediately, where the debtor has any enforceable property after the termination of the current enforcement proceedings. The court may do so if without instantly taking enforcement measures the property may be transferred, hidden, sold or destroyed.

In this way, the all-inclusive duty to discover the debtor's assets of Chinese enforcement courts could be transformed to a limited to-do-list of the enforcement officers. Then Chinese law is respectively of a mixed nature, namely firstly with an all-inclusive role then with relatively narrow duties when the entire enforcement is not successful. It is also argued that, based on comparative experiences in Europe, China should employ a separation model in relation to the civil enforcement power. According to one possible design, the declaration of failure of enforcement should be treated as the signal of this separation. After the termination of the current enforcement procedure, we should rely on the force of market and private sectors to continue discovering the debtor's assets.[62] Conversely, the other viewpoint may emphasize the temporary nature of this termination mechanism and insist on the importance to have a well-developed bankruptcy system.[63]

5 Conclusion

Good judicial service must be paid by someone, and who is to pay for it is a question which may have socio-economic meanings. The constitution, rate and amount of prepaid litigation costs and whether such costs are able to be shifted back afterwards to the winning party are key costs issues in civil proceedings which may have a great

[61] Administrative Document (法) No. 373 [2016] of the SPC.

[62] Chen (2018). On the recent privatization of the enforcement in China organ, Cao (2021c), pp. 111–116. Moreover on American self-help methods, Marcus (2022), pp. 66–68.

[63] Gao (2020).

influence on the access to justice. Compared to this, it seems that such issue does not arise when under Chinese law the enforcement creditor does not need to pay the relevant cost in advance. This feeling could be amplified when we consider the fact that the Chinese court play an all-inclusive role in discovering debtor's assets and solving the difficulty in enforcing substantive rights which have been confirmed with *res judicata* effect. However, if in practice, the enforcement creditor has to pay for additional expenses for some service which should have been provided by the enforcement *sua sponte* in the first place, the mitigation of the aforementioned all-inclusive role of Chinese courts may be acknowledged.

Such fundamental change in the judicial attitude toward the role of the court may have solid practical grounds. Considering the rapid increasing caseload of the courts at all levels and more crucially, the potential conflict between interests of general tax-payers who are paying the court's service and the interests of individual enforcement creditors who are making use of the court's service, a more privatized enforcement system could indicate the future of Chinese enforcement legal regime. Especially when the enforcement court has to terminate the current enforcement proceedings temporarily because no enforceable property of the debtor is found, it is understandable to transform a great deal of enforcement assignments to the side of enforcement creditors. The remaining issue is that under which test the enforcement proceedings could be temporarily terminated. In any event, this system should not be used as a short-cut to enable the enforcement court to evade the statutory duty to discover the debtor's assets positively and enforce the confirmed substantive rights on its own initiative.

References

Andrews N (2019) Andrews on civil processes. Court proceedings, arbitration & mediation. Intersentia, Cambridge

Baur F, Stürner R, Bruns A (2006) Zwangsvollstreckungsrecht. C.F. Müller, Heidelberg

Brox H, Walker W (2018) Zwangsvollstreckungsrecht. C.H. Beck, München

Cao Z (2021a) Civil enforcement rules and mechanism in China: the past, present and the future. Peking Univ Law J 9(1):23–44. https://doi.org/10.1080/20517483.2021.1978677

Cao Z (2021b) Evolution of online courts in China: situation and challenges. Int J Procedural Law 11(2):300–316

Cao Z (2021c) On the civil enforcement organ in China. China Leg Sci 4:106–129

Cao Z (2022a) Discovery of debtor's assets in the enforcement of monetary judgement in China. Ritsumeikan Law Rev 40:69–87

Cao Z (2022b) Online dispute resolution mechanism in China: principle of proceedings and impact of technologies. China WTO Rev 8(1):29–62

Chase OG (2005) Law, culture, and ritual: disputing systems in cross-cultural context. NYU Press, New York

Chen H (2018) Civil enforcement models in comparative perspective: focus on solving the problem of "civil enforcement difficulty" [Bi jiao fa shi ye xia de zhi xing quan pei zhi mo shi yan jiu——yi jiejue "zhi xing nan" wen ti wei Zhong xin]. Jurist 2:73–87. (in Chinese)

Clarke DC (1996) Power and politics in the Chinese court system: the enforcement of civil judgments. Colum J Asian Law 10:1–92

Deguchi M (ed) (2022) Effective enforcement of creditors' rights. Springer, Singapore
Freer RD (2017) Civil procedure. Wolters Kluwer, New York
Fu Y (2001) The nature of litigation fees and the allocation of litigation costs. Peking Univ Law Rev 4(1):239–274. (in Chinese)
Fu Y (2021) Class actions and public interest litigation in China. In: Uzelac A, Voet S (eds) Class actions in Europe. Springer, Cham, pp 369–400
Fu Y, Cao Z (2012) The position of judges in civil litigation in transitional China: judicial mediation and case management. In: Chen L, van Rhee CH (eds) Towards a Chinese civil code: comparative and historical perspectives. Martinus Nijhoff, Leiden, pp 495–519
Fu Y, Meng X (2016) Civil justice in China. BRICS Law J 3(4):94–124
Gao X (2020) Current situation and potential picture of the exit mechanism for cases undergoing "failure of enforcement" ["Zhi xing bu neng" an jian tui chu ji zhi de dang xia jing yu wei lai tu jing]. Academia Bimestrie 3:137–142. (in Chinese)
He X (2009) Enforcing commercial judgments in the pearl river delta of China. Am J Comp Law 57:419–456
Hess B (2010) Different enforcement structures. In: van Rhee CH, Uzelac A (eds) Enforcement and enforceability – tradition and reform. Intersentia, Antwerp, pp 41–61
Kennett W (2003) Enforcement: general report. In: Storme M (ed) Procedural laws in Europe: towards harmonisation. Maklu, Antwerpen, pp 81–111
Kennett W (2021) Civil enforcement in a comparative perspective. A public management challenge. Intersentia, Cambridge
Lei Y (2016) Fundamental role of civil enforcement [min shi qiang zhi xing zhi ji ben ding wei]. People's Court Daily, 7 September 2016, Beijing, p 8 (in Chinese)
Levy I (2017) Taking enforcement seriously. CJQ 36:127–132
Marcus RL (2005) Putting American procedural exceptionalism into a globalized context. Am J Comp Law 53:709–740
Marcus RL (2022) America's BYO approach to enforcing money judgments. In: Deguchi M (ed) Effective enforcement of creditors' rights. Springer, Singapore
Pajic N (2010) Avenues for enforcement and execution of judgments in the United States. In: van Rhee CH, Uzelac A (eds) Enforcement and enforceability – tradition and reform. Intersentia, Antwerp, pp 237–250
Peerenboom R (2001) Seek truth from facts: an empirical study of enforcement of arbitral awards in the PRC. Am J Comp Law 49:249–328
Peerenboom R, He X (2009) Dispute resolution in China: patterns, causes and prognosis. East Asia Law Rev 4:1–62
Reimann M (2012) Cost and fee allocation in civil procedure: a synthesis. In: Reimann M (ed) Cost and fee allocation in civil procedure: a comparative study. Springer, Heidelberg, pp 3–56
Rosenberg L, Schwab KH, Gottwald P (2018) Zivilprozessrecht. C.H. Beck, München
SPC of PRC (ed) (2019) Guidelines of the supreme people's court on deepen the judicial system reform with comprehensive integrated reforms of people's courts—framework of the fifth five-year judicial reform for people's courts (2019–2023). People's Court Press, Beijing
Stürner R (2016) Preliminary feasibility study on possible additional work on the development of principles of transnational civil procedure relating to effective enforcement (Governing Council 95th Session, Rome, 18–20 May 2016). UNIDROIT. www.unidroit.org/english/governments/councildocuments/2016session/cd-95-13add-02-e.pdf, pp 6–7. Accessed 24 Mar 2023
UNIDROIT (2021) Enforcement: best practices. UNIDROIT. https://www.unidroit.org/work-in-progress/enforcement-best-practices. Accessed 24 Mar 2023
Van Rhee CH, Uzelac A (2010) Enforcement and enforceability – an introduction. In: van Rhee CH, Uzelac A (eds) Enforcement and enforceability – tradition and reform. Intersentia, Antwerp, p xxi
Wang DT (2008) Judicial reform in China: improving arbitration award enforcement by establishing a federal court system. Santa Clara Law Rev 48:649–679
Wang F (2016) On cost-sharing in civil justice. Soc Sci China 2:93–113. (in Chinese)

Woo M (2018) Comparative law in a time of nativism. Hastings Int Comp Law Rev 41:1–30
Zhang B (2021) Third party funding for dispute resolution: a comparative study of England, Hong Kong, Singapore, the Netherlands, and mainland China. Springer, Singapore
Zhou Q (2019) Annual working report of the SPC [Zui gao ren min fa yuan gong zuo bao gao]. chinacourt.org. https://www.chinacourt.org/article/detail/2019/03/id/3791943.shtml. Accessed 24 Mar 2023 (in Chinese)
Zuckerman A (2021) Zuckerman on civil procedure: principles of practice. Sweet & Maxwell, London

Funding of Claims in Investor-State Dispute Settlements: Could Third-Party Funding Enhance Access to Justice?

Manfredi Marciante

Contents

Abstract This chapter addresses the issue of funding of claims in investor-state dispute settlement (ISDS), aiming to investigate whether the mechanism of "third-party funding" (TPF) could facilitate access to justice for a potential claimant. After a preliminary assessment on the role of the individual in the context of international investment law, the chapter will focus on the possible identification and recognition of the right of access to justice in investment arbitration, notably through the indirect analysis of denial of justice and the relevance of bilateral investment treaty provisions. Once the main aspects of access to justice in ISDS have been addressed, the problematic nature of high costs in investment arbitration procedures will be discussed, which sometimes represents a real obstacle to access to justice, especially for small and medium-sized enterprises (SMEs). Against this background, the

M. Marciante (✉)
LUISS Guido Carli University, Rome, Italy
e-mail: mmarciante@luiss.it

E. Storskrubb (ed.), *YSEC Yearbook of Socio-Economic Constitutions 2022*,
YSEC Yearbook of Socio-Economic Constitutions (2023) 2022: 291–320,
https://doi.org/10.1007/16495_2023_54, Published online: 30 July 2023

mechanism of TPF will be analyzed, first by defining the nature of the agreement underpinning it and then by looking at the potential legal implications might be. The overall conclusion reached is that, although TPF facilitates access to justice, there are several complexities that could make its use rather difficult in ISDS. The chapter ends with some recommendations to overcome the main obstacles.

1 Introduction

Over the years, the concept of individual access to justice has taken on countless legal implications in the context of international law. While the traditional state-centric[1] approach had restricted individual access to rare situations, the evolution of the discipline has progressively increased its attention towards the protection of the individual.[2] As a matter of fact, funding of claims entails the macro-argument concerning the legal protection of any individual, which is thus a cornerstone of the expansion of the rule of law, since the judicial organization is one of the fundamental functions of the state.[3] However, identifying and defining the concept of access to justice is quite challenging, considering its differing manifestations in national legal systems.[4] It is clear that each state is independent in organizing its judicial system in the appropriate manner, having regard to the principles that may indeed be acknowledged in different legal systems and traditions.[5]

One of the fundamental principles of a judicial system is undoubtedly the "right to take legal action", which enables any person to bring a claim before a judicial authority against a relevant counterparty to protect his or her rights. Taking legal action is often considered a constitutional right,[6] since it has a strong social dimension, expressing values that are now universally recognised.[7] Moreover, such a right has also gained importance at the international level, notably in EU[8] and international human rights instruments.[9] In this regard, the ECHR system, which is often considered to be the most consolidated human rights protection mechanism among

[1] Brown (1992), p. 204.

[2] Kotlik (2017), p. 93.

[3] Chavez (2008), p. 63.

[4] United Nations Development Programme UNDP (2005), p. 5.

[5] *Abdoella v. the Netherlands*, no. 12728/87, §24, 25 November 1992.

[6] Storskrubb and Ziller (2007), pp. 178–183.

[7] Cf., Human Rights Act 1998, Schedule 1, United Kingdom, 1998; Chapter II article 9, Sweden, 1974; Constitutión Española, arts. 54, 119, 241, 1171 and 1201, Spain, 1978.

[8] Gáspár-Szilágyi (2013), pp. 165–169.

[9] UDHR, 10 December 1948, article 8; ECHR, 4 November 1950, arts. 6, 13; ACHR, 22 November 1969, arts. 8, 25; ICCPR, 16 December 1966, arts. 2 (3), 9 (3), 9 (4); OPICCPR, article 2; ACHPR, 28 June 1981, articles 3, 7(1); CFR, 7 December 2000, article 47(2).

the regional treaty-based control systems,[10] has largely contributed to make the Convention's protection of individual claimants effective.

Therefore, access to international litigation arguably covers the set of both substantive and procedural rules enabling an individual to bring a claim under an international procedure that provides appropriate relief for alleged violations of personal and property rights. Nevertheless, while the identification of such a right is well known in the context of international human rights litigation,[11] it cannot be said to be equally well established in the framework of judicial mechanisms dealing with foreign investment disputes.

For these reasons, this chapter is structured in two mainparts. The first examines the role of the individual in international law and whether it is possible to assert access to justice in the investor-state dispute settlement system (hereinafter also referred as "ISDS"). In the second part, the analysis focuses on the high costs associated with the use of the ISDS system, as a barrier to access to justice, attempting to understand whether third-party funding (hereinafter also referred as "TPF") could effectively provide a tool to facilitate access to ISDS.

2 The Access of an Individual to International Litigation

In the international legal order states are the primary subjects of international law,[12] since they represent the main recipient of international rights and obligations.[13] Yet, the ongoing evolution of international law[14] has contributed to the emergence of other actors than states, so-called non-state actors, which have acquired in recent years a more prominent role in the international legal system.[15] Among the non-state actors, individuals, both natural and legal persons,[16] have assumed a significant role, thus evolving from their status as mere objects of the home state.[17]

It has been argued that direct access[18] of an individual to a body holding international jurisdiction constitutes a state's choice,[19] as there is no rule of customary law guaranteeing access to international jurisdiction. Nevertheless, through

[10]Pustorino (2023), pp. 55–56.

[11]Gerards and Glas (2017).

[12]Viñuales et al. (2020), p. 79.

[13]Crawford and Brownlie (2019), pp. 105–133.

[14]Sterio (2008), p. 213.

[15]Peters et al. (2009), pp. 1–33.

[16]Bantekas (2004), p. 309.

[17]Higgins (1978), pp. 2–5.

[18]Trindade (2011), pp. 17–49.

[19]Mills (2013), pp. 187–239.

participation in international treaties[20] and consent to jurisdictional mechanisms,[21] states may empower individuals to take legal action to demand justice against their state of origin, or in certain circumstances against other states, within the international community. Therefore, it seems appropriate to make some brief considerations to clarify whether, through the attribution of rights and obligations, an individual's access to international justice could currently be endorsed.

According to a contemporary overview of doctrine and case-law in the field of international law, the individual is deemed to have acquired a sui generis legal personality.[22] This may be inferred from the relevance that the academic community has recognized towards to this topic over the years,[23] thus fostering the development of a real change in international law, leading to what has been called humanisation of international law.[24] Although legal position of the individual in international law remains limited,[25] the gradual shift away from a state-centric perspective in recent years has expanded that legal position. Hence, the role assumed by individuals, including the opportunity to access international litigation, is expanding. Yet, an individual's right to litigate in international forums stil stems directly from international treaties, both as a defendant and as an alleged victim. Therefore, the impact of the right of access to international justice on this development is the key.

More precisely, the role of the individual is gaining importance in specific areas of international law,[26] especially in international investment law.[27] Such importance has clearly affected access to justice in international disputes, creating complexities especially when it comes to financing the cost of bringing international claims, which is particularly high in ISDS.

3 The Access of an Individual to an ISDS Mechanism

3.1 Background

A mechanism allowing direct access to international justice for the individual, both as a natural and legal person, is certainly provided by the ISDS system.[28] ISDS refers

[20] Sitaraman (2016), pp. 5–23.

[21] Hollis (2005), p. 137.

[22] Dörr (2005), pp. 905–916.

[23] Giorgetti (2018), p. 1085.

[24] Palombino (2020), pp. 745–750.

[25] Gärditz (2014), pp. 86–93.

[26] These concern two fields where the contribution of the individual has been particularly relevant, namely international human rights law, Pustorino (2022), pp. 269–271, and international criminal law, Aitala (2021), pp. 10–16.

[27] Mauro (2019), p. 87.

[28] de Oliveira and Hourani (2020).

to those disputes arising out of an investment made by an individual in a foreign country, where the investment may often be protected by an ad hoc agreement between the state and the investor, by an existing law of the state concerning foreign investment and, as will be explained below, by an international investment agreement (hereinafter also "IIA").[29]

ISDS is closely related to public international law, where the principle of sovereignty of states is one of the cardinal rules.[30] Thus, the legislative measures adopted by a state hosting a foreign investment do not often result in an automatic violation of the investor's rights, due to the possibility of the state to exercise its sovereign powers to perform its functions.[31] Therefore, the crucial issue arise when the right to regulate[32]—as an inherent power of sovereign states[33]—could lead to an international violation of binding rules and principles of international law.

Indeed, when there is a potential violation by the host state, the substantive and procedural rights of the investor come into play, thus creating an indirect and mitigated right of access to justice. Consequently, this is the only protection afforded to a foreign investor, because in the absence of principles of public international law, states would have no limits, and consequently they would potentially be able to trample on an investor's personal and patrimonial rights. Thus, in order to outline the most significant factors affecting the investor's access to justice in international investment law, it is arguably appropriate to reflect upon to two further linked perspectives, one from a general and the other from a specific point of view.

First, from a general perspective, a brief analysis of the principle of denial of justice is necessary to understand the international practice developed in relation to the right of access to justice. This analysis will adopt a deductive methodology. Second, taking a more specific perspective, it will be essential to examine the IIAs, with particular attention given to bilateral investment treaties (hereinafter also the "BITs"), to identify provisions addressing the right of access to justice.

3.2 Denial of Justice: An Indirect Recognition of Access to Justice

In international law, denial of justice[34] occurs when a state does not provide an adequate judicial organization to guarantee effective legal protection for the individual, thus causing an international violation against the state of nationality of the

[29] Schreuer et al. (2022), pp. 1–10.

[30] Boisson de Chazournes and McLachlan (2016), pp. 255–256.

[31] Viñuales (2014), pp. 317–362.

[32] Titi (2014).

[33] Korzun (2017).

[34] Although originally intended to be used in inter-state relations as a necessary condition for retaliation (Spiegel (1938), pp. 63–81), the concept subsequently evolved, meaning any

foreign citizen.[35] This is an undisputed principle of public international law,[36] which has also been applied over the years as a cornerstone in the field of international investment law for foreign investors.[37]

Indeed, several cases have arisen in the field of expropriation[38] and nationalization[39] of foreign assets in recent years, unfortunately without ensuring prompt and fair compensation to the investor in certain circumstances.[40] For these reasons, it seems necessary to clarify whether it is possible to consider the denial of justice as a principle aimed at ensuring access to justice in ISDS, taking into account the provisions contained in BITs and subsequent arbitral jurisprudence.

As a matter of fact, certain BITs relate to general principles recognised by customary international law, specifically on fair and equitable treatment ("FET"). In this respect, there may be an obligation upon states to avoid a denial of justice, which therefore becomes a positive requirement to ensure access to justice in all types of judicial proceedings.[41] For example, the recent Belgium-Luxemburg Economic Union (BLEU) Model BIT of 2019 provides for a breach of fair and equitable treatment by a contracting party when, one or more of the measures implemented result in a denial of justice or a breach of effective access to justice for the investor.[42]

Notwithstanding such rules aimed at protecting investors, there are nevertheless cases in which states have abusively exercised their authority by placing arbitrary conditions upon an individual's access to justice, thus affecting an investors' rights. Reference can be made to the case Lowen v. United States, in which although the plaintiff's application was rejected for failure to exhaust domestic remedies, the tribunal recognised a violation of access to justice. In this sense, the arbitral award, based on NAFTA Article 1105,[43] provides for a definition of what constitutes a denial of justice and this definition helped to guide subsequent arbitral case-law.[44]

---

internationally wrongful act against which diplomatic protection could be exercised, i.e., the action taken by one sovereign against another to obtain reparation, Focarelli (2012), para 6.

[35] International Law Commission, *Draft Articles on Responsibility of States for Internationally Wrongful Acts, with Commentaries*, November 2001, (A/56/10), where it is specified that: "[…] *Something further is required before international law becomes relevant, such as a denial of justice by the courts of the State in proceedings brought by the other contracting party.* […]", p. 41.

[36] Paulsson (2005), p. 5.

[37] Padilla (2011), pp. 296–297.

[38] Kammerhofer (2021).

[39] Yackee (2019), pp. 71–110.

[40] Francioni (1975), pp. 255–280.

[41] *Bilateral Agreement for the Promotion and Protection of Investments between the Government of The Republic of Colombia and The Government of the People's Republic of China*, signed on 22.11.2008 and entered into force on 02.07.2013, article 2 c) "*Promotion, Admission and Protection of Investments*".

[42] (BLEU) Model BIT 2019, article 4, para 3, lett. b), c) "*Promotion and Protection of Investments*".

[43] Article 1105 of NAFTA protects investors through the provision and enforcement of FET (fair and equitable treatment) and full protection and security, Dumberry (2014), pp. 47–73.

[44] *The Lœwen Group, Inc. & Raymond L. Lœwen v. United States*, ICSID Case No ARB(AF)/98/3, Award (26 June 2003), para 119.

Moreover, from the perspective of FET, attention should also be drawn to the reasoning of the ICSID arbitral tribunal in Metalclad v. Mexico. The tribunal found the procedure denying the construction permit to the investor unlawful, since the investor would have had no possibility to review the administrative decision directly affecting him, thereby leading to a denial of justice.[45] A similar view of denial of justice was adopted in Middle East Cement v. Egypt. The ICSID tribunal found that the investor had been deprived of access to justice following the seizure and sale of its ship. Specifically, the tribunal pointed out that the seizure and sale of such an important vessel should at least have been notified to the company, thus resulting in a denial of justice, because government authorities had acted in bad faith.[46]

Therefore, both the conventional and case-law elaboration of the principle of denial of justice have largely contributed to the modern definition of access to justice, albeit indirectly. However, whilst such analysis aims at providing a more general definition, attention should now be focused on the specific recognition of access to justice in BITs, as they represent the instruments upon which investors can mostly rely in order to access ISDS mechanisms.

3.3 *The Relevance of BITs: A Substantive and Procedural Recognition of Access to Justice*

Despite the aforementioned case-law having a significant indirect influence on the definition of access to justice in ISDS, it should also be considered that the ultimate recognition of a more specific right of access to justice is clearly embedded in IIAs, specifically through BITs.[47] As a result, the increasing protection afforded to investors through BITs has facilitated access to justice, thus allowing investors direct access to ISDS.[48] Therefore, with the so-called BIT proliferation,[49] a series of individual duties and rights have been recognised, which have increased the protection of the foreign investment.[50]

For the aim of the following analysis, it is thus necessary to understand the attitude of states in concluding BITs, briefly examining the evolution concerning the specific issue of access to justice. To that end, the investigation will include both

---

[45] *Metalclad Corporation v. Mexico*, ICSID Case No ARB(AF)/97/1, Award (30 August 2000), para 91.

[46] *Middle East Cement Shipping and Handling Co. S.A. v. Egypt*, ICSID Case No ARB/99/6, Award (12 April 2002), para 143.

[47] Bekker and Ogawa (2013), pp. 314–330.

[48] Deva and Van Ho (2023), pp. 413-414.

[49] Elkins et al. (2006), pp. 814–819.

[50] Nyombi and Mortimer (2018), pp. 46–53.

BITs and, to a more limited extent, so-called Model BITs[51] drafted by states. In this respect, the extent to which recognition of the right of access to justice has evolved over the years in such conventions (especially bilateral ones) over the years is impressive.

When referring to the very first treaties concluded to facilitate trade, navigation, and investment and to mutually protect individuals and the states parties, the so-called treaties of friendship, commerce, and navigation ("FCNs")—questions of interpretation and application were largely deferred to the jurisdiction of the ICJ.[52] Hence, these treaties included no direct recognition of the individual's access to international dispute resolution systems.[53] The same approach was adopted in the first BIT, which did not provide for ISDS but instead referred potential litigation to the jurisdiction of the ICJ or an arbitral tribunal.[54] However, over the years, this approach has been decisively superseded, limiting the interposition of states, and increasingly opening up the field to a direct recognition of the rights of an individual who may have suffered violations as a result of investing abroad.

In this context, it is worth noting that specific articles in BITs, sometimes directly entitled "Access to the Courts of Justice", provide that each contracting state must recognise the right of access to justice for investors, understood as access to courts or administrative agencies at all levels of domestic jurisdiction,[55] both in pursuing and defending rights.[56] Clearly, this represents a necessary consequence of the development of the principle of non-discrimination.[57] Such a concept, which provides that equal situations should be treated equally, can be easily identified in human rights systems, and therefore represents a legal standard, to be respected by the host state of the investment vis-à-vis the investor.[58] Moreover, access to justice is sometimes considered as a necessary consequence of investment protection, by explicit references to the laws and regulations of each contracting state, thus creating a

[51] "*Model Agreements*" or "*Model BITs*" are sometimes adopted by states as a reference model for negotiating or renegotiating their BITs, Nam (2017), pp. 1280–1282.

[52] Treaty of Friendship, Commerce and Navigation (with Protocol). Signed at Managua, on 21 January 1956 between Nicaragua and USA, art. 24, para 2.

[53] Vandevelde (2017).

[54] *Treaty for the Promotion and Protection of Investments (with Protocol and exchange of notes), Germany and Pakistan*, article 11, para 2, lett. a), b).

[55] Gáspár-Szilágyi (2020), pp. 389–415.

[56] *Agreement between the Argentina Republic and Japan for the promotion and protection of investment*, signed on 1.12.2018, Cap. I "*Investment*", art. 5 "*Access to the Courts of Justice*"; *Agreement between Japan and The Republic of Armenia for the liberalization, promotion and protection of investment*, signed on 14.02.2018 and entered into force on 15.05.2019, Cap. I "*Investment*", art. 5 "*Access to The Courts*".

[57] Bayefsky (2017), pp. 71–104.

[58] For example, the concept of fair and equitable treatment (FET) and most-favoured-nation treatment (MFN) stem from the notion of non-discrimination. On the first topic, see: Palombino (2018), pp. 19–56; for an analysis of the second topic see: Acconci (2012), pp. 363–406.

judicial guarantee for the investor to access to all legal authorities to protect the investment.[59]

Furthermore, again in a BITs context, it seems possible to recognise articles granting the investor's access to justice from the point of view of the treatment that should be accorded. Through an explicit reference both to the applicable international rules and to the rules provided for by the respective state in its own legislation, the investor is therefore guaranteed a "multilevel protection", thus ensuring a right of access to justice to secure its investment against measures which might impede substantial or procedural rights and thus lead to a violation of due process.[60]

Likewise, requirements contained in Model BITs point towards a recognition of the right of access to justice. Clearly, the inclusion of a provision in a Model BIT does not mean that every single state has approved it. However, it can certainly be argued that such prescriptions provide useful guidance as to the main guarantees which a state acknowledges in its own legislation and which, consequently, it would expect to see granted to an investor in a foreign country. For example, as early as 1985 the Asian-African Legal Advisory Committee, provided for the right of nationals (including state agencies and companies) of a contracting party to have access to the courts if there was a possible violation of a right relating to an investment.[61] Differently, the Chile Model BIT of 1994[62] and the Kenya BIT Model of 2003[63] introduce a reference to the right of access to justice for an investor who has suffered expropriation or a measure with the same purpose.[64]

Additionally, to address the recognition of the right of access to justice within BITs, it seems useful to refer to the recent Netherlands Model BIT of 2019[65] for two main reasons. First, the new text that replaces the Netherlands Model BIT of 2004,[66] provides for an article entirely devoted to the rule of law. Thus, this Model BIT serves an example highlighting the recent attention that states have devoted to the issue of access to justice.[67] Secondly, the new wording emphasises the right of

---

[59] Compare: *Agreement between The Government of The Republic of Armenia and The Government of The United Arab Emirates*, signed on 22.07.2016 and entered into force on 21.11.2017, art. 3, para 4, "*Protection of investments*" and *Agreement between The Republic of Rwanda and The United Arab Emirates on the promotion and reciprocal protection of investments*, signed on 01.11.2017, art. 3, para 4 "*Promotion and encouragement of investments*".

[60] *Agreement between Japan and The Republic of Kazakhstan for the promotion and protection of investment*, signed on 23.10.2014 and entered into force on 25.10.2015, art. 6 and art. 12, para 4.

[61] *Asian-African Legal Consultative Committee Revised Draft of Model Agreements for Promotion and Protection of Investments*, art. 9 "*Access to courts and tribunals*", 1985.

[62] Government of the Republic of Chile, 1994.

[63] The Government of the Republic of Kenya, Ministry of Foreign Affairs, 2003.

[64] See, respectively: *Chile Model BIT*, art., 6 para 3 "*Expropriation and compensation*" and the *Kenya Model BIT*, art. 5, lett. c) "*Expropriation and Compensation*".

[65] *Netherlands model Investment Agreement*, 22 March 2019.

[66] *Netherlands model Investment Agreement*, 22 March 2004.

[67] *Netherlands model Investment Agreement*, 22 March 2019, article 5 "Rule of law".

access to justice as the main corollary of the rule of law, underlining its importance from two points of view: (1) by stressing the necessary obligation of each contracting state to ensure that the investor has access to effective dispute resolution mechanisms;[68] and (2) by reaffirming that each contracting state has a duty to protect against human rights abuses arising from commercial activities, the new BIT Model obliges to ensure that victims of such abuses are granted access to an effective judicial remedy.[69]

In conclusion, evaluating the past situation and considering the rules today encompassed within BITs (and certain provisions of Model BITs), states are paying increasing attention to the needs of investors and implementing provisions concerning the right of access to justice. Although effective protection exists, it will now be necessary to further examine how this is translated into ISDS practice, analysing one of the core problems of the system, namely the high costs.

4 Setting the Scene

4.1 Introduction

Generally, one of the main obstacles for investors to access ISDS is the high costs of international arbitration proceedings, which results in two consequences. First, access is no longer completely free but substantially restricted, depending on the economic situation of the investor. Secondly, such restriction could affect the legal market, creating economic, social, and legal inequalities. For these reasons, it is necessary to classify the "costs" referred to in ISDS and identify the economic and legal actors most affected. Subsequently, this chapter will deal with the question of whether TPF can provide a possible remedy to overcome the problem of costs, thereby rendering access to justice effective through the funding of one party's costs. However, because TPF is based on a commercial transaction with the purpose of making a profit, several social, economic, and legal consequences may arise from the funding agreement, which will therefore necessarily have to be assessed in the overall context. Finally, remarks on the convenience of TPF in ISDS will be made in order to understand whether this instrument could really be considered as a facilitation of access to justice in the light of current legal and economic practice.

[68] *Netherlands model Investment Agreement*, 22 March 2019, article 5, para 2.

[69] *Netherlands model Investment Agreement*, 22 March 2019, article 5, para 3.

4.2 Costs in Investment Arbitration

Costs represent one of the main obstacles an investor faces to initiate proceedings,[70] since access to every legal procedure comes at a cost.[71] In international investment law, specifically in the field of ISDS, a type of private justice financed by the parties is quite often involved.[72] The litigating parties can customarily decide on the arbitral institution,[73] the applicable law[74] and the persons who will decide the dispute,[75] that are the arbitrators that will constitute the arbitral tribunal.[76] Traditionally, costs in arbitral proceedings are classified in two macro-categories. First, the costs that a party incurs related to the administration of the arbitral tribunal and the proceedings,[77] defined as "reliable costs".[78] Second, the costs generally related to the party's legal defence, i.e., "legal costs".[79]

Legal costs might depend on several factors, for example: how many professionals are included in the legal team; the quality of the lawyers chosen to represent the case; and the level of complexity of the dispute. These issues are embedded within an ultra-specialised legal market, that of ISDS, which requires specific knowledge to handle complex situations intertwining public international law issues with domestic law matters. For these reasons the involvement of big law firms is often necessary in ISDS, as they guarantee a high level of quality and expertise in handling cases. However, reconnecting to the issue of legal costs in ISDS, it is also clear that these law firms, both in terms of quality of work and number of staff involved, require not insignificant costs from the client. According to a recent study it was pointed out that the costs of paying the defence counsel would amount to an average of approximately USD 4–5 million for each party involved in the proceedings.[80] Hence, these are very high amounts, which—when added to the reliable costs—could hinder access to justice.

---

[70]Bradfield and Verdirame (2014), p. 411.

[71]Scholars, about cost relating to access to justice, contributed in a different way. See Barendrecht et al. (2006), who argue that cost of access to justice includes "[...] (all) *the barriers that people experience when they seek access to justice* [...]", including time spent on the case, costs resulting from delay, etc, p. 3. Gramatikov (2009) defines it as "[...] *all costs incurred on the quest to solve a legal problem, including out-of-pocket costs, opportunity costs, and intangible costs* [...].", p. 10.

[72]Kudrna (2013), p. 2.

[73]Clearly, parties are not always free to choose the arbitral institution to refer to.

[74]Bjorklund and Vanhonnaeker (2021), pp. 225–243.

[75]Giorgetti (2019), pp. 1–93.

[76]Tanzi (2020), pp. 57–75.

[77]These costs range from the first official act, which could often be the so-called 'notice of intent', to the rendering of the award.

[78]Clearly, such costs are not certain *per se*, but these expenses need to be considered.

[79]Benedettelli et al. (2017), p. 1160.

[80]Franck (2019), pp. 253–296.

As for reliable costs, i.e., costs related to the fees of individual arbitrators and those of the arbitral institution, it seems quite difficult to fix a determination criterion. An attempt to calculate "*an estimate of the likely costs*" is provided by the International Chamber of Commerce, which only relies on Secretariat and arbitrators' expenses[81] and by the European Court of Arbitration, specifying that it is still "[. . .] *a general idea of the costs and fees of arbitral proceedings administered by the European Court of Arbitration under the International Rules* [. . .]" and that the Secretariat of the Court will always be responsible for setting a precise amount.[82] As set forth in several arbitration rules, the parameter used to determine such costs is based on the dispute value and—where such value is indeterminate or cannot be determined—the responsibility for fixing such costs resides within the arbitrators' discretion.[83]

In line with a relevant classification discussed in the literature,[84] it seems possible to identify three approaches to calculate the cost of instituting international legal proceedings: the payment of a fixed sum, regardless of the total amount of the dispute;[85] the determination of a variable fee, to be fixed on the basis of the dispute value;[86] and, finally, the subscription of a so-called hybrid fee, composed of a fixed part and a variable part.[87] Whilst this classification could be considered as a useful tool, estimating the total amount of ISDS's cost is complicated, although several studies that have tried to do so,[88] sometimes managing to provide an indicative value that could be considered as an important step in decision-making.[89] In any case, these costs seem truly excessive[90] and also underline the need for a structural reform of the system, such as the one carried out within ICSID,[91] which has among its aims

[81] International Chamber of Commerce (2022), Cost calculator. https://iccwbo.org/dispute-resolution-services/arbitration/costs-and-payments/cost-calculator/. Accessed 27 Feb 2022. This seems a valuable indicator for access to justice: having a minimum idea of the costs involved, notably for companies operating on a balance sheet basis, could be decisive in deciding whether to engage in ISDS arbitration.

[82] European Court of Arbitration (2022), Cost Calculator. https://cour-europe-arbitrage.org/the-costs-of-arbitration/. Accessed 27 Feb 2022.

[83] Bühler (2005), pp. 179–182.

[84] Assareh (2012), p. 12.

[85] ICSID Schedule of Fees (2022).

[86] In pure variable fee forums, the cost of initiating legal proceedings varies directly according to the amount of the dispute.

[87] An interesting dynamic is that of hybrid forums, where the costs of initiating proceedings are calculated using a combination of variable and fixed fee formulas.

[88] According to research conducted in 2012, the average total costs of ISDS proceedings have averaged $8 million and, in very exceptional cases, over $30 million, see Gaukrodger and Gordon (2012), p. 19.

[89] Hodgson et al. (2021).

[90] Bottini et al. (2020).

[91] As well known, the amendment process began in 2016 and—after different suggestions with the aim of amending the rules—in 2021 the ICSID Secretariat published 6 working papers, see ICSID (2021), About the ICSID Rule Amendments.

that of reducing the costs of the procedure.[92] Clearly, although the ICSID Arbitration Rules are the most widely adopted in ISDS, in other contexts—such as those within UNCITRAL, SCC or ICC—it is possible to identify highly significant costs when comparing the respective cost-related provisions as well.[93]

Another problematic issues concerning the costs of access to justice in ISDS relates to the advance payment of costs.[94] Although it is true that the costs advanced will be assessed in the award and often ultimately borne by the losing party in the proceedings,[95] such advance payment could often consist in a request and a subsequent order of the Tribunal for security for costs.[96]

In the light of these considerations and of the problems that costs represent, three reflections can be made. Firstly, from a legal point of view, these costs represent the 'condicio sine qua non' for access to ISDS. Secondly, the social impact of high costs should not be underestimated. The more costs continue to rise, the more difficult it will be to create a legal market that even small and medium-sized enterprises can rely on. Finally, there is a problematic issue that represents a synthesis of the two issues addressed above, namely the economic problem, which affects small and medium-sized enterprises (hereinafter also "SMEs").

4.3 Cost Issues for SMEs: Barriers to Access to Justice?

Traditionally, international arbitration in contrast to domestic arbitration, where small claims may be involved, has covered larger transnational corporations and, consequently, larger litigated amounts. However, it should be borne in mind that SMEs are small compared to large multinationals and therefore the costs of initiating proceedings and the associated cost risk create a daunting and practically prohibitive burden.[97] Indeed, previous studies authorised by the European Commission (2011)[98] and, more recently, by the World Bank (2019)[99] confirms that especially for SMEs international litigation is an inadequate means of pursuing justice. Because of this situation, several companies do not often freely operate in the legal market and their

[92] Alarcon (2020).

[93] Hodgson et al. (2021), p. 8.

[94] ICC Arbitration Rules (2021), article 37.

[95] *Cement Investment & Trade S.A. v. Republic of Turkey*, ICSID Case No ARB(AF)/07/2, Award (13 August 2009), paras. 185–186.

[96] Camilleri (2021), pp. 851–862.

[97] Walton and Williams (2014), p. 304.

[98] European Commission, European contract law in business-to-business transactions: Summary (2011), https://europa.eu/eurobarometer/surveys/detail/965.

[99] World Bank and the International Finance Corporation Doing Business 2019 (2019), https://www.worldbank.org/content/dam/doingBusiness/media/AnnualReports/English/DB2019-report_web-version.pdf.

commercial growth remains restricted.[100] To that end, different and consequential examinations appear to be worthwhile, in close connection with issues related to access to justice in international arbitration, which will provide a preliminary discussion concerning the opportunity to fund of a dispute.

Facilitating access to arbitration for SMEs would be strategic. In doing so, the ISDS mechanism would avoid being perceived as the exclusive monopoly of the richest and largest companies.[101] It seems sufficient to consider, in this connection, that companies with an annual revenue of more than 1 billion dollars and private individuals with an income of more than 100 million dollars received approximately 94.5% of the total compensation following ISDS, and if interest before the award of the sums is included, the figure is still very high, at 93.5%.[102] In addition, SMEs as international investors can also face complications in planning, implementing, and managing an investment abroad.[103] The settlement of disputes with the host state of the investment is not only extremely burdensome, but requires particular legal expertise,[104] which as previously observed entails a considerable amount of legal costs.

The clear difficulties for SMEs outlined above are supported be a study conducted from 2008 to 2013, according to which the number of SMEs that had restored to international dispute resolution mechanisms accounted for only 15% of total disputes.[105] Therefore, it seems quite clear that the high costs of arbitration proceedings are not only a barrier to access to justice, but sometimes a real disincentive to use ISDS mechanism. Such a situation becomes even clearer when one considers that, in the classic hypothesis, the investor complains of having already suffered an economic loss due to a legal violation and would then find itself having to face the costs of an arbitration procedure from a loss-making balance sheet. Although very recent efforts have attempted to outline some options on how to provide economic and legal assistance to reduce costs by facilitating SMEs' access to justice in ISDS,[106] these situations have nonetheless created a demand in the economic-legal market. Such demand led to the intervention of various entities, who—attracted by the possibility of high profit margins with ostensibly limited investment risk—provide funding of the dispute, in exchange for a return of a financial nature. This is the phenomenon of TPF, which is increasing in importance, especially in ISDS.

---

[100] Butler and Herbert (2014), pp. 186–221.

[101] Walton and Williams (2014), p. 433.

[102] Van Harten and Malysheuski (2022).

[103] Karl (2017), pp. 245–249.

[104] Gebert (2017), pp. 292–293.

[105] Karl (2017), p. 261.

[106] Fach Gómez and Titi (2023), pp. 32–40.

5 TPF and Its Relevance in ISDS

5.1 Background

TPF is not a recent practice in litigation[107] and the function of this mechanism in domestic jurisdictions remains of major importance to both academics and practitioners.[108] Nevertheless, the issues concerning TPF overlapping with ISDS have recently attracted considerable attention,[109] since ISDS litigation strategy often deals with issues beyond the application of domestic law, incorporating matters that frequently have as their main reference the sovereignty of a state, and consequently the application of principles of international law.[110] As recognised by the ICSID tribunal in Giovanni Alemanni v. Argentina, TPF is a well-recognised practice also in the investment arbitration context,[111] which can therefore provide a practical implementation of the recognition of the right of access to justice in the ISDS. Therefore, balancing the interests of private funders with the main purpose of the funded entity, i.e. to be funded and thereby be able to access to justice, represents the core difficulty in ISDS system, in a context hiding many legal, economic and social pitfalls. Indeed, following the 2008 financial crisis, the legal market became an interesting strategic point for several economic speculators, realizing that with TPF[112] investments could be made with potentially moderate risks as well as potentially satisfactory possibilities of economic return.[113] Among the reasons behind this trend, importance should be drawn to the uncertainty surrounding the international regulation of TPF, which has prompted scholars to question its legal suitability in ISDS.[114]

To that end, this topic will be assessed evaluating three, consecutive, perspectives. Firstly, consideration will be given to the definition of TPF in relevant international instruments, with the purpose to outline, albeit indirectly, some of the key aspects surrounding the funding mechanism. Secondly, it will be necessary to evaluate which advantages and disadvantages TPF might create in the general context of ISDS, aiming to critically assess both the substantive and procedural law aspects. Finally, it will be possible to investigate some of the consequences the choice of TPF entails in ISDS practice, questioning whether such mechanism facilitates access to justice.

---

[107] Solas (2019), pp. 17–37.

[108] Latham and Ventures (2022).

[109] Kalyanpur and Newman (2021), pp. 773–790.

[110] Viñuales (2017), pp. 1071–1072.

[111] *Giovanni Alemanni and others v. Argentine Republic,* ICSID Case No ARB/07/8, Decision on Jurisdiction and Admissibility (17 November 2014), para 278.

[112] Santosuosso and Scarlett (2018), pp. 8–16.

[113] Garcia (2018), p. 2913.

[114] Guven and Johnson (2019), pp. 3–7.

5.2 *Defining TPF in ISDS: A Strategy for Clarity*

Although there is no statutory definition of TPF, in ISDS it is generally considered as a funding mechanism based on an agreement, where a private entity—i.e., the third-party[115] (also referred as the "funder")[116]—finances the costs of investment arbitral proceedings for a party in a dispute (or in a potential one). In return, the funder receives a percentage of the awarded compensation (if the claim is successful), gaining some degree of control over the case, the "litigation strategy", and/or the party's client.[117]

Considered in these terms, TPF could be a hypothetical win-win situation: on one hand, the funder carries out an investment with significantly high-profit margins; on the other hand, the funded party is secured the costly access to justice of ISDS mechanisms, with the possibility to receive an albeit lower percentage of the awarded compensation, should it win the case. However, as mentioned above, there are several complications related to TPF, mainly connected to the circumstances that this agreement and its regulation appear to be rather fragmented in the context of ISDS.

For example, there might be issues involving TPFs and legal costs, under three possible circumstances. Firstly, if the party intending to apply for funding does not have the financial means to obtain legal advice—even in the out-of-court phase, i.e., aimed at an assessment of whether initiate ISDS proceedings—TPF can be considered the only mechanism enhancing the right of access to justice. Secondly, it will be a matter of understanding whether the costs of paying the defence counsel would be included in the funding agreement. Such a choice can, therefore, influence the attitude of the funder, who could support—or in some cases replace—the counsel hired by the party wishing to apply for the funding. Another issue may arise regarding the payment of any adverse costs; the TPF agreement could cover the legal costs, but not costs in the event of losing the case, essentially leaving the funded party solely responsible for paying the costs. Consequently, states have conventionally regulated such a funding mechanism in different ways, according to different legal interpretations. Therefore, the lack of an unambiguous definition

[115] The term 'third-party' is used because it is a third party to the dispute between the state and the investor. These are usually private investment funds, which have found excellent investment opportunities in the current legal market, see for example the Omni Bridgeway Annual Report (2020), in section "Proceeds from litigation funding", pp. 6–7.

[116] In current market there are several third-party funders with a background in international litigations and arbitrations. In this respect, the work carried out by the "*TPF Observatory*", an independent initiative from the "*ICCA/QMUL Task Force on Third Party Funding*", is quite interesting. The Observatory created a list of TPF funders and TPF brokers (whose task is not to directly fund a dispute but to act as an intermediary between parties seeking funding and funders).

[117] The tasks carried out by the fund, particularly at the time when the funding opportunity is submitted, consists of due diligence work, see *Third Party Funders for International Arbitration*.

has given rise to several characterisations,[118] which will be necessary to examine below.

In treaties with investment provisions, reference can be made to the *EU-Canada Comprehensive Economic and Trade Agreement* (CETA),[119] where TPF

> [...] means any funding provided by a natural or legal person who is not a disputing party but who enters into an agreement with a disputing party in order to finance part or all of the cost of the proceedings either through a donation or grant, or in return for remuneration dependent on the outcome of the dispute [...].[120]

The CETA definition seems to be a rather clear and detailed description of the funding agreement, highlighting the typical aspects of TPF. However, besides the definition, what is striking within CETA is the disclosure policy, which obliges the funded party to disclose—both to the Court and to the counterparty—the name and address of the third-party funder.[121] Such specific obligation and, more generally, the TPF regulation within CETA, were not addressed in Opinion 1/17 of the European Court of Justice,[122] and this silence could legitimise the admission of private actors such as TPFs into the system.[123]

Moreover, in the *European Union-Vietnam Investment Protection Agreement* (EVFTA),[124] there is a quite similar definition of TPF,[125] and an almost identical disclosure obligation upon the disputing party benefiting from TPF,[126] which is therefore an extremely crucial requirement for investment agreements within the EU. However, what makes the EVFTA more peculiar with respect to CETA are the considerations on security for costs[127] and provisional award,[128] which allow to

[118] Park and Rogers (2015), p. 4.

[119] *Comprehensive Economic and Trade Agreement (CETA) between Canada, of the one part, and the European Union and its Member States, of the other part*, provisionally entered into force on Sept. 21st, 2017. For an overview, see Bungenberg and Reinisch (2022).

[120] CETA, Chapter eight "*Investment*", Section A "*Definitions and scope*", art. 8.1 "*definitions*".

[121] CETA, Chapter eight "*Investment*", Section F "*Resolution of investment disputes between investors and states*", article 8.26 "*Third party funding*".

[122] It concerns the request for an opinion, pursuant to Article 218(11) TFEU, submitted to the Court by Belgium, concerning the compatibility of some CETA's investment provisions (Section F, Chapter VIII) with the EU Treaties, including with fundamental rights. See C-1/17 EU:C:2019: 341 (30 April 2019) (Opinion 1/17).

[123] Fanou (2020), p. 16.

[124] *EU - Viet Nam Investment Protection Agreement (EVFTA) (2019)*, signed on 30.06.2019 and entered into force on 1.08.2020.

[125] EVFTA, article 3.28, lett. i), which defines TPF as "[...] *means any funding provided by a natural or juridical person who is not a party to the dispute but who enters into an agreement with a disputing party in order to finance part or all of the cost of the proceedings in return for a remuneration dependent on the outcome of the dispute, or any funding provided by a natural or juridical person who is not a party to the dispute in the form of a donation or grant* [...]".

[126] EVFTA, art. 3. 37, paras 1–2.

[127] EVFTA, art. 3.48.

[128] EVFTA, art. 3.53.

understand how in practice the issue of TPF is strictly connected, or in any case subject to an assessment by the Court, to provisional measures.[129]

Certainly, these investment treaties represent a significant breakthrough in the recognition and definition of TPF in the context of potential state-investor disputes. However, not the same kind of attention has been paid to it in BITs and in Model BITs. In addition to the definition of the TPF, there are agreements regulating the primary obligations of the different parties as well. In this respect, the Colombia Model BIT (2017)[130] represents one of the first instruments that outlined the TPF framework, including both a definition of the agreement[131] and an obligation of immediate disclosure when the claim is submitted,[132] as well as attractive considerations on monetary damages in the award.[133]

A few years later, thus demonstrating how the topic is being placed at the centre of the legal interest of states in investment disputes, the Netherlands Model BIT (2019), has not included in the text a definition of TPF, but a duty upon the claimant to disclose the third-party funder.[134] Furthermore, the same kind of disclosure obligations regarding TPF are also found in the Slovakia Model BIT (2019),[135] which become even more specific and appealing in the matter of provisional measures. Indeed, it is specified that the tribunal may issue an order of security for costs if there is a [. . .] *reasonable doubt* [. . .] that the funded party will not be able to fulfil the costs award.[136] This is certainly an important indication evaluating the extensive practice of TPF on security for costs, that however leaves some legal uncertainty behind the parameter of the reasonable doubt, which therefore could increase the—already very high—discretion of the arbitrators within the dispute.[137]

Finally, the Canada Model BIT (2021)[138] has embedded in its text an entire article dedicated to TPF as well, including more stringent factual and timing disclosure requirements than the examples of in the above-mentioned texts. There is indeed a specification to disclose the TPF agreement immediately or, if it has been arranged after the submission of the claim, within 10 days from when it was agreed.[139] Such an approach should be particularly encouraged, as clear terminology and timing on

---

[129] EVFTA, art. 3. 37, para 3.

[130] Colombia Model BIT (2017).

[131] Colombia Model BIT (2017), p. 5.

[132] Colombia Model BIT (2017), where it is also specified that the form must contain "[. . .] *any sort of financing agreement is reached, even if it takes place after the submission of a claim to arbitration, without delay as soon as the agreement is concluded* [. . .]", p. 16.

[133] Colombia Model BIT (2017), p. 21.

[134] Netherlands model Investment Agreement (2019), art. 19, para 8.

[135] Slovakia Model BIT (2019), art. 21, paras 1–2.

[136] Slovakia Model BIT (2019), art. 21, para 3.

[137] Vargiu (2021), pp. 13–15.

[138] Canada Model BIT (2021).

[139] Canada Model BIT (2021), article 42.

the disclosure obligation will be beneficial to the transparency of the funded party, thus helping the established arbitral tribunal.

While TPF is beginning to be increasingly defined in Model BITs, a similar situation cannot be observed in bilateral investment treaties. For example, the Argentina – United Arab Emirates BIT (2018) clearly forbids TPF.[140] The only one that stands out in this respect is the recent Colombia – Spain BIT (2021),[141] which not only reiterates the disclosure obligation on the funded party to the dispute,[142] but also specifies that if the funded party does not comply with the disclosure obligations (transparency), it will have to bear the costs and expenses of the proceedings regardless of the outcome of the award.[143] Similar considerations are adopted in the Indonesia-Switzerland BIT (2022), where although there is no definition of the TPF agreement, reference is made to an obligation for the funded party to notify the tribunal the name and address of the funder, as soon as the first notice is submitted or when the funding agreement is implemented.[144] Thus, albeit it is a limited disclosure concerning the existence of the agreement and the identification of the funder—and therefore not a full disclosure containing the details of the funding agreement—it is nevertheless a mandatory activity for the funded party. Indeed, should the funded party fails to disclose the existence of the TPF agreement, this could be assessed by the tribunal as an element for the determination of costs, or even order the suspension or termination of the proceedings.[145] However, it seems interesting to monitor how the arbitral tribunals appointed according to this BIT, will interpret such aspect, i.e., a lack of immediate disclosure, as the boundaries between the determination of costs and/or the interruption or suspension of proceedings are blurred, and may therefore prejudice the interests of the investor and the funder.

Against the background of these definitions and obligations concerning TPF, it seems possible to briefly make a few reflections. Firstly, it appears that the main focus regarding TPF is the disclosure duty/obligation, which therefore represents the first hurdle in ISDS litigation. The main reason behind is embodied in the more general necessity for transparency in ISDS, specifically concerning the need to avoid any potential conflicts of interest between all parties involved. As a matter of fact, in the event of non-disclosure, several implications may arise, concerning for example, prior relationships between the investment fund and one of the appointed arbitrators, which could increase risks of annulment of the award or denial of enforcement, based on the very existence of an undeclared conflict of interest. Secondly, it

[140] *Agreement for the reciprocal promotion and protection of investments between The Argentine and The United Arab Emirates*, signed on 16.04.2018, art. 24.

[141] *Acuerdo entre la República de Colombia y el Reino de España para la promoción y protección recíproca de inversiones* (2021), signed on 16.09.2021.

[142] Colombia – Spain BIT (2021), art. 22, para 4.

[143] Colombia – Spain BIT (2021), art. 33, para 5.

[144] *Accord entre le Conseil fédéral suisse et le Gouvernement de la République d'Indonésie concernant la promotion et la protection réciproque des investissement* (2022), art. 20, paras 1–2.

[145] Indonesia-Switzerland BIT, art. 20, para 3.

seems—comparing the high number of Model BITs to BITs—that the intention of states (taken individually) is to define the general scope of application of TPF, but this intention clashes with diplomatic realities when the funding agreement is to be included in a bilateral investment treaty. Thirdly, these are still sporadic episodes that do not regulate all the aspects—legal, economic, and social—related to TPF within the international legal market.

However, from the latter point of view, it should be noted that an example of good practice—aimed at outlining the most significant aspects and related impacts of TPF—comes from the European Parliament, through its recent "*Draft Report with recommendations to the Commission on Responsible private funding of litigation*".[146] This Report, supported by a well-defined and detailed study,[147] is currently the first real attempt to propose regulation for a wide scope of regarding TPF,[148] albeit within the vast legal and economic field of the EU. It will be worth noting the attitude of the main actors—funders and funded parties—towards such stringent proposed requirements, also considering the impact that the ISDS disputes have had in the European context after the well-known *Achmea* ruling.[149] With the main features of the TPF clarified, it is now necessary to understand its legal implications to lay the groundwork for the final considerations of this chapter.

5.3 TPF Main Implications: Between Disclosure and Security for Costs

The necessity to regulate the system behind the TPF has very precise practical reasons. In this sense, as mentioned above, the main consequence concerns the duty/obligation to disclose, both the existence of TPF and the details of a funding agreement. At this time, according to many international instruments, there is no such widespread obligation incumbent upon the funded party to disclose the existence—at the outset or during the arbitration proceedings—of the TPF agreement. However, it appears from the previous practice examined above, that states are increasingly pushing towards an obligation to at least disclose the major details of the agreement, but investment arbitration case-law on this matter is by no means consistent.

[146] European Parliament (Committee on Legal Affairs), 2020/2130(INL), (2021), available online https://www.europarl.europa.eu/doceo/document/JURI-PR-680934_EN.pdf.

[147] Saulnier et al. (2021).

[148] Some reference to the TPF can be found in the Directive (EU) 2020/1828 of the European Parliament and of the Council of 25 November 2020 on representative actions for the protection of the collective interests of consumers and repealing Directive 2009/22/EC, Official Journal of the European Union (2020), recital nn. 25, 52 and art. 10, para 2, (a) and 18.

[149] CJEU, Case C-248/16, Slovak Republic v. Achmea, ECLI:EU:C:2018:158.

As a matter of fact, arbitral tribunals have not found a uniform solution yet to resolve the obligation to disclose the existence of a TPF agreement. In the case S & T Oil v. Romania the Tribunal disclosed—for the first time—both the terms of the financing agreement and the identity of the funder;[150] the opposite reasoning was followed in the case Oxus Gold plc v. Republic of Uzbekistan, where the panel clarified that it was not necessary to identify the nature of the third party financing because the agreement would not affect the proceeding in any way.[151] Indeed, disclosure of the funder's identity has been ordered in few cases. In South American Silver v. Bolivia, [...] *for purposes of transparency* [...]—and considering that the claimant had not opposed disclosing the name of the funder—the tribunal ordered such disclosure by the claimant, but refused to disclose the content of funding agreement.[152] Similarly, in EuroGas v. Slovakia the tribunal ordered the claimant to disclose the identity of the funder who—as specified in its motivations—"[had] *the normal obligations of confidentiality* [...]".[153]

In contrast with the aforementioned cases, in García Armas v. Venezuela the tribunal, after an in-camera review of a redacted version of the funding agreement, went beyond ordering disclosure of the identity of the funder. Indeed, the tribunal decided to provide the respondent state the redacted version, thus protecting both parties interest at stake: on one hand, to safeguard the respondent's legitimate interest in the event of a favourable award on costs; on the other hand, to preserve claimants' legitimate interest to keep confidential certain information contained in the agreement.[154] However, one of the first cases where such agreement was found to exist was Kardassopulos and Fuchs v. Georgia,[155] where the existence of the funding agreement had been communicated to the arbitral tribunal. Notwithstanding the counterpart's arguments that it was not liable for legal fees because they were incurred by a third party unrelated to the dispute, the tribunal ruled that the existence of a funder did not affect the recoverability of the losing party's costs and ordered the respondent state to pay the established amount. Therefore, there is currently no proper obligation to disclose the existence of the TPF, as the funder is essentially not a 'party'—from a formal and substantive standpoint—to the proceedings.

---

[150] *S & T Oil Equipment and Machinery Ltd. v. Romania*, ICSID Case No ARB/07/13, Order of Discontinuance of the Proceeding (16 July 2010).

[151] *Oxus Gold plc v. Republic of Uzbekistan*, UNCITRAL Case, Final Award (17 December 2015), para 127.

[152] *South American Silver Limited v. Plurinational State of Bolivia*, PCA Case No 2013-15, Procedural Order No. 10 (11 January 2016) para 79.

[153] *EuroGas Inc and Belmont Resources Inc v. Slovak Republic*, ICSID Case No ARB/14/14, Transcript of the First Session and Hearing on Provisional Measures (17 March 2015), p. 145.

[154] *Manuel Garcia Armas et al v Bolivarian Republic of Venezuela*, UNCITRAL PCA Case No 2016-08, Procedural Order No 9, Decision on Request for Provisional Measures (original in Spanish), para 2–3.

[155] *Ioannis Kardassopoulos and Ron Fuchs v The Republic of Georgia*, ICSID Case Nos ARB/05/18 and ARB/07/15, Award (3 March 2010), para 691.

Although there are some cases where a voluntary disclosure has taken place,[156] in practice arbitral tribunals are more often the ones to order parties to disclose whether they use the TPF—for purposes related to the costs of arbitration—sometimes even adding to disclose the identity of the funder.[157] Nonetheless, there have also been some cases where the arbitral tribunals, besides disclosing the existence of the TPF and the identity of the funder, have ordered a party to reveal the content of the funding agreement as well. For instance, in Muhammet Çap. v. Turkmenistan, the state requested the disclosure of both the identity and the involvement of the third-party funders, as these matters were necessary to avoid hypothetical conflicts of interest and were necessary for a potential claim for security for costs. In that case, the tribunal—upholding the respondent state's requests—not only ordered the disclosure of the existence of the TPF and the identity of the funder, but also required the claimant to disclose the terms of the funding agreement as well, thereby creating a very important step in disclosure obligations in the matter of TPF.[158]

Considering these arbitral trends and, above all, state practice in BITs or investment treaties, it is certainly important to note that even disputes resolution centres (including arbitration institutes) are now moving forward to make disclosure mandatory for the funded party. In this sense, the recent ICC Rules of Arbitration, entered into force on January 1st 2021,[159] specify that

> [. . .] In order to assist prospective arbitrators and arbitrators in complying with their duties under Articles 11(2) and 11(3), each party must promptly inform the Secretariat, the arbitral tribunal and the other parties, of the existence and identity of any non-party which has entered into an arrangement for the funding of claims or defences and under which it has an economic interest in the outcome of the arbitration. [. . .].[160]

This is a different disclosure requirement from the more tempered disclosure requirements already in place,[161] but set from the perspective of a potential conflict of interest for arbitrators. More recently, the amended ICSID Arbitration Rules ("2022 ICSID Rules") have introduced a tailored disclosure obligation applicable throughout the arbitration proceedings. Nonetheless, some criticism[162] was raised since the new rules do not encompass any TPF guidelines going "beyond" the obligation to disclose.[163] However, in light of the above, it is reasonable to assume

---

[156] *Oxus Gold plc v. Republic of Uzbekistan,* Award, 17 December 2015.

[157] *Julio Miguel Orlandini-Agreda and Compania Minera Orlandini Ltda v. Bolivia*, Case No. 2018-39, 04.02.2019 (Procedural Order No. 1), para 11.

[158] *Muhammet Çap & Sehil In_aat Endustri ve Ticaret Ltd. Sti. v. Turkmenistan*, ICSID Case No. ARB/12/6, 12.06.2015 (Procedural Order No. 3), para 13.

[159] ICC Arbitration Rules (2021), International Chamber of Commerce.

[160] ICC Arbitration Rules (2021), article 11 para 7.

[161] For comparison, see SCC Policy disclosure of third parties with an interest in the outcome of the dispute (2019), Stockholm Chamber Commerce Board, where it is immediately specified that "[. . .] *Each party is encouraged to disclose* [. . .]", available online https://sccinstitute.com/media/1035074/scc-policy-re-third-party-interests-adopted.pdf.

[162] Portman and Muti (2022).

[163] See ICSID Arbitration Rules (2022), rule 14.

that a mandatory, prompt and full disclosure of the TPF agreement would be beneficial for all parties involved, for three main reasons.

Firstly, there would be clarity and transparency in the relationship between the funder and the funded party, in order to avoid cases where the tribunal might award costs directly to the party and the latter refuses to reimburse the funders.[164] Secondly, any conflicts of interest that might arise between the parties would be prevented at an early stage. The issue of conflicts of interest, already well known in investment arbitration, could in the case of TPF lead to difficulties of an objective nature especially for arbitrators.[165] Thirdly, it would be of great assistance to a tribunal, both in avoiding possible lengthening of the proceedings and in the decisional phase, as regards the allocation of costs in the final award.

However, if several issues regarding TPFs normally arise throughout the proceedings, in the particular context of a request for a provisional measure,[166] the funding mechanism is even more stressed. Indeed, the compatibility between TPF and security for costs represents a difficult balancing of rights that may arise in certain situations,[167] for example when a potential company finds itself in a less than positive financial situation because of the alleged illegal conduct of the state where it made the investment. As is well known, such application is made with the purpose—in those cases where there is a well-founded suspicion that one of the party may be insolvent and therefore unable to pay an adverse cost award—to request the constituted tribunal for security for cost order.[168] However, security for costs has not yet found much implementation within the TPF, therefore requiring the necessity to establish new rules governing the tripartite relationship between parties to the proceedings and third-party funders.[169]

For example, in Guaracachi Inc. v. Bolivia,[170] the respondent state requested the Tribunal the production of the TPF Agreement and further documentation, being one of the reasons behind the request for cautio judicatum solvi.[171] Although the Tribunal made it clear that

---

[164] This refers to the well-known events concerning the case *Waguih Elie George Siag and Clorinda Vecchi v. Arab Republic of Egypt*, ICSID Case No ARB/05/15, where the Tribunal decided in favour of the investor, which in turn would later have to reimburse its lawyers for financing part of the litigation. However, the company later decided to settle with the Egyptian state, thus having no obligation to reimburse the law firm, and this resulted in several difficulties and related further disputes between the company and the financing law firm.

[165] See both the IBA Guidelines on Conflicts of Interest in International Arbitration (2014), International Bar Association, General standard (7) "*Duty of the Parties and the Arbitrator*", and the recent Note to Parties and Arbitral Tribunals on the Conduct of the Arbitration (2021), International Chamber of Commerce.

[166] Pauciulo (2021), pp. 319–364.

[167] Storskrubb (2020), p. 115.

[168] Chun (2021), pp. 478–498.

[169] Shao (2021), pp. 445–447.

[170] *Guaracachi America, Inc. and Rurelec PLC v. The Plurinational State of Bolivia*, UNCITRAL, PCA Case No 2011-17.

[171] *Guaracachi America, Inc. and Rurelec PLC v. The Plurinational State of Bolivia*, UNCITRAL, PCA Case No 2011-17, Solicitud de *cautio judicatum solvi* (12 February 2013), paras 26–27.

> [. . .] The issue – analyzed by scholars and some tribunals – of the appropriate balance between the right of access to justice of entities that have been allegedly expropriated and the protection of States against alleged frivolous claims by parties who may not have sufficient assets to guarantee the payment of an adverse costs award is a serious issue [. . .][172]

However, it was specified that the role of an external funder in this case had a minimal impact on the overall analysis of the request for provisional measures—and thus the request for security for costs—by defining that the presence of a funder cannot in itself facilitate an order on costs.[173] In the case of RSM Production v. Santa Lucia, often considered as one of the most important cases on security for costs,[174] the tribunal pointed out that one of the reasons that led the arbitrators to order the payment of security for costs to the investor was precisely the presence of the third-party funder.[175]

In the end, it seems quite clear the existence of a strong connexion between the duty of disclosure and the possible request of security for costs, perfectly representing the connection among TPF mechanism with the issues concerning the right of access to justice. Indeed, in the event of an initial disclosure of the existence of the TPF, i.e., at the very beginning of the proceeding, the chance of a request to the arbitral tribunal for security for costs would be significantly reduced. Therefore, should the existence of a funder and its identity be disclosed from the outset, it would yield two types of advantages: firstly, potential conflicts of interest would be avoided from the initiation of the proceedings, facilitating the party receiving the funding; secondly, the arbitral tribunal's work would be considerably speeded up, as there would be no necessary interruption of the proceedings on the merits for a potential claim for security for costs.[176] Such an argument would only support the decision-making capabilities of the tribunal, which could therefore focus only on the merits of the claim asserted in arbitration.

6 Conclusion

Taking into account all the considerations made above, it seems appropriate to make three final remarks. First, there seems to be a trend among states to conventionally guarantee access to international litigation for the individual. However, such a

[172] *Guaracachi America, Inc. and Rurelec PLC v. The Plurinational State of Bolivia*, UNCITRAL, PCA Case No 2011-17, Procedural Order No. 14 (11 March 2013), para 9.

[173] *Guaracachi America, Inc. and Rurelec PLC v. The Plurinational State of Bolivia*, UNCITRAL, PCA Case No 2011-17, Procedural Order No. 14 (11 March 2013), paras. 6–10.

[174] Rosenfeld (2016), pp. 160–166.

[175] *RSM Production Corp v Saint Lucia*, ICSID Case No ARB/12/10, Decision on Saint Lucia's Request for Security for Costs (13 August 2014), para 83.

[176] Or, in the event of a request for security for costs, the tribunal's decision would be processed more rapidly, as it would not be necessary to disclose—as already known—both the existence of the TPF and the identity of the Funder.

guarantee often clashes with practical challenges, among them those related to the high costs of arbitration. These difficulties are intensified in the area of ISDS and commercial arbitration, as the investor is often at a crossroads: on the one hand, initiate arbitration to obtain compensation for possible violations committed by the investment's host state, thereby cumulating the associated costs plus any economic losses already suffered; on the other hand, bear the costs of the losses incurred as a result of the foreign investment and not worsen his financial situation by initiating arbitration proceedings.

In the first scenario, large multinational corporations should not face many problems in bearing the losses incurred because of the failed foreign investment, although in the event of an unfavourable arbitration award, these could be rather high financial losses. Clearly, this kind of scenario would be difficult to realise in the case of SMEs, hence jeopardising access to justice. In the second scenario, high costs would be a strong reason for hindering access to justice, with consequences that could therefore also undermine the investor's economic activity. Consequently, facilitating access to justice for investors, using the TPF, could be a solution to overcome the issue of high costs. However, it may not necessarily be the case that the TPF represents a useful tool only for SMEs or investors in financial difficulty. Indeed, according to a recent study, TPF should be a tool made available to all investors, thus substantiating its nature as a commercial decision, and not based on the investor's willingness to pay.[177] These considerations can only lead to one conclusion: TPF is a commercial solution that consequently may enhance access to justice for the investor by facilitating access to commercial and investment arbitration.

Secondly, if the TPF is understood to be a commercial decision, this means that it falls within the 'risks' the investor undertakes in its commercial operations. Although TPF should therefore be guaranteed, there are practical difficulties that not always make it an easy instrument to implement. In the light of the research carried out, these difficulties could be shortened in two stages, which are successive and consequential. The first difficulty may be found in the "identification of the funder". This activity is often left to the lawyers who look after the investor's interests or to the investor himself. Therefore, this is a challenge related to the lack of knowledge of the market where funders operate, which could result in a high expenditure of time, increasing costs for the investor.

The successive problem, once the funder has been identified, consists in the necessity for the investor to engage in actual negotiations to reach an agreement. Thus, this phase could be summarised as the "funder's discretion" because they will carry out due diligence research, often aimed, for example, at identifying: the arguments in favour and against the investor in a potential litigation; determining the balance between the costs of funding and the benefits should the investor win or lose in any arbitration procedure; and assessing the advisability of supporting the investor's lawyers with lawyers of its own choice. Therefore, these developments

[177] QMUL-CCIAG Survey: Investors' Perceptions of ISDS (2020), p. 18.

could lead to two consequences: on the one hand, the funder could decide against financing the investor in the dispute, de facto slowing down—or sometimes even precluding—access to justice; on the other hand, the funder could eventually decide to finance the dispute, assuming a discrete control in the management of the case, marginalising the role—and thus the choices, including in litigation—of the investor. Accordingly, these considerations make it even more evident that, although the TPF facilitates access to justice, it is still a commercial decision that entails risks—which may often materialise at the litigation stage—that need to be mitigated at the outset of negotiations to reach an agreement.

Lastly, while it is true that the TPF may facilitate investor's access to justice, it is nevertheless evident that—in the litigation phase—this mechanism could become a tool that might even undermine the entire procedure. The greatest risk, in this respect, would arise in the event of a conflict of interest between the funder and one of the arbitrators composing the arbitral tribunal, which could subsequently lead—depending on the case—to a suspension, revision or annulment of an arbitral award. To avoid these risks while ensuring access to justice through TPF, certain considerations on disclosure should be made. Assuming that there are conventional instruments forbidding the use of TPF or describing, to a greater or lesser extent, the various disclosure obligations of the funded party, it is necessary to address the hypothesis that the IIAs do not indicate the TPF mechanism at all. Therefore, to ensure that the TPF agreement guarantees effective access to justice—considering the orientation of the arbitral tribunals and the different provisions recalled governing the functioning of the TPF—the following approach could be envisaged.

Once the decision to initiate arbitration proceedings has been made, the funded party could provide notification of the existence of the TPF agreement and disclose the identity of the funder from the outset, e.g., already in the "notice of intent". This strategy could be defined as "prompt and voluntary disclosure" and may be derived from the principle of good faith, in a twofold capacity: both in the execution of the international agreement (i.e., substantial-good faith) and in the application of the agreement (i.e., procedural good faith). Such a strategy, in light of the scope of these obligations, could therefore create to the funded party certain benefits, such as: the immediate disclosure to the other party of the presence of a funder; the anticipation of possible conflicts of interest once the arbitral tribunal is constituted, also facilitating the work of the two arbitrators appointed by the parties in identifying a presiding arbitrator; and the reduction of the possibility of interrupting the proceedings by requesting provisional measures.

Clearly, providing this information does not mean conducting a "full disclosure" of the TPF. Indeed, the details of the TPF agreement—concerning e.g., costs, case management, and the funder's profit percentage in the event of a favourable award—would not be disclosed at all, thus ensuring absolute confidentiality. Such a strategy, subject to particular situations applied on a case-by-case basis, would allow the investor to: *(1)* overcome the problem of high costs by succeeding in enforcing his—conventionally recognised—right of access to justice; *(2)* avoid that the TPF agreement could be used as a tool to enforce potential conflicts of interest between the parties involved.

References

Acconci P (2012) Most-favoured-nation treatment. In: Muchlinski P, Ortino F, Schreuer C (eds) The Oxford handbook of international investment law. Oxford Academic, Oxford
Aitala RS (2021) Diritto internazionale penale. Le Monnier Università, Firenze
Alarcon MJ (2020) ICSID reform: balancing the scales? Kluwer Arbitration Blog. DIALOG. https://arbitrationblog.kluwerarbitration.com/2022/01/28/icsid-reform-balancing-the-scales/
Assareh A (2012) Forum shopping and the cost of access to justice-cost and certainty in international commercial litigation and arbitration. J Law Comm 31:1–44
Bantekas I (2004) Corporate social responsibility in international law. Boston Univ Int Law J 22: 309
Barendrecht M, Mulder J, Giesen I (2006) How to measure the price and quality of access to justice?
Bayefsky AF (2017) The principle of equality or non-discrimination in international law. In: Farrior S (ed) Equality and non-discrimination under international law. Routledge, London, pp 71–104
Bekker P, Ogawa A (2013) The impact of Bilateral Investment Treaty (BIT) proliferation on demand for investment insurance: reassessing political risk insurance after the 'BIT Bang'. ICSID Rev 28(2):314–350
Benedettelli M, Consolo C, Radicati di Brozolo L (2017) Commentario breve al diritto dell'arbitrato nazionale ed internazionale. Wolters Kluwer Italia, CEDAM, Milano
Bjorklund A, Vanhonnaeker L (2021) Applicable law in international investment arbitration. In: Lim C (ed) The Cambridge companion to international arbitration (Cambridge companions to law). Cambridge University Press, Cambridge, pp 225–243
Boisson de Chazournes L, McLachlan C (2016) Preface-the intersection of investment arbitration and public international law. ICSID Rev 31(2):255–256
Bottini G, Titi C, Aznar FP, Chaisse J, Jovanovic M, Sola OP (2020) Excessive costs and recoverability of costs awards in investment arbitration. J World Invest Trade 21(2-3):251–299
Bradfield M, Verdirame G (2014) Costs in investment treaty arbitration. In: Giorgetti C (ed) Litigating international disputes. Martinus Nijhoff, Leiden, pp 411–434
Brown BS (1992) The protection of human rights in disintegrating states: a new challenge. Chic Kent Law Rev 68:203
Bühler MW (2005) Costs of arbitration: some further considerations. In: Aksen G, Briner R (eds) Global reflections on international law, commerce and dispute resolution Liber Amicorum in Honour of Robert Briner. ICC Publication, pp 179–190
Bungenberg M, Reinisch A (2022) CETA investment law: article-by-article commentary. Nomos, Baden-Baden
Butler P, Herbert C (2014) Access to justice for small and medium sized enterprises: the case for a bilateral arbitration treaty. N Z Univ Law Rev 26(2):186–221
Camilleri SP (2021) Between rags and riches: rethinking security for costs in international commercial arbitration. Arbitr Int 37(4):851–862
Chavez RB (2008) The rule of law and courts in democratizing regimes. In: Caldeira GA, Kelemen RD, Whittington KE (eds) The Oxford handbook of law and politics. (online edn). Oxford Academic, Oxford
Chun YH (2021) 'Security for costs' under the ICSID regime: does it prevent 'arbitral hit-and-runs' or does it unduly stifle third-party funded investors' due process rights? Pepp Disput Resolut Law J 21:477
Crawford J, Brownlie I (2019) Brownlie's principles of public international law. Oxford University Press, New York
de Oliveira LVP, Hourani S (2020) Access to justice in arbitration: concept, context and practice. Wolters Kluwer
Deva S, Van Ho T (2023) Addressing (in)equality in redress: human rights-led reform of the investor-state dispute settlement mechanism. J World Invest Trade 24(3):398–436
Dörr O (2005) Privatisierung "des Völkerrechts". JuristenZeitung 60:905–916

Dumberry P (2014) Denial of justice under NAFTA Article 1105: a review of 20 years of case law. ASA Bull 32(2)

Elkins Z, Guzman AT, Simmons BA (2006) Competing for capital: the diffusion of bilateral investment treaties, 1960–2000. Int Organ 60(4):811–846

Fach Gómez K, Titi C (2023) Facilitating access to Investor-State Dispute Settlement for small and medium-sized enterprises: tracing the path forward. Eur Bus Law Rev 34(7) (forthcoming)

Fanou M (2020) The CETA ICS and the autonomy of the EU legal order in opinion 1/17 – a compass for the future. Camb Yearb Eur Leg Stud 22:106–132

Focarelli C (2012) Denial of justice. In: Encyclopedia of public international law. Oxford University Press, Oxford

Francioni F (1975) Compensation for nationalisation of foreign property: the borderland between law and equity. Int Comp Law Q 24(2):255–283

Franck SD (2019) Arbitration costs: myths and realities in investment treaty arbitration. Oxford University Press, Oxford

Garcia FJ (2018) Third-party funding as exploitation of the investment treaty system. Boston Coll Law Rev 59:2911

Gärditz KF (2014) Bridge of Varvarin. Am J Int Law 108(1):86–93

Gáspár-Szilágyi S (2013) EU Member State enforcement of 'mixed' agreements and access to justice: rethinking direct effect. Leg Issues Econ Integr 40(2):163–189

Gáspár-Szilágyi S (2020) Let us not forget about the role of domestic courts in settling investor-state disputes. Law Pract Int Courts Trib 18(3):389–415

Gaukrodger D, Gordon K (2012) Investor-state dispute settlement: a scoping paper for the investment policy community. OECD Working Papers on International Investment. https://www.oecd-ilibrary.org/finance-and-investment/investor-state-dispute-settlement_5k46b1r85j6f-en

Gebert A (2017) Legal protection for small and medium-sized enterprises through investor-state dispute settlement: status quo, impediments, and potential solutions. In: Rensmann T (ed) Small and medium-sized enterprises in international economic law. Oxford Academic, Oxford, pp 291–308

Gerards JH, Glas LR (2017) Access to justice in the European Convention on Human Rights system. Neth Q Hum Rights 35(1):11–30

Giorgetti C (2018) Rethinking the individual in international law. Lewis Clark Law Rev 22:1085

Giorgetti C (2019) The selection and removal of arbitrators in Investor-state Dispute Settlement. Brill, Leiden

Gramatikov M (2009) A framework for measuring the costs of paths to justice. J Juris 2:111

Guven B, Johnson L (2019) The policy implications of third-party funding in investor-state dispute settlement. Columbia Center on Sustainable Investment, CCSI Working Paper

Higgins R (1978) Conceptual thinking about the individual in international law. Rev Int Stud 4(1): 1–19

Hodgson M, Kryvoi Y, Hrcka D (2021) Empirical study: costs, damages and duration in investor-state arbitration. The British Institute of International and Comparative Law (BIICL). DIALOG. https://www.biicl.org/publications/empirical-study-costs-damages-and-duration-in-investor-state-arbitration

Hollis DB (2005) Why state consent still matters-non-state actors, treaties, and the changing sources of international law. Berkeley J Int Law 23:137

Kalyanpur N, Newman A (2021) The financialization of international law. Perspect Polit 19(3): 773–790

Kammerhofer J (2021) International investment law and legal theory: expropriation and the fragmentation of sources, vol 158. Cambridge University Press, Cambridge

Karl J (2017) Enterprises in international investment law. In: Rensmann T (ed) Small and medium-sized enterprises in international economic law. Oxford Academic, Oxford, pp 241–266

Korzun V (2017) The right to regulate in investor-state arbitration: slicing and dicing regulatory carve-outs. Vand J Transnatl Law 50(2):355–414

Kotlik M (2017) Defying the theoretical constraints of state-centric approaches: a review of non-state actors in international law. Isr Law Rev 50(1):87–105

Kudrna J (2013) Arbitration and right of access to justice: tips for a successful marriage. New York University Journal of International Law and Politics (JILP) Online Forum. https://blogs.law.nyu.edu/transnational/2013/02/arbitration-and-right-of-access-to-justice-tips-for-a-successful-marriage/

Latham S, Ventures A (2022) The third party litigation funding law review, 6th edn. The Law Reviews

Mauro MR (2019) Diritto internazionale dell'economia. Teoria e prassi delle relazioni economiche internazionali. Edizioni Scientifiche Italiane, Napoli

Mills A (2013) Rethinking jurisdiction in international law. Br Yearb Int Law 84(1):187–239

Nam J (2017) Model bit: an ideal prototype or tool for efficient breach. Georget J Int Law 48 (4):1275–1308

Nyombi C, Mortimer T (2018) Rights and obligations in the post investment treaty denunciation period. Int Arbitr Law Rev 21(2):46–53

Padilla C (2011) Denial of justice to foreign investors. Cuad der transl 3(1):296–301

Palombino FM (2018) Fair and equitable treatment and the fabric of general principles. T.M.C. Asser Press/Springer, The Hague/Berlin

Palombino FM (2020) Revisiting the 'humanization of international law' argument through the lens of international investment law. Dir comm internaz 2020(3):745–750

Park WW, Rogers CA (2015) Third-party funding in international arbitration: the ICCA Queen-Mary Task Force. Austrian Yearb Int Arbitr:14–67

Pauciulo D (2021) Provisional measures in ICSID arbitration proceedings: between the current legal framework and the proposed reform. In: Palombino FM, Virzo R, Zarra G (eds) Provisional measures issued by international courts and tribunals. Springer, pp 319–364

Paulsson J (2005) Denial of justice in international law, vol 17. Cambridge University Press, Cambridge

Peters A, Koechlin L, Förster T, Zinkernagel GF (eds) (2009) Non-state actors as standard setters. Cambridge University Press, Cambridge

Portman S, Muti N (2022) Increased transparency under the new ICSID rules: a way forward for ISDS legitimacy. Jus Mundi Blog. Available via DIALOG. https://blog.jusmundi.com/increased-transparency-under-the-new-icsid-rules-a-way-forward-for-isds-legitimacy/. Accessed 12 Jun 2023

Pustorino P (2022) Tutela internazionale dei diritti umani. Cacucci Editore, Bari

Pustorino P (2023) Introduction to international human rights law. T.M.C. Asser Press, The Hague

QMUL-CCIAG Survey: Investors' Perceptions of ISDS (2020). https://arbitration.qmul.ac.uk/media/arbitration/docs/QM-CCIAG-Survey-ISDS-2020.pdf

Rosenfeld F (2016) Security for costs in ICSID arbitration: *RSM Production Corporation v St Lucia*. Arbitr Int 32(1):157–166

Santosuosso T, Scarlett R (2018) Third-party funding in investment arbitration: misappropriation of access to justice rhetoric by global speculative finance. Boston Coll Law Rev 60:8

Saulnier J, Koronthalyova I, Müller K (2021) Responsible private funding of litigation: European added value assessment. EPRS | European Parliamentary Research Service. DIALOG. https://www.europarl.europa.eu/RegData/etudes/STUD/2021/662612/EPRS_STU(2021)662612_EN.pdf

Schreuer C, Kriebaum U, Dolzer R (2022) Principles of international investment law. Oxford University Press, Oxford

Shao X (2021) Disrupt the Gambler's Nirvana: security for costs in investment arbitration supported by third-party funding. J Int Disput Settlement 12(3):427–447

Sitaraman S (2016) State participation in international treaty regimes. Routledge, London

Solas GM (2019) Third party funding. Cambridge University Press, Cambridge

Spiegel HW (1938) Origin and development of denial of justice. Am J Int Law 32(1):63–81

Sterio M (2008) The evolution of international law. Boston Coll Int Comp Law Rev 31:213

Storskrubb E (2020) Emergency arbitration: a maturing and evolving procedure. In: Calissendorff A, Schöldström P (eds) Stockholm arbitration yearbook 2020. Wolters Kluwer

Storskrubb E, Ziller J (2007) Access to justice in European comparative law. In: Francioni F (ed) Access to justice as a human right. Oxford University Press, Oxford, pp 177–203

Tanzi A (2020) On judicial autonomy and the autonomy of the parties in international adjudication, with special regard to investment arbitration and ICSID annulment proceedings. Leiden J Int Law 33(1):57–75

Titi C (2014) The right to regulate in international investment law. Hart, Oxford

Trindade AAC (2011) The access of individuals to international justice. Oxford Academic, Oxford

UNDP, HDR (2005) Programming for justice: access for all. A practitioner's guide to a human rights-based approach to access to justice. Bangkok. https://www.asia-pacific.undp.org/content/rbap/en/home/library/democratic_governance/programming-for-justice.html

Van Harten G, Malysheuski P (2022) Who has benefited financially from investment treaty arbitration? An evaluation of the size and wealth of claimants. In: Behn D, Fauchald O, Langford M (eds) The legitimacy of investment arbitration: empirical perspectives (studies on international courts and tribunals). Cambridge University Press, Cambridge, pp 394–423

Vandevelde KJ (2017) The first bilateral investment treaties: US postwar friendship, commerce and navigation treaties. Oxford University Press, Oxford

Vargiu P (2021) Stakeholders of investment arbitration: establishing a dialogue among arbitrators, states, investors, academics and other actors in international investment law. In: Fach Gómez K (ed) Private actors in international investment law. Springer, pp 5–25

Viñuales JE (2014) Sovereignty in foreign investment law. In: Douglas Z, Viñuales JE, Pauwelyn J (eds) The foundations of international investment law. Oxford University Press, Oxford, pp 317–362

Viñuales JE (2017) Sources of international investment law: conceptual foundations of unruly practices. In: Besson S, d'Aspremont J (eds) The Oxford handbook of the sources of international law. Oxford Academic, Oxford, pp 1069–1094

Viñuales JE, Gaeta P, Zappalá S (2020) Cassese's international law. Oxford University Press, Oxford

Walton J, Williams DA (2014) Costs and access to international arbitration. Int J Arbitr Med Disput Manag 80(4)

Yackee J (2019) Investor-State Dispute Settlement at the dawn of international investment law: France, Mauritania, and the nationalization of the MIFERMA iron ore operations. Am J Leg Hist 59(1):71–110

Part II : General Part

Protecting Social Rights: A Fine Balance Between the 'Golden Rule' and the 'Golden Principle' in Greece

Styliani Christoforidou

Contents

Abstract This paper will examine the way that the constitutional protection of decent living emerged in the Greek legal order, initially through constitutional interpretation and after through constitutionalization in the recent constitutional amendment, all against a backdrop of severe budgetary deficits and strict financial obligations. The paper will first provide the context and background on state social policy up to the beginnings of the financial debt crisis in 2011. Thereafter, the discussion will turn to the crisis period itself and the fiscal EMU rules, and in particular the Golden Rule which obliged the adoption of austerity measures that adversely impacted social rights. Compliance with the Golden Rule found a counterbalance in the decent living principle as far the protection of social rights was concerned. The broad scope and means of implementing the decent living principle rendered as a Golden Principle in the face of the austerity measures adopted for financial reasons and placed a severe burden on social rights. Through the interpretive construction of the principle of fiscal sustainability, the courts found the way to implement the content of the Golden Rule which is not constitutionalized in the

S. Christoforidou
Hellenic Open University, Patra, Greece
e-mail: christoforidou.styliani@ac.eap.gr

E. Storskrubb (ed.), *YSEC Yearbook of Socio-Economic Constitutions 2022*,
YSEC Yearbook of Socio-Economic Constitutions (2023) 2022: 323–340,
https://doi.org/10.1007/16495_2023_47, Published online: 11 May 2023

Greek legal order. Rather, eventually it was the Golden Principle that found its way to constitutionalization after 10 years of systematic implementation by the national courts under the judicial review of the constitutionality of the austerity measures. Finally, this paper will endeavour to show how the Golden Rule and Golden Principle—the former through constitutional interpretation, the latter through constitutionalization—established post-crisis a balance between the dual needs of establishing a robust state budget while maintaining strong social protection and social justice.

1 Introduction

1.1 The Protection of Social Rights Before the Financial Crisis

Until the outbreak of the financial crisis in 2008 going back the mid-70s Greek governments followed more or less the Keynesian model for the adopted socioeconomic policies. Through the expenditure of the state budget financed by loans from the private sector, the national economy was enhanced in various ways. Wages, mostly in the public sector, pensions, benefits, and other forms of cash income were provided by the state in order to stimulate consumption and strengthen the internal market. Additionally, the state retained for itself public enterprises, provided public services at low cost for users (i.e. public transportation, energy etc.), as well as universal social services in sectors such as health and education with free access to the citizens.[1]

Under State protectionism and intervention to protect the social whole, the state took initiatives—principally nationalization—to shield so called 'troubled' businesses engaged in activities of social and public interest. Law 1386/1983 "On the Organization for Economic Reconstruction of Businesses" provided that in cases of failing businesses, the management came under the Organization for the Economic Reconstruction of Businesses which operated under the supervision of the state.[2] The Organization served the public and social interest of establishing the financial consolidation of such a business. Beyond the significance of the services provided for the social whole on the socio-political level, rescuing failing companies also took on the goal of saving jobs and protecting their employees.

This then was a period (1975–2008) marked, in contrast with the time of the financial crisis and after, by the protection of social rights passing primarily through legislative initiative and adopted socio-economic policies towards intervention into

[1] Chrysogonos and Vlachopoulos (2017), p. 382.

[2] Chrysogonos and Vlachopoulos (2017), p. 236.

the markets, relying much less on judicial protection.[3] Exercising judicial control to protect social rights mainly focused on the part concerning benefits policy towards citizens, whereby, in application of the general principle of equality, it was reviewed whether certain groups of the population with identical features were being unjustifiably excluded from receiving benefits enjoyed by other population groups.[4] It should however be stressed that these state-centric policies, aiming at social growth in conjunction with an expanded public sector, according to the Greek literature are associated with populist agendas to ensure the re-election of the government of the day, and are accused of creating the budgetary deficits that led to the financial crisis.[5]

During this period, in 2001, Greece became a member of the Eurozone where strict fiscal rules apply.[6] Greece had always been blighted by fiscal mismanagement and budgetary deficits.[7] Very soon after joining Eurozone, the country was put under the excessive deficit procedure. In particular, in 2004, the Council confirmed the existence of an excessive deficit in Greece.[8] This was the first time that Greece went through this procedure. The second time, the most crucial, was in 2009,[9] where the Council decided that an excessive deficit had existed in Greece since 2007 as revealed by the October 2008 correction of notified data.

1.2 The Financial Crisis as a Turning Point for the Adoption of the Golden Rule and the Golden Principle

The outbreak of the global financial crisis in 2008 found Greece with budgetary deficits and with serious debts that lead to loss of credibility of the world markets.[10] In order to restore credibility and regain the interest of private sector investments, as well as to safeguard the sustainability of the euro area, three bailout programs were

[3]This is of interest since it reappeared once more during the pandemic, whereby the state adopts anew the policy of benefit support to support those people adversely affected by the measures taken to protect public health, that is to say, companies, the self-employed and workers whose stores and offices remained closed to stop the spread of COVID-19.

[4]Papadopoulou (2004), p. 4.

[5]Petrakos et al. (2021), p. 33.

[6]See Article 126 of the Treaty on Functioning of the European Union (TFEU) together with the Protocol No 12 on the excessive deficit procedure 12008M/PRO/12, Official Journal 115, 09/05/2008 P. 0279–0280.

[7]Papadopoulou (2014), p. 224.

[8]2004/917/EC: Council Decision of 5 July 2004 on the existence of an excessive deficit in Greece. ELI: http://data.europa.eu/eli/dec/2004/917/oj.

[9]2009/415/EC: Council Decision of 27 April 2009 on the existence of an excessive deficit in Greece. ELI: http://data.europa.eu/eli/dec/2009/415/oj.

[10]Pagoulatos (2018), p. 6.

applied in Greece as a debt country, the so-called Economic Adjustment Programs.[11] The first program agreed in 2010 between Member States of the eurozone, the International Monetary Fund (IMF) and Greece, the second one in 2012 between the IMF, the European Financial Stability Facility (EFSF) and Greece, and the third one in 2015 with the European Stability Mechanism (ESM).[12] All three programs paved the way for fiscal consolidation according to the EMU fiscal rules, the financial crisis having spread rapidly to more eurozone countries, through the adoption of the six-pack and two-pack measures and the international Treaty on Stability, Coordination and Governance in the Economic and Monetary Union (TSCG).[13] The main rule of the TSCG is for a balanced state budget and the obligation of the state to adopt the balanced budget obligation in the domestic legal order, preferably in the Constitution, the so-called Fiscal Compact, also known as the Golden Rule.[14]

This same Golden Rule was not eventually adopted in the Constitution, as will be examined in part two, albeit there was an intervening constitutional review in 2019. Despite that, its supremacy over legislative law is not doubted as evidenced by a raft of fiscal measures taken on and aimed at complying with this rule. Indeed, the courts recognized the importance of prioritizing the country's economic rescue, at least, at the first years of financial crisis, as will be analysed in the same part. The Greek Court of Audit shaped through constitutional interpretation the "Principle of Fiscal Sustainability", being the closest expression of the Golden Rule at a constitutional level, while at the same time accepting that said constitutional principle does not have precedence over other constitutional principles, including that of the human dignity principle. Thus, as will be examined in part three, when the adopted financial measures began to seriously impinge on a series of social rights, the courts formulated interpretively the notion of decent living, which functions as a constitutional limitation to the adopted financial policies.

The protection of decent living initially finds its legal grounds in Article 2(1) of the Constitution which establishes the human dignity principle, which was later enshrined in the Constitution through the constitutional review of 2019. It does not follow that this constitutionalization vitiates the Golden Rule or alters the quality of the protection of social rights, which is based on the formulation of the new constitutional provision emerging from a system of minimum guaranteed income. However, as this study argues, this constitutes the coalescence of two opposing obligations of the state, whereby the honouring of one obligation finds as the limit the honouring of the other. In other words, this is the expression of mutual compromise at a constitutional level, and thus the principle of decent living is characterised in this paper as the Golden Principle.

---

[11] Ruffert (2020), p. 35.

[12] Pagoulatos (2018), p. 7.

[13] Peers (2012), p. 404.

[14] Adams et al. (2014), p. 2; Papadopoulou (2014), p. 230.

This study seeks to highlight the way in which decent living, that is to say, the Golden Principle, mediates in a period, that of economic crisis, between the retreat of social protection and the application of strict fiscal rules, employing the analytical method and monitoring the course of social rights through the implementation of the rules of fiscal discipline on the one hand and judicial protection of social rights on the other.

2 The Golden Rule in the Greek Legal Order

2.1 The Legal Status and Implementation in the Field of Social Rights

It is of some interest that the adoption of the Golden Rule according to Article 3 of the TSCG was preferable at the constitutional level.[15] Since the ratification of the Treaty, Member States must follow the legally binding rules provided. Insofar as concerns the Greek legal order, according to Article 28 of the Greek Constitution, international treaties once ratified are considered as part of domestic law and cannot be repealed by any national legal provision.[16] The TSCG was ratified by Law 4063/2012, and therefore, the Golden Rule can be considered as a legally binding provision of the national legal order. Besides, the pressure exercised at the political level was so great vis-à-vis the risk of state bankruptcy that it was absolutely certain that the political leadership of the country would follow the instructions of the lenders.[17] Indeed, hundreds of legislative measures were adopted under the requirements of the lenders to achieve fiscal consolidation according to fiscal rules of the European Monetary Union (EMU).[18]

In particular, according to the first Article of Law 3845/2010 "Measures for the implementation of the support mechanism of the Greek economy by Member States of the Eurozone and the International Monetary Fund", parts of this law appear in the Declaration of the 25th March 2010 between the Member States of the Eurozone. Under this Declaration, a support mechanism for the economic and fiscal stability of the euro area would be created. Under the Declaration of 11th April 2010 of the Member States of the Eurozone, it was decided that this mechanism be activated to support Greece, and the program 'Economic and Financial Policy Memorandum and Memorandum of Understanding in the Specific Economic Policy Conditions' would be implemented for this support. In the following years, the TSCG was ratified by Law 4063/2012, as already mentioned, two more Memoranda of Understanding

[15] Papadopoulou (2014), p. 240.

[16] Venizelos (2021), p. 163; Contiades et al. (2019), p. 676.

[17] For another perspective, i.e. the problem of conditionality of the "new economic governance" in the eurozone, see Poulou (2014), pp. 1148–1154.

[18] Contiades and Tassopoulos (2013), p. 197.

were adopted under laws 4046/2012 and 4336/2015, and the Medium-Term Fiscal Strategy Framework 2012–2015 were adopted under Law 3986/2011.[19]

Among the measures adopted under Law 3845/2010 were apprenticeship contracts for workers up to the age of 24 with a minimum wage 20% less than the minimum wage, the increase of the redundancy limit in cases of collective redundancies, the calculation of the amount and the manner of payment of redundancy compensation, employment conditions and the minimum wage for young people under the age of 25 entering the labor market for the first time.[20] Law 4172/2013 abolished collective bargaining regarding wages in the private sector while the minimum wage was set by law according to the poverty threshold and taking into consideration the economic growth and the financial stability of the enterprise.[21]

Apart from the measures that changed the legal framework of labor and increased employer flexibility, also adopted were measures to reduce public spending. All wages in the private and public sector, pensions, and benefits were reduced while some benefits were completely abolished. The pension system was re-structured radically, the retirement age increased, and pensions were calculated based on the poverty threshold.[22]

Through the adopted measures, an attempt was made to increase public revenue. All indirect taxes rose, some tax exemptions regarding direct income tax were abolished and tax scales changed, losing their proportional character. For example, all the self-employed without exception were targeted for tax evasion. Due to the irrefutable presumption of tax evasion, they were charged with additional income tax, the so-called minimum income tax, which was imposed in addition to the income tax of individuals, even if they had made losses (Article 31 Law 3986/2011). More precisely, all the self-employed burdened with a same amount of tax, regardless their personal tax capacity, tax burden that according to the Court does not violate the tax justice and equality principle, because based on common experience and the extent of the tax evasion phenomenon, everyone is able to fulfill this tax obligation.[23]

Because of this treatment, legal entities enjoyed more favorable tax treatment than that of the self-employed, despite the fact that they, as natural persons, are protected by the human dignity principle. Furthermore, in 2013, regarding the incomes of the self-employed, the tax scale that applied provided that every income between 1 euro and 50,000 euros was burdened with 26% income tax, which in practical terms means that the poor and the rich were treated in the same way without any exception

---

[19] Venizelos (2020), p. 296.

[20] See for an extended analysis, Poulou (2014), pp. 1161–1169.

[21] Achtsioglou and Doherty (2014), p. 220.

[22] According to the explanatory memorandum to the law "Unified Social Security System - Insurance-pension system reform" (page 2), "[The] establishing of the national pension at 384 euros was based on 60% of earnings according to the European Union", whose rules refer to the quantitative techniques of poverty measurement. In fact, 60% of the [median equivalent] income is the poverty threshold.

[23] Greek Council of State [GC] 2527/2013, para 14.

for covering the basic needs. In addition, a new tax on real estate was adopted through Law 4223/2013, which burdened even the property used as the main residence. Consequently, rented houses raised the problem of homelessness. Other measures included liberalizing 'closed' professions, such as the lifting of the restrictions on the minimum wage for lawyers or the minimum distance between pharmacies, enhancing the private sector, mostly through privatizing public infrastructure and other public assets, simplifying and accelerating the licensing process of companies, industrial activities and professions, and liberalizing the activities of the electricity and gas sectors.

The aim of all these measures was initially to reduce the state budget deficit and, gradually, to balance the budgets without creating deficits, aligning the state function with the European fiscal rules as a whole, regardless the source of the (binding) rule (MoU, Fiscal Compact, etc.).[24] However, these measures drastically changed the social policies adopted up to that point, destabilizing the social safety net and hugely impacting the standards of living,[25] leading a significant portion of the population into poverty and many companies to bankruptcy.

All in all, through the abolition of state protectionism, what was mostly at stake was the welfare state as a social safeguard. Social justice, mainly redistributive justice, was also put in doubt, mostly due to the adopted tax system that no longer could be considered as proportional despite the constitutional obligation of Article 4 (5) of the Greek Constitution.[26] From this point of view, fiscal EMU rules did not only narrow the range of appreciation regarding the adoption of fiscal policies as such from an abstract or theoretical point of view,[27] but, because of the limited actual capacity of the Government to adopt effective social policies to address the severe social problems that emerged,[28] put at risk the real social peace and cohesion. Within this context, the adopted deregulation measures and the opening up to the free global market did not actually create new opportunities for the citizens, but for foreign investors, because citizens by losing the social protection net, also lost their business capacity. From the perspective of protecting social rights, the self-employed, small and very small enterprises and/or sole traders, all of which make up a characteristic feature of the Greek economy, were unable to seek protection through the courts. What was attempted in general terms was to protect judicially the amount of various forms of income in terms of the protection of a decent living, as analysed below.[29]

In this context, the question regarding the adoption of the Golden Rule at the constitutional level is not so crucial given that its binding force is not questioned while, at the same time, a judicial review of constitutionality is rather difficult to

[24] Contiades et al. (2019), p. 679.

[25] Contiades and Tassopoulos (2013), p. 198.

[26] See for the constitutional obligation of the tax progressivity Karagiorgas (1981), p. 278.

[27] Calliess (2012), p. 104; Fabbrini (2013).

[28] Despite the fact that the austerity measures appeared as products of national legislation, as Poulou points out (2017), p. 1015.

[29] See at Sect. 3.

perform while measures are actually being adopted which burden the state budget. The legal status that the Golden Rule enjoys based on the Article 28 of the Greek Constitution is quite similar to the status of constitutional provisions. The Golden Rule as content of the ratified treaty has precedence over national legal provisions, which means that these provisions cannot include content contrary to its own. That said, the constitutionalization of the Golden Rule would not ensure precedence of any kind over other constitutional principles and rules.

2.2 *The Problem of Adjudication. Towards the Social Rights' Protection*

Though in theory it could be argued that the exercise of a judicial review of constitutionality regarding the compliance of national law with the Golden Rule cannot in principle be excluded,[30] the main problem regarding the adjudication of the Golden Rule is that in the Greek legal order there is no Constitutional Court, which entails that the judicial control that is exercised is, in principle, *ex post* and *in concreto.*[31] In other words, the problem of the judicial enforceability of the Golden Rule is that measures that could possibly breach the content of the rule cannot come before the national courts because it is very difficult for an applicant to establish its personal legal interest and to prove personal damage because of those measures.[32] Furthermore, financial policy is a political matter which requires that the judge abstain from it.[33] Most crucially, the Golden Rule does not bring any rights to citizens, which, were this the case, judicial control would be exercised for their protection.[34]

In contrast, the implementation of the Golden Rule did have a severe impact on social rights which led to citizens seeking protection before the national courts, based their claims on the violation of the human dignity principle (Article 2(1) Gr. Const.) and the Article 1 of the First Protocol of the ECHR. Hence, the social rights' judicial protection took an income-based turn, far from the general principle of equality,[35] by seeking the grounds for the adjudication of the social rights in the legal nature of each income as property.

In light of the above, the Golden Rule came before the national courts because they had to exercise judicial review of the constitutionality of the austerity measures regarding social rights linked with some kind of an income, such as cuts in pensions, salaries etc. Among the three Supreme Courts of the Greek judicial system (the

[30] Papadopoulou (2014), p. 244.

[31] Vlachopoulos (2019), p. 8.

[32] See for the judicial system of the control of constitutionality, Skouris (1989), p. 180.

[33] Contiades et al. (2019), p. 669.

[34] Vlachopoulos (2019), p. 10.

[35] See above at Sect. 1.1.

Council of State for disputes under public law,[36] Areios Pagos for disputes under private law,[37] the Court of Audit for control of state expenses[38]), only the Court of Audit attempted to construct interpretively a legal rule with a content similar to the Golden Rule, named the principle of fiscal sustainability. The Council of State and Areios Pagos treated the fiscal problem as a fact, mainly as an emergency situation,[39] without any attempt to move towards a legalization of the concept.[40] In other words, it was the emergency in Greece's fiscal situation, according to jurisprudence, that offered the grounds to justify the adopted austerity measures and not any legally binding force that created the obligation to adopt such measures.[41]

Only a little later was this emergency transformed by the Council of State to the so-called "fiscal interest", a kind of overriding public interest,[42] which means a

[36] Article 94 para 1 of the Greek Constitution: "1. The Supreme Administrative Court and ordinary administrative courts shall have jurisdiction on administrative disputes, as specified by law, without prejudice to the competence of the Court of Audit.".

[37] Article 93 para 1 of the Greek Constitution: "1. Courts are distinguished into administrative and civil and criminal courts, and they are organized by special statutes.".

[38] Article 98 of the Greek Constitution: "1. The jurisdiction of the Court of Audit pertains mainly to: a. The audit of the expenditures of the State as well as of local government agencies or other legal entities subject to this status by special provision of law. b. The audit of high financial value contracts in which contracting partner is the State or any other legal entity which in this respect is equated to the State, as specified by law. [...] f. The trial of disputes concerning the granting of pensions as well as the audit of accounts under section (c). g. The trial of cases related to liability of civil or military servants of the State, as well as of civil servants of local government agencies and of the other public law legal persons, for any loss that through intent or negligence incurred upon the State, the local government agencies or other public law legal persons. 2. The jurisdiction of the Court of Audit shall be regulated and exercised as specified by law. The provisions of article 93 paragraphs 2 and 3 shall not be applicable in the cases specified in (a) through (d) of the preceding paragraph. 3. The judgments of the Court of Audit in the cases specified in paragraph 1 shall not be subject to the control of the Supreme Administrative Court." in conjunction with the Article 100 para 1 e: "1. A Special Highest Court shall be established, the jurisdiction of which shall comprise: [...] e. Settlement of controversies on whether the content of a statute enacted by Parliament is contrary to the Constitution, or on the interpretation of provisions of such statute when conflicting judgments have been pronounced by the Supreme Administrative Court, the Supreme Civil and Criminal Court or the Court of Audit".

[39] Greek Council of State [GC] 668/2012, [GC] 431/2018, 2705/2014.

[40] For example, according to the decision no 3177/2014 of the Greek Council of State [GC], the deterioration of salary arrangements is not, in principle, contrary to any constitutional provision or constitutional principle, as the legislator, assessing the prevailing conditions and taking into account the fiscal situation of the country, can reform the salary of employees of the public sector, within reasonable limits.

[41] In many cases, it was accepted that in cases of prolonged economic crisis, the legislator may adopt measures to reduce public expenditure which entails a serious financial burden for large parts of the population and, in particular, those receiving a salary or pension from the public treasury due to the immediate application and effectiveness of such measures regarding the reduction of the government deficit. See, for example, Greek Council of State [GC] 668/2012, 4741/2012.

[42] Greek Council of State [GC] 1286/2012, para 13, where according to the reasoning, the reduction of the benefits is a general measure of fiscal consolidation within the regulatory framework of the broad set of economic policy measures. This measure, which is part of the Medium-Term Fiscal

public interest with priority above all other reasons that could justify the public interest.[43] At first, it was considered that the fiscal interest was a way for the court to gain access to some form of judicial control upon the fiscal rules by constructing a new legal term. Finally, the fiscal interest served as a ground to justify austerity measures and not as a way to exercise judicial control over political decisions of the legislature.

On the contrary, the principle of fiscal sustainability which originated from the Court of Audit allowed the court to exercise intensive control on the measures, while taking into consideration all the parameters, i.e. the whole system of constitutional rules and principles, including the human dignity principle. According to the Court of Audit jurisprudence, the fiscal sustainability principle derives from Article 79 of the Greek Constitution, which determines the voting procedure for the budget in conjunction with the Article 73(2) of the Constitution which establishes the procedure prior to the adoption of pension bills with long-term budgetary implications and Article 75 of the Constitution which sets out the obligation of a preliminary report regarding the expenditure for bills with budgetary implications. All these constitutional provisions imply the constitutional obligation for financial management and for establishing specific procedural guarantees for financial planning. Consequently, and taking into consideration that public funding is not infinite, public funds must be distributed in accordance with the fiscal sustainability principle, which is constitutional and a component necessary to ensure continuity in the economic operation of the State and the execution of its mission.[44]

It must be underlined that the Court in its reasoning included no mention of the Fiscal Compact or the EMU fiscal rules but found the grounds of the principle solely in the constitutional provisions. Despite that, since the court accepted that the fiscal sustainability principle is a principle of constitutional status, it noted that the legislature is obliged to take it into consideration together with the other constitutional principles (equality principle, legal certainty principle, human dignity principle) and strike a fair balance between them during the adoption of legislative measures. In particular, despite the fact that it also accepted, as the Greek Council of State, that in cases of prolonged economic crisis, the legislator may adopt measures to reduce public expenditure which entail a serious financial burden for large parts of the population, it added in its reasoning that the legislator does not have a totally free hand when adopting measures with budgetary significance: the legislature is still limited by constitutional principles, such as the human dignity principle, proportionality, legal certainty, equality principle, etc. Therefore, any legislative intervention into rights for budgetary purposes, even in order to ensure fiscal

Adjustment Program of the country, seeks to increase revenues and reduce expenditures in order to save the resources necessary to ensure the sustainability of social security, the achievement of the defined fiscal targets and, in particular, the reduction of the general government deficit, including the deficits of the social security funds. In the light of the above, the adopted measure serves the above overriding public interest and for that reason does not violate any constitutional provision.

[43] Giannakopoulos (2012), p. 100.

[44] Greek Court of Audit [GC] 244/2017.

sustainability, must not violate constitutional principles. Furthermore, according to the proportionality principle, a fair balance must be struck between the rights of citizens and the public interest which is served by the imposition of such measures. According to its reasoning, the severity of the crisis and the need to address it immediately to ensure fiscal sustainability is a criterion which is taken into account during the review of the conformity of the measures adopted with the above principles. In any case, fiscal emergency situations, or even the fiscal sustainability principle, is not a legitimate mechanism for reducing the substantive and procedural constitutional guarantees.[45]

It would appear that the Court of Audit managed to apply the desirable constitutional gravity to the Golden Rule, according to the text of the TSCG, though without any explicit mention of the rule, but rather shaping the same content through interpretation of constitutional provisions. Nevertheless, regardless of the "indirect" constitutional recognition, it did not recognize priority or any manner of precedence over other constitutional principles. The paradox is that the desirable "priority" of the Golden Rule over the decision-making was finally achieved through the notion of the "fiscal interest" by the Greek Council of State, despite the fact that the "fiscal interest" is not a principle nor a rule of constitutional value. In any case, the fact that the national courts did not have to exercise control of conformity of the national legislation with the Golden Rule, but control of constitutionality of the measures adopted according to that rule, gave rise to the emergence of the decent living protection.

3 The Golden Principle and the Protection of Social Rights

3.1 The Emergence of the Decent Living Principle

After 10 years of jurisprudence, it can be concluded that the Council of State achieved the purpose of fiscal consolidation and refrained from exercising intensive judicial control regarding the protection of social rights more than any other Greek Supreme Court,[46] at least, during the first phase of the financial crisis in Greece between 2011 and 2015. For example, regarding measures adopted by Law 3986/2011, the Council of State stated that the choices of the legislator were duly justified, and for this reason they were not subject to judicial control, which is restricted only to estimate if the aim served by them exceeds the extreme logical limits of the concept of public interest.[47] Consequently, during this period, conditions in the

[45] Greek Court of Audit [GC] 244/2017.

[46] Contiades et al. (2019), p. 680.

[47] Greek Council of State [GC] 734/2016.

country regarding the living conditions of the population changed drastically,[48] almost the one third of the population dropping below the poverty threshold.[49]

Over time,[50] in this context, the Council of State jurisprudence produced a new notion, that of the 'decent living protection' as a safeguard of social rights with the obligation of the state,[51] while downplaying the importance of public fiscal interest.[52] The decent living protection was adopted by the Council of State as an interpretative loan from German jurisprudence.[53] It is actually the transformation of the notion of the Existenzminimum into Greek legal culture.[54] In German legal order the protection of the Existenzminimum applies in cases of the social welfare system.[55] In Greek legal order decent living protection was expanded in every field with income-based characteristics: tax exemptions,[56] wages of civil servants,[57] pensions,[58] confiscations,[59] social benefits,[60] etc.

It is worth noting that in the Greek literature, even before the outbreak of the financial crisis, it was argued that the state's obligation to protect decent living conditions of its citizens belongs to the core of social rights.[61] Regarding the scope of the implementation of the decent living protection, the range of the content of the decent living notion is rather too extensive and broad as the core of social rights, whereby one would expect the core of social rights to be narrower and more specific in scope. Furthermore, it must be taken into consideration that the notion of decent living derives interpretatively from Article 2(1) of the Greek Constitution which

[48] See, for example, K. Chrysogonos (European Parliamentary Member), Question for written answer E-004784-18 on Excessive taxation hampering a recovery in Greek economic output and competitiveness to the Commission under the Rule 130, 24.9.2018.

[49] According to Hellenic Statistical Authority, Reports 2013–2018, available at www.statistics.gr.

[50] First time appeared in dissenting opinion of the decision of the Greek Council of State [GC] 668/2012. As cornerstone, it is considered the decision of the Greek Council of State [GC] 2287/2015.

[51] Greek Council of State [GC] 1906/2014, regarding the privatization of water.

[52] In the decision no 2193/2014 [GC] the Greek Council of State estimated that the public interest served by the new reductions were imposed, was not as strong as the one that justified the adoption of the initial measures of Laws 3833/2010 and 3845/2012 which, according to the legislator, were taken before the risk of immediate bankruptcy and the country's exit from the eurozone.

[53] Explicitly the decision no 2287/2015 of the Grand Chamber of the Greek Council of State is referred to the *Hartz IV*, the well-known decision of the German Federal Constitutional Court (BVerfG, Judgment of the First Senate of 9 February 2010—1 BvL 1/09—paras. 1–220, http://www.bverfg.de/e/ls20100209_1bvl000109en.html).

[54] Christoforidou (2021), p. 34.

[55] Leijten (2015), p. 24.

[56] Greek Council of State [GC] Decision no 1087/2017, dissenting opinion.

[57] Greek Council of State [GC] Decision no 1286/2012, dissenting opinion.

[58] Greek Council of State [GC] Decision no 2287/2015.

[59] Greek Council of State [GC] Decision no 532/2015, 359/2018.

[60] Greek Council of State [GC] Decision no 719/2018.

[61] Sotirelis (2022), p. 348.

establishes the human dignity principle.[62] Therefore, decent living should be treated as a special aspect of the human dignity principle.

The decent living principle obliges the state to take appropriate measures to protect decent living conditions.[63] This form of protection applies to measures that safeguard decent living (social security) and enhance decent living (social growth). Additionally, the state is obliged to abstain from measures that deprive someone's decent living conditions, mostly in cases of taxation or confiscation.[64]

Consequently, what emerged from the political, social and legal upheaval during the financial crisis was the 'golden' principle of decent living. The decent living principle, mostly after 2015, served as a counterbalance in the face of austerity measures adopted for financial reasons. Both the Golden Rule, or the fiscal sustainability principle as it has been called by the Greek Court of Audit, and the decent living principle have almost the same wide content and scope while the decent living principle is sufficiently concrete so as to apply directly to measures adopted for fiscal purposes with adverse effects on a kind of income.

In this context, the judicial review of constitutionality on the fiscal measures progressed on two different levels:

(a) In terms of the principle of proportionality, it was checked, at an abstract level, if other 'softer' fiscal measures existed which could be adopted without hurting financially the same sections of society whose living standards had already deteriorated substantially through the successive fiscal measures already adopted and implemented.[65]
(b) In terms of the protection of decent living itself, it was checked if, from the implementation of fiscal measures in the specific and individual case before the court, the decent living of the claimant was under threat. It should of course be pointed out that the court has never quantified the threshold of a decent living but has adopted the definition of German case law for Existenzminimum in order to describe the situation whereby not only the material limits are safeguarded but also a minimum possibility of social participation.[66]

3.2 *The Constitutionalization of the Golden Principle*

The constitutionalization of the Golden Rule has never become a serious issue of public debate. In particular, despite the fact that just 1 year after the country regained its credibility in the global markets and the excessive deficit procedure stopped, the

62 Greek Council of State Decision no 359/2018.

63 Greek Council of State Decision no 359/2018, [GC] 2287/2015.

64 Greek Council of State Decision no 359/2018, [GC] 1087/2017.

65 Kaidatzis (2021), p. 279.

66 Greek Council of State [GC] Decision no 2287/2015.

fourth constitutional amendment was made. According to Article 110 of the Greek Constitution, a constitutional amendment can only be made after 5 years have elapsed since the previous one. During the recent constitutional amendment, concluded in 2019, no one political party proposed the introduction of the Golden Rule in the constitutional text, which means that any attempt at the constitutionalization of the Golden Rule must wait at least 5 years, and, in practice, at least 8 years.

Indeed, on the contrary, three political parties proposed the entry into the Constitution of the state's obligation to safeguard decent living conditions for the citizens. The obligation of the protection of decent living, from a substantive perspective, can be seen as functioning as the counterbalance to the Golden Rule. Especially, in cases where the implementation of the Golden Rule implies wage and/or pension cuts or any other form of income which serves as a means for a living, the decent living protection sets the limits on interventions into income in order to protect the human dignity principle.[67] So, taken from this perspective, it can be assumed that some political parties chose to constitutionalize that form of protection of social rights, after a period of strict implementation of the Golden Rule which put most of them at risk, in order to protect these social rights.

Indeed, the constitutional amendment of 2019 was a cornerstone for the decent living principle. the new constitutional provision of Article 21 (1, b) provides that "the state is obliged to safeguard decent living conditions for all its citizens, through a minimum guaranteed income system".

The wording of the provision, however, provoked some reactions from political parties in opposition. In particular, the fact that the constitutional provision did not stop at the point of the recognition of the state's obligation to safeguard decent living conditions, but continued to the specification of how it will be fulfilled, i.e. "through a minimum guaranteed income system" brought some fears to the opposition parties that could be interpreted in such a way that could lead to a form of 'liquidation' of social rights,[68] by replacing public and universal social services, such as health system or education, with a cash benefit to the poor in order to safeguard their access to respective services of private sector. In other words, there was concern that the provision for the system of minimum guaranteed income implies the adoption of the notion of basic income.[69]

The basic income notion serves to promote the liberalization of the market economy and the stripping down of social systems.[70] It offers the state the chance to withdraw from any attempt to regulate the market or any other kind of protectionism, such as statization, and to stimulate only the citizens' ability to consume.

[67] For example, according to Decision no 1716/2010 of the Administrative Court of Appeal of Athens, the confiscation of a pension may serve reasons of public interest, such as the recovery of public claims, but given that it is imposed on a person who has no other means to live on, it violates the human dignity principle.

[68] See, for the term 'liquidation' regarding social rights, Moyn (2018), p. 71.

[69] According to the Proceedings of the Constitutional Amendment of the Greek Constitution (in Greek), XI Period, Session B: 26.9.2007.

[70] Groot (2004), p. 27.

That said, from the neo-liberal, perspective, even the basic income benefit could be considered as a form of intervention into the markets because by intervening in the capacity to consume changes the manner in which supply and demand function. In fact, as the very next crisis—the pandemic—proved, there is no way that the state can abandon the key-role activities vital for the whole of society, such as the health system, without putting the effective protection of social rights at risk.

Within this context, what must be borne in mind is that the constitutional amendment of 2019 achieved recognition for the golden principle, introducing in the constitutional text a special form of human dignity principle in the area of the social welfare system as far as concerns financial issues. This means that since then the state can restructure the social welfare system but explicitly cannot abolish it. Moreover, benefits must serve the purpose of decent living which means that they must be adequate to safeguard decent living conditions. At the same time, the decent living principle as derived from the human dignity principle still stands and applies to every other sector in addition to social welfare.

The human dignity principle shapes the content of the decent living principle in conjunction with Article 4(5) of the Greek Constitution which imposes tax progressivity[71] and Article 5 (1) of the Constitution which provides the freedom of social participation of everyone.[72] Together those provisions denote that decent living conditions are not tantamount to poverty prevention, i.e. a mere physical existence, since they include the possibility to social participation.[73] In addition, with regard to cash benefits, everyone shall be treated according to their personal means, consequently, can neither be excluded from a form of social protection nor treated in the same way when compared with someone with different personal means.

The above constitutional interpretative directions are restricting the universal and mostly the unconditional dimension[74] of the notion of basic income, because they impose a gradation, which means a progressive form of social protection, without exclusions but without across-the board treatment either. Hence, it can be concluded that the recent constitutional amendment attempted to combine two, in principle, opposite purposes in the same provision: on the one hand the decent living protection while on the other the surplus budgets through the simplification of the income-based pillar of the social welfare system and the adoption of a system of basic guaranteed income, which would further reduce the number of persons eligible for a specific (income) benefit, since for the first time income criteria for those who might be eligible would be envisaged in the Greek legal order. That said, the new

---

[71] Article 4 para 5 of the Greek Constitution: "5. Greek citizens contribute without distinction to public charges in proportion to their means.".

[72] Article 5 para 1 of the Greek Constitution: "1. All persons shall have the right to develop freely their personality and to participate in the social, economic and political life of the country, insofar as they do not infringe the rights of others or violate the Constitution and the good usages.".

[73] Gruner (2009), p. 207.

[74] The unconditionality of basic income has the meaning that personal means such as property or incomes are not taken in consideration or shape the amount of cash benefit, Zelleke (2005), p. 4; Torry (2019), p. 24.

constitutional provision will be subject to further constitutional interpretation and through its implementation may lead in the future to different results, given that the final outcome of every case before the courts depends on more parameters than what this new constitutional provision includes.

4 Concluding Remarks

There is little doubt that the Golden Rule and, consequently, a robust state budget without real social protection and social justice has no real value, and vice-versa: a social system without a robust state budget would be equally catastrophic. It seems that finally, after the first shock, the Greek judicial system and, subsequently, the constitutional amendment, the Greek legal order in general, struck a balance between the Golden Rule and the Golden Principle, as far as the protection of social rights is concerned.

The fiscal problems that the country faced triggered the enhancement of social protection, despite, or perhaps because of the fact that the courts placed priority on budgetary consolidation in the first years of the financial crisis. Over the years that followed, the same courts prepared the ground for the constitutionalization of the decent living principle, which cannot be considered merely as an "answer" to the Golden Rule. The case law of the courts during the whole of that period created a legacy, attempting to balance on the one hand fiscal sustainability while on the other the enjoyment of citizens' social rights, taking care from a financial perspective to distribute the economic burden fairly amongst the people,[75] and from the perspective of protecting social rights to distribute these rights in a way in which their decent living is not in jeopardy.

References

Achtsioglou E, Doherty M (2014) There must be some way out of here: the crisis. Labour rights and Member States in the eye of the storm. Eur Law J 20(2):219–240

Adams M, Fabbrini F, Larouche P (2014) Introduction. In: Adams M, Fabbrini F, Larouche P (eds) The constitutionalization of European budgetary constraints. Hart, pp 1–17

Calliess C (2012) From fiscal compact to fiscal union? New rules for the Eurozone. Camb Yearb Eur Leg Stud 14:101–117

Christoforidou S (2021) The constitutional protection of decent living. Nomiki Vivliothiki (in Greek)

Chrysogonos K, Vlachopoulos S (2017) Civil and Social Rights. Nomiki Vivliothiki (in Greek)

Contiades X, Tassopoulos I (2013) The impact of the financial crisis on the Greek Constitution. In: Contiades X (ed) Constitutions in the global financial crisis: a comparative analysis. Routledge, pp 195–218

[75] Kaidatzis (2021), p. 277.

Contiades X, Papacharalambous C, Papastylianos C (2019) The Constitution of Greece: EU Membership perspectives. In: Albi A, Bardutzky S (eds) National constitutions in European and global governance: democracy, rights, the rule of law. T.M.C. Asser Press, The Hague, pp 641–683
Fabbrini F (2013) The fiscal compact, the 'Golden Rule' and the paradox of European federalism. Boston Coll Int Comp Law Rev 36:1–38
Giannakopoulos K (2012) The public interest during the financial crisis. Efimerida Dioikitikou Dikaiou 1:100–112. (in Greek)
Groot LFM (2004) Basic income, employment and compensatory justice. Kluwer
Gruner A (2009) Der verfassungsrechtliche Anspruch auf Gewährleistung des Existenzminimums. Journal für Rechtspolitik 17:202–213
Kaidatzis A (2021), Socioeconomic rights enforcement and resource allocation in times of austerity: the case of Greece 2015–2018. In Farahat A, Arzoz X (eds) Contesting austerity, Hart, p 275-294
Karagiorgas K (1981) Public Finance II, The financial institutions. Papazisi (in Greek)
Leijten I (2015) The German right to an existenzminimum, human dignity, and the possibility of minimum core socioeconomic rights protection. German Law J 16(1):23–48
Moyn S (2018) Not enough. Human rights in an unequal world. Harvard University Press
Pagoulatos G (2018) Greece after the bailouts: assessment of a qualified failure, Hellenic observatory discussion papers on Greece and Southeast Europe. GreeSE paper no 113, LSE
Papadopoulou L (2004) The principle of equality in the Greek Constitution. In: Weber A (ed) Fundamental rights in Europe and North America, Part BIII: the individual rights, supplement 7. Kluwer Law International, pp 1–75
Papadopoulou L (2014) Can constitutional rules, even if 'Golden', tame Greek public debt? In: Adams M, Fabbrini F, Larouche P (eds) The constitutionalization of European budgetary constraints. Hart, pp 223–247
Peers S (2012) The stability treaty: permanent austerity or gesture politics? Eur Const Law Rev 8(3):404–441
Petrakos G, Rontos K, Vavoura C et al (2021) Political budget cycles and effects of the excessive deficit procedure: the case of Greece. Reg Stat 11(2):32–51
Poulou A (2014) Austerity and European social rights: how can courts protect Europe's lost generation? German Law J 15(06):1145–1176
Poulou A (2017) Financial assistance conditionality and human rights protection: what is the role of the EU Charter of fundamental rights? Common Mark Law Rev 54:991–1026
Ruffert M (2020) The future of the European Economic and Monetary Union: issues of constitutional law. In: Bignami F (ed) EU law in populist times: crises and prospects. Cambridge University Press, pp 33–66
Skouris V (1989) Constitutional disputes and judicial review in Greece. In: Landfried C (ed) Constitutional review and legislation. Nomos Verlagsgesellschaft, Baden-Baden, pp 177–200
Sotirelis G (2022) Constitution and democracy in the era of globalization. Papazisi (in Greek)
Torry M (2019) The definition and characteristics of basic income. In: Torry M (ed) The Palgrave international handbook of basic income. Palgrave Macmillan, pp 15–29
Venizelos E (2020) The impact of the financial crisis on the constitutions of Eurozone Member States under rescue programs - Greece as a laboratory of constitutional theory 1. Eur Rev Public Law (ERPL) 32:295–342
Venizelos E (2021) Lessons of constitutional law. Sakkoulas, pp 307–330 (in Greek)
Vlachopoulos S (2019) The constitutionality control in the Greek legal order. IRP 77
Zelleke A (2005) Distributive justice and the argument for an unconditional basic income. J Socio-Econ 34(1):3–15

MIX
Papier aus verantwortungsvollen Quellen
Paper from responsible sources
FSC® C105338

If you have any concerns about our products,
you can contact us on
ProductSafety@springernature.com

In case Publisher is established outside the EU,
the EU authorized representative is:
Springer Nature Customer Service Center GmbH
Europaplatz 3, 69115 Heidelberg, Germany

Printed by Libri Plureos GmbH
in Hamburg, Germany